Lecture Notes in Computer Science 1031

Edited by G. Goos, J. Hartmanis and J. van Leeuwen

Advisory Board: W. Brauer D. Gries J. Stoer

Springer

Berlin
Heidelberg
New York
Barcelona
Budapest
Hong Kong
London
Milan
Paris
Santa Clara
Singapore
Tokyo

Marcel Toussaint (Ed.)

Ada in Europe

Second International Eurospace—Ada-Europe
Symposium
Frankfurt/Main, Germany, October 2-6, 1995
Proceedings

 Springer

Series Editors

Gerhard Goos
Universität Karlsruhe
Vincenz-Priessnitz-Straße 3, D-76128 Karlsruhe, Germany

Juris Hartmanis
Department of Computer Science, Cornell University
4130 Upson Hall, Ithaca, NY 14853, USA

Jan van Leeuwen
Department of Computer Science, Utrecht University
Padualaan 14, 3584 CH Utrecht, The Netherlands

Volume Editor

Marcel Toussaint
Eurospace
16 bis, Avenue Bosquet, F-75007 Paris, France

Cataloging-in-Publication data applied for

Die Deutsche Bibliothek - CIP-Einheitsaufnahme

Ada in Europe : ... international Eurospace Ada Europe
Symposium ... ; proceedings. - Berlin ; Heidelberg ; New York
; Barcelona ; Budapest ; Hong Kong ; London ; Milan ; Paris ;
Santa Clara ; Singapore ; Tokyo : Springer
NE: European Industrial Space Study Group
2. Frankfurt, Germany, October 2 - 6, 1995. - 1996
  (Lecture notes in computer science ; 1031)
  ISBN 3-540-60757-9
NE: GT

CR Subject Classification (1991): D.2, D.1.2-5, D.3, D.4, C.3

ISBN 3-540-60757-9 Springer-Verlag Berlin Heidelberg New York

© Springer-Verlag Berlin Heidelberg 1996
Printed in Germany

Typesetting: Camera-ready by author
SPIN 10512415   06/3142 – 5 4 3 2 1 0   Printed on acid-free paper

Preface

The 'Ada in Europe 1995' Conference held in Frankfurt on the Main from 2nd to 6th October 1995 was the second Conference organised jointly by Eurospace, the organisation of the European space companies, and Ada-Europe.

The Conference was chaired by Mr. John Barnes, chairman of Ada-Europe.

The Conference has been the first since the official issue of Ada 95 - the work of the Ada 9X project having happily been completed since the 'Ada in Europe 1994' Conference held in Copenhagen, Denmark in September 1994. (The revised ISO standard was published on 15th February 1995.)

Significant features of the new version of the language were naturally presented in several sessions, as well as the approach developed by various actors to bring Ada 95 to a broader audience than Ada 83.

However, as in previous conferences, applications, in particular to aerospace projects, represented the majority of the papers presented.

Also, and again as already noticed in previous conferences, it could be seen that the attention of those involved in applications tended more and more to shift from the language itself to the more general aspects of software engineering.

The present volume gives the text of all papers presented as well as the proceedings of the round table discussion that took place on October 4th on "Tools and Design Methods".
The question and answer sessions after the presentation are not reported.

The papers have been grouped into 11 sessions:

Session 1 : Ada 95: the Future
Session 2 : Safety
Session 3 : Language (First session)
Session 4 : Applications (First session)
Session 5 : Language (Second session)
Session 6 : Applications (Second session)
Session 7 : Distribution
Session 8 : Methods and Tools
Session 9 : Design Methods
Session 10 : Life Cycle
Session 11 : Real-Time
Session 11 : Methods.

Many people contributed to the success of the 'Ada in Europe 1995' Conference. The role of the Programme Committee and its energetic chairman and vice-chairman was, of course, decisive. A special mention must also be made of Ms. Rosy Plet, from Eurospace, who took the responsibility for the Conference logistics, and of Ms. Claire Guilly, also from Eurospace, who did most of the work involved in the preparation of this volume.

October 1995

Marcel Toussaint
Director of Studies
Eurospace

Chairmen and Programme Committee

Chairman: John Barnes, Consultant (Ada-Europe President)

Vice Chairman: Finn Hass, C.R.I.
(Chairman of the Eurospace 'Ada and Software Engineering Panel')

Programme Committee Members:

Ms.	M. Aleyrangues	Matra Marconi Space (France)
Messrs.	D. Alzerra	Dassault Electronique (France)
	L. Asplund	Uppsala University (Sweden)
	J. Barnes	John Barnes Informatics (UK)
	R. Borcz	Daimler-Benz Aerospace (Germany)
	F. Ciceri	Laben (Italy)
	X. Cusset	3ip (France)
	R. Flabat	SHAPE (Belgium)
	A. Fodde	Alenia Spazio (Italy)
	R. Gerlich	Dornier Satellitensysteme (Germany)
	G. Guarrera	Alenia Spazio (Italy)
	F. Hass	C.R.I. (Denmark)
	C. Joergensen	C.R.I. (Denmark)
	B. Källberg	Celsius Tech Systems (Sweden)
	P. Lacan	Aerospatiale (France)
	R. Landwehr	Competence Center Informatik (Germany)
	J. Lee	Logica UK (UK)
	G. Macchia	Space Software Italia (Italy)
	K. Mangold	ATM Computer GmbH (Germany)
	P. Mazal	CNES (France)
	A. Moya	European Union (Belgium)
	P. Panaroni	Intecs Sistemi (Italy)
	C. Rolls	ESA-ESTEC (The Netherlands)
	J.P. Rosen	Adalog (France)
	E. Schonberg	New York University (USA)
	J.S. Stevens	British Aerospace (UK)
	A. Strohmeier	Swiss Federal Institute of Technology in Lausanne (Switzerland)
	M. Toussaint	Eurospace (France)
	G. Valentiny	ESA/ESOC

Contents

Ada: A Sceptical Assessment

Jean-François Kaufeler
ESA/ESOC

Presentation Content

- Why this opening address
- ESOC experience with Ada
- Lessons learned
- ESOC view on Ada

Why this opening address

- Ada seems to be a sensitive subject
- Face Ada community with other views
- Enable to understand these other views
- Trigger useful discussions
- Find elements for future consideration by the Ada community

ESOC experience

- Limited to 2 domains

    - In the S/C simulator (to simulate on-board logic when its is implemented in Ada)
    - In Mission Control Systems MCSs (within the Operation WorkStations)

- Exposed case is: MCS

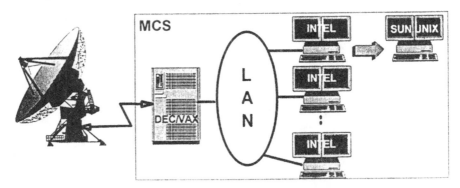

Project History

- Project started in 1990 and completed in 1994
- Why have we chosen Ada?
  - ESA planned future IOI infrastructure (Hermes, Columbus, APM, DRS)
  - Need to rationalise on-board SW
    Ada --> HOOD --> ESSDE
- More a consideration of trend than real technical reasons
- Interest in new technology in the direction of Object Orientation

Problems encountered: ours

- Combined two steps:
  - Go for radically new technology
  - Try to expand largely the functional domain
- Two teams (not collocated)
  - One specialised in Ada
  - One with expertise in the domain area

Problems encountered: Ada?

Ada concept	Our environment
1 program	distributed
1 environment	open

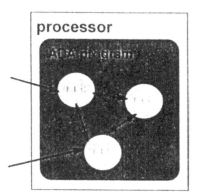

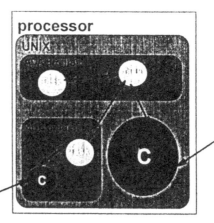

ESOC's Ada assessment

- +
  - . Extension of the PASCAL language spirit
  - . Enables to develop rigorously clean code
  - . Well suited for embedded systems

- -
  - . Not ideal for distributed and open systems
  - . Does not fully support all O-O concepts
  - . No favourable market trend
    - $\Rightarrow$ cost increase (products, maintenance)
    - $\Rightarrow$ dependency on vendors increases
    - $\Rightarrow$ limited number of application enabling to interface Ada

ESOC future MCS systems

- Decision to go for C++ (also for stations, flight dynamics systems, ...)
- Full O-O approach from requirements to design
- Client/Server --> distributed and open
- No heavy SW development tools (only OMT, Requirement DataBase)
- Stick strictly to a method (Rumbaugh)
- Stick strictly to the PSS-05 standards;

Ada95 -
An Approach to Overcome the Software Crisis ?

Karlotto Mangold

ATM Computer GmbH

Konstanz

Abstract:

The first part of this paper tries to characterise the notorious software crisis. Some of these characteristics are: Programming in the Large, Distributed Development, Configuration-Management, Object-Oriented Analysis, Design and Programming, Consistency of Interfaces, Life cycle and Maintainability, Reusability, Portability.
The second part discusses some "prejudices" about Ada, such as military language, complex, expensive, inefficient, old-fashioned, not object-oriented, not open to integrate COTS-products.
The third part presents some highlights of Ada95 which may contribute to overcome this crisis.

Preliminary Remarks

During the development of the programming language Ada, there were three major milestones which were visible to the public. In 1980 the first definition of Ada was published as MIL-Std 1815 [1]. After a period of public comments and a subsequent revision phase a modified language was published in 1983 as MIL-Std 1815A and as an ANSI-Standard [2]. This version of the language was adopted without any changes in 1987 as an ISO-Standard [3]. It took more than six years of work for a full-time team and a group of international experts till a new revision of Ada was published in early 1995 as an international (ISO-) Standard [4] and an ANSI-Standard. It will be adopted as a number of national standards in near future. If in this paper differences are of any importance, the three versions will be called Ada80, Ada83 and Ada95. In all other cases only Ada is used as reference.
This paper is not intended to present the language Ada. For those who want to see the exact features of Ada the language reference manuals (LRM), which are identical to the above mentioned standards documents, give a precise definition. To see the principles of the language and some background information the Rationale document [5] for Ada95 is recommended. For those who only want to get a short overview or some highlights, there are text-books available or some documents published during the revision process e.g. [6], [7], [8], [9], and [15].
Technical information in the most actual form and also information about GNAT are available on the internet from the Ada-Server located at Ecole Polytechnique in Lausanne Switzerland, abbreviated EPFL. The home-page can be reached by "http://lglwww.epfl.ch/Ada/". Besides this there are also a lot of different national mirror sites.

I. The so-called Software-Crisis

More than 25 years ago at the Garmisch conference in 1968 the term *Software-Engineering* was established. From that time on up today the aim of software engineering has been to produce software in a more professional way like all other technical products. Some years after that famous conference nearly no improvements were visible and therefore the so-called "software crisis" was mentioned in a lot of publications. There have been a lot of approaches to overcome this crisis in between. Among them were *Structured Programming, artificial intelligence, 4th* or *5th Generation Languages*.

All these approaches promised an end to the crisis, but each of them ended with the hope that the next version of the different tools would offer the expected improvement. This promise and also the expectations have seemed constant for years.

Until now there has been for example no German translation of the term *Software Engineering*. This may be an indicator that developing software is quite different from engineering other technical stuff.

There are two major differences between software and other engineering disciplines:

First of all at a very early stage of software development CASE, computer aided software engineering, was introduced. I would like to say that this happens even before software engineering was really understood and known. Therefore CASE offered such solutions which could be solved by computers and not those which improved the engineering process. Now the problem is recursive and very difficult to solve.

The other difference is the fact that there are different groups of engineering disciplines as architecture, electrotechnics, etc. according to the different problem areas, whereas in the area of software always one approach should cover all the different application areas and should offer solutions to the wide range of problems.

In this paper I'll try to identify some of the most important problems and look for stand-alone solutions. This may improve the situation even a little bit.

Programming in the Large, the Problem of Size

During the past twenty-five years there was a tremendous growth in computing power and memory size (main memory and secondary memory). But with this growth in hardware capabilities there was a growth in the size of the problems too, and also in the size of software needed to solve these problems. This growth of the problems took place at least at the same or even a higher speed than the growth of the hardware facilities. Consequences of this growth were that the problems to be solved were too complex for one programmer and even one team. To solve those large problems in an appropriate time frame it was necessary to start with distributed development, which causes several problems. In architecture it has been well known for centuries, that it is impossible to build up a house in one day even by one hundred workers. What are the consequences in SE? At an early stage modules were introduced, but for a long time there were no concepts and no tools to support consistency between these modules which where developed in a distributed environment. Configuration management and change control is very important during the development process already. It must be guaranteed by the computer, that only actual versions are used, otherwise the same errors must be located several times.

The Problem of Interfacing

A second aspect of this modular development is the consistency of interfaces between the modules. It is often appropriate to change an interface during the development phase. How can it be assured however, that all users get knowledge of such a change and adopt their modules to the modified interface? Such a check should be automatically done with the actual version whenever it is used by another module. These checks should be done by a computer at compile time to avoid expensive run-time tests to find the differences in the interfaces.

Reusability

A third aspect of this problem of size is the reuse of modules. Large hardware systems (not only computers) are built up from components. One principle is to minimise the number of different components. To reach this goal, the same elementary components are used whenever possible. There are a lot of books and papers published on reuse and reusability, but during software development similar modules are often re-implemented without knowing anything about the existence of each other. As it is often difficult to find and identify reusable components, there is a need for "standardised" interfaces and functional specifications as well as a concept of templates in addition to existing library concepts.

The Software Life Cycle

There are two major differences between hardware and software:
- Software can be modified very easily and without difficulties.
- There is no wear and tear of software and therefore no need for maintenance.
Conclusions from these facts are that software can be changed during the development process very often without any consequences and software can be frozen after putting the system into operation. In fact a lot of errors and problems including missing deadlines are caused by these changes which were not well published through the distributed development. On the other side, the acceptance of a system by the user is depending on the possibility to adopt the system during the life-cycle to the changing requirements of the users. Software must be maintained during the whole life-cycle of a system and tools must be available to do this.

Portability

Very often - especially in embedded systems - software is used to control complex hardware systems. In this case, the system has a life-span which is much longer than the life-span of the computer used for controlling the system. After some time there will be no spare parts available for the computers and therefore the computer must be replaced even if there is no functional need for such a replacement. In this situation the software - which is still working - must be ported to the new computer. But to do this, the software must be portable and there must be at least a compiler available which translates the "old" language onto the new computer system.

Object Oriented Programming

The most recent approach to overcome the software crisis is the object oriented paradigm. If problems arise in a project not using this paradigm, the reason for the problem seems to be clear. But I think this kind of reasoning is too simple. There are of course areas as e.g. Graphical User Interfaces (GUIs), which can be handled by object-oriented methods rather efficiently, but it is probably not adequate to solve all the different software problems with this approach. One problem of class libraries are the different views they offer, depending on the application area they were developed for. Consequences from this observation are the need of using paradigms which are appropriate to the problem and avoiding to adopt the problem to an existing solution.

II. What People Say about Ada

Ada is a Military Language !

Depending on the definition of a "military language" this statement is true and false. It is true that the US Department of Defense has contracted the development of all three versions of Ada. But COBOL for example, which is very widespread in information systems and in commercial applications was developed by the US Navy. Obviously a client specifies the work to be done, but Ada does not contain any specific military keywords or programming structures. There is also no specific support for military specific actors or sensors. Ada was developed in the late seventies and now modified to Ada95 to support the implementation of embedded systems on one side and to handle large projects on the other. In between some of the constructs of Ada83 as e.g. exception handling were adopted by other programming languages. There is only one speciality of military systems the long life space supported by the design of Ada. Ada supports the maintenance of such systems. On the other side there are a lot of throwaway programs which are not of any interest if they once have calculated their (hopefully correct) result. But nowadays - regarding product liability regulations - a lot of these programs must be kept for evidence. A lot of industrial systems as aeroplanes, steel mills and power plants have about the same life span and also the same type of criticality. Therefore quite similar requirements have to be fulfilled by a programming language used in these application areas.

Ada is far too complex

I think the first issue discussing complexity should be the complexity of a problem. If there is a complex problem, the adequate description of this problem will be complex too. The complexity of a problem, its description and the solution is about the same size of complexity. If there was a large difference between these, information would be lost or added. Both cases would either simplify or complicate the solution in a way that the solution would lose its relation to the problem. Unfortunately there is a tendency to seek simple descriptions and solutions for describing and managing complex situations. To model a complex world or non-trivial parts of it, the tools used must offer about the same complexity as the reality has, otherwise there are huge discrepancies between the reality and the model. Such differences would reduce the acceptance of the model by the user dramatically. Obviously there can be reductions in complexity if the complex reality is reduced to one or two specific views. But to offer Ada as a language to model and to control complex structures it must have a similar complexity. Quite another issue is whether all the language features are needed in every program. Obviously the implementors of a system should restrict themselves to the features necessary for a specific problem.

Looking at the Language Reference Manuals of Ada83[2] and Ada95[4], these are quite thick. Comparing these definitions for example with the definition of ALGOL60 [11] published about 35 years ago, consisting of about 35 pages there is an expansion factor of about 15. During these years all the programming languages have expanded their functionality, not only Ada. Comparing this with the expansion of computing power and memory size - and also with the size of solved problems, this growth can be called moderate. Another aspect of the complexity of a language is the difference between active and passive vocabulary. Programmers often use a subset of the language sufficient to solve the problems. They normally don't try to explore all the edges of a language. There is a general tendency in every programming language to adopt all existing paradigms from other languages to offer all these features to the programmer. On the one hand Ada95 has adopted also some new features, but on the other hand it offers standardised interfaces to programs implemented in other languages. Generally there must be a decision between one universal language which offers facilities to express all problems and a bunch of specialised languages which are problem-oriented and offer the possibility of interfacing with one another. Until now Ada95 has been the first language to my knowledge which offers these interfacing in a standardised way (see Annex B [4]).

Ada is too difficult to teach, to learn, to use ...

To teach and to learn Ada in so far as to be able to write a simple program, the effort is about the same as in any other programming language. There are often complaints about the need of generic instantions of I/O packages, but not only for didactic purposes it is wise to use predefined instantiated packages in a project, which are the same for the whole project. Therefore there is no need to start with these features at the very beginning of an Ada training course. If the only task is to print "Hello Ada-World", this can be done be a simple echo-command and there is no need to learn Ada or any other programming language.

Tasking and rendezvous are concepts which are difficult and error-prone. But if there is a need to model several activities which are executed in parallel, with communication and synchronisation, this is a difficult task which may cause problems. As many languages don't offer tasking, there are many programs which don't need tasking. It is ridiculous to calculate primes or factorial by using several tasks. If you don't have tasking facilities within your programming language and you need parallel processes, you have to access specific run-time-libraries or the operating system directly. Dealing with these libraries or with several different operating systems is more difficult and error-prone than to understand the Ada tasking model.

A detailed look at Ada83 tasking shows that the only basic construct, the rendezvous, as synchronous, asymmetric, and one-sided anonymous construct, has some deficiencies to model the real asynchronous world. Of course it is possible to build packages using the rendezvous to offer other "asynchronous" communication mechanisms. But this approach ignores performance issues and causes also some unnecessary difficulties in building up such systems especially as such packages are not offered in a standardised way as e.g. the I/O packages. To overcome these problems Ada95 offers protected types to model a data-oriented synchronisation in addition to the task-oriented rendezvous.

Another approach to express complexity is the number of iterations necessary to compile a program without error messages. If this were a real aim , the simplest way to reach it would be to implement compilers without any error messages. This would make implementing compilers much easier. In contrary the aim should be to detect all errors as early as possible and in this sense it is cheaper to detect any error at compile-time than at link-time or even at run-time.

Ada is too expensive

In the past, Ada Development Environments (Hardware prices plus software licenses) were rather expensive compared with development platforms for other languages. In addition the hardware platforms used for Ada must be more powerful (computing power, main memory and disk capacity) than those for the other languages.

In these comparisons often UNIX or DOS Systems with the standard C-Compiler were taken as representatives for the other languages. It was normally not calculated, that in large projects there is a need for a powerful file server to keep all sources consistent and it is not adequate to supply each of the let's say fifty programmers with a stand-alone PC. Such an approach would cause an immense integration effort. It is even not sufficient to connect these isolated PCs via Ethernet. There is also a need for a centralised library- and module management system and also for a powerful configuration management system. This configuration control should be applied during the development phase. Most of the development tools offer a central database for design and specification documents, but object management is often done by a simple make-utility without any consistency checks.

Another aspect is maintenance of the compiler which includes correction of errors and com-piling of a stable language in different compiler versions. In classical engineering and produc-tion processes the tool smith plays a very important role, but in software development processes the costs of such a tool smith are often too high. Consequences of switching over to a new - hopefully better - but certainly different version of a tool are ignored as well as those of keeping an old version with known bugs. It is also important to make sure that all necessary tools, especially the compilers are available for the whole life of the software, where mainte-nance is needed. It is necessary to guarantee that the executable programs can be reproduced and produce the same results.

It is difficult to compare the quality of different tools. The validation of Ada compilers which is required in definite intervals guarantees the quality of an Ada compiler in two aspects. First the language constructs accepted by different compilers or versions of one compiler are the same. Second the validation suite checks the compiler and guarantees that not only simple programs are correctly translated into executable programs.

In addition to licensed products offered by compiler vendors there is an Ada95 compiler, the GNU Ada Translator (GNAT) which was sponsored by AJPO and which is distributed accord-ing the GNU Public Licence (GPL) regulations [12] of Free Software Foundation. As a con-sequence there is an Ada compiler available for free for the major development systems. For education and training purposes as well as for small projects this is a chance to start with Ada and gain own experiences. I personally know a lot of software developers who were a bit reluctant to start with Ada, but after their first experiences they were convinced!

Using Ada Causes Inefficiencies

Comparing Ada programs with programs in other languages, the size of memory used by an Ada program is acceptable. Especially as memory gets cheaper and cheaper on one side and the shortage in addressable space does not exist anymore.

There are published experiences (e.g.[13]) which report on better run-time performance of Ada programs compared with C programs. If Ada programs are executed slower due to the power-ful language constructs, this is the price for higher reliability of those programs. Another aspect concerning execution time is the concept of exception handling in Ada. This concept reduces the need of explicit, dynamic checks and improves the execution speed of all cases where no exceptions occur.

Training in Ada is too expensive

To teach and learn that "subset" of Ada which is equivalent to most of the other languages, the effort is about the same. To get specific know-how as inter-task communication and synchronisation there is a need to learn the underlying operating system. These functions are normally hidden in some libraries or include files and it is more difficult to understand these concepts than to have them included in the language, where the compiler can check syntax and semantics. Another issue is the fact that this knowledge is only valid for one operating system and should be renewed for every new operating system. As most of the other languages don't have these constructs, learning them should not be treated as part of learning the language.

As Ada does not support cryptic programming, (the contrary of self-documented programs), there is a chance to write readable programs. Those readable programs can be easily understood by another programmer to guarantee the maintainability for the life-time.

As Ada offers a lot of basic principles of software engineering, it could be used as a tool to teach and demonstrate software engineering principles. If this took place in a wider range, learning Ada would be much simpler for those who know these principles

Ada is old-fashioned, modern concepts are not included in the language

First of all the long life-time of embedded software systems must be considered. The software must be maintained during the whole life-time of the system. The need of changes requires software modifications and re-compilations of at least small software modules.

Extensions or modifications of a programming language imply at least a new version of the compiler. As every new version of a compiler offers the risk of new errors all programs have to be verified with the new version even if they remain unchanged in the actual modification of application software. This program verification may be a very expensive process, which should be avoided whenever possible. Another problem of language modification are incompatibilities which may cause unwanted software modifications, too. Therefore a stable development environment is required for the whole usage of the software system.

Ada is not object-oriented

Strong typing, abstract data-types and generic units offer object-based programming in Ada83. In Ada95, so called *tagged types* are introduced. They offer object-oriented and class-wide programming with dynamic binding. Even if there is no keyword object in Ada, the functionality is available. Ada95 is the first object-oriented programming language which is standardised world-wide by ISO.

Ada is exotic and does not fit into COTS-Software

Ada83 [2] assumed a pure Ada-World. The basic assumption was that everything could and should be implemented in Ada. Therefore in Ada83 as in most other programming languages there was no need to interface programs written in other languages. The Ada programming model often assumed a bare machine concept, where the compiler and the linker generate a tailored application system comprising application-, run-time-, and operating system. Nevertheless it was possible in principle to write a package specification in Ada and to implement the body in any other languages and to call procedures implemented in other languages in that way.

The possibility of machine-code insertions was useful to implement hardware or machine specific instructions, but it was not a real approach for interfacing.

The normative Annex B of Ada95[4] specifies the interfaces to other programming languages. C, COBOL and FORTRAN are named explicitly. To do this there are two pragmas: *Import* to use objects defined in another language from an Ada program and *Export*, to offer Ada defined objects for use in other languages. The Pragma *Convention* allows the definition of language specialities such as calling conventions or column wise storing of matrices in FORTRAN.

This annex opens Ada95 to other languages in a unique way. It offers the possibility to integrate existing program packages (COTS-products) into Ada-programs in a standardised way and increases the reusability of these programs.

III. Some Essentials of Ada95

Ada95 consists of a kernel language and so-called special-needs annexes. The kernel must be supported by all validated compilers. These annexes support the areas of systems programming, real-time programming, distributed systems, information systems, numerics, and safety and security. They may be implemented by specific compilers only, but if an annex is supported by a compiler, all features of this annex must be supported.

The kernel of Ada95 is an upward compatible extension of Ada83. There are publications [14] which list about 40 incompatibilities, but most of them are either formal ones, which can be solved nearly automatically by an intelligent editor or are very sophisticated, and I don't expect, that these are used in real projects.

There is one new, highly important feature in Ada95. *Tagged types* support object-oriented programming with type extensions, inheritance, class-wide programming and late or dynamic dispatching. In addition to this new feature, there are hierarchical packages which also support the management of objects and classes in a much better way than it was in Ada83.

In addition to the synchronous rendezvous Ada95 offers data-oriented synchronisation by means of *protected types*. Besides these extensions there are a lot of clarifications and corrections.

As already mentioned there is a normative annex, which specifies the interfaces to other programming languages as C, C++, COBOL and FORTRAN. This offers a chance to integrate existing software in a standardised manner.

IV. Conclusions

As mentioned in this paper, Ada95 has at least some features which support modern software engineering principles. I am not going to promise that Ada95 will overcome the software crisis with all its different problem areas, but I really expect, that on one hand, Ada can offer solutions to some of the problems in software engineering which sum up to the software crisis and on the other hand at least some of the opinions which prevented potential users from programming in Ada are not correct. Both aspects could lead to broader acceptance of Ada and thus contribute to a solution of some software problems. But the results of a marketing survey, done in the US in spring 94, show that even if decision makers have about the same, widely accepted criteria to select a programming language, they were not aware of the properties of Ada. Therefore we must try to bring some knowledge of these principles and highlights of Ada to a much broader audience than we did until now.

References

[1] Ada Reference Manual (July 1980), New York, Heidelberg, Berlin, 1980
[2] Reference Manual for the Ada Programming Language, ANSI/MIL-STD-1815A , Washington D.C., January 1983.
[3] ISO 8652 1987 Programming language Ada, ISO, Geneva, 1987
[4] Ada Reference Manual. International Standard for Information Technology - Programming Languages - Programming Language Ada , Language and Standard Libraries, ANSI/ISO/IEC 8652, February 1995.
[5] Ada95 Rationale The Language, The Standard Libraries, Intermetrics, Cambridge Ma., January 1995.
[6] Introducing Ada9X, Ada9X Project Report.Office of the Under Secretary of Defense for Acquisition, Intermetrics Inc., Second printing, May 1993
[7] Baker, T.P., Pazy, O.: The Systems Programming Annex of the proposed Ada9X Standard, in: [10] pp. 65 - 73.
[8] Pazy, O., Baker. T.: The Real-Time Systems Annex of the proposed Ada9X Standard, in: [10] pp. 75 - 97.
[9] Gargaro, A.: Distributed Programming in Ada9X, in: [10] p 99 - 113.
[10] Loftus. C. (ed): Ada Yearbook 1994, Studies in Computer and Communication Systems. Amsterdam, Oxford. Washington, Tokyo, 1994
[11] Revised Report on the Algorithmic Language ALGOL60, Numerische Mathematik 4 (1963), S. 420 - 453
[12] Stallman, R.M.: Using and Porting GNU CC, Free Software Foundation, December 1992
[13] Lawlis, P.K.. Elam. T.W.: Ada Outperforms Assembly: A Case Study, in Engle, C.B.jr (ed) TRI-Ada'92, Conference Proceedings. New York, 1992, p334 - 337.
[14] Taylor, B.: Ada9X Compatibility Guide, Version 4.0. Nov. 1993 in [10] pp 295 - 343
[15] Barnes, J.: Programming in Ada95, Addison-Wesley, Wokingham UK, et al. 1995

Safe Ada Executive : An Executive for Ada Safety Critical Applications

Marc Richard-Foy

Thomson Software Products / Alsys

66-68 Av. Pierre Brossolette, 92247 Malakoff, France

Tel : 33 (1) 41481137

Fax: 33 (1) 41481020

E-Mail : richafoy@alsys.fr

Abstract

*This paper presents the SAE **project** (Safe Ada Executive) which deals with the **DO-178 B** certification for safety critical systems which use **COTS** (Commercial Off The Shelves) software components such as the **Ada Run Time System**. Traditionally safety critical systems avoid parallelism or rely on cyclic dispatcher to achieve determinism. At the opposite this project shows that it is possible to use the **preemptive scheduler** of the Ada Run Time System for safety critical systems. The proposed model of the Safe Ada Executive is designed to support a predictible subset of the Ada tasking. This real time executive allows to support applications developped with the **RMA** (Rate Monotonic Analysis) methods and an appropriate coding style. We point out this approach which allows to separate applications from the real time executive and to minimize the **certification** costs. Anyhow, the SAE project, based on the Ada83 revision of the language, has a stronger support with the **Ada95** revision.*

1. Introduction

The use of software has grown over the last decade with the availability of low cost and high performance hardware. Flexibility is the major attraction of software. However it involves a greatly increased risk of errors. The avionic industry which is a pionner for safety critical systems has early defined software recommendations [DO178B] to provide the aviation community with guidance material for determining - in a consistent manner and with an acceptable level of confidence - that the software aspects of systems and equipment design meet the certification requirements.

If these procedures do not need any specific development methods, on the other hand, they require stringent software life cycle control and software verification, and this impacts significantly the software architecture. The more safety critical the software programs are, the simpler, the more modular and the more sequential they must be to be easily proved. Contrary to the reliability requirements which need powerful languages, they are often programmed in assembly language to minimize complexity. It is paradoxal to note that when high level languages are used, it is in a poor manner because certification authorities are afraid of powerful features such as Object Oriented Programmation or tasking, because their dynamic and implicit behaviour makes them difficult to prove. The situation is the same for real time executives based on priority preemptive scheduling : deterministic cyclic dispatchers are generally preferred.

Although the Ada language is an excellent support for developping safety critical software, this matter of fact makes it difficult to use. To adopt a coding style only using a language subset is not sufficient, the Ada executive correctness must be proved since DO-178 recommendations apply to any kind of software including COTS (Commercial Off The Shelves).

To bypass this difficulty, Ada suppliers have proposed proprietary reduced Ada Run Time Systems supporting Ada language subsets which eliminate dynamic features and unpredictible constructs. Thus, Thomson Software Products/Alsys has developped the C-SMART run time executive used in some of the most critical systems, such as the power generation, the brakes and steering control system and the Global Positionning System of the B777, the newest Boeing aircraft.

However this approach which allows to develop Ada software for the most critical level is not totally satisfactory. It is interesting to support Ada tasking, or at least some of its characteristics, for instance for less critical systems or to drop cyclic dispatchers. Indeed, if cyclic dispatchers introduce a kind of deterministic parallelism, unfortunately they are not reusable since they are built-in within a very application. The solution would be the use of a predictible Ada tasking subset. It is exactly the purpose of the SAE project : to build an approach allowing the use of the Ada tasking in systems to be certified at the highest criticity level.

2. The SAE project (Safe Ada Executive)

The French Armament Board (DGA) initiated the SAE project and financed the study of a Safe Ada Executive (SAE) usable in current and future defense projects. The purpose is to reduce the certification costs thanks to a widely used Ada executive within a given defense project being re-usable in new projects. The project which started in 1994 (still in progress when this paper is written) relies on the Ada83 revision of the Ada language [ARM83]. The study is handled by both the companies Thomson Software Products/Alsys and Sextant Avionique. The former is in charge of the SAE executive development, the latter has to develop representative safety critical avionic applications. The project consists of two steps: a feasibility study and then the development of the SAE executive itself. To achieve the feasibility, we successivly examine the language, the RMA technics (Rate Monotonic Analysis) and the existing Ada run-time implementations. At the end of this stage, the SAE specifications are defined. The Ada executive is developed according to the DO-178 recommendations for the highest critical level (5 levels of criticity for these systems : A, B, C, D and E). It is planned to prototype a software coverage analysis tool and also a schedulability analysis tool for the testing period. The Ada executive is first developped for a Motorola MC68040 target, it is ported then to a RISC Power PC target. Throughout the whole project, an observer group composed of avionic companies which might use the SAE executive, is kept informed of the project. Finally, the project is audited by the defense certification authorities to check the DO-178 B compliance.

2.1 The RMA approach

RMA originated with rate monotonic scheduling (RMS) theory. In 1973, LIU and Layland wrote a paper on a scheduling theory [LIU73] that provided mathematical conditions for assessing the schedulability of a set of tasks. These results could be used only if all tasks were periodic (with period at the end of each period), perfectly preemptible, independent (or noninteracting), and scheduled using the rate monotonic scheduling algorithm. Recently, the rate monotonic scheduling has been extended from its original form of scheduling independent periodic tasks to scheduling [KLEIN93]:

- Both periodic and aperiodic tasks

- Tasks with synchronization requirements

- Tasks with mode change requirements

- Tasks with deadlines before the end the period

- Tasks with deadlines after the end of the period

The impact of this theory is now very broad and allows a better analysis of the real time systems. This is the reason why the RMA approach has been retained as a guideline for the design of applications running under SAE.

First, the RMA techniques have been examined to determine their applicability to the avionic systems. It has been found out that the avionic systems usually are a combination of most of the RMA real time situations but rarely only one of them. Then, a survey to define features of common real time systems was led within the observer group. Desired information deals with:

- DO-178 B criticity level of applications.

- The maximum number of tasks.

- Arrival pattern of events (periodic, irregular, bounded, bursty or unbounded).

- Period and deadline values of tasks.

- Shared resources.
- Aperiodic events.

With this information it was possible to identify, among the set of applications proposed by Sextant Avionique, four models representative of the most common avionic real time situations. This classification gives a gradual complexity:

First model:

This model consists of six independent periodic tasks with non harmonic periods and with deadlines matching the end of periods.

Second model:

This model consists of six interacting periodic tasks. Three tasks share resources. Task periods are not harmonic.

Third model:

This model consists of five periodic tasks and two aperiodic tasks. In both aperiodic processings it exists a minimum inter-arrival time between two consecutive aperiodic events (bounded arrival pattern).

Fourth model:

This model consists of twenty tasks and fifteen shared resources. It combines both periodic and aperiodic tasks. Aperiodic arrival pattern events are both bounded or bursty. The bursty mode is when the next event can occur arbitrarily close to the previous one, but the number of events over a specified period of time is restricted. Bursty arrival patterns are characterized by an event density.

All these models come from real avionic systems; they are analysed according the RMA approach, then they are programmed according to the following rules.

2.2 The Ada Language

The language has been examined on one hand to define a safe Ada programmation guideline [Which89] and, on the other hand, to identify the necessary constructs to program the RMA models. Choices which have been made regarding the memory model, the exception mechanism and the tasking aim to define a predictible way of programming.

The memory model:

The goal was to defined a coding style allowing a predictible heap management. This predictibility implied two strong requirements. The first one is the underlying implementation supports time-bounded allocation/deallocation memory algorithms. The second one is a guaranteed availibility for memory allocation when sufficient free space can be collected over the heap. This last point assumes memory allocation algorithms which are not fragmentation-prone. The survey of most of the common algorithms for dynamic allocation of variable size objects did not allow us to find a general algorithm meeting these two requirements. So we have chosen some programmation rules which only allow static objects allocation onto the heap. Such objects are allocated once for ever; they are never released all over the program lifetime. These objects which are allocated onto the heap have a global scope, they depend on library units and they are never released via the *Unchecked_Deallocation* function. However if these rules satisfy the language viewpoint they are not sufficient regarding the implementation. Indeed, the implementation may require heap memory allocation for its own. This is the case for instance of functions returning unconstrained type objects making the compiler allocate implicitly onto the heap temporary objects. Modifying the compiler to remove this kind of memory allocation is out of the scope of the SAE project, so we have introduced additional programming rules to prevent implicit heap object allocation.

Exceptions :

The exception processing includes two mechanisms : the exception raising and its propagation. We have only kept the first one : the exception raising. The reasons we have removed the propagation mechanism are first, the difficulty to trace code which can be left at any time due to an exception occurrence and then, the impossibility to guarantee bounded response time for the propagation, this time depending upon the application structure.

Finally, only the raising of predefined exceptions has been authorized. This choice has introduced an additional implementation requirement to give the control to an application subprogram when an exception occurs, so the whole program can be stopped.

Tasking :

Choices made for heap allocated objects apply also to task objects. So, only static tasks are supported, that is to say those whose scope is the program's. In addition, some tasks synchronization rules regarding RMA programmation models have been set. The set of tasking rules are :

- Tasks are activated when library packages or subprograms are elaborated.

- Tasks have the program lifetime and never terminate.

- Tasks have no dependent (no tasks hierarchy)

- The alternative *terminate* and the *abort* statement are not supported.

- The *delay* statement is not supported. A similar structure to the *Delay Until* statement of the new language revision [ARM95] will be prefered instead.

- The package *Calendar* will not be used for monotonic time. A package like *Real_Time* of the real time annex of the Ada95 language will be used instead.

- *Select* statements with a *delay alternative* are not supported.

- The *pragma Priority* is not supported. (Priority assignment is implementation defined; an Ada95 like solution is recommended).

- Task attributes : *Callable*, *Terminated* and *Count* are not supported.

2.3 The Run-Time Executive services

The programmation rules above allow to simplify significantly the Ada executive services. The exception propagation function is removed, the heap management just supports a function for allocating global objects since functions for allocating local or temporary objects and all the deallocation functions are removed. Regarding tasking, the task attributes and the hierarchy functionality are removed (*terminate*, *abort*) or simplified (task creation and termination). *Rendezvous* constructs become very simple and the *delay* statement is removed.

At the opposite, the programmation of the RMA paradigms introduces new requirements on the Ada executive services. Periodic tasks need a service like the Ada95 *Delay Until* statement. Resources sharing use RMA protocols such as the Priority Inheritance Protocol (PIP), the Priority Ceiling Protocol (PCP) or the Highest Locker Protocol (HLP). These three protocols have been evaluated and the two first have been dropped. Indeed, the priority inheritance makes the *rendezvous* implementation more complex and impedes the performance. On the other hand, it does not prevent from dead lock when several resources are shared unlike the PCP or HLP protocols. These two last protocols are globally equivalent except that the PCP requires a run-time support whilst the HLP can be entirely supported with the standard *rendezvous* mechanisms. Regarding aperiodic processings, the RMA paradigms are the polling servers or the sporadic servers which do not need a specific Ada run_time support, apart from an efficient interrupt processing. Another RMA outcome is that the *pragma Priority* has been replaced by a *Set_Static_Priority* mechanism which might be achieved in Ada95 with the help of task discriminants.

The Ada Executive is then composed of two parts: the classical Ada83 Run Time System which has been simplified at the most and an extension including the non supported Ada83 services (*Delay Until, Set_Static_Priority ...*)

2.4 The Coverage Analysis Tool - AdaCover

The revision B of DO-178B recommendations contains hard requirements about the program coverage analysis. For the most critical systems (class A), it is necessary to demonstratre that the instructions - at the code generated level and the modified conditions/decisions coverage - are met. A condition is a boolean expression containing no boolean operators. A decision is a boolean expression composed of conditions and zero or more boolean operators. A boolean without a boolean operator reduces to a condition. The modified condition/decision coverage is achieved when every point of entry and exit in the program has been invoked at least once, every condition in a decision in the program has taken on all possible outcomes at least once, every decision in the program has taken on all possible outcomes at least once, and each condition in a decision has been shown to independently affect that decision's outcome.

These two requirements - instructions coverage at the code generated level and the modified condition/decision coverage - are rarely or even never satisfied by COTS. For this reason, one of the objectives of the SAE project is to produce a software coverage analysis tool which meets the DO-178 requirements. The prototype of this tool is based on the same concept as the AdaCover tool, already been experienced in the B777 project in the C-SMART environment. The functionality of this tool has been extended to the Ada tasking. The concepts of this tool are the following :

The modules to be tested are encapsulated into a harness. The purpose of the harness is to activate at the module's beginning the trace mode of the processor (if it exists); for every executed instruction, the program instructions table is updated. In this table containing as many entry points as instructions in the program, two types of information are recorded : on one hand, the boolean result of the execution of the corresponding instruction, and on the other hand, the value of the condition code if the instruction is a conditional instruction. At the end of the module to be tested, the trace mode and the table update are switched off, then the table is transferred to the host. On the host, a process analyses the content of the table; it consists of annotating the compiler code generated listing with the two kinds of information extracted from the table. It is then possible to determine the instructions and the modified conditions/decisions program coverage. The tool is composed of a monitor residing on the target which updates the instructions table and of a process on the host machine which analyses the instructions table.

2.5 The Schedulability Analysis Tool - AdaSchedule

The RMA analysis methods allow to determine whether a system is schedulable in a predictible way, however their scope is limited to the design stage. Indeed, the RMA techniques rely on the a-priori knowledge of execution time and on the blocking time of each task of the system. These times must be known when being designed and must be the same at execution time. So, it is necessary to check that the implementation does not introduce bad side effects on these values and estimated design times are still valid at the execution time. The purpose of the AdaSchedule tool is to check the execution time and the blocking time at posteriori for each task of the program. This tool has the same structure as AdaCover : a monitor residing on the target which records times, then a process on the host machine which analyses them. The Safe Ada Executive records the corresponding times for each task and at each system event occurrence, (preemption, suspension, task activation, ...). However the user determines the worst cases scenarii of its program. It is important to note that the SAE time recording function is always embedded. Only the transmisson and the analysis functions can be disconnected. So, we are sure the SAE code is the same during the development and the operational stages.

2.6 Certification

At the end of the project, the SAE executive will not be certified though the certification authorities audited it according to the DO-178B procedures. A software component is never certified itself, only the equipments in which it is embedded are certified. Nevertheless the audit work which will have been done might be re-used by the certification authorities when a future system based on SAE will be certified. This assumes that the SAE Executive has a well-defined and stable interface whatever the system which uses it. The SAE executive interface has been defined this way, to avoid *dead code* and to minimize *deactivated code*. Indeed, according to software configurations, it is possible that some services of the Executive are not used. In that case, the corresponding code which is not executed is (and must be) deactivated. The operational configuration needed for operational configuration of this code should be validated during testing phases.

At the end, the certification will be carried out by the equipment supplier who uses the SAE executive. Thomson Software Products/Alsys will provide auditors with the material required for the executive SAE.

3. Conclusion

This project started with the Ada83 revision of the language and will end with the Ada95 revision. It is interesting to note that the results of this study **will take advantage of the new language revision**. First of all, the *pragma Restrictions* could be used to transform the programmation rules proposed by the SAE executive use. The proposed restrictions do not match exactly those proposed in the « Real Time » annex, nor in the « Safety and Security « annex, but instead are a combination of both of them. The following Ada95 restrictions apply to SAE :

- *No_Task_Hierarchy*
- *No_Nested_Finalization*
- *No_Abort_Statements*
- *No_Terminate_Alternatives*
- *No_Implicit_Heap_Allocations*
- *No_Asynchronous_Control*

- *Max_Asynchronous_Select_Nesting => 0;*

- *No_Local_Allocators*

- *No_Unchecked_Deallocation*

- *No_Exceptions*

- *No_Delay*

- *No_Io*

- *No_Recursion*

Regarding the Ada executive, an interesting feature of Ada95 is the *protected types* which might replace the *rendezvous* currently recommended for programming *polling servers, sporadic servers* or the *Highest Locker Protocol.* This feature is not mandatory but it would allow performance enhancement. Finally with the Ada95 revision, it will not be any longer necessary to maintain Ada executive extensions to support a construct such as *Delay Until* or a service allowing to assign different task priorities for a given task type.

Independently of the Ada language, the major interest of the SAE project is the challenge regarding the certification process. If this project achieves its goals, it will demonstrate that it is possible to certify - at the highest critical level - equipments using tasking software based on preemptive scheduling. This will allow to drop cyclic dispatchers and to use COTS instead and to introduce a separation between the application and the executive. This separation will enable to **better re-use application software.**

The **cost reduction of certification** will be another result of the SAE study.The SAE COTS will have been audited once for ever and, whatever is its re-use, the equipment supplier will take advantage of it. Re-using the applications will be also a cost reduction factor.

Références

[ARM83] « *Reference Manual for the Ada Programming Language* », ANSI / MIL-STD 1815, January 1983.

[ARM95] « *Ada 95 Reference Manual* », International Standard ANSI/ISO/IEC-8652:1995, January 1995.

[KLEIN93] Mark H Klein, Thomas Ralya, Bill Pollak, Ray Obenza, Michael González Harbour, « *A Practitioner's Handbook for Real-Time Analysis: Guide to Rate Monotonic Analysis for Real-Time Systems* », Kluwer Academic Publishers, 1993.

[LIU73] Liu, C. L. and Layland J. W, « *Scheduling Algorithms for Multiprogramming in a Hard Real Time Environment* », JACM 20 (1): 46-61, 1973.

[WHICH89] B.A. Whichmann, « *Insecurities in the Ada Programming Language* », National Physical Laboratory, Report DITC 144/89, 1989.

[DO178B] DO-178B/ED-12B, « *Software considerations in airborne systems and equipment certifications* », RTCA/EUROCAE, December 1992.

Developing Fault Tolerant Software in Ada for Real-Time Dependable Systems

P. David, T. Planche, A. Correge, J.F. Chane

Matra Marconi Space Toulouse, France

Key-words: Ada for dependable software, Software Implemented Fault Tolerance Techniques, Defensive Programming, On-Board Computer System Software, Error Confinement area, Error propagation.

Forewords

The Ada language has been used in the Space industries since approximately 1988. Lots of investments industrial investments have been made on the Ada development environment but also on the accompanying upstream design methods and the downstream test and validation means. This design and development environment will continue to be used for the development of our future Space Systems. But once again, why using Ada? Simply because it helps getting more reliable software through the simple use of a compiler. This is a fundamental property of the Ada language which follows a more general trend towards procuring more dependability. In the near future, the dependability of the objects of our everyday life will be significantly enhanced; even, dependability will be more than today the keyword for marketing products.

Starting from this idea, this paper presents three examples of the dependable computing systems that MATRA MARCONI SPACE is preparing for the future Space Applications. Through these examples, it demonstrates that the Ada language has taken the right direction in promoting the image of dependability for programming and this still needs to be reinforced. Our experience in the development of such dependable systems has generated some propositions for enhancing the dependability features of the Ada language or of Ada libraries which are presented in section 3 of the paper. It does not mind if they will be retained or not by the Ada community, in doing so, we had the only objective of highlighting today the needs that will be encountered tomorrow in the development of the future dependable computing systems.

The first section of the paper introduces the *strategic interest* of MATRA MARCONI SPACE for using *dependable data processing* for its future systems. In particular the use of software implemented fault tolerance techniques is emphasized.

The second section presents three projects conducted by MATRA MARCONI SPACE which include fault tolerance properties. Firstly the project "Fault Tolerant On-Board Software systems" is presented, it has been performed during the 93-95 period under an ESTEC contract with the associated partners LAAS-CNRS and SIEMENS Österreich; the aim of this project was to define a generic architecture including fault tolerance techniques targeted to the management of autonomy in a modern telecommunication satellite. Secondly the project "Unité de Surveillance et de Reconfiguration" (Monitoring and Reconfiguration Unit) is presented, it has been running since 92 under a CNES contract and has defined a fault tolerant computer system which is dedicated to the operations of on-flight maintenance on-board a satellite. Thirdly the project "Manned Support Transportation Program" is presented, it is currently running as a follow-on of the HERMES program under an ESA/CNES contract and it has demonstrated the data processing functions which are necessary for managing the safety critical mission of a space plane.

The third section details the fault tolerance mechanisms which have been implemented in Ada on these three projects and gives the *lessons learned* from these three projects. Ideas and propositions are added for enhancing the dependability features of the Ada technology in order to be ready for the development of dependable software systems.

1. Introduction

Since 1980, MATRA MARCONI SPACE has been designing Fault Tolerant systems for the on-board computing functions of its satellites, and an important evolution of the fault tolerance properties of the Space Systems have been performed since that time. Fault tolerance was originally limited to the automatic switch to a survival mode whose goal was to keep the satellite in a state operable by the ground, in addition the on-board pieces of equipment were redunded and their reconfigurations were managed by the ground through the telemetry/telecommand link. This simple architecture has evolved into three main directions.

The first evolution of space systems is the use of more software instead of hardware for implementing the on-board functions. Putting on-board more and more complex functions has led to the creation of a dedicated management of on-board faults using error detection mechanisms, fault localization, error compensation, fault treatment. Implementing this function by software has brought the required advantage of getting a system with a high level of configurability and easiness of use. The second evolution is the modification of the way the functions are distributed between the ground and the space system. Today, the satellites are becoming more autonomous than the past generation, this is due to economical reasons whose origin is the cost of the man power in the control station on-ground. In order to lighten these tasks on-ground, we are putting more intelligence on-board the satellite so that it can detect its failure and can try to recover automatically. To allow such an autonomous management, the satellite shall be equipped with a dedicated processing support including fault tolerance which shall keep the autonomy features active whatever the situation is. The third evolution is oriented towards all the applications which deal with man in space. In this area which is very promising for the future, all the functions whose failure may endanger the life of the crew are classified as safety critical. The execution of the embedded safety critical functions requires a dedicated fault tolerant support because their availability shall remain constant even in the presence of errors.

Even if the needs for fault tolerance are different between satellites and manned systems and lead to different architectures, the underlying technology in particular the software technology remains the same. All these systems shall be able to run significant amount of software because today, the trend is to integrate all the functionalities of the on-board computing system into a single computer (centralized architecture). Furthermore, the economical and industrial parameters such as reusability and flexibility require now, undoubtedly, the implementation of fault tolerance techniques in software rather than in hardware.

MATRA MARCONI SPACE shows in this paper the fault tolerant architectures which will certainly be the basis of the future Data Management System Software for the next generation of space systems. Associated to these system architectures, a new software architecture based on an innovative concept of integrity domains and which makes intensive use of defensive programming techniques is proposed.

This new software architecture forces the designers of space applications to think about the error handling, how the system can fail, how the errors propagates at the same time he is defining the functional system.

2. The Strategic Interest in the Use of Fault Tolerant Software

MATRA MARCONI SPACE-FRANCE has designed Fault Tolerant Computers for the Earth Observation satellites and the Telecommunication satellites, they are now flight proven with numerous years of commercial use. But the satellite market is still evolving towards the definition of new products which are cheaper, adaptable, lighter and which allow to embed more commercial pay-loads. The other evolution we have seen in the previous chapter is to require from the new satellites more autonomy for getting more availability of the services like telephone, television, imaging, this evolution implies to embed more intelligent and more dependable functions.

The way to make these two evolutions fitting in together, i.e. being less expensive and more dependable, is to use more software techniques for both, implementing the functions and the dependability mechanisms.

However, a lot of problems are raised in employing the software technology. In particular, the main drawback of the integration on the same CPU of software functions is that in the case of an error such as software design error or hardware error, no mechanism exists today which prevents the error from propagating into all the parts of the software. The building of a dependable centralised system is then a challenge because it requires to use technologies which are well mastered by the research domain and which need now to be transferred to the industry. In particular, making a fault tolerant design requires to systematically study the classes of errors which can be encountered and to include in the design the corresponding detection mechanisms and firewalls for avoiding the global pollution of the satellite by a minor event. A software system able to properly handle all the classes of errors will optimize significantly the resource management of the satellite by avoiding a too quick loss of some resources or being able to recover from a faulty state using a better management scheme.

2.1. The FTOBS project, Fault Tolerant On-Board Software Systems

The "Fault Tolerant On-Board Software Systems" study has been conducted by MATRA MARCONI SPACE-FRANCE with SIEMENS ÖSTERREICH and LAAS-CNRS under an ESTEC contract from 93 to 95 [5]. Three main objectives were assigned to the FTOBS project. The first one was the systematic and justified provision of dependability for the On-Board Computer System of a telecommunication satellite (OBCS), in order to enhance it into a fault tolerant Data Management System architecture (FTOBCS) mainly by adding software implemented Fault Tolerant Mechanisms. The second objective was the definition of a validation tool able to evaluate the efficiency of the dependability of the fault tolerant mechanisms included in the FTOBCS. This tool implements the method of dependability evaluation through fault injection. Finally, the third objective was a theoretical one whose aim was to make an overview of the techniques devoted to software dependability analysis.

2.1.1. The FTOBCS System architecture

The synthesis of the FTOBCS *hardware architecture* which has been retained as the reference FTOBCS architecture for an autonomous telecommunication satellite is shown in figure 1.

The CPU module is built around a MA3-1750 component performing 1.0 MIPS at least. It is able to switch ON and switch OFF any of the other modules of the FTOBCS. The two CPU modules are managed in a cold redundancy mode. The MEMory modules are replicated, they are managed in a hot redundancy mode and protected with an EDAC. A MMU (Memory Management Unit) allows to replace a failed memory chip by a spare one located at a different physical address and to map it on the same logical address. The MMU implements protection mechanisms. The MEM modules constitutes a central point in the management of the software context of the application when an error occurs. The IO modules are the controller of the system bus, they are managed in a cold redundancy manner. The IO module contains a TM/TC interface implementing the satellite CCSDS protocol. It contains also direct acquisition and direct command line. The system bus is a 1553B bus or a OBDH bus running a full duplex physical protocol.

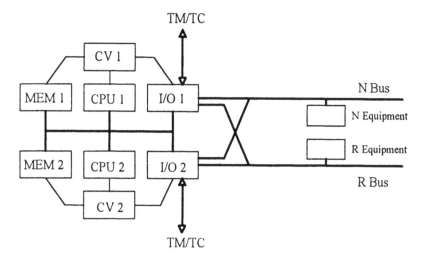

Fig. 1. The hardware architecture for the Fault Tolerant On-Board Computing System

The *software system* is arranged in hierarchical domains. Three domains are defined according to their criticality and the kind of resources they use. Each of these three integrity domains ensures the non-propagation of its errors to the other domains.

The definition of the contents of a domain is based only on the safety analysis of the functions and has no connection with the classical software layering based on a functional decomposition. The level of criticality is derived from the capability that the software components have in managing the hardware and software resources of the system. For instance, several kinds of software can be found each with a different responsibility in managing the hardware resources: the Attitude and Orbit Control software (AOCS), the Attitude and Orbit Control FDIR software, the Data Management System (DMS) FDIR software. FDIR stands for Failure Detection, Isolation and Recovery. The AOCS software is in charge of computing the control laws; it does not need to manage resources and it has only to interface functionally with the actuators and sensors. The error detection of the AOCS (FDIR of the AOCS) is responsible for detecting the equipment items (actuators and sensors) which are in error and for reconfiguring them to replicated equipment items. The AOCS FDIR software is then responsible for the management of the actuator and sensor resources. The DMS FDIR software is in charge of managing the DMS functions and the DMS resources, the responsibility of the DMS FDIR is to detect errors and to reconfigure the DMS in order to allow the AOCS software and the AOCS FDIR software to continue their activities.

Software components such as the AOCS FDIR or the DMS FDIR which are able to induce a reconfiguration of the On-Board equipment and of mission modes are considered as critical pieces of software and must have dedicated properties. In particular, they must be protected against internal design faults but also against error propagating from lower criticality components. This analysis has motivated the definition of the software architecture, as shown in figure 2, which groups the various functions of the satellite into domains which confine the errors and which contain firewalls avoiding error intrusions.

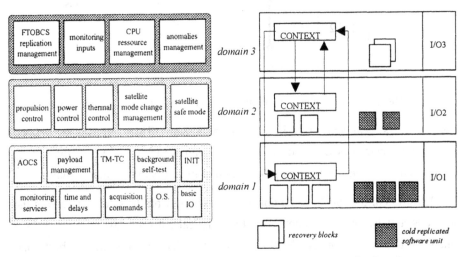

Fig. 2. On-Board Software Architecture decomposed into integrity domains

In addition to the confining technique and firewall, the domain shall ensure the availability of the functions it encapsulates, this is achieved in monitoring the software with techniques such as control flow monitoring, execution timing monitoring, data monitoring. In case an error is detected, it is compensated and a fault treatment strategy is applied which allows to recover the function, in managing the software replications and the functional context.

The integrity domain 1 contains the lowest critical software and the most complex software in terms of size and of algorithm. It is built of several tasks implementing the classical satellite functionalities. It is cold replicated, i.e. another version of this software is loaded but not executed. The cold version is functionally equivalent to the active one but it has followed a completely separate development process. The domain 1 software is developed using defensive programming techniques, it is monitored by the domain 3 software through data flow and control (path and timing) flow checks. It is reconfigured by the domain 3 software; in this case, the domain 1 software starts by recovering its context provided by the domain 3 software.

The domain 2 software contains a more critical part of the software, it is the mode management of the satellite and also the management of the safe mode of the satellite. This software is simple, it inherits from the domain 1 properties: cold replication, data flow and control flow checks. The recovery of its context is performed like for the domain 1. Moreover, the domain 2 software is developed using formal specification and automatic code generation and it is PROMed.

The domain 3 software is the most critical since it is in charge of reconfiguring the FTOBCS. It contains all the recovery logic concerning hardware as well as software errors and it manages the context data of the domain 1 and domain 2 software units in order to perform error compensation on context data. It allows fault treatment through up-loading of new pieces of software by the ground. The domain 3 software unit is not allowed to fail; so, in addition to the technique of data and control flow checks, it features the recovery blocks technique to continue running properly as long as possible when an error is detected.

The coexistence in the centralized OBCS (same CPU) of these 3 software components, each with a different level of criticality, implies to control strictly the exchange of information between these domains. The approach retained in the FTOBCS software architecture is based on techniques used to ensure security and confidentiality in military data processing systems [1,2].

2.1.2. The Mechanisms to ensure the integrity of the domains

The use of code and data within an integrity domain must be checked (check on memory utilization and check on IOs data) because this can be a source from which the errors propagate. To this concept of integrity domain, let us add the notion of **Active objects** and **Passive objects** in which a software item can be decomposed. An active object corresponds to a process and all the code which is linked to it. A passive object is a set of data which are computed by an active object or which come from IOs. A passive object belongs to only one integrity domain. To each object is associated the integrity level (IL) of the domain it belongs to. Active objects and passive objects interact in the following way:

An A object may read from a P object, only if ILP ≥ ILA.

An A object may write on a P object only if ILA ≥ ILP.

An A object may request a service from a A object only if

ILA (requester) ≥ ILA (server).

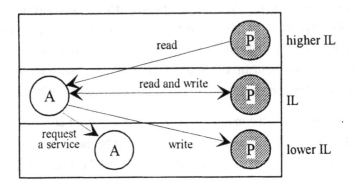

Fig. 3. Rules to ensure a safe communication between integrity domains

The protection of the communication between objects is achieved by means of privileges, access rights and dynamic memory ownership. Each active object has a set of privileges which determine the services it is enable to request. Each active or passive object has a set of access rights which determine which active object is allowed to request the service by comparing the access rights to the privilege of the caller.

To guarantee the integrity of an object, the memory shall be divided into segments. To each segment shall be associated dynamically the notion of ownership. The segment is owned by an object where are located its data and/or code. The owner object is the only one authorized to use its segments. For communication between Active objects (processes), the use of common segment is precluded (no shared memory), a dedicated inter-process mechanism is implemented in order to perform the service request.

Following these rules, three memory area are defined, corresponding to the 3 integrity levels, all of them are then protected against false access request coming from lower level software. In order to detect as soon as possible the intrusion of an error inside a domain or the arrival of an error in the function of a domain, complementary fault tolerant mechanisms have been applied, they are described in the following lines.

Detection of error on data by Executable assertions

The defensive programming technique is applied for including assertions. Two kinds of assertions are used, the structural checks verifying the integrity of the data (Ada checks). The Reasonableness checks which are using functional redundancy. The specification of mission applications often contain mission monitoring requirements. This monitoring is implemented by executable assertions included in the code of the AOCS tasks for instance and related to the dynamic behaviour of the satellite, such as pointing convergence time, reasonableness of the AOC mode with the sensors measurements, etc. This kind of monitoring is mission-dependent.

Detection of error on code, Control flow monitoring

Significant locations called Trace Points are selected in the code and used to monitor the execution of the software tasks by comparing the trace points reached with the expected trace points list. The control flow monitoring process is using these trace points. it is implemented by a dedicated task. This task is awaken by trace point messages issued from the active tasks, it compares then the execution path of this task with the expected execution graph in order to detect the execution of a wrong path in the control flow.

Detection of error on timings

Worst Case Execution Time data are checked between Trace Points by using watch-dogs and timers.

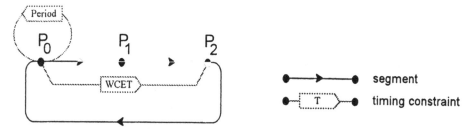

Fig. 4. The trace point mechanism for monitoring the timings and the control flow

Each time an active task encounters a trace point, and if the timing check flag is set, the execution duration between the two last trace points is compared with the expected duration for this task. A watch-dog is managed for each task in order to allow the checking of the period of the task or to detect infinite loop in the software.

Error Processing Techniques

It comprises 3 steps:

(a) collection of the error messages sent by processes upon the detection of an error,

(b) classification and filtering of the collected error messages if any,

(c) making up of a diagnosis and execution of a recovery according to the diagnosis.

In the FTOBS the error processing task is cyclically activated inside the highest critical domain at the highest functional frequency. All the possible error messages can be gathered quickly and classified into error classes according to their symptoms and then an adequate recovery strategy is selected.

Error Recovery techniques

To recover from software errors, the on-board software system must be diversified. The simplest diversification, inspired by hardware replication, consists in providing a spare software unit, which will replace the nominal one if the latter is declared faulty, just like the spare CPU can replace the nominal CPU. In this strategy, the nominal and the spare software units are executed in an exclusive manner, and the nominal software unit is abandoned after software reconfiguration.

2.1.3. Budgets

The major part of the FTOBS demonstrator is written in Ada. The corresponding source (specifications and bodies of Ada packages) comprises 10,000 lines (including comments) composing 4500 Ada statements. The rest is written in assembler and corresponds to the real-time operating system kernel (ASTRES). The total size of this software unit is 20,000 16-bit words.

In the nominal modes (when no error have been detected), the highest CPU occupancy is about 45 %, i.e., within one second, the CPU is executing tasks other than the background task (empty loop) during 450 ms, apportioned among the integrity domains in the following manner:

ID3:   290 ms

ID2:   10 ms (safe mode AOC and mode changer)

ID1:   150 ms (telemetry and nominal AOC)

An outstanding figure is the time spent on control flow monitoring (170 ms) which is high, even in a nominal case (17 % of the CPU time). This is explained by the high number of monitoring items in this function. Indeed, control flow monitoring in the FTOBS demonstrator concerns 27 different trace-points and 25 different monitored execution times attached to cyclic tasks; then, within one second, up to 88 trace-points are hit and 101 watch-dogs are armed/cancelled. So, this represents a heavy processing.

In addition, the performance of the used OBC, based on a F9450 processing unit, is low (300 kips) because of its high number of wait states (11) and low clock frequency.

When stepping to a new OBC architecture based on processors like MA3-1750 or SPARC which will increase the available CPU power, these techniques will become affordable as they have been successfully demonstrated on a low CPU power architecture.

2.2. The MSTP project, Fault Tolerant Architecture for Manned Systems

Since 1986, MATRA MARCONI SPACE-FRANCE has been involved in the studies and pre-development activities of the Fault Tolerant Computers for Manned Space applications like HERMES. These computers are safety critical, they are managing the electrical commands of the space plane by computing the stabilization of the plane as well as the control laws for the launching phase, the landing phase, the re-entry phase, etc.

The concepts on which are based the dependability of these computers makes intensive use of fault tolerance techniques. During the design period of the HERMES demonstrator, from 1986 to 1992, the trend was to integrate all these specific and critical features in the hardware in order to achieve the highest level of dependability. However, the experience got on the development and validation of the HERMES demonstrator system has shown that the integration of fault tolerance techniques in the hardware is necessary but still most of the work has to be done by software in order to keep the necessary level of flexibility which is required for such a system. The current state of the technology is then to build such safety critical system as a software intensive system. The techniques dedicated to the handling of fault tolerance are implemented in software and supported when necessary by specific hardware fault tolerant features.

2.2.1. The MSTP System Architecture

The data processing architecture which has been studied by MATRA MARCONI SPACE-FRANCE [3] for procuring intensive dependability for the guidance, navigation and control of the manned space plane is presented in the figure 5.

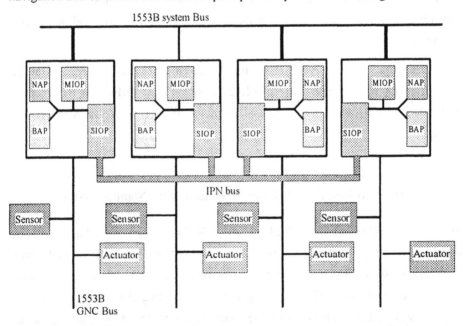

Fig. 5. Retained hardware architecture for the safety critical manned application.

The functioning of the dependable pool of computers is based on three principles. The first principle is the run of four computers in parallel and in tight synchronisation. The second principle is the majority voting of the commands and of all the intermediate values in order to detect failures and to avoid sending false commands. The achieved outage is null with regard to the computer activities and is less than 100 milliseconds with regard to the IO activities. The pool shall cope with the requirement to be tolerant to two computer failures which are not correlated, consequently, it is made up of four computers. The third principle is the execution in the same time of two versions of the software in order to be tolerant to one software design error. The nominal software is monitored and when a software error is detected, it is switched to the hot back-up version.

The Inter Processor Network (IPN) supports the communication between the computers, it is used to broadcast to the three other computers the input data which are acquired by each computer on its 1553 GNC bus. The results of the processing are also exchanged on this bus in order to prepare the majority voting of the output data which ensures the masking of the hardware failures.

Each computer is based on a modular design which implements the physical segregation of the functions inside one computer. The problem of error propagation is solved here by segregating physically the functions onto dedicated processor boards.

One computer is constituted of the following functional blocks:

- 2 application functions named NAP (Nominal Application Processor) and BAP (Back-up Application Processor) which contain respectively the nominal application software and the Hot Back-Up application software. These two redundancies of the application allows to tolerate one software design errors, they are hosted on 2 SPARC boards.

- the SIOP (Safety critical Input/Output Processor) manages the IO to/from the 1553B GNC bus as well as the exchanges on the IPN. The Fault Management software is also hosted on this board, it is built around a 1750A microprocessor and an intelligent DMA device.

- the MIOP (Management Input/Output processor) contains the non critical part of the I/O. It manages the communication between the computer pool and the other sub-systems of the plane.

2.2.2. The MSTP Software Architecture

The figure 6 and the following lines describes the different functions which are distributed inside one computer of the pool.

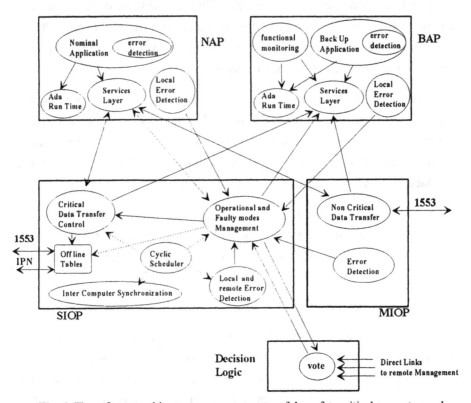

Fig. 6. The software architecture on one computer of the safety critical computer pool.

The software architecture is in charge of supporting the execution of the functions of Guidance, Navigation and Control (GNC) of the manned space transport vehicle. On the other side, the software architecture shall cope with stringent real-time constraints and heavy RAMS requirements.

This architecture shall be generic enough to be the basis from which will be derived the architectures of the next programs such as the Crew Transport Vehicle (CTV) and the Automated Transfer Vehicle (ATV), it benefits from all the knowledge which has been gained during the HERMES program.

The Fault Management Software

The Fault Management function involves many sub-functions (error detection, error filtering, fault isolation, error masking, error recovery) which are split in the various software units inside a computer. The figure 7 details all the error management mechanisms which are used at the various stage of the fault tolerance process.

<u>LOCAL DETECTION</u>

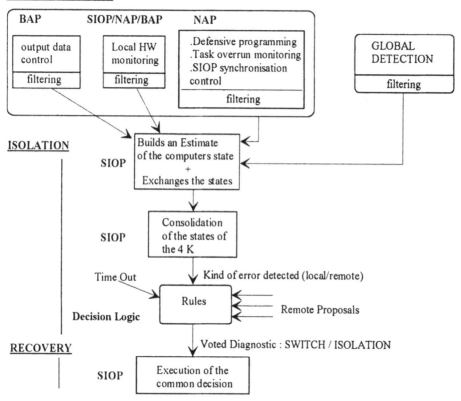

Fig. 7. The error management which goes from the error detection to the reconfiguration.

The management of the errors is decomposed in several parts. Firstly, each function detects the errors at its level by monitoring its own activity. Secondly, in the SIOP, the functional data computed by the NAP or BAP of the four computers are voted by the remote error detection function in order to mask potential hardware failures. Thirdly, the error status coming from the monitoring of the functions or issued by the remote error detection are used to localize the origin of the error. At this stage, in the presence of an error, the system is able to distinguish a software design fault from an hardware error. Depending from the kind of fault which has been detected, the right reconfiguration is applied.

In order to reconfigure the pool, a Decision Logic has been implemented on the four computers. It interfaces the Fault Management software of the four computers to allow the pool to decide the passivation of one faulty computer or to agree on the switching of the pool to the Back-Up software in case a software fault has been identified.

The SIOP Software

The SIOP software is a single point of failure in this architecture, it is not diversified and consequently it shall be design and developed without fault. A dedicated development process has been followed to develop it but the use of a structured high level language as Ada has been the necessary basis to reach the objective of a fault free software.

In such heavily real-time constrained environment, the risk of using the full Ada run time has not been taken, the solution of a procedural Ada associated to a specific Operating System has been retained. This solution allows the exhaustive validation of the SIOP software, in particular with regard to the real-time requirements.

The Application Software

The Defensive programming techniques have been used for the development of the NAP and BAP software in order to introduce in-line error detection. Some Ada facilities have been directly used such as exceptions: Constraint error, Numeric error, Program error, Storage error, Tasking error.

The NAP and BAP software are implemented in full Ada using the RATIONAL SPARC Ada cross compiler. This environment offers some CIFO primitives, in particular the mailbox and semaphore services for inter task communication and synchronisation have been very useful. Such set of CIFO primitives fills the gap between the procedural Ada solution which is commonly used in very deterministic systems and the full Ada solution.

In order to build the firewalls in charge of avoiding errors to propagate in the whole system, the notion of package has been used to support the encapsulation of critical data.

Nevertheless the lack of a dynamic debugging tool and the lack of a schedulability analysis tool remain and need to be solved soon.

2.3. The USR project, a Fault Tolerant Architecture for Autonomous Spacecrafts

Since 1992, MATRA MARCONI SPACE-FRANCE has developed, under a CNES contract, a fault tolerant computer whose purpose is to support the in-flight maintenance of the satellite. The USR, for "Unité de Surveillance et de Reconfiguration", is designed for being included in any kind of electrical architecture such as satellites or robots without major impact on the design of the host system. Inside the host system, the USR is responsible for the monitoring of the system and for the automatic reconfiguration in case of failure. The USR provides to the system the autonomy and the availability properties which are required now in modern satellite systems.

2.3.1. The USR System architecture

The design of the USR computer pool has been optimised to ease its embedding in any kind of system in order to provide it with more autonomy and availability. The characteristics of the USR system are the following:

- Probability of sending a false command < 10^{-8}/h;
- Outage = 0 considering the computer activities, outage = 100 ms considering the IO activities;
- Tolerance to two computer non correlated failures;
- Probability of occurrence of a single point failure < 1-0.995;
- Reliability = 0.985 over 10 years;

The USR is a maintenance processor for a satellite and as such, it shall be tolerant to its own errors in order not to propagate false commands to the host system and to stay available in all circumstances for reconfiguring the satellite. Such a system is very much constrained by the requirements about power consumption, mass and cost and it necessitates a completely new design to be attractive for satellite builders. The figure 8 shows the hardware architecture of the USR.

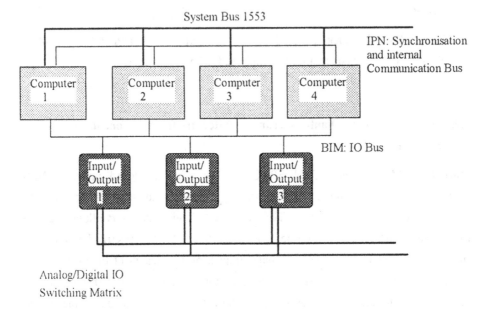

Fig. 8. The retained hardware architecture for the USR.

The USR is a small fault tolerant system which has concentrated all the good properties that help for embedding it in the architectures of the satellites. Its design has been based on the concepts of the MSTP thus getting a very strong and well proven capability for tolerating the errors. As the USR needs to be included in several kinds of electrical architectures to monitor and reconfigure them, it provides a generic way of supporting various applications of monitoring and reconfiguration which is based on the notion of a *software bus* upon which the application software is plugged. Furthermore, the USR is built upon the same CPU board which is MA3-1750A based and the same components (ASIC, memory, bus drivers) than the MATRA MARCONI SPACE computers for satellites.

As the USR is a subsystem whose dependability shall be as high as possible, we have included in the design of the hardware some supports for several specific dependability features. They comprise the spying of the activities of the inter computer IPN bus, the parallel management of the 1553 protocol on the System Bus by all the active computers of the USR pool, the protection of the power converters, the capability for a majority of computers to isolate or to switch off a faulty computer by the mean of hardware voters, the capability to vote by the mean of a hardware voter the switching of a relay through an Arm/Verify/Fire protocol.

The design of the USR has been driven by an analysis of the error confinement area which ensures that hardware errors such as bus failures or power supply errors will not propagate out of their area.

In spite of its small size which is approximately 10 litres and 10 kilograms for the complete box, the USR comprises 256 Kw of RAM on each computer boards. Even in such a small system, software is the most suitable tool, as in the MSTP, for implementing the fault tolerance techniques which uses or complements the hardware voters and all other hardware features dedicated to fault tolerance. The software dependability is also tackled through one fundamental property of the USR, which is to support the N-version programming of the application software.

2.3.2. The USR Software Architecture

The Software developed in the frame of the USR project consists of a set of generic services, which is able to support any kind of mission application. It is therefore supposed to provide an open architecture, in which the applications and the services shall be as independent as possible. In particular, all references to the applications within the services are avoided. The applications are declared to the services via cold entry-points which are initialised in the bootstrap. After the activation of each cold entry-point, the application declares itself to the operating system and services. The analogy with a software back-plane can be made with the applications which are plugging themselves on it. The software bus mechanisms allow the in-flight upgrading of the system by loading a new software part and "pseudo-elaborating" it by calling its cold entry-point.

The software architecture follows a classical layered structure. The mission applications communicate through the software bus using the agencies it provides as an extended operating system with large mailboxes, events, shared memory buffers and memory pools.

The USR software uses a freeware operating system, ASTRES-1750, and procedural Ada. No Ada run-time is embedded, which means that Ada tasking, exceptions, delays, etc, are replaced by ASTRES agencies. The ASTRES operating system has been extended by three low-level services: the cyclic sequencer, the extended memory management and the hardware interface service. The Service layer includes all the I/O objects, and several service to support the applications such as monitoring, on-board time. It includes also all the services which are dedicated to the fault tolerance: the voter, the USR mode management and the USR internal resource management.

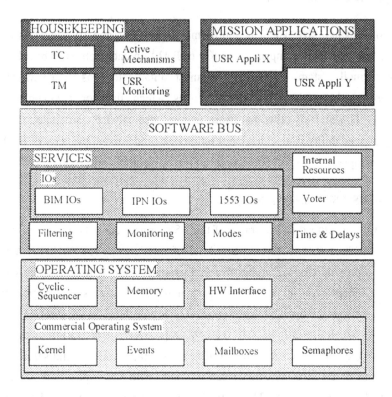

Fig. 9. The USR software architecture based on the software bus.

The Mission applications are the main part of the USR, it has been designed to support their execution in a dependable manner. The various applications which can be embedded on the USR depend very much on the host system. It can the maintenance of a robot such as a Lunar rover or a scientific probe or a civil or military satellite. The application layer includes also the Housekeeping of the USR itself which is built of the Telemetry and Telecommand processes and various autonomous activities such as the inter-processors synchronisation algorithm and the monitoring of USR by itself. All the applications have access to all the services via Ada calls to the *software bus* but the direct access of a task to another task is forbidden when it is not performed through the software bus mechanisms. All communication between tasks shall be made through the software bus, using the operating system and services.

2.3.3. The Software Implemented Fault Tolerance mechanisms

Control flow monitoring

The control flow monitoring technique consists in checking that the chaining of functional software blocks is correct, from two points of view: sequencing and timing. It uses time-tagged traces whose principle is similar to the one of FTOBS. Trace points are inserted in the source code (inside functional blocks), and their execution is signalled to a dedicated automaton. These trace points are part of the possible automaton states, which has a knowledge of all the allowed transitions between them. When a trace point is executed, the monitoring mechanism consists in checking the validity of the transition. The tracing is activated on a given state of the automaton (start state), and can be deactivated on a set of final states. Furthermore, a timer may be associated to each transition of the automaton, in order to check on each state reached by a trace that the time spent since the activation of the last trace is not inferior to a given limit.

This mechanism is then able to detect errors as bad logical chaining (invalid jump or branch) or temporal errors (late delivery of a result or late activation of a task). It is very useful in a real-time context, even if some invalid jumps could impair data, and thus be also detectable by assertions checking the data integrity.

Data integrity monitoring

The data used by the various software objects are checked before use. In particular, the parameters provided to Services and Operating System through the application calls, or the messages received from the external world or other CPU boards on the internal IPN bus are closely verified.

Voting

The voter is invoked each time a majority is required to take a decision. The voter is used when comparing data emitted by each CPU board, namely the on-board time, the USR configuration and the monitored hardware registers. The result of the vote (majoritary value) is accompanied by a diagnosis which shows which

CPU card has failed (in the case of 1 error within 3 or 4 values). If a CPU is detected in error, a passivation is applied by sending a passivation request to the other CPU's, this request is voted between the CPU boards before being applied using the hardware voters for isolation or switching off.

Real-Time Determinism

The real-time behaviour of the system is primarily driven by the I/O coprocessor, which is an ASIC able to autonomously execute I/O tables and to raise interrupts to the software when an I/O is performed. This feature has been used to trigger the software tasks in a deterministic way (as far as possible); the software shall be considered as I/O driven.

I/O BIM bus spying

On the I/O BIM bus, there is only one CPU board which is master at a given time and the other CPU boards have the capability to spy the Master's activity. An error is detected when the spying board does not agree on what the master has done. This leads to a reconfiguration request for changing the master CPU which is exchanged on IPN and voted. It is to be noticed that this spying activity on the BIM implies a strong synchronism and determinism within all the CPU boards.

2.3.4. Results from the USR demonstrator

Budget

The major part of the USR software is written in Ada. The corresponding source (specifications and bodies of Ada packages) comprises 17,000 of Ada lines (without including the comments). The rest is written in assembler and corresponds to the real-time operating system kernel (ASTRES) plus 5,000 lines written in assembler and devoted to the built-in-test of the USR. The total size of this software unit is 35,000 16-bit words of code.

The execution of the USR services requires 50% of the MA3-1750 CPU running at 5 Mhz and giving approximately 500 Kips.

Validation

The validation of the USR fault-tolerance concepts requires a dedicated validation bench with fault-injection capabilities. Some fault injections can be implemented by test scenarios run in the software, such as heterogeneous I/O activities raising, spying problems or SW data inconsistency. Some others can only be implemented by hardware, such as permanent physical bus failure. A specific test tool for supporting the fault injection has been developed by MATRA MARCONI SPACE-FRANCE. It has been connected to the Ada environment to allow the real-time debugging of the software and the error injection using an Ada symbolic debugging manner.

Fault Tolerant Mechanisms

The results on the USR demonstrator have shown the great efficiency of the various mechanisms listed in the previous chapter.

The *control flow monitoring* is able to detect very precisely bad functioning of the predetermined scheduling scheme. The cost of the most complete version of the control flow monitoring including state transitions and timing checks, in terms of CPU load is around 22%.

The *data integrity monitoring* rejects erroneous services requests and ill-formed data packets.

The *Real Time determinism* of the software architecture is a great support for the proof of the behaviour of the software architecture. In particular when a cyclical task consumes data which are produced by an automatic DMA and if the phasing between this task and the predefined I/Os of the DMA has not been exactly settled, the data will not be consumed correctly and the error will be detected by the data integrity monitoring. As the number of tasks in the USR software is not important, an intellectual analysis and a set of measures allows to assert that this case shall not happen. But for complex mission application with a lot of IOs, the proof of the Real Time activities shall be achieved via modelling techniques or the support of the Hard Real Time theory and corresponding tools.

The *I/O bus spying* is a performant tool to "cross-check" the CPU boards activities. It is entirely automated by the hardware and the software is only awoken when a problem raises. The cost in term of CPU load is null.

3. Lessons Learned on using Ada for real-time dependable Systems

3.1. Real-Time Operating System Kernel

The Software Bus

The software bus is an elegant way to provide an open architecture in which the applications and the services are as independent as possible. The software bus is built from simple mechanisms which include large mailboxes, events, shared memory buffers and memory pools. All the applications have access to all the services via Ada calls to the software bus but the direct access of a task to another task is forbidden, all communication between tasks shall be made through the software bus, using the operating system and services.

The differences between the software bus and the Ada Run-Time System (RTS) are mainly twofold. Firstly, the software bus provides asynchronous inter-task communication. Using these tools, it is very easy to build any kind of software architecture as well as it becomes possible to maintain dynamically the software configuration by plugging in-flight a new software component. Secondly, the property of the software bus for keeping the applications and the services independent is a very important difference with the RTS and it is very valuable to ease the validation of the dependability of the whole system.

Ada and the Real-Time

In a real-time system, the measure of the execution timings is very important as it is the basic information with which the designers and the validaters are working. The production of this timing information shall be performed in the compiler in order to be generated at the same time than the object code. The execution timings need only to be pessimistic estimates of the real value. These estimated timing figures are very useful in the early phases of the design to validate the dynamic properties of the software architecture and to define the parameters for the defensive programming techniques which are devoted to the monitoring of timing data.

Implementation of the integrity domains

In the theory of the integrity domains, the code of an active object belongs to only one domain. In the FTOBS demonstrator, this requirement is fulfilled, except for the real-time operating system kernel (RTOSK). This kernel provides a set of operations used by all integrity domains and then constitutes a 'shared library' apart from these domains.

In order to avoid such a derogation, one RTOSK can be implemented in each domain, but this leads to a complex design. A shared RTOSK is the right way to implement the inter-domain communications. But as this shared piece of software is a single point of failure in the software architecture, the RTOSK shall be proven as the highest criticality device in the system.

So, if the sharing of the RTOSK between the various integrity domains is retained for future applications using this concept, the technology of RTOSK shall be adapted mainly on two points:

inter-domain communication by operations which monitor access rights in order to avoid error propagation.

- it shall be validated as a highly critical component.

Implementation of the Control flow monitoring

The control flow monitoring process is implemented by a dedicated task which is awaken by messages containing either the coordinates of the occurred execution event, or the identifier of an expired monitoring timer. It monitors the measured execution timings by comparing them to the Worst Case Execution Timings that have been estimated or ideally computed by the compiler. This task could be fruitfully included in the Run-Time for two reasons, firstly because it uses data structures as the control flow graph which is already built by the compiler and which could be included in the Run-Time System (RTS) data and secondly because as it is very often activated, it can be significantly optimised when integrated in the Run-Time System.

3.2. New Ada features for the dependability

Implementation of the Access rights

The monitoring of the access rights on data must be supported by a hardware memory protection unit, otherwise, it will not be able to prevent an unauthorized process from reading or writing the protected variables.

So, to be effective, access right monitoring shall be supported by a memory management unit (MMU). But, in order to be fully operational, the corresponding software tools for programming the MMU shall exist, in particular it is necessary that they will be integrated in the Ada development environment.

In order to implement this access right monitoring it would be necessary to define a generic representation in software of a MMU, it could be a virtual memory management unit including privilege management and access authorization. This software representation of a MMU should be taken into account by the compiler when the user wants to define the memory protection scheme. Furthermore, a code generation shall exist to map this virtual memory model onto the existing hardware MMU components such as the 1750A MMU and the SPARC MMU for instance.

The software tools corresponding to the management of this MMU shall then comprise the additional compiler services for defining the required protection scheme from the high level description of the Ada language and the code generator for programming the MMU.

Implementation of the Executable assertions

The specification of mission applications often contains mission monitoring requirements. This monitoring is implemented by executable assertions included in the code which verifies dynamically the evolution of the data structure according to evolutive thresholds. The evolution of the thresholds could be related to other parameters such as the dynamic behaviour of the satellite, etc. An executable assertion raises error exactly as an exception when the monitoring conditions are not fulfilled. The executable assertion mechanism could be implemented in modifying the exception mechanism in two ways, firstly by allowing the declaration of complex conditions which may evolve dynamically, secondly by not propagating the exception but better in storing it in a reserved system area accompanied by an identifier and a time stamp.

Support for the Error Processing

The Error processing impacts the system by putting two major requirements which are attached to this highly critical function:

1. The Error processing shall not be blocked by the failing of low criticality process,

2. The Error processing shall not prevent the other processes from running by monopolizing the CPU resource.

In the FTOBS demonstrator, requirement (1) leads to implementing this function by a high priority task cyclically activated at the highest functional frequency. This task is in charge of collecting all the error status that have been raised by other tasks. This mechanism corresponds to the cyclic management of exceptions which have not been propagated but which have been stored in the local task in a reserved system area. This new exception handling mechanism could then be just the setting of an error status in the task control block, in a reserved area, the error manager being a system task coming cyclically for polling this area in each task.

To cope with requirement (2), the number of error messages processed by this error manager task at each activation shall be limited. Obviously, the execution of the error manager task shall also be monitored using the timing monitoring.

3.3. Connection of Ada with dependability procurement tools

Support for the validation

The validation of the fault-tolerant systems as FTOBS, MSTP or USR requires to use the fault injection technique in order to force the exact error case that will lead to the expected reconfiguration. A specific tool is necessary for supporting a complete fault injection campaign, MATRA MARCONI SPACE-FRANCE has developed such a validation bench for these three projects. In the case of the FTOBS system which is running on a single CPU, the validation tool consists of an hardware device which looks like a logic analyser. It is able to freeze the system giving to the user a confortable access to the memory and to the registers of the CPU. It resumes the FTOBS exactly in the state it had been frozen.

The USR validation bench is built on the same principles than the FTOBS one but the four hardware validation devices, one per CPU are synchronized together in order to allow the user to freeze and resume the complete pool.

In MSTP, on the SPARC, we have evaluated the benefit of integrating JTAG features in the CPU boards. The JTAG bus allows to prepare a test without disturbing the real-time, when the test case is ready to be forced onto the target, it freezes the CPU, the test patterns are injected and the CPU is resumed. This JTAG environment needs to be connected to an Ada symbolic debugger in order to simplify a lot the test preparation process.

On all of these validation benches, it is required that the Ada symbolic debugger be open enough to be retargeted to one of these test environments which are very similar to a CPU emulator.

Ada and the Formal Specification

For the development of safety critical software, the use of formal specification and automatic generation of code is recommended. Ada remains the industrial reference for developing space application software, it shall then be connected to formal specification tool in order to be included in a full automatic code generation process. In particular, many fault tolerance techniques dedicated to error detection and error recovery could be automatically generated in using information located in the specification. This process of automatically including executable assertions directly from information located in the specification will reinforce both the fault prevention and the fault avoidance for the production of dependable software in order to approach as closely as possible the objective of a design error free software. Specification language such as B, Z or VDM could be fruitfully connected to a reliable Ada translator.

Connection with a real-time schedulability analyser

For constrained real-time software, fault prevention was limited to the static description of the architecture using design methods such as HOOD. With regard to the dynamic behaviour of the software it is possible today to describe it and to validate it in using the Hard Real-time Hood method (HRT). But this method is not accompanied by sufficiently mature tools to be operationally used. However, it is a very promising area.

References

[1] C. Beounes, Y. Deswartes, J.-C. Fabre, P. Thevenod-Fosse, "Coexistence of Software Programs with Different Levels of Criticality", *LAAS Report no. 94-515*, 1994. (In French)

[2] K.J. Biba, "Integrity Consideration for Secure Computer Systems", *Tech. Rept. no. MTR-3153*, The MITRE Corp., 1975.

[3] C. Guidal, P. David, P. Humbert, "A Highly Dependable Fault-Tolerant Computer System for European Manned Space Transportation Vehicles3, *Proc. 45th Int. Astronautical Fed. Congress*, Jerusalem, Israel, 1994.

[4] J.-C. Laprie (Ed.), *Dependability: Basic Concepts and Terminology*, Springer-Verlag, Vienna, 1992.

[5] T. Vardanega, P. David, J.-F. Chane, W. Mader, R. Messaros, J. Arlat, "On the Development of Fault-Tolerant On-Board Control Software and its Evaluation by Fault Injection", *Proc. FTCS-25*, pp. 510-515, IEEE, Pasadena, California, 1995.

The Practical Application of Safety Techniques on an Ada based Project

Rupert Brown

Logica UK Ltd, Byron House, Business Park 4
Randalls Way, Leatherhead
Surrey, KT22 7TW, England

E-mail : brownrw@logica.com

Abstract. Two techniques are used to analyse a computer based system from a safety perspective. The first identifies those user requirements which encapsulate the safety-related nature of the system. These requirements are tracked through analysis, design and coding, resulting in the identification of safety-related components throughout the project lifecycle. The second technique seeks to examine the effect of failures of system components as they emerge from the design activity. The results produced from both activities are compared and combined. Design changes are made to eliminate "weak points", and the degree to which components can affect safety is constantly monitored. Safety-related components are handled with greater care and subjected to more intense development and testing rigour than non safety-related components.

1.   Introduction

Ensuring the safe operation of software based systems is becoming an increasingly important task for software developers. Typically, this task falls to those who develop using Ada, as the language is a natural choice for safety related systems. The Ada language and its use in safety related systems has been the subject of much study. An obvious example of this is the work which culminated in the SPARK subset[1]. The techniques used to determine whether a system, or parts of a system, are safety related have received less attention. This paper describes the practical application of safety analysis techniques on an Ada based project.

2.   System Overview

The Système pour Coordination, Traitement et Visualisation (SCTV) project is one of the systems currently being developed as part of the Year 2000 Investment Programme for the Guyana Space Centre (CSG), PICSG 2000. The main aim of the programme is to provide the ground infrastructure for the Ariane 5 launcher programme for the next fifteen to twenty years.

The SCTV system is distributed across several sites and over several computers within each site. In total, SCTV is made up of fourteen DEC Alpha workstations, three DEC VaxStations and three DEC rmVAX real-time computers. The language of choice for all software is Ada, although some of the software is written in C and

FORTRAN. Most of the FORTRAN software is existing code "industrialised" as part of the project. The system has been under development since November 1993 by an international consortium consisting of Logica and Sema teams in France, England, Italy and Spain. The French National Space Agency CNES, based in Toulouse, are managing the procurement of the system and the final users will be CSG in Kourou.

Fig. 1 Overview of the SCTV system

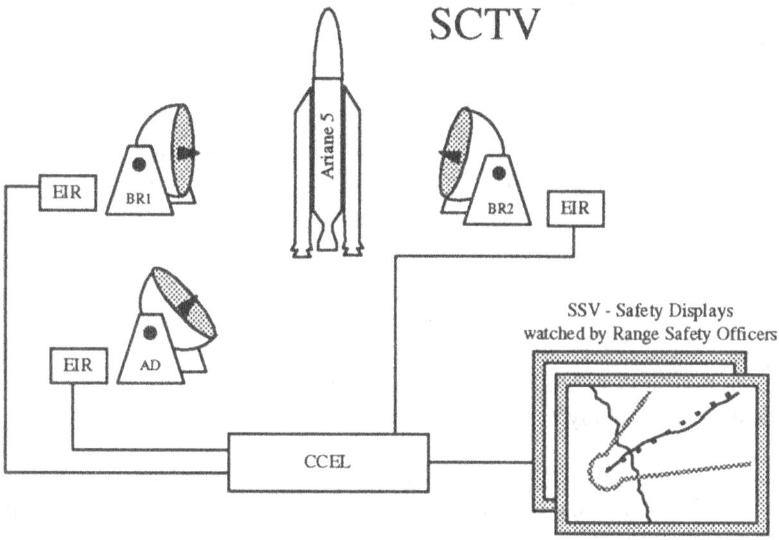

The main purpose of SCTV is to monitor the trajectory of Ariane launchers throughout their flight. Telemetry systems and radars positioned around the launch site feed SCTV with data describing the launcher's position. This information is used to determine whether the launcher is behaving normally i.e. whether it is following a nominal and safe trajectory. If the launcher is shown to be deviating in a dangerous way, then the range officers, who monitor the information provided by SCTV, have the power to destroy the launcher in the air before it can cause loss of life or damage to people and equipment on the ground.

3. Safety Levels

CNES have defined a series of high level fault trees for PICSG 2000. These fault trees show how failures within SCTV (called mission critical events) could lead to one or more "feared events" which sit at the top of the fault trees. Feared events include loss of human life, destruction of ground systems and incorrect destruction of a launcher. Comparison of these fault trees and the ESA safety standard for space systems and equipment[2] show that a failure of SCTV could not on its own lead to a catastrophic event. Catastrophic in this sense may be related to integrity level 4 of the IEC standard[3] (but note CNES have defined their own failure probability requirements). This comparison sets the overall level for safety analysis work.

It is necessary to employ safety analysis techniques to ensure that the delivered system offers as little risk of failure in operation as possible. It must be accepted that perfect safety is not possible. Given that fact, safety analysis has two important goals to achieve. Firstly it must ensure that the overall safety of the system as designed meets the safety thresholds mandated for the project (the ALARP principle[4]). Secondly, by identifying the "safety drivers" of the project it allows a greater proportion of the available project resources to be focused on those elements. This holds out the prospect of improved levels of safety being achieved within the finite resources available to the project. Safety analysis requires conscientious pragmatism.

4. Safety Requirements

Safety requirements are expressed as a set of high level safety related functions; functions that must be performed in order that the range safety officers can fulfil their role during launches. The safety related functions on SCTV are a small subset of the total required functionality.

In addition, a set of high level "mission critical events" (MCE) are defined for SCTV. These MCEs are the shown on the high level fault trees mentioned in section 3. The design of SCTV should ensure that the risk of one of these mission critical events actually happening is acceptably low.

Functions can fail in different ways, and combinations of failures can lead to MCEs. The following sections describe the techniques employed on SCTV to determine how these failures could occur and to mitigate both the chances of occurrence and their consequences.

5. Analysis Through the Lifecycle

SCTV follows a conventional project lifecycle. Yourdon and SADT were used to perform the functional analysis, describing system functions derived from user requirements. These functions were translated into operations within objects, captured using HOOD. Software components were produced from the objects, and the software was subjected to verification and validation.

Safety analysis develops through the lifecycle as the project develops. At the beginning of the lifecycle, safety analysis concentrates on requirements, because that is all that is available. As the project progresses, safety analysis examines and influences the design and then goes on to determine the level of development and testing rigour appropriate for individual software (and hardware) components. SCTV uses two primary safety analysis techniques :

1. the identification, allocation and tracking of safety related functions,
2. the examination of the effects of failure modes.

These two techniques cross-reference and support each other in a manner which is described below.

6. The Identification and Tracking of Safety Related Requirements

Section 4 describes how safety related functions are identified. A process that continues throughout the lifecycle is the identification and tracking of the functions, then objects and finally software and hardware components that realise these safety related functions. This identification and tracking process ensures that components which realise safety related functions are handled with an appropriate degree of rigour throughout the lifecycle.

7. The Examination of the Effects of Failure Modes

A parallel analysis activity determines the effect of failure modes of functions, then objects and finally software and hardware components. The Failure Modes, Effects and Criticality Analysis (FMECA) is used to determine failure modes (Fig. 2). Fault Trees (Fig 3) combine failure modes to reveal possible outcomes of those failures, and how combinations of failures can lead to MCEs. This analysis feeds back to influence the project at the next stage of the lifecycle. For example, as the design becomes more detailed it is possible to identify and modify parts of the design to remove single points of failure and other areas of potential weakness. In this way risks are assessed and action taken to mitigate those risks. This is an iterative process.

Fig. 2 An example of a FMECA table.

No.	Name	Function	Failure Mode	Effects	Detection	C	Comments
14	Real time clock	Synchro.	Intermittent or total failure.	Loss of time signal leading to a loss of the machine.	System error message.	2	Redundancy supplied by the other chain.

C = *level of significance.*

8. Combining the Techniques

The identification and tracking of safety related functions results in some of the Yourdon functions being marked as safety related. The objects that are allocated these functions are then also marked as safety related. The software produced from these objects is considered to be safety related software. Not all software is marked as safety related. Safety categories are allocated to software components. This is discussed later. At each stage a check is made to ensure that the safety related functions are being properly identified and tracked at the transitions between different requirements and design representations (e.g. Yourdon to HOOD).

At the same time, the "effects of failure modes" analysis is performed. The results of this analysis should confirm that functions, objects and software components, marked as safety related, can have a significant impact on the successful operation of the system. If it becomes obvious that the failure of an object, which is marked as safety related, would have no impact on the system whatsoever, then the object is re-examined to see if it can be marked as not safety related. Conversely, an object that has been ignored in safety terms but which, through a failure mode, could cause the whole system to fail, would have to be marked as safety related.

Fig.3. An example of a Fault Tree.

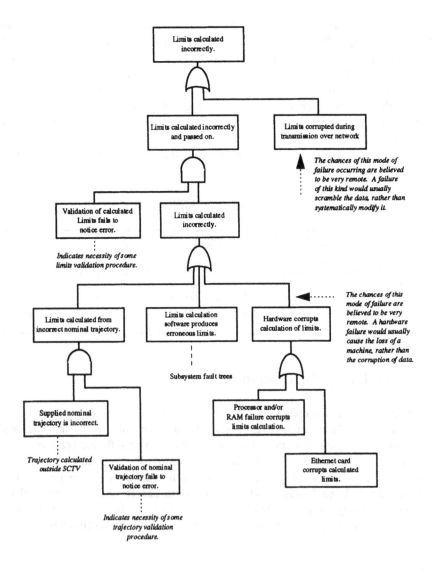

In this way the two techniques cross check each other. The "effects of failure modes" analysis should also show where redesign would help mitigate risk of failure. The way and extent to which the risk is mitigated determines the cost to the project. A compromise has to be reached between acceptable risk and affordable cost.

It is vital to start this kind of analysis work as early as possible. The later safety related problems necessitate design changes, the more expensive to the project the change becomes.

9.   Safety Categories

The techniques described identify both those components which pose the greatest risk to the system should they fail, and those whose failure would represent a loss in functionality, but which might not lead to a serious situation. This means that components have different levels of significance with regards to safety. It follows that it is possible to categorise components depending on their different levels of safety significance.

On SCTV, we have defined three levels of safety related significance, category 1 being the least safety significant, category 3 being the most significant. Software components that are identified as being more significant in safety terms, are being developed and tested in a more rigorous way; in a way that increases confidence in their ability to function correctly. Rigour is enhanced through the use of :

1. greater controls during detailed design and coding - specific rules for safety software contained within the Ada coding standard,
2. the use of automated standards checking (AdaTest),
3. formal inspections (Fagan Inspection Technique),
4. enhanced levels of testing (for example 100% condition coverage as opposed to simply statement coverage).

The result is that software realising safety related functions should be less susceptible to failures than software in other parts of the system.

10.   Conclusion

The application of these techniques results in the creation of a trace from high level safety functions to the safety categories assigned to individual software components. The trace continues through inspection and testing records demonstrating that the appropriate level of rigour has been applied to each component.

The techniques discussed represent a two-part approach to the safety related software developed as part of the SCTV project. Firstly, a thorough analysis of risks allows weaknesses to be designed out of the system. Secondly, development and testing rigour is determined by the safety category allocated to each software component. The visibility and ownership of this analysis by the project team enables thorough checking of the developed system against project standards throughout the project lifecycle. It also ensures the audit trail of implementation standards is clearly marked. The approach taken thus maximises project management and client confidence that the system will meet its safety requirements.

References

1   B A Carré and T J Jenning, 'SPARK - The Ada Kernel'
2   'System safety requirements for ESA space systems and associated equipment', ESA PSS-01-40 Issue 2 September 1988.
3   IEC 65A WG9 'Draft International Standard for Software for Computers in the Application of Industrial Safety-related Systems'.
4   'Guidelines on Risk Issues', The Engineering Council and Lloyds Register.

Ada in Mixed Language Applications

G. Taurisano

Logicasiel, Cso. Svizzera, 185
10148 TORINO
Italy

Internet: taurisanog@logica.com

I. Williams

Logica UK Ltd, Byron House,
Business Park 4
Randalls Way, Leatherhead
Surrey, KT22 7TW, England

Internet: williamsi@logica.com

Abstract

The development of large systems more and more often requires the interaction of different parts of software written in different languages.

The following paper analyses this aspect of Ada describing the different methods which can be used to accomplish this difficult task. Some of those methods have been successfully experimented with during the development of a large safety-related system. The advantages and disadvantages of the various approaches will also be outlined.

1.   Introduction

The problem of making Ada interact with other languages arises especially in those projects which, by their very nature, are the result of cooperations between different countries and contractors and which involve different and very specialised code sources. In these cases, the choice of the language to be used may be related to the kind of functionality to be implemented and to the peculiarities of the language itself or may be driven by external factors such as the existence of legacy software. Thus, we increasingly encounter large systems with a mixed language environment. It is therefore useful to analyse this aspect of Ada. In fact, some of Ada's well known characteristics make it suitable to be used with other languages, while others cause problems. Understanding these features becomes urgent in such a scenario.

Ada '83 provides the INTERFACE pragma to allow interaction with code written in other languages. However, this is inadequate in many cases, as it does not allow Ada procedures to be used from other languages, nor does it allow the parameter passing mechanism or linker symbol of a procedure to be specified. For this reason, implementors of Ada compilers have often provided additional non-standard facilities. DEC Ada, for example, offers a pragma IMPORT_FUNCTION which enables the parameter passing mechanisms to be specified [DEC Ada Language Reference Manual].

Because of this lack of standardisation, the set of interfacing pragmas has been extended in Ada '95 to provide many additional facilities, so in the future, non-standard pragmas will no longer be required.

It should also be noted that the way in which the interaction (or binding) is implemented is often constrained to comply with code rules, especially in safety related systems (sometimes, in these cases, the use of some pragmas has to be avoided). This is because the integration between Ada and other languages is further complicated by the safety, maintainability and portability problems related to the use of these non-standard built-in facilities. While some of these may be solved by using Ada '95, many of the safety problems associated with mixed language programming will always be relevant.

The main aim of this paper is to analyse methods of interfacing Ada programs with other languages such as SQL, PV-WAVE, DATAVIEWS, FORTRAN, C, Lex-Yacc, X-Designer and other GUI builders, and systems such as OSF/1, UNIX (mainly), X-Windows, with reference to our experience in the development of a large distributed system (SCTV project) for the provisioning of part of the ground infrastructure for the Ariane 5 launcher. As this system will be maintained for the next 20 years, the following paper will analyse briefly how Ada '95 (previously Ada 9X) faces a mixed environment.

2.   The SCTV System: a Mixed Language Application

The SCTV system (Système pour Coordination, Traitement et Visualisation) is one of the systems currently being developed as part of the Year 2000 Investment Programme for the Guyana Space Centre, PICSG 2000. It has been in development since November 1993 by an international consortium consisting of Logica, Sema and other contractors in France, England, Italy and Spain and Germany. Its main task is to provide the operators of the Space Centre with the information they need to perform their vital functions.

The system will be highly distributed over several sites in French Guyana and over several computers within each site. In total, SCTV is made up of fourteen DEC Alpha workstations, three DEC VaxStations and three DEC rmVAX real-time computers.

The main functions of the SCTV are:

- radar control and data acquisition

- computation of launcher trajectory from radar data

- computation of launcher trajectory from inertial telemetry

- display of trajectory data

- computation of predicted impact point from computed launcher trajectory

- display of impact point for range safety officers

- distribution of pointing angles to radars and other external equipment

Since we have started to develop it, we have met with the problems related to a mixed language environment.

The language we use for most of the software is Ada. The choice of this language has been dictated by the nature of the system itself. In fact, Ada is the language that fits the best for developing safety-related systems. As far as the use of other languages is concerned, we can identify several reasons why non Ada elements are desirable:

- The Unix system libraries, and X-Windows and Motif libraries, are written in C, and have C interfaces. While these can be accessed from Ada, code which intensively uses these facilities is much easier to write in C. In this case, the consistency of the interfaces can be checked to some extent by the ANSI C type checker. Also, the style of programming required to use these interfaces (involving the use of pointers, null terminated strings, pointers to functions, and dynamic memory allocation) is difficult to replicate in Ada.

- It is common-place in large systems to use a GUI-builder application such as UIMX or X-Designer to prototype and generate the user interface interactively. These applications usually generate source code modules written in C or C++, which must be included in the final system. It is impractical to translate these into Ada, both because of the effort involved, and because of the risk of introducing errors. It should be noted that some GUI builders such as TeleUse can generate Ada code, but these are generally more expensive and may be undesirable for other reasons.

- Higher level languages such as SQL and PV-WAVE, can be used to dramatically reduce the coding effort. They providing powerful facilities tailored to specific functional areas, which are applicable to many systems: e.g. database access (SQL) or graphics and visualisation (PV-WAVE). Using these languages can be seen as a form of re-use of software, which together with commercially available libraries of routines, is a more popular mechanism than Ada's package model.

- Existing source code, written in many different languages, must often be incorporated into new systems. In the case of SCTV system, Trajectory Analysis software written in FORTRAN and C, was provided by CNES. To translate this software into Ada would be expensive and commercially undesirable.

Therefore, in theory, the system could be divided into a number of well defined sub-systems, each of which can be written in a different language. The core of the application, and especially any safety critical sections, would be written in Ada. This approach is complicated by the following factors:

- It is inevitable that some modules of common software will be required to be used by more than one sub-system. These must either be re-written in each of the languages required, or written in one language with an interface to each of the others.

- The division of a software system into sub-systems must often be done on criterion other than the language to be used.

The resulting mix of languages even within sub-systems, means that mixed language programming issues can influence a large proportion of the software design.

Having briefly depicted the environment, we can proceed in presenting our study. Note that the study so far has a general character even if during our analysis we will frequently refer to the system just presented.

3. Mixing the languages: methods and examples

There are several ways in which the integration between Ada code and other language codes can be achieved. Most of these are strictly related to the implementation, the compiler and the provided linking systems. It is therefore necessary to consider the different methods in order to choose the most suitable accordingly with the characteristics required for the application to be developed. It is not by chance, in fact, that so many research groups are studying and developing bindings between Ada and other standards and that most of the literature concerning these subjects shows different approaches all developed for a specific machine (or compiler).

The main aim of the following sections is to provide an overview of the various techniques and to point out relative pros and cons. As already stated in the previous paragraphs, we will refer to our experience in interfacing Ada with the following languages and applications:

- PV-WAVE: interpreted graphics language based on APL language [Ref. PV_WAVE]
- DATAVIEWS: C library providing data visualisation facilities [Ref. DATA_VIEWS]

- Applixware : Word processor for work stations based on ELF macro language [Ref. APPLIX]
- C
- FORTRAN
- X-Designer: GUI builder which generates C code modules [Ref. X-Des]
- Lex-Yacc: compiler generator which produces C code [Ref. Lex-Yacc]
- SQL: database query language [Ref. SQL]
- POSIX: standard operating system interface based on UNIX system [Ref. POSIX]

3.1 Procedure and function bindings using pragmas

The easiest way to interface a language with another, is to use the built-in facilities provided by the language itself. Ada provides the *pragma INTERFACE*. It is mostly used to interface Ada with C or FORTRAN. Its use is described in the Ada Language Reference Manual. The main point is that *"all communication is achieved via parameters and function results"* [LRM]. This means that a "mapping" has to be defined between the different data-types (in the two languages) of the parameters and function result.

The task of constructing a data-type mapping is not always easy to achieve. Consider, for example, the difficulty of representing C data-types such as pointers, callbacks and void types in Ada '83. Ada '95 presents less problems because of its richer type model (e.g. access to pointer types), and the provision of standard packages (*Interfaces.C* and its children) to map and convert basic C data-types. Vice-versa the creation of interfaces for Ada in another language, such as in C, often presents problems in the replication of the Ada module hierarchy and in the mapping of some types such as unconstrained arrays.

It can also be very difficult, for example, to export a foreign language function with writable (**out** mode) parameters to Ada '83 where this mode is illegal for functions.

The integration of two different languages makes it impossible for any single compiler to perform any kind of check during the integration phase. So the system we obtain is, in general, less reliable than one written only in one language. This point is of special importance if the system we are developing is a safety-critical system.

The pragma INTERFACE does not provide any facility to interface with routines with mixed case names or, more generally, Ada ('83) does not allow the association of an external symbol with the internal Ada name for the subprogram or object. This leads to very serious problems when interfacing Ada on a UNIX system because:
- the UNIX linker is case sensitive
- some standard UNIX routines have names which are reserved in Ada (e.g. **exit**)

The problems stated above show the insufficiency of the standard and, we believe, are the main causes for the development of software which heavily uses either compiler dependent pragmas or other non-standard methods.

We provide the following example of the use of DecAda compiler pragmas in the SCTV system:

```
function XDVVIEWUPDATE ( WIDGET : XT.WIDGET_TYPE;
                         READ_DATA : DV_TYPES.DV_Integer;
                         USER_DATA : SYSTEM.ADDRESS )
                  return DV_TYPES.DV_Integer;
pragma INTERFACE ( C, XDVVIEWUPDATE);
pragma IMPORT_FUNCTION ( XDVVIEWUPDATE, "XdvViewUpdate",
                         MECHANISM =>(VALUE,VALUE,VALUE),
                         RESULT_MECHANISM => VALUE );
```

where the pragma IMPORT_FUNCTION allows the association of an external symbol ("XdvViewUpdate") with the internal Ada name (XDVVIEWUPDATE).

3.2 Executables

It is particularly useful to have an Ada binding for either the ANSI C library function "system", or the POSIX "exec" functions (or their equivalents on other operating systems), as shown below:

```
function SYSTEM ( COMMAND : string ) return integer;
pragma INTERFACE ( C, SYSTEM );
```

Software written in another language can then be encapsulated in an executable, and used without the need to produce any more Ada bindings. This has several advantages:

- The foreign program cannot corrupt the memory of the calling Ada program.
- The calling program will be protected from crashes or core dumps in the foreign code.
- The Ada program can protect itself from non-terminating programs by setting an alarm.
- The parameters are passed as ASCII strings (using Ada's IMAGE attribute) - a simple mechanism which is less prone to errors of interpretation than binary data.
- Any executable program can be used without producing a binding.
- The calling Ada program need not concern itself with the internal design and modular break-down of the foreign code, since it has no effect on the compilation or linking of the Ada process.

Unfortunately, the cost of making a call to a new process, in terms of CPU time and memory required, is many orders of magnitude greater than calling an ordinary function or procedure. This method of interfacing, therefore, would not be appropriate within a tight loop, or in a time-critical section of code.

We have found it a very useful method however, for calling legacy software written in other languages, which is considered less reliable than the core Ada program, but which is too large and complex to re-implement or fully re-test.

The following is an example in which Ada interacts with Applixware using the method just described. The same method has been used to interface Ada with PV-WAVE.

```
procedure RUN_APPLIX (
    CONFIG: in  SRV_SYSTEM.T_SRV_CONFIG;
     MACRO : in  SCTV_SYSTEM.T_STRING;
     RPT_FILE: in CCEL_TYPES.ST_FILENAME) is

    -- Define name of file holding status string, and types to open them
    C_STATUS_FILE : constant SCTV_SYSTEM.T_STRING :="applix_status.text";
    STATUS_FILE_TYPE : TEXT_IO.FILE_TYPE;
    C_MAX_STATUS_RECORD_LENGTH : constant SCTV_SYSTEM.T_INTEGER := 80;
    STATUS_RECORD : SCTV_SYSTEM.T_STRING (1..C_MAX_STATUS_RECORD_LENGTH);
    STATUS_RECORD_LENGTH : SCTV_SYSTEM.T_POSITIVE;

begin
    -- Set the license manager environment variable for the Applix
    -- license file
    ..........
    -- CALL srv_system.system to invoke applixware with the
    --     specified macro
    STATUS := SRV_SYSTEM.SYSTEM (
                 C_APPLIX_DIR & "/applix -nobackground -
                    macro " & MACRO & " -pass " &
                 CONFIG.MISSION_ID  &
                 CONFIG.ACTIVITY_ID &
                 CONFIG.SUBACT_ID &
                 CONFIG.PROCESS_ID & ' ' & RPT_FILE);
    if STATUS /= 0 then
       raise ERR_SYSTEM_CALL_FAILURE;
    end if;

    begin
       -- IO exception frame, to read the Applixware status file
       -- open Applixware status file
       TEXT_IO.OPEN(STATUS_FILE_TYPE,
                   MODE => TEXT_IO.IN_FILE,
                   NAME => C_STATUS_FILE);

       -- read status message
       TEXT_IO.GET_LINE(STATUS_FILE_TYPE,
                       ITEM => STATUS_RECORD,
                       LAST => STATUS_RECORD_LENGTH);

       --close the file
       TEXT_IO.CLOSE(STATUS_FILE_TYPE);

    exception

       -- IO errors occurred when reading status file
       when others =>
          raise ERR_SRV_FILE_ERROR;

    end; -- IO exception frame

    if STATUS_RECORD(1 .. 7) /= "SUCCESS" then
       raise ERR_APPLIX_FAILURE;
    end if;
```

```
      -- exception handler

end RUN_APPLIX;
```

The function SYSTEM returns an error code which could be mapped to an appropriate Ada exception to control the behaviour of the system avoiding dangerous crashes and allowing error recovery.

Because both Applixware and PV-WAVE allow good control over errors, the following strategy has been adopted.
Applixware, as well as PV-WAVE, writes a log file during its execution. This log file is read after the completion of the system call to check if an error has occurred. In fact, the system call can only capture errors which cause the severe termination of the application. Any other error which does not prevent the application from ending its execution "normally" but which can produce incorrect results can only be handled by the application itself and eventually logged. So, for example, it is possible to log errors related to missing files that should be linked during the report generation because this kind of error does not stop the operation and the Ada routine interfacing with it would wrongly notify a success.

3.3 RPCs

Although not used in the SCTV system, the "Remote Procedure Call" mechanism could be used to interface between languages (although usually it is used to interface two modules written in the same language) [NISTIR 5277 Comparing Remote Procedure Calls, John Barkley -October 1993].

The interface for the procedure call is written in an interface description language, which is then processed by a special RPC tool into two modules written in another programming language (usually C) - called the client stub and the server stub. The calling module interfaces with the client stub, and the called module with the server stub, both using ordinary procedure calls. The stubs are responsible for translating these calls into network communication or IPC, to allow the calling module (client) and called module (server) to communicate as if they were calling each other directly.

Although we know of no such system, it would be possible for the client stub and server stub to be generated in different languages (e.g. Ada and C). This would allow Ada and C programs to interact as if calling each other directly, but without the problems of data representation associated with procedure bindings - the client and server stubs communicate using a data representation protocol such as XDR.

The X-Windows protocol uses a similar strategy, although the stubs need not be automatically generated. On some systems, Xlib (the X-Windows client stub) is written in Ada, while the X-Server (the X-Windows server and server stub) is written in C. This mechanism allows seemless integration between C and Ada code.

An increasing number of commercial applications provide built-in facilities to allow interapplication communication based on this technique, for example, PV-WAVE (*CALL_UNIX* and *CALL_WAVE* routines) and Applixware (*RPC_CALL@*, *RPC_START_SERVER@*, *RPC_CONNECT@* for example).

3.4 Dynamic Links

Another way to interface Ada with other languages is to use dynamic links. This technique is particularly useful for calling Ada routines from an interpreted language such as PV-WAVE.

A dynamic link allows your application to call a routine in an external sharable object. We can say that this is "midway" between the system call method and the use of bindings.

The Ada routines to be called are linked into a shareable image. The PV-WAVE programs can access these routines by dynamically linking this sharable image into the PV-WAVE interpreter process. This is done the first time an Ada routine in the image is accessed, and is similar in terms of overhead to executing a new process. Thereafter, however, the Ada routine can be accessed just like an ordinary procedure within the same process, which is much less time-consuming.

The dynamic linking method is a recent addition to most operating systems, and therefore is not standardised even between different versions of UNIX. Consequently, programs which use this interfacing mechanism will be less portable.

3.5 Preprocessors

It is sometime useful to embed the foreign code directly into the Ada routine and to precompile the resulting source code. Precompilation causes the embedded code to be translated into calls to the preprocess runtime library procedures that handle the interaction between Ada and the foreign code. The result of precompilation is, then, compiled by the supported Ada compiler. Embedded code usually consists of a declarative part, to define the foreign objects and precompiler pragmas and of executable statements which result in calls to the external application and return codes and data. The precompiler generally provides error handling mechanisms to detect and recover from the executable statement errors.

This approach can be used to easily interface Ada with SQL, for example. There are some precompilers such as Pro*Ada which allow this kind of interaction. The main problems are the cost of this kind of commercial application and the fact that they are usually designed to work with a particular server (for Pro*Ada it is ORACLE7) and on a particular platform. This, of course, does not enhance the portability of the software [Ref. Pro*Ada and Oracle Precompilers].

3.6 Standard Interfaces

The ideal way in which to interface to a library written in another language is to use a set of validated or well tested bindings provided by someone else, preferably free of charge. Bindings are not only the most common method of interfacing, they are also a pre-requisite for some of the other methods (e.g. system call, RPC, dynamic linking).

Public domain bindings for many APIs are available on the internet, such as for POSIX, X-Windows, and SQL. Others are available from compiler vendors and other software product suppliers. Bindings written in Ada 83 necessarily apply only to one Ada compiler, and moreover only to one Operating System and CPU architecture.

Therefore when building systems using Ada we often find that no bindings are available for the library we wish to interface to, or for the platform we are using. This was certainly the case on SCTV. We were able to use the DEC Ada bindings to interface with X-Windows libraries and the POSIX interface. Ada bindings for Dataviews were available from Dataviews Inc (who supplied the libraries), but at significant cost, and not for the Alpha OSF platform.

In such a situation we are faced with two choices: to write the bindings from scratch or to modify bindings from another platform. For libraries such as X-Windows and Dataviews, the types, constants, and sub-programs in an API actually used by even a large application such as SCTV (a few hundred in the case of SCTV and Dataviews), is a small subset of the total number available (which can be many thousands). In the absence of pre-existing API bindings, it is preferable to avoid spending the time to produce or verify those interfaces which are not used.

On SCTV we adopted the second of these approaches for interfacing to the Dataviews library. We secured an agreement with Dataviews whereby they supplied us free of charge with Ada bindings for their product, for use on an HP platform. In return, we were to modify the bindings so that those interfaces used by our software worked on our Alpha platform, and then return the modified bindings to Dataviews for use by their other customers.

Some of the changes required could be spotted immediately by running the Ada compiler on the bindings: differences between compiler specific interfacing pragmas, and inconsistencies in record representation clauses caused by the Alpha's 64 bit pointers. Others, such as the effect on the representation clause of big-endian/little-endian byte ordering, and more subtle assumptions in the bindings, were spotted at run time during unit testing.

Many of the problems of portability of Ada bindings concern the representation of types: specifying the correct representation in Ada to match basic types in other languages, and the field sizes and offsets in a record representation clause.

Any errors in the representation clause used in Ada bindings are difficult to detect without exhaustive testing. For this reason they should preferably be generated in an automated way, with the help of a compiler for the other language. Consider, for example, the C program below.

```
typedef struct { char a; short b; int *c } t;

#include <stddef.h>
#define SHOW_FIELD( record, field )                        \
        printf("%s at %d range 0 .. %d;\n",                \
                #field, offsetof(record,field),            \
                sizeof(((record*)0)->field)*8-1)

int main() {
        SHOW_FIELD(t,a);
        SHOW_FIELD(t,b);
        SHOW_FIELD(t,c); }
```

When compiled and executed on any system, it prints the correct record representation clause for an Ada interface to the record type **t** above. On a DEC Alpha running the OSF1 operating system it gave the following results:

```
a at 0 range 0 .. 7;
b at 2 range 0 .. 15;
c at 8 range 0 .. 63;
```

A more sophisticated strategy would be to parse a C program for type definitions. A program similar to the one above would be generated, compiled, and executed for each record type as it was encountered. The results would be used to help generate an Ada interface.

Ada 95, with its package of types corresponding to C basic types, and its **convention** pragma, which enables the representation of a record type to be specified as the same as a C compiler, without explicitly specifying the field offsets, will enable portable interfaces to be developed.

4.   Conclusions

As it has just been stated, a mixed environment can be due to the choice of using Ada for the safety-related software and of using other languages for their best suitability to perform particular functions.

The disadvantages related to having such an environment can be summarised as follows:

- it is necessary to develop the software to interface the different code sources. Moreover, some of the types allowed by one of the language could not have a correspondent type in the other (the unconstrained types in Ada and the difficulty to map these types in C, for example).

- a safety-critical system developed both in C and Ada is less reliable than one developed using just Ada. This is due to the impossibility of using a compiler to perform type checking between the two languages.

- mixed language software is less portable because language interfaces depend on machine specific data representation and on compiler and linking specific facilities.

The advantages are mainly the following:

- no need to translate every code source into one language

- the ability to perform specialised operations more effectively in different languages

- easier reusability of the different code

References

APPLIX :   **Applix macros** manuals version 4.0

DATA_VIEWS :   **DV-Tools user's guide**, V.I. Corporation version 9.5

PV-WAVE :   PV-WAVE Advantage **PV-WAVE Command Language**, Visual Numerics version 4.2, 1993

X-Des :   **X-Designer User's Guide, release 3** Imperial Software Technology, DataViews V.I. Corporation, August 1993

SQL :   **PL/SQL User's Guide and Reference**, version 2 ORACLE, December 1992

POSIX :   **IEEE Standard Portable Operating System Interface for Computer Environments, Part 1: System**

Application Interface (API) [C Language]
Institute of Electrical and Electronics Engineers, Inc.,
1990

Pro*Ada :   **Programmer's Guide to the Pro*Ada Precompiler
version 1.5,**
ORACLE, 1992

Oracle Precompilers :   **Programmer's Guide to the Oracle Precompilers
version 1.5,**
ORACLE, 1992

NISTIR 5277   **Comparing Remote Procedure Calls**, John Barkley -
October 1993

Heterogeneous Data Structures
and Cross-Classification of Objects with Ada 95

Magnus Kempe

Swiss Federal Institute of Technology in Lausanne
Software Engineering Laboratory
EPFL–DI–LGL
CH–1015 Lausanne, Switzerland

e-mail: *Magnus.Kempe@di.epfl.ch*

Abstract. The implementation of ADTs for homogeneous data structures has become a classic example of ADT in Ada 83. With some effort, it was also possible to implement a restricted form of heterogeneous data structures, based on variant records. We show that various approaches in implementing flexible heterogeneous data structures with Ada 95 are now possible. One of these approaches is generalized to create heterogeneous catalogues of cross-referenced objects, thus implementing one kind of multiple classification.

Keywords. Abstract Data Types, Ada 95, Heterogeneous Collections, Classification, Catalogues.

1 Introduction

It has long been known how to implement various homogeneous data structures with Ada 83 (e.g. stacks of integers, or lists of characters). However, it is sometimes necessary to collect polymorphic items in one data structure, i.e. in a heterogeneous container ADT. Since each object in Ada has one specific type, the question is then how to build a collection of objects which do not all have the same specific type, while remaining within the frame of Ada's strong typing.

In other words, is it possible to create dynamic data structures with elements of various kinds in Ada? This paper demonstrates how, using Ada 83 mechanisms only [1], this could be done with some difficulty and much inflexibility, and then goes on to show several alternative and flexible approaches using new Ada 95 constructs [2].

First, we show how to use variant records, i.e. record types with discriminants.

Second, we explain how tagged types, class-wide access types, and genericity can be used.

Third, we describe an alternative design using tagged types and class-wide access types, but no genericity, to create a type-extensible framework.

Finally we develop an extremely versatile technique, based on self-referential types (with access discriminants). This technique has the additional benefit of offering a straightforward approach for cross-referencing catalogues or, in more general terms, for multiple classification.

This tour of techniques for implementing heterogeneous data structures in Ada 95 shows that the revised definition of the language provides a set of extremely powerful constructs, and that this set is more than adequate to solve many advanced design and coding problems.

2 Variant Records

The programmer can apply a technique to implement heterogeneous data structures simply with the constructs offered by Ada 83, namely with variant records. This technique requires both the declaration of an enumeration type which lists the different kinds of items to be dealt with, and the declaration of a record type with a discriminant of the enumerated type such that each variant in the record type corresponds to the representation of one kind of item.

For instance, considering a very simple case in which one would like to implement a list mixing integers with characters, one could write the following declarations (for presentation purpose, we choose to present a simple array and ignore issues of information hiding):

```
type Kind_Type is -- two kinds of items: integers and characters
  (K_Integer, K_Character, K_Null);

type Item_Type (Kind : Kind_Type := K_Null) is -- default: no value, no kind
  record
    case Kind is
      when K_Integer
        => I : Integer;
      when K_Character
        => C : Character;
      when K_Null -- default variant: undefined value
        => null;
    end case;
  end record;

type Bounded_Array_Type is
  array (Positive range <>) of
    Item_Type;
```

Figure 1. Heterogeneous array, with variant records.

With such declarations, one could also instantiate e.g. a generic list ADT:

```
generic
  type Item_Type is private;

package Lists_G is
  type List_Type is limited private;
  procedure Insert_Front
    (X : in Item_Type;
     L : in out List_Type);
  ...
end Lists_G;
```

```
package List is
  new Lists_G (Item_Type);
```

Figure 2. Heterogeneous list, with variant records as item type.

Note that the generic list ADT is not, and need not be, specially designed for use as a heterogeneous data structure. It is simply the same as what used to be seen as a homogeneous list in Ada 83.

Unfortunately, this technique has several drawbacks.

First, each time one wants to add a new kind of item, one has to update the type Kind_Type and then propagate the change to the variant record type Item_Type as well as to the case statements likely to appear in the code to distinguish between kinds of items. Such modifications are not always possible or desirable. For instance, it would be better if we could avoid changing existing code, since there would be no consequent need to recompile it and everything that depends on it.

Second, the use of variant records is not necessarily space-efficient, since the compiler is likely to systematically reserve as much space as needed for the largest variant. Depending on the differences in size between variants, this may turn out to be a heavy penalty to pay in terms of memory usage.

If an access type is declared, it is possible to directly use this access type to instantiate the required (Ada83-style) ADT, with better average use of memory as a consequence (but with additional headaches due to memory management):

```
type Reference_Type is
  access Item_Type;

package List is
  new Lists_G (Reference_Type);
```

Figure 3. Heterogeneous list, with access to variant records as item type.

3 Tagged Types and Class-Wide Access Types

With the advent of tagged types in Ada 95, a new kind of access types has also been introduced: *class-wide access types*. A class-wide access type is associated to the root of a hierarchy of tagged types (i.e. the root of an inheritance tree), and its values may designate objects of any specific type within that hierarchy.

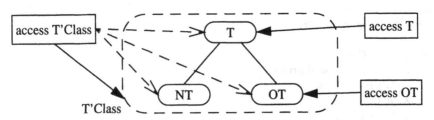

Figure 4. "T'Class" as covering a hierarchy of specific types; contrast between "access T" and "access T'class".

In figure 4, we show with dashed lines that, given an inheritance hierarchy with two types (NT and OT) derived from a root type T, the class-wide type T'Class covers values of all three specific types and a class-wide access type ("access T'Class") would cover values like those of specific access types (e.g. "access T").

This leads to a simple solution in order to implement heterogeneous data structures: create a hierarchy of tagged types, each one corresponding to a separate kind of items to be handled, and work with a related class-wide access type. This creates a *constrained* heterogeneous data structure, because *only* items belonging to a given class are allowed in the structure. The tag of each item corresponds exactly to the discriminant of the first example.

A combination of the examples shown in figures 1 and 2 and a translation to use tagged types and class-wide access gives:

```
type Item_Type is -- parent of all kinds of items
   abstract tagged null record;

type Integer_Type is -- first kind: integers
   new Item_Type
   with record
      I : Integer;
   end record;

type Character_Type is -- second kind: characters
   new Item_Type
   with record
      C : Character;
   end record;

type Reference_Type is -- access any kind
   access Item_Type'Class;

type Bounded_Array_Type is
   array (Positive range <>) of
      Reference_Type;
```

Figure 5. Heterogeneous array, with class-wide access as item type.

Again, the access type can be passed directly to the required generic list ADT. The values stored in the ADT are access values to objects within the Item_Type'Class hierarchy of types:

```
package List is
   new Lists_G (Reference_Type);
```

Figure 6. Heterogeneous list, with class-wide access as item type.

An obvious advantage of this technique is that it is possible to declare new types within the hierarchy without any changes to the declarations already shown. A noteworthy difference and potential advantage is that the kinds of items are not linearly enumerated but can be organized in a hierarchy of kinds, if a taxonomy is needed.

In addition, the space requirements are strictly related to the actual type of each item stored in the container. This is a direct consequence of the level of indirection introduced by the class-wide access type which is used.

Most object-oriented programming languages do in fact automatically create a level of indirection to represent objects, which explains why many also offer heterogeneous data structures by default. Ada's advantage in this context is that the programmer is *free* to decide whether he wants a homogeneous or a heterogeneous data structure, and then the language enforces that decision.[1]

It is possible to design a new breed of container ADTs, one which is specifically tuned to working with heterogeneous collections implemented in the form of hierarchies of tagged types.

We present for instance the specification of a generic heterogeneous stack ADT, which, given some tagged type T used as an actual parameter to instantiate the ADT, will store and return objects of any type in the class rooted at T (i.e. in T'Class):

```
generic
   type Item_Type is
      tagged private;

package Heterogeneous_Stacks_G is
   type Stack_Type is
      private;

   procedure Push
      (X : in Item_Type'Class;
       S : in out Stack_Type);

   function Top (S : Stack_Type)
      return Item_Type'Class;

   procedure Pop
      (S : in out Stack_Type);

private
   type Reference_Type is
      access Item_Type'Class;
   ...
end Heterogeneous_Stacks_G;
```

Figure 7. Explicitly heterogeneous stack ADT.

---

1. To some, this may be seen as a drawback, since the programmer is required to decide which to use...

4 Type Extension Framework

A different technique relying on tagged types is to create a framework, with a non-generic ADT exporting a tagged type that the programmer will extend to create the various kinds of item types he needs.

Here is an example specification of a singly-linked list, with just one operation profile shown, "insert in front of the list":

```ada
package Heterogeneous_Lists is
   type Item_Type is -- parent of all kinds of items
      abstract tagged private;

   type List_Type is
      limited private;

   procedure Insert_Front
      (X : in Item_Type'Class;
       L : in out List_Type);
   ...
private
   type List_Type is
      access Item_Type'Class;

   type Item_Type is
      abstract tagged
      record
         Next : List_Type;
      end record;
end Heterogeneous_Lists;
```

Figure 8. Explicitly heterogeneous singly-linked list ADT.

This technique is quite unusual for someone who is accustomed to working with generic ADTs written in Ada 83, but it is not an unusual OO programming technique. Here, the client programmer is able to define the kind of items to store in the list by externally deriving a new type from Item_Type (and defining appropriate additional components and/or operations):

```ada
type Integer_Item_Type is
   new Heterogeneous_Lists.Item_Type
   with record
      I : Integer;
   end record;
```

Figure 9. A new kind of items for the heterogeneous list.

As in section 3, since new types may be created by extending Item_Type to create a hierarchy of types rooted at Item_Type, the list data structure implemented above is heterogeneous in a *constrained* but *open-ended* fashion. It is not "arbitrarily" heterogeneous in the Smalltalk way [5].

There is no apparent advantage or disadvantage in using this version, except for a potential obstacle: an existing inheritance hierarchy would have to be modified at the root to derive from the ADT's Item_Type; the problem comes from trying to use inheritance to achieve multiple, distinct goals.

The raw interface to Item_Type is very limited, but it is possible to get to the properties of the derived types either by declaring a root user type derived from Item_Type, with dispatching to subprograms common to all kinds of items to be defined, or by using the membership test operator "**in**" and type conversions with run-time checks.

One difference with the technique presented in section 3 is that genericity is not used here, but exclusively type extension and a class-wide access type. This may be taken as yet another illustration of the extreme flexibility inherent in both the mechanisms of genericity and inheritance.

5 Self-Referential Types

There is yet another technique for the implementation of heterogeneous data structures, based on self-referential types (with access discriminants).

The construction is similar in spirit to one used by [6] in order to automatically collect all instances of a given type. An object which should be contained in some ADT has a component of type Hook_to_*ADT*, and that component has an access discriminant designating the enclosing object—thus allowing both ADT traversal and access to the object enclosing each node acting as a hook.

The example we will use is a representation for heterogeneous binary trees.

```
type Node;
type Node_Ref is access Node'Class;
type Node is -- similar role to that of Item_Type in figure 8 (heterogeneous list ADT)
   abstract tagged
   limited record
     Parent,
     Left_Child,
     Right_Child : Node_Ref;
   end record;
```

Figure 10. Heterogeneous binary tree data structure.

The next figure shows how to add a new kind of items given the definition of heterogeneous tree presented above:

```
type T;
type Hook_to_Tree (Outer : access T) is
   new Node
   with null record;
type T is -- T may appear in a tree
   limited record
     ...
     Tree_Hook : Hook_to_Tree (T'access); -- self-reference
   end record;
```

Figure 11. Item type T in heterogeneous binary tree.

If T was defined as a tagged type, we could derive a new type NT with a second hook, thus defining a kind of item that may appear twice in a tree or simultaneously in two trees:

```
type T is -- T may appear in a tree
    tagged limited record -- assume we use T'Class in access discriminant of the hook
        ...
        Tree_Hook : Hook_to_Tree (T'access); -- self-reference
    end record;

type NT is -- may appear twice in a tree, or in two separate trees
    new T
    with record
        Second_Hook : Hook_to_Tree (NT'access); -- second self-reference
    end record;
```

Figure 12. *Item type NT potentially twice in a tree.*

Any type having a component of a hook type (derived from Node) can thus be part of the heterogeneous tree structure. This provides *unconstrained* and *open-ended* heterogeneous data structures, without any restriction to types within an inheritance hierarchy (such as the ones based directly on class-wide access types have, as presented in sections 3 and 4). Also, note that type T need not be tagged.

This kind of classification is different from the usual "class" concept: objects can in their lifetime belong to various catalogues [4]. A *catalogue* is a collection of references to objects; the objects are described in the catalogue but exist independently and remain external to it, unlike objects which are included in and parts of a collection.

This technique is rather complex to design and implement, but it is easy to understand and apply. To turn it into standard practice, it is best to abstract the structure with a generic unit; thus we will create a "framework" that captures this "pattern."

We now demonstrate multiple classification on the basis of mixins [3, 7] with the following specification:

```
package Heterogenous_Trees is
    -- same as before: pointer structure of a binary tree
    type Node;
    type Node_Ref is access Node'Class;
    type Node is
        abstract tagged
        limited record
            Parent,
            Left_Child,
            Right_Child : Node_Ref;
        end record;

    -- generic "add a kind of items"
    generic
        type T is -- to be derived from and extended with a hook
            tagged limited private;
```

```
package In_Tree_G is
  -- a hooking node with access discriminant to T'Class objects
  type Hook_to_Tree (Outer : access T'Class) is
    new Node
    with null record;

  -- a new kind of T, self-referential through a hooking node component
  type Tree_T is
    new T
    with record
      Tree_Hook : Hook_to_Tree (Tree_T'Access);
    end record;
end In_Tree_G;


end Heterogenous_Trees;
```

Figure 13. Heterogeneous tree ADT with mixin hook.

On the first hand, this technique has the disadvantage that it is applicable exclusively to limited types, since a component with an access discriminant is limited, the container type is limited too. However, self-referential objects must be of a specific nature, viz. they must have complete by-reference semantics. To simultaneously belong to several collections, an object has to be shared by reference, i.e. copy semantics would violate the referential integrity of the object; thus "**limited**" is necessary to enforce the desired integrity.

On the other hand, this approach has the definite advantage that it allows us to get out of the "constrained heterogeneous" and tagged type frame, since any type which contains an appropriate hook component can be added to our heterogeneous container without interference with already existing inheritance hierarchies. An additional advantage is that this technique renders multiple classification fairly easy. For instance, some items could be defined as potentially belonging to either a list or a tree, or to both at the same time and independently.

It is interesting to note that, where available, multiple inheritance (MI) is often used for the purpose of such multiple classification, i.e. for cases of multiple, cross-referencing catalogues. But MI is not necessarily the best tool, since for instance a famous area of dispute is what "repeated inheritance" should mean. By contrast, with the technique presented in this section, an item may have as many hook components as necessary, and the meaning of each component is immediately clear. E.g. an item containing two hooks may appear twice in a catalogue or in two otherwise unrelated catalogues.

6 Conclusion

We have described solutions and options in the implementation of heterogeneous data structures with Ada 95. The initial design and implementation may seem complex, but understanding and applying the techniques developed here is straightforward, especially if these techniques (or "patterns") are captured by frameworks available in the form of generic packages.

There are several alternative approaches that one may choose from, depending on specific requirements; these approaches all remain safely within the context of Ada's strong typing.

A generalization of the self-referential technique presented in [6] leads to a clean concept and implementation of multiple classification. This is achieved through the disciplined composition and application of self-referential types, not with multiple inheritance.

7 Acknowledgments

The author would like to thank Stéphane Barbey, Gabriel Eckert, and Robb Nebbe for very helpful comments and discussions which helped improve this paper.

8 Bibliography

1. *Reference Manual for the Ada Programming Language*. ANSI/MIL-Std-1815a, 1983

2. *Programming Language Ada: Language and Standard Libraries*. ISO/IEC 8652:1995. Ada 9X Mapping/Revision Team, Intermetrics, Inc., 733 Concord Avenue, Cambridge, Massachusetts 02138, MA, USA, January 1995

3. G. Bracha and W. Cook. *Mixin-Based Inheritance*. In *Proceedings of the OOPSLA/ ECOOP'90 Conference*, ed. by N. Meyrowitz, Ottawa, Canada, 21-25 October, 1990, ACM SIGPLAN 25(10):303-312

4. G. Eckert. *Types, Classes and Collections in Object-Oriented Analysis*. In *Proceedings of First International Conference on Requirements Engineering*, Colorado Springs, Colorado, Apr. 18-22, 1994, IEEE Computer Society, pp. 32-39

5. A. Goldberg and D. Robson. *Smalltalk-80: The Language and its Implementation*. Addison-Wesley 1983

6. M. Kempe. *Abstract Data Types Are Under Full Control with Ada 9X*. In *Proceedings of the TRI-Ada'94 Conference*, ed. by C. Engle Jr., Baltimore, Maryland, November 6-11, 1994, pp. 141-152

7. M. Kempe. *The Composition of Abstractions: Evolution of Software Component Design with Ada 95*. In *Proceedings of the TRI-Ada'95 Conference*, ed. by C. Engle Jr., Anaheim, California, November 5-10, 1995

An ANDF Based Ada 95 Compiler System

Jørgen Bundgaard

DDC-I A/S
Gl. Lundtoftevej 1B, DK-2800 Lyngby, Denmark

jb@ddci.dk

Abstract. An Ada 95 compiler system which uses the Architecture Neutral Distribution Format (ANDF) as an intermediate program representation form is presented. ANDF was originally designed and developed for use in C compilers, but has now been extended to support other high-level languages efficiently, including Ada 95.

The main difference between ANDF and conventional intermediate program forms is that ANDF represents an abstraction of the high-level language while the others typically represent an abstraction of the target architecture. One of the advantages of using ANDF is that high quality final code generators already exist for a number of popular platforms. That gives a potential for bringing Ada 95 rapidly to these platforms.

1 The ANDF Concept

Traditionally, when N high-level languages shall cover M target machines, this requires N times M compilers. However, with the existence of a universal intermediate language supporting the N high-level languages and covering the M target machines, the number of compilers could be reduced to N plus M. ANDF is such an intermediate language.

```
High-level language
        |
     Producer
        |
      ANDF
        |
     Installer
        |
Target machine code
```

In the ANDF terminology a compiler translating from a high-level language to ANDF is called a *producer*, and a compiler translating from ANDF to target machine code is called an *installer*.

Currently, installers are available (or under development) for the following platforms:

Architecture	Operating Systems					
386/486	SVR4.2	SCO	Solaris	NT	Linux	
Pentium	SVR4.2	SCO	Solaris	NT	Linux	Sinix
680x0	HP-UX					
HP-PA	HP-UX					
SPARC	SunOS4	SVR4.2	Solaris	NT		
MIPS	Ultrix	SGI-Iris	NT			
Alpha	OSF/1					
RS6000	AIX					
PowerPC	AIX	PowerOPEN				
ARM	-					

Currently, a producer is available for C. Producers are under development for C++, Ada 95, Dylan/Lisp, and FORTRAN 77.

2 The ANDF Language

ANDF is an abstraction of high-level languages. Its definition contains abstractions for common programming language concepts such as data structures, procedures, numbers, conditionals, loops, labels, jumps, etc. The intention of ANDF is to retain all the information in the programming language being compiled to ANDF which can then be used by code optimizers in the installers. In this way it is equally applicable to any new architectures as to any existing ones.

ANDF constructs have been designed so as to be able to accommodate the particular variants found in different programming languages. However, ANDF cannot guarantee coverage of new programming languages as it can for architectures. New languages might contain novel features that are not efficiently implementable using existing features of ANDF. Extensive research has therefore been undertaken to ensure that ANDF is an efficient target for the compilation of Ada 95.

ANDF contains for example EXPs (abstractions of expressions an statements), SHAPEs (abstraction of types) and TAGs (abstraction of variable identifiers). In general form it is an abstract syntax tree which is flattened and encoded as a series of bits, called a CAPSULE. A number of CAPSULEs may be combined to form a single CAPSULE. This fairly high level of definition (for a compiler intermediate language) means that ANDF is architecture neutral in the sense that it makes no assumptions about the underlying processor architecture.

ANDF has a parameterization mechanism via TOKENs. Virtually any node of the ANDF tree may be a TOKEN: a place holder which stands for a subtree. Before the ANDF can be decoded fully, the definition of this TOKEN must be provided. The TOKEN definition is then macro substituted for the token in the decoding process to form the complete tree. Tokens may also take arguments.

The specification of ANDF takes the form of an abstract syntax with the semantics described in English. Here is an extract of the specification of the constructs assign, top, pointer, and alignment:

assign
      arg1: EXP POINTER(x)
      arg2: EXP y
          -> EXP TOP

The value produced by arg2 will be put in the space indicated by arg1.

top
          -> SHAPE

TOP is the SHAPE that describes program pieces which return no useful value.

pointer
      arg: ALIGNMENT
          -> SHAPE

A POINTER is a value which points to space allocated in a computer's memory. The pointer constructor takes an ALIGNMENT argument.

alignment

An ALIGNMENT gives information about the layout of data in memory and hence is a parameter for the POINTER and OFFSET SHAPES.

The construct *assign* takes two arguments each of sort EXP; the sort of *assign* is itself an EXP; the SHAPE of assign is TOP, it performs the assignment but does not deliver any useful value. There are more than 100 different EXPs, and there are ten different basic SHAPEs. The specification of ANDF also concerns the memory model (that is what the *alignment* constructors are used for), error handling, order of evaluation, representation of integers and floating point values. The complete specification of the ANDF language is found in [4]. This informal specification of ANDF is supplemented by a formal specification [9], using the style of Action Semantics [6].

The ANDF concept was originally invented by the British MoD Defence Research Agency (DRA) for solving portability problems with software written in C, including the problems of name clashes in different APIs and much, much more. The paper "TDF and Portability" [1] provides a deep insight.

These true powers of ANDF are really not unleashed until the Ada 95 vendor, in this case DDC-I, attempts to port an Ada binding from one platform to another, using the available system libraries. In all other respects, ANDF can be regarded as Yet Another Compiler Intermediate Language, but one with the thrilling feature that a host of code generators happen to exist.

3 ANDF Compared to other Compiler Intermediate Languages

Intermediate Languages (IL) are typically compared on the basis of the achievable efficiency of the final code, the ease of targeting from a high-level language, the ease of mapping to a new architecture, the cost and availability of the technology, and finally on the level of standardization. For compiler system vendors who support multiple high-level languages and/or multiple target platforms, the choice of IL is of strategic importance.

There are several alternative IL designs: Three-address code, abstract stack machine code, Register Transfer Lists (RTL) (the interface between the GNU NYU Ada Translator (GNAT) and the GNU gcc back end) and even shrouded C!

The main difference in design between the usual IL choices and ANDF is that the usual choices represent an abstraction of the architecture while ANDF represents an abstraction of the high-level language.

No IL design has yet proven to be superior with respect to efficiency of the final code because some information present in the source code is bound to be lost in either end of the abstraction scale. However, ANDF based C compilers are as good as the best traditional C compilers. This is documented in [3].

The ease of targeting from a high-level language favors ANDF once ANDF has been properly extended for the purpose. The cost of extending ANDF for a new high-level language includes effectively the cost of enhancing all dependent installers.

The development time for a new high quality installer (for a new architecture) is one to two person-years. A lot of code can be reused for similar architectures. The retargeting time for the GNU gcc back end is known to depend very much on the implementors' experience with that very same component. Anything from a couple of days to a year has been quoted. The retargeting time for a proprietary IL is typically a well guarded secret!

There is an important difference between proprietary ILs, ANDF, and RTL in terms of availability: Code generators for proprietary ILs are typically either not commercially available, or are only available from a single source. The GNU back end is free "Copyleft" software, but using it implies that the entire compiler source code must also be given away for free to anyone who asks for it. ANDF installers are available on commercial terms for the highly optimizing ones from at least two vendors while the "standard" ones are in the public domain.

ANDF is the only IL for which a formal standardization has begun (ISO and X/Open). RTL is a sort of de facto standard set by the GNU community.

All in all, the choice of IL lies with the compiler vendor, and the combinations of high-level languages and architectures to support now and in the future must be used to guide decisions.

It is clearly interesting for DDC-I to build a compiler system which includes a translator from Ada 95 to ANDF, because the availability of installers will reduce the cost and time for bringing DDC-I Ada 95 technology to many platforms.

4 Usefulness of the ANDF Technology

ANDF has proven to be a very versatile technology for C. OSF Research Institute, France, and Defence Research Agency (DRA), UK, as well as other collaborators around the world, have made numerous advances through the use of ANDF. Until now the technology has proven to be very useful in the following areas:

- For developing and testing portable software (the ANDF technology requires conformance to API specifications, so it also serves as a good portability checker).

- As an open compiler technology (a baseline for developing a compiler family). In particular for new non-interpretive languages, portable compilers may find ANDF a more preferable intermediate language than say C source code.

- For software distribution (the original ANDF objective).

- As a more formal and machine manipulable way of expressing the static aspects of APIs.

OSF also foresees interesting usages in the following areas:

- ANDF as a representation of parallel programs.

- As a format to represent and manipulate code in CASE tools.

5 Will ANDF be Useful for Ada as well?

It has yet to be demonstrated that ANDF is also a very versatile technology for Ada 95. This will partly depend on the quality of the Ada 95 front end for ANDF (being developed as part of the OMI/GLUE project), partly on the quality and availability of installers.

The most important message is that there is definitely a great potential for bringing Ada 95 rapidly to a lot of popular platforms via the ANDF technology.

This is important because there are clear indicators that ANDF candidates for an important role in multi-language development environments and in projects which deal with porting legacy software to new hardware platforms:

- New architectures emerge (Alpha, PowerPC)

- COTS software is (re)used through interfacing

- Applications are more long-lived than hardware

- APIs being offered on more platforms

6 About the OMI/GLUE Project

The Open Microprocessor Initiative (OMI) is a 250 million dollar technology programme which involves many large IT companies within the European Community. The hardware part of OMI operates with a "macrocell" concept which enables VLSI designers to combine different CPU architectures, storage units, communication devices, and other function units on single chips.

The OMI/Global Language and Uniform Environment (GLUE) project is a 17 million dollar project in the software part of OMI. It aims at providing a choice of advanced languages for the software developers within the OMI and allows the most suitable language to be used in a given application. The development of an Ada 95 producer is such an example. The project also aims at consolidating the ANDF technology within OMI. This means development of installers for the architectures supported by the OMI.

The partners in the OMI/GLUE project are:

- Etnoteam SPA, Italy,

- DDC-I A/S, Denmark

- Harlequin Ltd, UK

- Defence Research Agency (DRA), UK

- OSF Research Institute, France

The starting point for the OMI/GLUE project was a production quality C producer and several ditto installers developed by DRA.

In addition to development of new producers and installers, the project includes formal and informal specification of ANDF, development of test suites and validation capabilities, portability checking tools, technology consolidation for conventional languages (C & Fortran 77), extension of ANDF for advanced languages (Ada 95 and Dylan/Lisp), and proposing ANDF extensions for parallism. From the diagram below you can probably see why the project's logo is an hourglass!

Programming languages supported

```
Ada 95   C/C++  F77  Dylan/Lisp
          \   |   /
          Producers
           \ | /
           ANDF
           / | \
          Installers
          /  |   \
i386/486 680x0  SPARC  MIPS  PowerPC
Pentium  RS6000   HP-PA   Alpha   ARM
```

Target architectures supported

The OMI/GLUE project will be finished by September 1995. Several follow-up projects, under the Esprit programme as well as funded by private companies, are under preparation.

International standardization of ANDF will be handled by the newly formed ISO working group: ISO/IEC JTC1/SC22 WG15 ANDF/Virtual Binary Interface.

Standardization under X/Open (which is likely to be achieved much faster than ISO standardization) is currently under consideration.

7 Efficient Support for Ada 95 in ANDF

As part of the OMI/GLUE project, ANDF has been extended in order to support advanced languages like Ada 95 better. Initially ANDF was not sufficient to fully support Ada 95, or at least was not sufficient to support an acceptable implementation. The areas concerned are: functions returning dynamically sized objects, stack checking, and out parameters.

These areas are now fully support by ANDF:

- Functions returning dynamically sized objects: A new return construct makes it possible to preserve the stack of the called function.

- Stack checking: A stack limit to be used in stack checking at procedure calls and dynamic stack allocation can be set by a new construct.

- Out parameters: A new generalized procedure call construct makes it possible to access parameters after the call.

A few other areas have still not quite optimal implementations:

- The stack limit to be used in stack checks must be set at each context switch, since the installer has no knowledge of what the current task is.

- The stack frame layout cannot be sufficiently controlled, which means that redundant information must be stored for each procedure activation.

- Labels cannot be used as constants, which means that labels to which the exception manager will long jump must be provided as run-time values.

- Subunits in Ada require the use of frame offsets of local variables from other ANDF capsules. ANDF has a construct that can provide frame offsets from the capsule in which the construct is applied. This means that frame offsets to be used in subunits must be stored as constants that can be accessed in the subunit rather than being directly accessible.

The more or less sub-optimal implementation in these areas is due to limitations of ANDF, or the architecture neutral nature of ANDF.

Other new language constructs introduced by Ada 95 did not require changes to ANDF. Run-time dispatching is for example already supported indirectly in ANDF through subprogram pointers (which are needed for C).

ANDF has no heap concept or tasking concept. Heap storage management and tasking will therefore be handled through external calls to a Run-time System.

Error handling for numeric overflow and stack overflow is supported by ANDF, while subtype check is not. Explicit ANDF code must therefore be generated for subtype checks. This has the advantage that a producer can omit a check if it can be determined at compile time that the check is superfluous [7].

ANDF supports data types in the form of SHAPEs: top, bottom, bitfields (bit-strings), compounds (records), floatings, integers, nofs (one-dimensional arrays), offsets, pointers, and procedures as required to model the Ada 95 data types.

Not all issues are equally important. DDC-I had, for example, suggested introduction of a fixed SHAPE (for fixed point types). That would have made the job simpler for the Ada producer, but there would be no differences at run-time. The additional cost imposed on all installers to support SHAPE fixed could therefore not be justified.

Alignment of objects is handled by the installer, including alignment of record components. This implies that it is the responsibility of the installer to choose the kind of alignment that gives the most efficient access to objects on the given target machine. The benefit is that the producer can be simpler and that the result in theory should be better. The downside is that there may be (yet to be shown) cases where the installer makes a bad choice of alignment with a resulting negative effect on the run-time performance.

8 Components of the ANDF Based Ada 95 Compiler System

The ANDF based Ada 95 Compiler System consists of the following major components:

- Compiler
- Linker
- Standard libraries

The design of the compiler system is presented in [2].

As we shall see below, the components are a little more complicated than normally due to the use of ANDF as intermediate language and due to the use of third party installers. Also, the CPU time and other resources used to activate the ANDF linker will come in addition to what is normally required.

However, from a functional point of view, the user should not be able to tell a difference between an ANDF based and a "normal", native Ada compiler system.

9 The Compiler

The compiler has a front end which maps Ada 95 source to a High-Level Intermediate Language (HLIL) which is essentially an abstract syntax tree where all name resolution and type matching has been done and where a number of attributes have been set to guide the code generation. The compiler has also a back end which first maps HLIL to ANDF and then calls an installer to map ANDF to object code for the desired target architecture.

When a compilation unit is compiled, an ANDF capsule is generated. If the compilation unit contains entities that may become visible to other units, then a second capsule is generated for these entities (this corresponds to a .h (=header) file in C).

Conversely, when the installer generates object code for a compilation unit, it is necessary to have the ANDF context capsules available for the Ada units mentioned (transitively) in the context clause of the compilation unit, including any parents.

In addition, it is necessary to have a header capsule available for describing target entities (e.g. size of predefined type Integer). This is the ANDF counterpart to the definitions in the predefined package Standard.

Finally, it is necessary to have header capsules available describing the APIs used on the platform, including the Ada 95 RTS.

The ANDF context capsules are identified (in the Ada 95 program library) by the compiler front end as part of locating the corresponding HLIL representations of the Ada context units. The remaining ANDF capsules reside in the compiler's system directory. Several ANDF capsules can be combined by an ANDF linker to form a single capsule. This means that only a single capsule is fed into the installer. All current installers generate assembly code which is fed directly into the system assembler.

To summarize the steps in the compile process:

Ada compile:

> translator:
> > Ada 95 compilation unit ->
> > > ANDF source capsule +
> > > ANDF header capsule (if required)

> ANDF linker:
> > API headers +
> > source capsule +
> > context headers +
> > target entity header -> installable capsule

> installer:
> > installable capsule -> assembly source file

> system assembler:
> > assembly source file -> object code file

10 The Linker

The Ada 95 linker has a front end which determines the units necessary to build a partition, extracts the required object files from the program library, and builds a main ANDF capsule that deals with elaboration code and elaboration order. Object code is generated for the main capsule and all the object files are given to the system linker which generates the executable.

To summarize the steps in the link process:

Ada link:

> extractor:
> > partition specification -> elaboration order +
> > > > unit object files of partition

> ANDF main generator:
> > elaboration order -> main capsule

> installer:
> > main capsule -> main assembly file

> system assembler:
> > main assembly file -> main.o

> system linker:
> > rts.o +
> > main.o +
> > unit object files of partition -> executable

11 The Standard Libraries

The standard libraries are supported via an Ada 95 "root" program library containing HLIL and ANDF header capsules for all compilation units (and for package Standard) as defined in Annex A of the Ada Reference Manual [5].

In addition, but hidden to the user, there are ANDF capsules representing the target entities (numeric types, addresses, etc.), the system header files and the header files of the APIs supported on the platform. The target entity capsule is essentially derived from the predefined package Standard. System header files and API header files are supplied (for the platform) by the system vendor, while the corresponding capsules are generated with a tool set accompanying the ANDF technology.

Finally, and also hidden to the user, there is the Ada 95 Run-time System which includes the tasking kernel, heap storage manager, exception manager, and other DDC-I specific code generator support.

The use of ANDF capsules to represent System header files and API header files makes it simpler for DDC-I to move the Standard Libraries to other platforms because the capsules can be made to be architecture neutral.

12 Current Status

At this time the development of the Ada 95 to ANDF mapping is well under way. The environment issues, such as library management, automatic recompilation, linking and integration of installers are working.

The compiler does not yet produce code for sufficiently many Ada constructs to accomplish meaningful run-time performance measurements using the standard benchmark programs. However, installers used as back ends in C compilers developed by DRA and others have shown performance results that are fully comparable with native C compilers. So why not be optimistic about Ada 95? On several occasions the ANDF based system outperformed the "default" native C compilers [3].

13 Example

This example shows the ANDF code and SPARC assembly code generated for setting up a dispatch table, and for a nondispatching and a dispatching call.

ANDF has no direct support for run-time dispatching, so ANDF code must be generated to set up a dispatch table with addresses of primitive operations of a tagged type. ANDF code must also be generated for making an indirect call via the dispatch table. Consider the following program:

```
package P is
    type T is tagged null record;
    procedure A( X : T );
    procedure B( X : T );
end P;

with P; use P;
procedure Q is
    Obj1 : T;
    Obj2 : T'Class := Obj1;
begin
    A( Obj1 );   -- Nondispatching call
    A( Obj2 );   -- Dispatching call
end Q;
```

A and B are primitive subprograms of type T. Their addresses are inserted in the dispatch table for type T together with the addresses of artificial subprograms generated for computing 'Size of objects, for Initialization of objects, for Assignment, and for Equality. In the first call to A the controlling operand, Obj1, is statically tagged. The controlling tag value is determined statically, so the address of the called subprogram can be determined statically and the call will be nondispatching. In the second call to A the controlling operand, Obj2, is dynamically tagged. The controlling tag value is determined dynamically by the tag of the controlling operand Obj2. The address of the called subprogram must be determined dynamically and the call will be dispatching.

High-Level Intermediate Form

The compiler front end produces an attributed tree representation of the program where tagging information is attached to the call-nodes for the benefit of the back end.

Source form:

```
A( Obj1 );    -- Nondispatching call
A( Obj2 );    -- Dispatching call
```

HLIL form generated by the front end:

```
mk_Procedure_call_statement(
    dynamically_tagged_parameter: Null
    procedure_name: mk_Id( A, [pointer to declaration of subprogram A] )
    actual_parameters:
    <  mk_Parameter_association(
          selector: [pointer to declaration of formal parameter X]
          named: FALSE
          defaulted: FALSE
          actual_parameter: mk_Id( OBJ1, [pointer to declaration of object Obj1]))
    > )


mk_Procedure_call_statement(
    dynamically_tagged_parameter:[pointer to param. association (X =>Obj2)]
    procedure_name: mk_Id( A, [pointer to declaration of subprogram A] )
    actual_parameters:
    <  mk_Parameter_association(
          selector: [pointer to declaration of formal parameter X]
          named: FALSE
          defaulted: FALSE
          actual_parameter: mk_Id( OBJ2, [pointer to declaration of object Obj2]))
    > )
```

Note that in the HLIL form the only difference between a dispatching call and a nondispatching call is the value of the field 'dynamically_tagged_parameter' in the call node. The front end does not generate any parts of the dispatch table.

ANDF Form

The compiler back end generates ANDF code to set up the dispatch table for type T. The table is an ANDF 'compound' construct which contains a size and a list of pairs (offset, value). The all information in the dispatch table is static.

Source form:

```
type T is tagged null record;
procedure A( X : T );
procedure B( X : T );
```

ANDF form generated by the back end:

```
T_DISPATCH_TABLE (variable) is :
make_compound(
   offset_add(                       -- specify the size of the dispatch table for type T
      offset_pad(
         alignment(proc),
         offset_add(
            offset_zero(
               alignment(pointer(dispatch_table_alignment*))),
            shape_offset(
               pointer(dispatch_table_alignment*)))),
      shape_offset(
         nof(6,proc))),
   offset_zero(
      alignment(pointer(dispatch_table_alignment*))),   -- parent table link offset
   make_null_ptr(
      alignment(pointer(dispatch_table_alignment*))),   -- parent table link value
   offset_pad(                                          -- entry table offset
      alignment(proc),
      offset_add(
         offset_zero(
            alignment(pointer(dispatch_table_alignment*))),
         shape_offset(
            pointer(dispatch_table_alignment*)))),
   make_nof(                         -- entry table value
      obtain_tag(~temp_9),           -- address of 'Size
      obtain_tag(~temp_10),          -- -        - Initialization
      obtain_tag(~temp_10),          -- -        - Assign
      obtain_tag(~temp_11),          -- -        - "="
      obtain_tag(A),                 -- -        - procedure A
      obtain_tag(B)))                -- -        - procedure B
```

The parent table link is used for tag checks, for example in view conversions.

The compiler back end generates ANDF code for the two calls:

Source form:

```
A( Obj1 );    -- Nondispatching call
A( Obj2 );    -- Dispatching call
```

ANDF form generated by the back end:

```
identify(                          -- temp_10 := address of Obj1
    ~temp_10,
    obtain_tag(OBJ1),
        apply_proc(                -- call
            obtain_tag(A),         -- procedure value
            obtain_tag(~temp_10))) -- actual parameter = address of Obj1


identify(                          -- temp_11 := address of OBJ2
    ~temp_11,
    obtain_tag(OBJ2),
        apply_proc(                -- call
            contents(              -- read the procedure address from the dispatch table
                proc,
                add_to_ptr(
                    contents( -- read Ada 95 tag value of temp_11 = address of Obj2
                        pointer(dispatch_table_alignment*),
                        obtain_tag(~temp_11)),
                    offset_add(    -- find the dispatch table offset for procedure A
                        offset_pad(
                            alignment(proc),
                            offset_add(
                                offset_zero(
                                    alignment(pointer(dispatch_table_alignment*))),
                                shape_offset(
                                    pointer(dispatch_table_alignment*)))),
                        offset_mult(
                            offset_pad(
                                alignment(proc),
                                shape_offset(proc)),
                            make_int(unsigned_int32*,4))))), --procedure A has index 4
            obtain_tag(~temp_11))) -- actual parameter = address of OBJ2
```

We can also say that the address of procedure A is calculated as:

```
a == t_dispatch_table.entries[ 4 ]
```

The tag value of Obj2 is simply the address of the dispatch table for type T. It is important to note that the offset of the address of A from the start of the dispatch table is static.

Sparc Assembly Code Form

The SPARC installer generates assembly code to set up the dispatch table:

```
_T_DISPATCH_TABLE:
     .align   4
     .align   4
     .word    0        -- parent table link
     .align   4
     .align   4
     .align   4
     .word $$3         -- address of 'Size
     .align   4
     .word $$4         -- address of Initialization
     .align   4
     .word $$4         -- address of Assign ( here same as Initialization )
     .align   4
     .word $$5         -- address of "="
     .align   4
     .word _A          -- address of A  (offset 20 in dispatch table)
     .align   4
     .word _B          -- address of B
```

Note that the installer can generate a static dispatch table. Note also that the Initialization and the Assign procedures are equal in this example. However, two different entries are needed because the two operations are different if objects of the type have variable sizes.

The SPARC installer also generates assembly code for the two calls:

Source form:

```
A( Obj1 );   -- Nondispatching call
A( Obj2 );   -- Dispatching call
```

Assembly code form generated by the installer:

```
add %fp,-16,%o0    -- set up parameter. Obj1's address is fp -16
call _A,1          -- call A
nop                -- delay slot
add %fp,-8,%o0     -- set up parameter. Obj2's address is fp -8
ld   [%o0],%g4     -- g4 := Obj2.tag (= address of the dispatch table)
ld   [%g4+20],%g5  -- g5 := dispatch table[20] ( = address of A )
call %g5,1         -- call A (indirectly)
nop                -- delay slot
```

A total of ten clock cycles is used for the two calls. Due to the use of register values immediately after they are loaded, the "ld"s take two cycles each. The nondispatching call uses three cycles. The dispatching call uses seven cycles.

To be honest, the following code sequence would have been better; it is two clock cycles faster:

```
call _A,1          -- call A
add %fp,-16,%o0    -- use delay slot to set up parameter.
                   -- Obj1's address is fp -16
ld   [%fp-8],%g4   -- g4 := Obj2.tag (= address of the dispatch table).
                   -- Obj2's address is fp -8
ld   [%g4+20],%g5  -- g5 := dispatch table[20] ( = address of A )
call %g5,1         -- call A (indirectly)
add %fp,-8,%o0     -- use delay slot set up parameter.
                   -- Obj2's address is fp -8
```

The system assembler can normally optimize constructs like the nondispatching call to take advantage of a delay slot, so that takes care of half of the possible improvements.

Even though there is some room for improving the use of delay slots, we conclude that using ANDF as intermediate code form does not result in unacceptable final code for dispatching and nondispatching calls on the SPARC architecture.

14 How to get ANDF Information and Documentation

There is now an ANDF home page located on the OSF RI World Wide Web server at URL:

  http://riwww.osf.org:8001/andf/index.html

Here you will find a brief overview of ANDF, additional information about OSF experience with ANDF, as well as pointers to a collection of ANDF related papers which may be either viewed on-line or printed. All of the papers from the "ANDF Technology Collected Papers" series, currently four volumes, are contained on the server.
For those who are not Mosaic users, the ANDF papers may also be obtained from the OSF RI anonymous FTP server:

  ftp://riftp.osf.org/pub/andf_coll_papers

Requests for ANDF information may be sent to:

  andf-tech-request@osf.org.

There is also an ANDF Frequently Asked Questions document [8].

References

[1]   Andrews, Robert. "TDF and Portability", Defence Research Agency, Malvern, UK. 1994.

[2]   Bundgaard, Jørgen. "The Design of an Ada 95 Compilation Environment", Proceedings of the Fourth "Ada in Aerospace" Symposium in Brussels, 1993.

[3]   DRA. "TDF Facts and Figures", Defence Research Agency, Malvern, UK. 1995.

[4]   Edwards, Peter. Foster, Michael. Currie, Ian. "TDF Specification 4.0", Defence Research Agency, Malvern, UK. 1995.

[5]   ISO/IEC 8652:1995(E) "Ada Reference Manual", 1995

[6]   Mosses, Peter. "Action Semantics", Number 26 in Cambridge Tracts in Theoretical Computer Science. Cambridge University Press, 1992.

[7]   Møller, Peter: "Run-Time Check Elimination for Ada 95", Proceedings of the TRI-Ada '94 Conference, Baltimore, ACM, 1994

[8]   Peeling, N.E. et al. "Frequently Asked Questions about ANDF", Defence Research Agency, Malvern, UK. 1993.

[9]   Toft, Jens-Ulrik. "Formal specification of ANDF semantics", ESPRIT Project 6062 OMI/GLUE, DDC-I, 1995.

Performance Tuning of a Check-Out System Coded in Ada

Bernt Rognes and Per Ivar Skinderhaug

Cap Computas AS, Space Skill Center,
P.O.Box 3765 Granaaslia,
N-7002 TRONDHEIM,
NORWAY
Telephone: +47 73 90 36 00
Telefax: +47 73 90 36 49

Abstract: This paper describes possible ways to tune the performance of existing Ada code. Theories for performance improvements are described and advices are given for programmers who want to code performant Ada or to tune existing code. The theories presented have been applied to a project under the Columbus Programme. The measures taken in this project are presented with illustrating code examples. Finally, some figures for the achieved results are given.

1 Introduction

The basis of this paper is Cap Computas' experience from the Columbus Ground Software (CGS) project, which is the check-out (ground testing) system for the European part of the international space station (Alpha). The complete CGS comprises software developed by several companies in Europe, with Daimler-Benz Aerospace in Bremen (DASA-RI) acting as Prime contractor and being responsible for the integration.

1.1 CGS

The CGS incorporates all processes used in support of ground based test operations performed by various human users in different roles. The philosophy of the CGS check-out environment is to allow user-tailored testing using purpose-built test systems. The CGS check-out system will make the configuration of Electrical Ground Support Equipment (EGSE) transparent to the test operator, allowing re-use of automated test procedures at several test levels and within different test configurations.

The CGS supports a wide variety of common and routine check-out tasks, such as test setup, control and monitoring of the unit under test (UUT), manually as well as automated, on-line data visualization and off-line evaluation, from subsystems up to fully integrated flight configurations.

In that view, CGS provides the core check-out functionality to be configured and tailored, in hardware and software, to individual demands of an EGSE. Additional hardware, called front end equipment (FEE) provides for physical connection to the UUT, whereas special application software (SAS) establishes the interface to the CGS check-out software driving and controlling the FEE.

A stand-alone check-out configuration, dedicated to subsystem testing, consists of a single test node, one or more workstations and a database server node all together operating in a LAN based environment. In contrast, the distributed configuration, mostly dedicated to simultaneous subsystem or flight configuration testing, can consist of several nodes and work stations performing relevant check-out tasks in parallel, in the same environment. However, the full range of check-out functions are available in any configuration.

1.2 TES

The Test Execution Software (TES), an integral part of each CGS test node, provides core services, configured by data during initialization, to command and control the UUT connected to the EGSE, containing basic logic processes needed by the test conductor.

TES allows check-out to be carried out under control of commands supplied as automated procedures (APs) written in User Control Language (UCL) as well as interactive commands given by the test operator. High Level Command Language (HLCL) commands are used for test system control. It is possible to reuse the same commands at different test levels, and the EGSE configuration details are transparent to the test operator.

TM and measurement data from the UUT and EGSE data, such as housekeeping data, will be received by TES and monitored in real time, i.e. compared with expected values previously defined in a configuration database. Conditionally, depending on the values of the monitored parameters, recovery and saving actions, also pretest specified, may be automatically initiated by TES.

The test operator can control all UUT functions via telecommands or other stimuli transmitted through the frontend equipment(s).

TES allows the test operator to control all UUT functions via telecommands or other stimuli transmitted through the frontend equipment(s).

1.3 Operating Modes of TES

In the test environment, TES can be operated in three different modes; Normal, Simulation and Replay mode.

In Normal Mode, TES receives spacecraft and EGSE data in real time, either as LAN packets or from standard bus interfaces. In parallel, TES dispatches processed data, logs events and provides data archive services for later analysis and replay purposes.

In Simulation Mode, data to be received by the test node are simulated in a very simple way, allowing to create specific test scenarios. The simulation speed of data may be altered by the user; simulated data can be archived.

In Replay Mode, instead of receiving data from the frontend equipment, the UUT and EGSE data are read from previously archived data, stored in files. The replay speed of received data may be altered by the user.

1.4 TES Services

The following services are provided by TES:
- Interpretation of Automated Procedures written in UCL
  TES provides services to interpret and execute Automated Procedures written in UCL (User Command Language).
- Monitoring of Unit Under Test and Test System
  TES provides services to monitor the status of the Unit Under Test and Test System. Telemetry data, measurement data and status messages from the test node(s) are input data for monitoring.
- Data Dispatch Service to other CGS nodes
  TES provides services to dispatch data (Telemetry data, Measurement data and Test System status) to any requesting source, e.g. other test nodes, HCI and SAS.

1.5 Generic approach

The flexible solution that is specified for CGS requires a wide utilization of the generics and tasking features provided by Ada. Generic types, abstract data types, tasking and task types are extensively used in the current implementation.

The distributed CGS also required a communication solution. This has been implemented as a separate product within CGS; the Common Services. The Common Services hide the Network Software which facilitates the connection and data transfer to other nodes. Common Services also include all common type definitions and procedure libraries.

1.6 Performance Requirements

The performance requirements to TES are very strict. A defined baseload shall be handled, with only 45% of the CPU capability available. The baseload comprises running APs, generating telecommands and stimuli (20 per second), aquiring telemetry and measurements (910 enditems every second), calibration, monitoring, archiving and logging of acquired data, plus data dispatch to users.

The V2-version of TES was delivered in 1994. This version did not meet all its performance requirements, hence some performance improvements were required. The time frame and budget available for the next version was very limited (8 months). A full redesign was therefore not feasible. The only possible approach was to tune the existing Ada code aiming at performance improvement.

1.7 Technical Environment

The software has been designed using the Hierarchical Object-Oriented Design Method (HOOD) and coded in Ada with the SunAda compiler on Sun Sparc and the Alsys compiler on HP 9000/800 series.

2 General Remarks on Ada Performance

There are in general two ways to increase the performance of an Ada program:

- Modify the 'environment' of the Ada program, i.e. tune the computer, utilize different kinds of compiler and linker options and strategies.
- Modify the Ada code.

The first method will always give some improvements, but only to a limited extent. Modification of the Ada code includes a lot more possibilities for performance improvements, and is the most interesting method, as seen from an Ada programmer's point of view. Therefore, we have looked closer to the last method. Ada has strengths for real-time applications, but some powerful abstractions that help solve generalized problems carry a cost in efficiency. In the following, some of the Ada constructs and their impact on the performance will be pointed out.

2.1 Memory usage

The Ada language has many explicit and implicit memory requirements. Explicit requirements include object declarations and the "new" allocator. Implicit requirements include queues and blocks for tasking control and intermediate storage for initializations.

Memory requirements are met from one of three areas:

- static data,
- the program stack, and
- the program heap

Use of static data is restricted to what can be allocated at compile time. For instance global variables in the package specifications and the bodies are placed in the static data segment.

The program stack is typically restricted to local usage because stack offsets must be known. Variables declared in procedures are typically placed on the program stack.

The program heap is the most flexible one. It can be used for any memory requirements, but excessive heap use can degrade performance.

With this in mind one could introduce the following rules:

- Avoid usage of the heap, to reduce the overhead of managing dynamic objects on the heap.
- Use short-lifetime local variables. This will minimize the use of global data and reduce the size of the executables.

2.2 Unconstrained types

An Ada package containing unconstrained types will be of dynamic size. From a performance point of view, such objects are more costly to use than an object of static size, for two reasons:

- The dynamic object requires execution of code in order to allocate the object on the stack or heap. If the object is allocated on the heap, the object will also be explicitly deallocated.

- A descriptor must be built and referenced for the dynamic attributes of the object.

When the performance is critical it is a general advice to avoid the usage of unconstrained types and dynamically sized objects whenever possible.
This is an example of dynamically sized arrays:

```
N : INTEGER := 20;

type T_DYNAMIC_ARRAY_1 is array (1..N) of INTEGER;
type T_DYNAMIC_ARRAY_2 is array (INTEGER range <>) of INTEGER;

ARRAY_1 : T_DYNAMIC_ARRAY_1;
ARRAY_2 : T_DYNAMIC_ARRAY_2 (1..N) := (others => 111);
```

2.3 Unbounded records and arrays

Ada allows the definition of record objects whose size can change during the lifetime of the object, i.e. *discriminant records*.

Since the size of such a variable will vary during the execution of the program, dependent on assignments done at run-time, a discriminant record will always be placed on the heap. Assignments to this kind of variables are time consuming; the dynamic nature of the variable normally requires several heap operations.

If the value of the type discriminant is explicitly set at the declaration of a discriminant record it cannot change size (at run-time). If the variable declared has a relatively small size, it is put on the stack. Assignments of this kind of variables are therefore faster than assignments to discriminant records on the heap.

A general advice is to avoid the usage of unbounded records and array types when performance is critical.

The usage of unbounded records and arrays will be explained by an example:

```
type STRING_RECORD( DEFAULT_LENGTH : INTEGER := 80 ) is
record
        STRING_COMPONENT : STRING(1 .. DEFAULT_LENGTH);
end record;

STRING_1 : STRING_RECORD;     -- this string can change size
```

The size of the object STRING_1 can be changed by a complete record assignment:

```
STRING_1 : STRING_RECORD;        -- can change size
STRING_2 : STRING_RECORD( 90 ); -- larger than STRING_1,
                                 -- cannot change size
begin
        STRING_1 := STRING_2;
end;
```

The assignment above is slow because several heap operations are required to change the size of STRING_1. Note that the object STRING_2 cannot change size because the value of the type discriminant is explicitly set at its declaration. Because STRING_2 has a relatively small size, it is put on the stack. For this reason, assignments of these objects are faster. For example:

```
DEFAULT : INTEGER range 1..80 := 80;

STRING_1 : STRING_RECORD;        -- can change size, in heap

STRING_2,
STRING_3 : STRING_RECORD( 90 );          -- larger than STRING_1,
                                         -- cannot change size,
                                         -- on stack

STRING_4,
STRING_5 : STRING( 1.. DEFAULT ); -- cannot change size, on stack

begin
        STRING_1 := STRING_2;  -- slowest
        STRING_4 := STRING_5:  -- faster
        STRING_2 := STRING_3;  -- fastest
end;
```

Note that unconstrained array objects can appear implicitly as function results. Such objects have all runtime overhead associated with unbounded records. One common case of this is the use of STANDARD.STRING as the result type of a function. The performance will improve if the size of the string is constrained. For example, if the string corresponds to a line of text with a fixed size of 80 caharacters, defining an array type using this fixed size is more efficient than the standard string type.

```
function GET_A_LINE return STRING;     -- slow

subtype STRING_80 is STRING( 1..80 );
function GET_A_LINE return STRING_80; -- faster
```

2.4 Exceptions for normal processing

The performance of the Ada exception mechanism becomes important when exceptions are used programmatically. Exceptions are handled in software. Using an exception to exit a loop is significantly slower than using an explicit exit statement.

2.5 Tasking

There are characteristics of tasking programs that cause the programs to execute slower than equivalent sequential programs. In addition, tasking constructs themselves are generally slower in relation to sequential constructs because of the task synchronization required by the Ada language. For example, an entry call is slower than a procedure call, because of the overhead necessary to synchronize the calling task and the accepting task.

When an Ada program activates multiple tasks, compiler-generated calls to the runtime for heap and I/O operations are affected. In general, I/O operations are affected marginally, while heap operations are affected significantly. These operations are slower because the runtime must protect non-reentrant critical regions within itself.

2.6 Separates

Separates minimize recompilation time (for individual files) and help break the code up into smaller and more manageable pieces. However, the use of separates also prevents some optimizations from being made on variables across the call to a separate unit. Moreover, the use of separates increases the size of the executable and also increases the overall compilation time for a system extensively using separates.

3 Performance Improvements

With these general considerations in mind we analyzed the code in order to identify the critical parts which could be considered candidates for optimization with respect to performance.

3.1 General strategy

The starting point for our work was a running system, fulfilling all functional requirements, but lacking in performance. Due to the limited budget and time available, we decided to keep the system running and do only small incremental changes to the existing code in order to increase the performance.

A general strategy for increasing the performance was established:

- Be sure that the code is correct before trying to make it more efficient.
- Locate the bottlenecks. The major part of the problem arises from a small part of the code.
- Make only small incremental changes, and analyze the results of each. Retest. Did the change help? Is the code more efficient? Is the code still correct?

The bottlenecks of the software could then be pointed out and changed, without disturbing the overall system functionality.

3.2 Memory usage

In our case, the size of the executable code was about 2 Mbytes, excluding dynamically allocated data space. Dynamically allocated data resided in primary memory and the swap area. Bursts of processing and communication caused the dynamically allocated data space to grow. At the most, the core process required about 40 MB of memory.

In other words, our implementation made extensive use of the program heap. There are mainly two types of Ada constructs which are responsible for the heap usage:

- Dynamically instantiated classes, which include instantiations of
- generic packages,
- generic packages with task,
- generic packages with task type
- Abstract Data Types (ADTs) using the heap for its variables and data structures.

We had to analyze more closely which data structures that could use static data instead of dynamic data.

3.3 Re-structuring of the internal database

All run-time data are pre-loaded into an internal database, residing in memory. The accesses to this database are controlled by an object called Kernel. The following measures for optimization of the Kernel were suggested:

- Do the processing where the data is and thereby avoid copying of data between objects. This should be implemented for all data structures used in the internal database.
- Pre-process some of the data at load time. Extract information frequently used and place it in static data structures easily accessible at run time. Data in the description ADTs could for instance be loaded into static arrays. This should reduce the time needed during processing.
- Place the internal database in a shared memory segment. This would allow programs running in other OS-processes access the database directly, and the overhead introduced by communication services would be eliminated.

3.4 Internal ADTs

The software used a lot of internal ADTs. Most of these ADTs define dynamic objects or data structures which are placed on the heap. For instance all of the data structures used in the internal database in the Kernel are dynamic data types.

Many of the ADTs used a lot of other ADTs and most of these ADTs were generics which had to be instantiated with the appropriate parameters before they could be used. This was very flexible and supported re-use of code. However, it is a drawback with such general constructs that they introduce an overhead for frequently used data structures.

The following steps were considered to increase the performance of the ADTs:

- Remove the discriminant records. This requires that the interface to the ADTs have to be changed.
- Introduce composite operations where appropriate.
- Make the components of the ADTs visible, i.e. remove the 'private' declarations in the package specifications. The components of the (ADT) records will then be directly accessible. Then they are no longer true ADTs, but this will reduce the number of procedure/function calls, and increase performance where the ADT operations are called frequently. For instance in tight loops.
- Joining of ADTs. The ADT hierarchy consisted of 5 levels; one ADT at the top level used many ADTs internally. This entailed many procedure calls to set/get data from ADTs used. This was flexible, but introduced an overhead when the ADT operations were called frequently. A more efficient solution is to join some closely related ADTs into one ADT. Then the data would be directly accessible inside the ADT.
- Usage of representation clauses to reduce time and cpu spent on packing/unpacking when transfering ADTs between different HW platforms.

3.5 Tasking

The design consisted of a great number of tasks. The execution time in the Ada Runtime system is mainly determined by the number of rendez-vous, and is rather independent of the number of tasks. But we also know that use of the Ada tasking model requires experience and care. When the software design does not acknowledge the limitations in the characteristics of the tasking model it will lead to weak performance. Task blocking, combined with vagaries in the specifications of task scheduling and with code flexibility within an accept clause, can lead to significantly poor performance of a tasking based implementation.

Tasking implementations that hide tasks under objects are likely to perform quite poorly. Hidden tasks usually incur excessive blockage because subsequent requirements to employ tasking rendez-vous are lost.

3.6 Separates

Most of the procedures in the software were separate procedures. As indicated before, use of separates prevents some optimizations from being made on variables across the call to a separate unit. But separates minimizes recompilation time for individual files and help break the code up into smaller and more manageable pieces. We therefore made a script which gathered the separate files into their appropriate body files, so that the delivery should not consist of separate procedures. It is not clear how much performance one may gain by this, but some improvement is expected.

3.7 Generics

When browsing the code we found that declarations and instantiations could be made more efficient by following these general rules:

- Avoid instantiations of generics inside frequently used operations. Move these local instantiations to a global location, in the body of the package.
- Avoid declarations of huge ADTs inside frequently used operations. This applies especially for ADTs using discriminant records, because these variables are allocated on the heap.

The two test programs below runs a declaration of discriminant records, outside and inside the declaration of an operation, respectively:

```
-- TESTING DISCRIMINANT RECORDS OUTSIDE THE OPERATION DECLARATION

with text_io;
with testpack3;
with calendar;

procedure test3 is
   start_time, end_time : calendar.time;
   package real_io is new text_io.float_io(float);
begin

   start_time := calendar.clock;

   for i in 1..10000 loop
      testpack3.testproc1;
   end loop;
```

```
    end_time := calendar.clock;

    real_io.put(float(calendar."-"(end_time, start_time)),5, 10, 0);
    text_io.new_line;
end test3;
```

```
with text_io;

package testpack3 is

    procedure testproc1;

end testpack3;
```

```
with text_io;

package body testpack3 is

    type strrec(d : integer := 80) is
    record
        s : string(1..d);
        p : string(1..d);
    end record;

    b : strrec(80);
    c : strrec;
    d : strrec;
    e : strrec;
    f : strrec;
    g : strrec;
    h : strrec;
    i : strrec;
    j : strrec;
    k : strrec;
    l : strrec;
    m : strrec;
    n : strrec;
    o : strrec;
    p : strrec;
    q : strrec;
    r : strrec;
    s : strrec;
    t : strrec;

procedure testproc1 is
begin

    b.s := (others => ' ');

end testproc1;

end testpack3;
```

-- TESTING DISCRIMINANT RECORDS INSIDE THE OPERATION DECLARATION

```
with text_io;
with testpack4;
with calendar;

procedure test4 is
    start_time, end_time : calendar.time;
    package real_io is new text_io.float_io(float);
begin

    start_time := calendar.clock;

    for i in 1..10000 loop
        testpack4.testproc1;
    end loop;

    end_time := calendar.clock;

    real_io.put(float(calendar."-"(end_time, start_time)),5, 10, 0);
    text_io.new_line;

end test4;
```

```
with text_io;

package testpack4 is

    procedure testproc1;

end testpack4;
```

```
with text_io;

package body testpack4 is

    type strrec(d : integer := 80) is
    record
        s : string(1..d);
        p : string(1..d);
    end record;

procedure testproc1 is
    b : strrec(80);
    c : strrec;
    d : strrec;
    e : strrec;
    f : strrec;
    g : strrec;
    h : strrec;
    i : strrec;
    j : strrec;
    k : strrec;
    l : strrec;
    m : strrec;
    n : strrec;
    o : strrec;
    p : strrec;
    q : strrec;
    r : strrec;
```

```
    s : strrec;
    t : strrec;
begin

    b.s := (others => ' ');

end testproc1;

end testpack4;
```

The first test (with testpack3) took 7 msecs to execute, while the second test (with testpack 4) took 162 msecs to execute. Consequently, the code is more efficient when the variables are declared in the package body and not locally, in the operations, especially when the variables are dynamic.

A similar experiment was run for one of our more complex ADTs:

1.   The ADT was declared locally and included a discriminant record
2.   The ADT was declared globally and included a discriminant record
3.   The ADT was declared locally and the discriminant record was replaced by a regular record.
4.   The ADT was declared globally and the discriminant record was replaced by a regular record.
5.   The ADT was declared locally and the discriminant record was replaced by an integer.

The following results were achieved, in terms of milliseconds elapsed to run the test:

1.   346
2.   256
3.   56
4.   11
5.   8

References

1.   Bruce E. Krell, Developing with Ada, Life-cycle methods, Bantam Books, 1992.

2.   AdaWorld for HP 9000 Series 700/800, Development Environment Manuals, Volume 1, Version 5.5.2

Ariane 5: Development of the On-Board Software

Jean-Noel Monfort and Vinh Qui Ribal

Aerosptiale - Espace & Defense
Route de Verneuil BP2
78133 Les Mureaux Cedex
France

1-INTRODUCTION

The first ARIANE 5 launch is expected in 1996 and the development phase of the flight program is now coming to an end. Before Flight Program, a significant program/application was developed to test the Cryogenic Propulsion Stage (EPC). In November 1994 this on board software named PBEL ignited the EPC 's motor, deflected the nozzle activation and shutdown the engine after 270s. Since this date seven successfull tests have been performed using PBEL which was regularly updated to take into account the changes resulting from EPC test analyses.

So some months before the first launch of ARIANE 5, the PBEL software had demonstrated the maturity of the ARIANE 5 on board software development process. It is a major event when considering the complexity of this application and the use for the first time of new software methodologies. It was the first time in the ARIANE program that on board software developed in the Ada language and using Ada tasking had been used in operational conditions. The experience gained with PBEL underpins other ARIANE 5 on board software which uses the same methodology (Flight Program, Launcher integration softwares).

This paper presents the main characteristics of ARIANE 5 on board software development, and the choices made for the design and code phases of PBEL.
We conclude this report of PBEL experience by discussing the suitability of HOOD and Ada in the development of critical real time software.

2- ARIANE 5 ON BOARD SOFTWARE DEVELOPMENT

2.1- ARCHITECTURE OF THE ARIANE 5 ON BOARD SOFTWARE

The ARIANE 5 target computers are based on the Motorola 68020 processor and 68882 coprocessor, with 512 Kbytes memory. Appendix 1 present the architecture of the ARIANE 5 Data Management System.
The on board software of ARIANE 5 has been divided into three levels, which facilitates the parallel development and validation of the different levels, and allows the reusability of the two lowest levels between different applications (Flight Program, Launcher or Stages integration software, PBEL). This structure is also very efficient to encapsulate a set of functions in different independent software components which have an acceptable level of complexity.

2.1.1- First level (LN1)

The first level (LN1) includes all low level services which manage :

- communications between the computer and the electrical system via the duplicated 1553 bus.

- timing services specified to offer an on-board time management with 10 μs of accuracy, and delays management services with or without suspension of the calling task. These services were specified because the timing management services offered by the standard real time kernel did not suit the accuracy and performance required of the on board software.

- interrupt handling, this covers interrupts linked with the communication system or with the application processor (coprocessor exceptions, ...).

The LN1 was developed in Ada with a small part written in Assembler (to obtain the best performance for services called frequently).

2.1.2 Second level (LN2)

The second level (LN2) includes all the services for the ARIANE 5 duplex redundant Electrical System, managed via the 1553 bus.

Some services manage the commands to actuators, the checking of these commands, and the actions to manage a single failure of an actuator.

It manages the interface with the sensors providing the functional measurements used by LN3 algorithms, the conversion to floating point and Standard Units and, the validation of these measurements (analysis of the communication status report, filtering of invalid measurements,...).

This level was developed in Ada, and in assembler for small part requiring high performance.

2.1.3 Third Level (LN3)

The third level (LN3) gathers the various algorithms associated with the flight control (navigation, guidance, autopilot), the management and the monitoring of the stages (monitoring of engines, pressurisation of tanks, detection/commutation of nozzle actuators), and the different configuration changes of the launcher (release of stages or payloads).

Several LN3 applications are being developed for ARIANE 5. This paper is essentially based upon our experiences during the development of the LN3 named PBEL.
This application is responsible for the following functions :

- Ignition and shutdown of the cryogenic engine, this function commands servovalves or pyrotechnic charges at specific times. These times must have an accuracy of 10 ms.

- Engine monitor, which acquires cyclically a set of measurements every 18ms or 72 ms, and checks that their values remain within thresholds. In case of anomalies the software must activate an emergency shutdown with a reactivity of less than 40 ms.

- The monitoring and pressurisation of the tanks (H_2, O_2, He) is checked every 72 ms. Using measurements from the tanks, servo-valves are commanded to keep the pressure within safe tolerances. The required reactivity of such commands is less than 50 ms.

- The commanding of nozzle actuators is done every 7.2 ms. The monitoring of actuators is done every 72 ms and will activate the redundant equipment in case of failure.

- monitor of ground requests and shutdown of engine with a reactivity of 18 ms.

All this software is developed in Ada.

2.2- DEVELOPMENT CHOICES AND RULES

2.2.1- DESIGN PHASE

At the beginning of development following ESA recommendations, we studied the suitability of the HOOD (Hierarchical Object Oriented Design) method for the design of the ARIANE 5 on board software.

This study concluded :

- the method is appropriate to design the LN2 , for the LN3 part managing stages functions, but less appropriate for the LN3 part managing the flight control program,

- the method is appropriate to design the software but not the real time architecture. A specific Structural document was created in addition to the HOOD document, describing in detail the tasking design.

- the method is appropriate for maintenance

The study underlined the lack of readability and weakness of the HOOD design documentation.
The lack of automatic cross checks for consistency between code and design was also a weakness for the tools then available on the market.

2.2.2- CODE PHASE

In 1988 studies and prototypes were made to choose the development language and to demonstrate the suitability of tasking to schedule on-board software. Considering the results of these studies it was decide in 1989 to use Ada, including tasking, for ARIANE 5 on-board software. Ada is a high level language which enables data abstraction, encapsulation, maintenance, portability and support well the HOOD method.

At the same time the choice was made to use the ALSYS cross compiler Ada/68020 and the Alsys Real Time Kernel(ARTK) to develop the software of the application processing unit (UT). The choice of the ARTK was taken despite the problems raised during the earlier studies concerning the timing performance, the memory size increasing and the lack of garantee of ARTK validation. We made the assumption that the widespread used of this product on similar projects will allow to increase our confidence during the ARIANE 5 development.

For the Input/Output processing unit (UES) it was decided to use the ADA language essentially for exchange memory data structures, and assembler for the UES software and SMART. The UES real time part was implemented as an automaton process scheduled by several hardware timers.

It was a major step to use this methodology for the on-board software development, in particular the use of tasking. In our experience of on-board software development in earlier projects, the real time management was always performed by a specific scheduler managing the activation of predetermined slices of the software. This design method was applied to facilitate testability and reliability, but was difficult to maintain and was not optimised for CPU load. This development process works well and is the best one when the size and the complexity of on-board software is small.

For ARIANE 5 the complexity and the number of functions managed by the on-board software increased greatly compared with our earlier on-board software development(migration of functions from equipment to software, duplex redundancy management, management of engine,...). These additional requirements increase the size of the code and the real time complexity. All these changes justify the need to use a high level language and tasking to facilitate the development and for the flexibility of maintenance.

2.3 RULES OF DEVELOPMENT

A Design and Coding Standard document has been written giving guidelines for Design and Coding phases. It defines a subset of Ada features and rules to be applied in the design and code phases.

2.3.1 REAL TIME RULES

In order to control the reliability and the testability of the software, a set of rules were defined :

- the use of tasks was forbidden for the lowest levels (LN1 and LN2), in order to encapsulate the real time design only in the application part.

- definition of specific LN1 services consistent with the tasking design of LN3 and the performance or precision required(reading of on board time, delays with or without task suspension, handling of interrupts, handling of Input/Output with or without suspension, ...),

- the number of tasks was specified to be less than ten.

- the communication between tasks must be minimised to save CPU time and to control testability (6 entry points maximum per task for PBEL)

- the number of semaphores must be minimized, and their effect analysed with care, as they are a frequent source of dead lock (3 semaphores for PBEL)

- the dynamic allocation of tasks is forbidden.

- the communication of data using rendez-vous is forbidden

2.3.2 CODING RULES

- CPU performance and memory size management were our major worries during development. We managed this with a Resource Allocation Document, to assign and to readjust performance criteria along each phase of development. At the beginning it was particularly difficult to have realistic estimates of CPU time and memory size considering our lack of informations in Ada and in the code generation mechanism of the Alsys Ada compiler. For the Flight Program, the experience gained from PBEL allowed us to manage this activity precisely, allowing us to take decisions in time.

- Due to the lack of compiler documentation and information from the supplier support, it was necessary to make our own researches into the mechanism of code generated. This survey covered several Ada features (types definitions, genericity, ...), as well as compilation and bind options.

We defined from this study a subset of Ada features compatible with our safety criteria (no dynamic allocation) and with our performances constraints. Thus, for enumeration types, the use of the pragma NO_IMAGE allowed us to save a lot of memory.
The real effects of optimisation options at compilation time and at bind time (eg. unreachable code removed) were also studied due to the need for optimized code with a high performance.

- Ada is a strongly typed language and several verifications are done at compilation time. Ada checks are very useful for debuging, but generate a large amount of code and time taken. As testing is rigorously performed during unit test and integration, we reduced, for the operationnal binary code, Ada checks by using only the compiler option CHECK=STACK which only checks for the stack overflow. In case of exception the nominal on-board computer is switched on the redundant on-board computer.

3- REPORT OF PBEL EXPERIENCE

3.1 SUITABILITY OF HOOD METHOD

3.1.1 PROBLEMS

Three main problems were met in the operationnal use of the HOOD method.

The first problem was the quality of the tools itself. At the beginning of development the tools available on the market was not mature. The first tool used in the project, was adequate for a small application and allowed the development the UES and LN1 software. But several problems were found with larger software (LN2) and lead us to choose another tool. The IPSYS HOOD tool was chosen to develop LN2, LBEL and the flight program.

A second problem is the HOOD document itself. Each tool has developed its own interface to input the textual descriptions. But the quality of the Man Machine Interface and combined with the documentation layout do not provide for a good readable design document. These problems added to the very complicated documentation structure implied by the HOOD Standard, lead to poor readability.

The third problem is the impossibility of maintaining consistency between design and code. It is not a specific problem of the HOOD design method, but considering the large amount of information input into the tool, it should be possible to have an automatic update of design and code consistency, particularly for the detailed design part.

3.1.2 ADVANTAGES

The use of an object oriented method, structuring the software to reflect objects in the real world was particularly efficient for LN2 (objects VALVE, PYROTECHNICS, NOZZLE ACTUATORS, ...) and for the PBEL functions (TANKS, ENGINE, ...) see APPENDIX 2. The HOOD design method enabled us to obtain a software structure with a clear mapping between functions and objects. It allowed us to easily localise the impact of functional changes.

Another important advantage of the method is that we obtain a clear definition of the design to the coders.
Also the encapsulation in one object of functions matching the technical specialities, improve communications between coder, designer and technical experts in charge of the corresponding objects (nozzle actuators, engine, ...).

The HOOD design also provides a clear manner to delimit the different phases of testing. The unit tests are done object by object, the integration must verify the interfaces between different objects (including environment objects) or between tasks.

3.2 Ada TASKING

3.2.1 REAL TIME DESIGN OF PBEL

Seven tasks are necessary to encapsulate the real time requirements of PBEL (see APPENDIX 3). We describe briefly the role of each task.

- CYCLIC EXECUTIVE : this task schedules the cyclic operations of PBEL. The main characteristic of this task is that all operations called will have no task suspension. This task contains 1 entry point and has the priority 5.

- ACYCLIC EXECUTIVE : this task schedules the acyclic operations (engine ignition,...). This task contain two entry points and has the priority 11.

- SHUTDOWN MANAGER : this task executes the shutdown of the engine at the required date or immediately in case of critical anomaly. Having a higher priority (14) than ACYCLIC or CYCLIC EXECUTIVE, this task will preempt them to immediately shutdown the engine. This task contain 1 entry point.

- ANOMALY HANDLER : this task, in the event of a system anomaly occurring, assesses the anomaly's criticality. In the case of a critical anomaly, this task will release the SHUTDOWN MANAGER thus enabling the shutdown sequence to be executed. This task contains 6 entry points and has the priority 20 (the highest).

- MV SERVER TASK : this task is used only to manage the electrical redundancy logic for mono-stable servovalve commands requested by CYCLIC EXECUTIVE. This task contains 1 entry point and has a priority 8.

- BV SERVER TASK : this task is used to order the bistable servovalves requested by CYCLIC EXECUTIVE, because the protocol of commands include a large delay and so a long suspension. This task contains 1 entry point and has priority 17.

- DEAD LOCK TASK : this task implemented as a non terminal loop within the main procedure, is required to ensure that ARTK does not enter a "dead lock" state as a result of having no task to run.

The PBEL software makes use of tasks and rendez-vous, but it also it uses three semaphores. One semaphore is to protect critical regions of software in which an operation can cancel a started delay. The second semaphore is used to protect the software against parallel requests of the same electrical equipment disconnection. The last semaphore protects the sofware where there exists a non reentrant protocol to acquire a functionnal measurement from a particular sensor.

3.2.2 PROBLEMS

Our experience highlights four main problems :

- The compiler documentation does not provide enough usable information to monitor tasks.

For example we had to obtain from our compiler supplier the TCB (Task Control Block) structure that provides important information for task monitoring such as the current priority, current state and substate (running, in rendez-vous, at select, ...), the stack start address, ... This kind of information should be provided with the compiler documentation.

- It remains a very difficult problem to estimate the size necessary for the heap and the stacks. The TCB only provides the stack start address and the allocated size, but not the actual used size. For the PBEL software we had enough spare memory to allocate large size, for the Flight Program it is a greater problem.

A specific tool measures, after each run on target, the percentage of remaining memory in each heap. Nevertheless the worst case heap size needed is very difficult to define, and we must provide a large safety margin.

So it is very important that the companies developing the real time kernel, provide reliable information on estimation of stack and heap memory size needed for a given application.

- The third problem is the validation of the real time kernel. It is the first time that we have developed safety critical on-board software that uses, in operational conditions, a critical subpart not specifically developed for our application. The same applies with the use of the Ada mathematical library.

At the moment we have developed four operational software products (including PBEL) using Ada tasking, no problems were detected concerning the ARTK (we use only a set of the ARTK's primitives). This development represents more than 50 hours of ARTK used on rigs without problem, which is around 70 times the duration of an ARIANE 5 flight. These figures will increase a lot after taking into account the test phases of the flight program, are a good indicator of confidence in the standard real time kernel ARTK. Nevertheless we get only a feeling of confidence, but not a formal validation of this software as is the case for the other parts. To enforce our confidence it would be very useful if the real time kernels available on the market have standard validation rules in order to certify the quality of such software.

- The fourth problem is the maintenance of the ARTK. Using a commercial real time kernel raises the problem of the support for this issue of software that must be maintained for several years. It could be impossible to update the ARTK in case of a blocking problem detected later.

This problem can also be generalized for the compiler versions maintenance. Indeed, PBEL used the compiler release V5.1.7 and the Flight Program the release V5.5.1. The supplier no longer maintains release V5.1.7 and so, each time we had any problem we had to find ourself a workaround.

Currently there is not adequate solution for this problem, this is true for all equipment or tools used for the software development.

3.2.3 ADVANTAGES

The experience of on-board software using Ada tasking is very positive for the following reasons :

- The four applications including PBEL that we developed allowed us to refine progressively a reference design, respecting our goals of optimisation and testability. These successive refinements allowed us to prepare for the design phase of the Flight Program.
Today the Flight Program real time design can be considered as a robust reference design (using tasking). For later projects it could be considered as an acceptable level of complexity for a real time critical software. This reference design will form the basis when building future electrical and data management system.

- Another advantage of Ada tasking is the simplicity and flexibility of design over a specific scheduler. The Ada rendez-vous mechanism allows the classification of tasks as client or server. Moreover, it is a powerful way to synchronize tasks.
During PBEL development we needed to update several times the real time design to take into account new requirements. One of the changes lead us to add a new task, because it was the simplest solution and better for non regression validation, rather than increasing the complexity of existing tasks and modifying a specific scheduler.
So it was confirmed that the use of Ada tasking is very useful when considering the complexity of the ARIANE 5 software and the great number of changes occurring within the development phase of PBEL and later in its maintenance phase.

- A very great advantage of Ada tasking is the possibility to validate the tasks independently during integration, this method was applied to PBEL reducing the difficulty of integration and optimising the planning. For example we integrated separately and in parallel the tasks ACYCLIC, CYCLIC and SHUTDOWN.

3.3 Ada LANGUAGE

3.3.1 PROBLEMS

- One problem is that Ada allows the definition of complex data structures (for example variant records), this feature is not always consistent with our constraints of performance, memory size and also not always very readable. The Design and Coding Standards gives guidelines to the developers.

- A major problem of the Ada compiler is the weakness of documentation concerning the compilation or bind options. It was necessary during our development to do this analysis by ourselves through a lack of clear information. For example, it is not easy to know how to suppress in the binary code all symbolic names for debug information. On this problem, we spent a lot of time to understand the effect of a bind option (HISTORY=NO), that was not documented.
So the effects of optimisation are not sufficiently documented, to study the risk implied in an on-board software build process.

One specific problem of our on-board application is the need to have an invariant part of the code that we qualify, and a set of data customized for each flight. We have a major problem because in the process of a binary build there are several steps that modify the invariant part, even though we have not changed the Ada source code. We discovered for example that a change of value of one constant can modify the binary code, another example is that the date of bind is inserted in the binary code changing the checksum of the software produced from the same Ada sources.

The compiler producers are unsufficiently aware of the problems that arise in the development of critical real time software, of the need to provide a detailed documentation on memory management, and the effects of optimisation.

- At the beginning of the project a major problem was the lack of availability of an Ada debugger for our target (68020 processor). For approximately three years we have been using a LAUTERBACH emulator with satisfaction. Nevertheless it is very important to state this point about the small number of Ada debugger/emulator available on the market. There are a lot of problems in developing such debuggers/emulators considering, the fact that the standard format definition (IEEE,...) does not provide all information necessary to develop a good target debugger for an Ada cross compiler.

3.3.2 ADVANTAGES

- The type definition features and the encapsulations with clear interface, is the first quality of Ada. A lot of problems are detected during compilation, saving a lot of time later in unit testing and integration.

- Both compiler checking and Ada checks are of great help for validation in the unit test phase as well as in integration on the target. These checks, are removed to produce the operationnal on-board code (option check=stack). Our approach for unit test and integration was to do each test systematically with and without the Ada checking. The time gained in debugging is significant and it is the major important point of Ada language.
In addition, if the Ada seems to be very difficult to beginners or to a coder with a practice of another language, it is due to its combination of strong type verification, its data abstraction and encapsulation mechanisms. All these features save a lot of time during the development and test phases (separate compilation, checks done at compilation time, safety of data access ...).

- Excluding the problem of complex data structures, one of the good points of Ada is its readability. The association of the HOOD method and Ada allows the people involved in the different development phases (design, integration, functional validation) or managing the activities, to be able to review very easily the code, and to detect easily major discrepancies with the design or the specification.

- Both the HOOD design method and the Ada language are a great help identifying the impact of changes and to appreciate the workload.

- Ada has a very good portability, only a very small part of Ada is depending of implementation. We used successively this very important feature of Ada.

We develop on different platforms with different compilers (for instance, VAX Ada is used for unit tests and Alsys Ada for target tests). We have had no significant problems in changing from one platform to another.

4- CONCLUSIONS

At the beginning of the ARIANE 5 project we took the decision to improve the method of on-board software development, considering the increase of complexity of ARIANE 5 Flight Program. Our objective was to manage this change while keeping or improving the level of reliability we had in our preceding on-board software projects.
Today with the PBEL experience and Flight Program progress, we control the process of development, using HOOD design method, Ada language and Ada tasking.

The HOOD method permits structuring of software, but is not sufficient to design completely the software particularly the real time part. The HOOD design is probably the best method to design software developed in Ada.
We are very disappointed by the readability of the HOOD documentation and by the tool itself.

The Ada has proved to be a suitable choice for on-board software development.

Tasking is an acceptable solution regarding the increase of flexibility of design in comparison with a specific scheduler. However the validation of the standard real time kernel remains a worry, especially for critical real time software.

The Ada language is not so difficult in itself but the Ada development environment specifically the compiler. To continue with Ada, compilers and run-time suppliers have to cooperate with industries and take into account their needs and concerns.

In any case it is clear that the choice of the language shall be the best compromise taking into account the processor, the compiler, the real time kernel and the host/target debug tools. Our experience highlighted that the design of the electrical and data management system for any project must take into account the acceptable limit of complexity for a critical real time software, performing in a centralized Data Management architecture.

APPENDIX 1 – ARIANE 5 DATAS MANAGEMENT SYSTEM

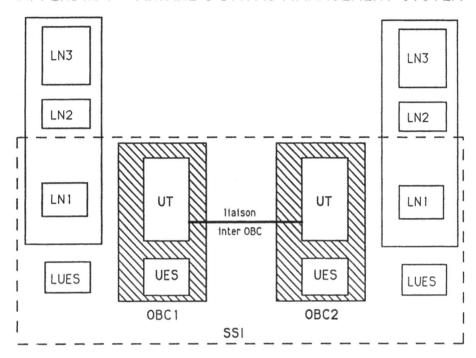

APPENDIX 2 - HOOD DESIGN PROCESS TREE

LBEL (ACTIVE)
    AUTOPILOT
    COMMUNICATIONS
        GROUND
        TELEMETRY
    CONTROL (ACTIVE)
        ACYCLIC EXECUTIVE (ACTIVE)
        CYCLIC EXECUTIVE (ACTIVE)
    CR_PROCESSING
    GAM
    LN3_PROFILE
    PROPULSION
    SIMULATION MANAGER
    SYSTEM_STATE (ACTIVE)
        ANOMALY_ HANDLER (ACTIVE)
        APPLICATION_STATE
        CONTEXT
    VALVES (ACTIVE)
    VULCAIN (ACTIVE)
        IGNITION_MANAGER
        SHUTDOWN_MANAGER (ACTIVE)
        SUPERVISE_MANAGER

A5RTK (ENVIRONMENT)
A5_EXCEPTIONS (ENVIRONMENT)
A5_MATHS (ENVIRONMENT)
A5_TYPES (ENVIRONMENT)
INFORMATION SUBSYSTEM (ENVIRONMENT)
LAUNCHER (ENVIRONMENT)

APPENDIX 3 - PBEL REAL TIME DESIGN

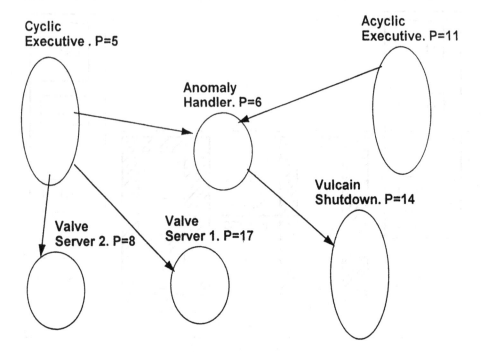

PRONAOS Ground Control Center :
First Operational Ada Application in C.N.E.S.

André LAURENS

PRONAOS Project, C.N.E.S.[1]
18, avenue Edouard Belin
31055 Toulouse, FRANCE
e-mail : andre.laurens@cst.cnes.fr
phone : 33-61-27-46-42 - fax : 33-61-28-20-08

Abstract. The computer team of the French PRONAOS project decided in 1990 to develop its whole ground control center software in Ada on PC calculators, thus becoming the first operational Ada application in C.N.E.S. After a brief description of the project, this paper will explain the reasons of Ada choice, then describe environment, architecture and main design features of the application software. Then, it discusses the methodological frame of this software development and, as a conclusion, draws the lessons of this experience.

1. The Project and its Constraints

PRONAOS[2] is a French science project in which C.N.E.S. and three laboratories of C.N.R.S.[3] work together (I.A.S.[4], DEMIRM[5] and C.E.S.R.[6]), and whose purpose is the cold universe survey, by observation in the submillimetric wavelengths (100 μm < λ < 1 mm, i.e. between far infrared and radio wavelengths). Two scientific instruments have been developed that will fly each one in its turn on a stratospheric balloon-borne gondola. This gondola has been developed by C.N.E.S. itself and provides accurate pointing (typically 5 arc seconds rms.) to a payload made of a 2-meter telescope and the focal instrument.

The on-board computer subsystem (and mainly the central on-board software, described in [LAU 92]) realises the following functions : monitoring of the gondola devices, rough and accurate pointing modes (90% of its activity), configuration management (such as folding or unfolding the payload), telemetry emission and telecommand reception and processing. This highly automatic flight segment leaves

---

[1] Centre National d'Etudes Spatiales : *French Space Agency*

[2] Projet National d'Astronomie Submillimétrique : *National Project for Submillimetric Astronomy*

[3] Centre National de la Recherche Scientifique : *French Scientific Research Council*

[4] Institut d'Astrophysique Spatiale : *Space Astrophysics Laboratory*

[5] Département Matière Interstellaire Infra Rouge et Millimétrique de l'Observatoire de Paris : *Infrared & Millimetric Interstellar Matter Department of Paris Observatory*

[6] Centre d'Etudes Spatiales des Rayonnements : *Space Radiation Laboratory*

to the ground segment the high level control functions : fine gondola monitoring (and particularly for the pointing subsystem), global flight control (for instance, starting to unfold the payload), scientific observations management (uploading parameters, start and stop).

The gondola is controlled by a ground control center (CCNT[7]), that provides the usual functions of telemetry acquisition, real-time trending and display, and telecommand emission. Its first distinctive feature is to be easily carried to the launch site : at the beginning of the project, it was planned to launch the gondola from 2 sites (both desert and having very rustic equipment) for 24-hours flights, once a year during 10 years, CCNT being moved on the launch site during each campaign. The choice of PC calculators has been made partly for these reasons, but mostly for cost reasons.

CCNT has been used for operational purpose during the last level of gondola tests (4 months in Toulouse), gondola assembly on the launch site (2 months) and for PRONAOS first flight, which took place in September 1994, in Fort Sumner (New Mexico). Next flight is planned for May 1996 in Fort Sumner.

2. Why Ada?

Though no one in C.N.E.S. had, at the time of this choice, any experience in such an operational Ada software development, we decided to use Ada for the following reasons :

- Ada provides elegant solutions for multi-tasked applications on PC/DOS computers, at least better than UNIX (that was very uncomfortable on PCs) or than many exotic runtime kernels that can be found in the PC world;

- Ada was felt as a good methodological answer to the lifetime and maintainability constraints of this application;

- the team was willing to test in full size a language that looked like a technical innovation. Such innovations are allowed only on science projects, not on application programs (such as telecommunication or earth observation satellites), that demand well-known solutions (even old-fashioned). So it has been decided to use *full Ada and only Ada*.

An operational development cannot be lead without a strict and suitable design method. After our first Ada mock-ups, we made sure that it was impossible to develop an operational Ada application without a dedicated design method. This is the reason why we chose HOOD[8], and we were helped in this way by the C.N.E.S. Ada group.

---

[7] Centre de Contrôle Nacelle - Télescope : *Gondola & Telescope Control Center*
[8] *Hierarchical Object Oriented Design*

3. CCNT Environment

The above requirements are very common for a ground control center. Nevertheless, CCNT differs from our satellite ground control centers for various environment reasons, such as data links and formats, or operational usage.

3.1. External Data Flows

They are carried by RS422 serial links and very simple home-made protocols (one byte-oriented protocol, two packet-oriented protocols, with or without CTS/RTS signals handshake). But, as seen by the end user, telemetry and telecommand flows are structured in packets with various sizes, formats and frequencies :

Telemetry

- about 40 telemetry packets carrying some 520 parameters, size : few bytes to few tens of bytes, periodicity : 1s, 10s, 1 min, aperiodic, are transmitted by the standard telemetry channel (called TM),

- high frequency current acquisition on each of the 16 high voltage power lines, are transmitted by another telemetry channel (called TM_EDE) in a single telemetry packet emitted every 200 ms.

Telecommand

- analog commands (less than 10), are available for some basic operations such as telemetry channel switching or on-board computer power on or reset,

- numeric telecommands, processed by the main on-board software, are divided in 5 groups :

  - mission control commands : high-level orders such as running the payload unfolding automatic procedure, or starting a scientific observation,

  - parameter upload commands : scientific source coordinates, scientific observation modes, technological parameters such as magnetometer correction offset, etc.

  - manual mode commands : sort of macro-commands used to fix problem occurring during an automatic procedure (e.g. manually modifying star tracker detection threshold and retry an aborted star acquisition),

  - miscellaneous commands : for instance, enabling/disabling communication on a test port, asking for immediate sending of specific telemetry packets,

  - direct commands : almost all gondola devices (sensors, actuators) are connected to the on-board central computer via micro controllers (named BEs[9]), used as multiplexers. A command of this kind is passed by the on-board central computer to the corresponding BE, that issues an information or acknowledge answer, sent in a telemetry packet. These commands are

---

[9] Boîtiers Electroniques : *Electronic Racks* - there are 5 of them on the gondola

used to do some specific on-off, or to gather basic information if a problem occurs during the flight.

Numeric telecommands represent over 70 high level telecommands, plus as many equipment-specific (direct) telecommands. Telecommand emission uses and end-to-end control protocol, by the mean of acknowledge telemetry packets, carrying transmission errors or telecommand authorisation errors (the on-board software implements an authorisation automate, that enables or disables the processing of telecommands in each of the 23 on-board software modes that represent the various gondola configurations). There is no automatic telecommand re-emission upon negative acknowledge.

A test bed (named BIC[10]), usually connected to the test port of the on-board computer during the gondola assembly phase, is connected to CCNT, in order to keep, during the flight, the capability of direct communication with gondola devices, through the telemetry-telecommand link. This test bed sends BE commands to CCNT, that passes them up to the gondola as direct commands. The telemetry-carried BE answer is passed back by CCNT to BIC, that displays it.

3.2. The Operational Point of View

CCNT end users are very few (the initially planned operational team consisted in 5 persons) and represent the different trades of the project (mechanical and thermal engineering, optics, electronics, automatics and computing). Moreover, the use of CCNT is limited to assembly and test phases, and to the flight itself, which represent few months a year. Thus, easy use and configuration were strong requirements for the software development.

4. Architecture Overview

CCNT consists in 5 main workstations, each one built with a 486 PC, a colour screen and a line printer :

- "*Frontal*" workstation : telemetry acquisition on TM channel, storage and distribution to the other workstations, with a replay capability (real-time or not, during the flight or later),

- "*Energie*" workstation : telemetry acquisition on TM_EDE, storage, merging with some TM packets acquired from *Frontal*, and distribution to the *Servitudes* workstations, with a replay capability (real-time or not, during the flight or later)

- "*Conduite*" workstation : telecommand emission, processing and display of telemetry parameters concerning flight control, i.e. telecommand acknowledge, mechanical devices status, gondola modes, configuration changes (folding or unfolding the payload) and scientific observations, gondola trajectory tracking, etc.

---

[10] Banc d'Intégration et de Contrôle : *Assembly & Control Bed*

- *"Spécialiste - Servitudes"* workstation : processing and display of basic telemetry parameters (temperatures, power consumption, voltage of power lines, etc.),

- *"Spécialiste - Pointage"* workstation : processing and display of telemetry parameters related to stabilisation, pointing and star tracker subsystems.

As shown by fig. 1, CCNT has some extra computers :

- *Pointage* workstation is duplicated, on the same serial link, in order to increase the surface of display,

- *Servitude* workstation is duplicated, on separate serial links, in order to keep real-time display (on *Servitudes_TR* workstation) when processing replayed telemetry (on *Servitudes_Rejeu* workstation),

- BIC is connected to *Conduite* workstation,

- a backup computer, named *Sécurité*, acquires telemetry from both channel and stores it in a rough format, in order to keep a safe copy of telemetry flows, even if *Frontal* or *Energie* workstations hang.

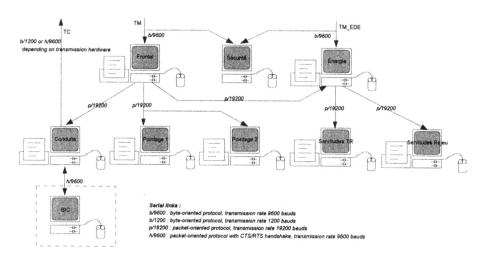

Fig. 1. CCNT general layout

5. Software Architecture

5.1. Guidelines

At top level, there are 4 main different software applications (i.e. executable files) :

- *"Frontal"* application,

- *"Energie"* application, that shares with *Frontal* application all packages related to telemetry storage, distribution, and replay,

- "*Spécialiste*" application : all *Spécialiste* workstation run the same software but process different telemetry packets,

- "*Conduite*" application : it is a *Spécialiste* application with 2 extra functions : telecommand emission and communication with BIC.

Sécurité software is a very simple C program that will not be described thereafter.

These main applications share common software layers, that are, bottom-up :

- general purpose packages :
  - hardware & O.S. interface : generic, interrupt-driven serial link handlers, various device handlers (line printer, interrupt controller, UARTs, etc.), file system interface (directory and file names management),
  - date and time computation, angular computation, management of strings, words, and various other data structures, definition of physical units;
- man-machine interface (M.M.I.);
- operational tools (logbook, interface to O.S. services such as file copy or delete, external links definition, etc.);
- telemetry format description and common telemetry processing (transfert functions, ground-computed parameters[11], monitoring), real-time display of telemetry parameters.

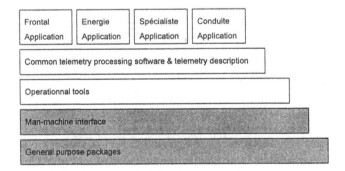

Fig. 2. CCNT software architecture

Changes and additions to the architecture

For the first flight, the processing of TM_EDE channel was not yet developed, so there was no *Energie* workstation and *Frontal* was sending telemetry packets directly to a single *Servitudes* workstation. TM_EDE processing has been developed with

---

[11] also called pseudo-parameters, these parameters are real-time computed from telemetry parameters, for instance : amplitude and period of the rocking movement of the gondola are computed from gyrometer raw data with a FFT on a 30 second sliding window.

minimal additions to existing software, thus reusing existing telemetry archive file management and telemetry processing software.

After the first flight, a telemetry extraction utility has been developed, using the above common software : it is a batch program that read telemetry archive files, processes the telemetry just like in the real-time application, and prints the parameters values in an ASCII file instead of displaying them to screen.

Various other off-line utilities have been added to the operational applications, all of them using existing software :

- *telemetry archive files manipulation* : merging, slicing, getting information such as beginning and end dates, number of packets, etc.,

- *telecommand batch files generation*, interactively or from files issued by the flight preparation software[12].

5.2. The M.M.I. : a Common Reusable Service

Because of the lack in "off-the-shelf" M.M.I. generation tools for PC (at the beginning of CCNT development, *MS-Windows* was in version 2), we were to develop a home-made M.M.I., real-time compatible and Ada callable. We decide to develop a mini window-manager, with some restriction such as : no window overlapping nor resizing, no compound event (such as multi-click, drag-and-drop), no notifier (mouse and keyboard events are processed by polling).

Of course, this M.M.I. has been designed to meet the application needs, but with a constant will of generalisation, that makes it application-independent and thus, reusable for other PC Ada applications, real-time or not. The M.M.I. is full Ada and uses an Ada callable off-the-shelf graphic library (*Halo Professional*). It has been developed separately of the application.

The M.M.I. is structured in 4 layers, bottom-up :

- HALO library interface, that makes the M.M.I. library-independent. It encapsulates all Halo requests, initialisation, start and stop of the graphic kernel, what was easy since we use only basic routines such as drawing a box, a line or a graphic text, such features being available in any graphic library;

- event manager : catches mouse and keyboard events and passes them up to requesting graphic objects (by a blocking read), and schedules drawing requests to the screen (in a semaphore-like manner);

---

[12] this software, distinct from CCNT, is used by the project scientists to plan the scientific observations to be made during a flight. It consists in input of submillimetric source characteristics, choice of associated tracking star, selection of time and mode for observation, control of visibility (related to earth rotation, sun and balloon / gondola technological constraints). Once the flight plan validated against these constraints, a report is issued as well as a file describing each observation. This file is used by CCNT to build the associated telecommand batches.

- graphic object manager : basic "widgets" are boxes, buttons, windows, texts, text boxes, scrollable text panes, curve drawing panes, etc.;

- high level widget managers : button menus, dialogue boxes, message boxes, choice lists, etc.

The basic widget manager is the core of our M.M.I. It provides such services as creation, deletion, move, activation, read on widgets located in a tree that implements two kinds of hierarchical relationships :

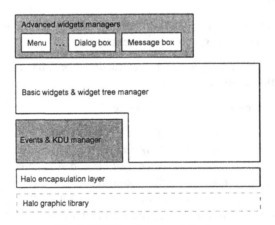

Fig. 3. M.M.I. software architecture

- membership : a window is made of a frame, a header and a canvas, which are 3 boxes,

- location : the W window contains the T text box, the R radio box and 2 buttons : B1 and B2.

These relationships and tree navigation are useful to implement such features as widget overlapping control, inherited visibility, relative/absolute coordinate systems, collective (subtrees) deletion.

All high level widgets are implemented as generic units, creating and managing composite widgets by assembling basic widgets. For instance, a button menu is a generic package, the generic argument of which is an enumerated type : the possible actions.

Ada83 lacks some object-oriented features such as heritage and polymorphism, so we were bound to some implementation tricks in order to represent both common and specific widget properties, and to make work together common services (delete, move, erase, ...) and specific ones (create, display, status read, event transmit, ...). Nevertheless, once these features properly encapsulated, Ada revealed a better tool than traditional procedural languages (such as C), as well for writing M.M.I. software, and for M.M.I. usage in the application software. Ada helpful features are, in this case, strong typing, overloading and generic units.

5.3. Telemetry Trending in Ada

Telemetry description and processing

Essentially, Ada is very helpful to describe telemetry formats (representation clauses prevent from writing software to decode telemetry fields). Nevertheless, Ada implementation of telemetry processing itself, based on such a static description, leads to a true dilemma :

- generalised algorithms, based on descriptors of transfer functions and monitoring laws (something usual in satellite GCCs), need data un-typing (or, at least, loose typing),

- hand-coded specific algorithms allow to keep Ada strong typing but may represent a hard work to write, and to maintain.

We have been reinforced in our "ideological" preference for strong typing, by a quick statistic on the different kinds of transfer functions : 85% of the 520 telemetry parameters have specific transfer functions, so it was not worth using descriptors. Moreover, the 110 ground-computed parameters have also specific computation algorithms, thus generalised processing was not useful.

In order to ensure the consistence of the various data structures used by the different steps of telemetry processing (monitoring tables, display units and formats, etc.), the initialisation software for this kind of data was not hand-coded. These informations are given in a unique ASCII file (edited by the CCNT configuration operator), and "compiled" to generate Ada code (package specifications for declaration and initialisation of the constant structures). The transfer functions remain hand-coded, but we were helped by Ada strong typing in defining such basics as Ohm's law, and making the compiler verify units in equations. Of course, the parameter description compiler is written in Ada.

The keystone of parameter modelisation in our software, is the kind of physical value (temperature, voltage, current, etc.), defined as an enumerated type, and used as a discriminant of all data structures. This discriminant is checked in a big 'case' at each time a parameter value is being read, written or computed : this is nothing more than Ada95 object tags. Of course, it would have been easier for us to develop such a software with the help of Ada95 object-oriented programming features, but it points the fact that object-oriented programming may be helpful for telemetry processing, as an alternate solution to descriptor-driven loose-typed algorithms.

Real-time display

The requirements for real-time telemetry parameter display consisted in alphanumeric display of parameter values (with a color signal of monitoring status : red = alarm), graphic display of parameter evolution vs. time (scrolling curves) or vs. another parameter (dot cloud graphs).

For this purpose, we have developed an off-line interactive display panel editor, using our M.M.I. and the above parameter description data structures. A display panel consists in a window, containing text boxes and curve panes, and is represented by data structure giving parameter identifiers and widget properties (size, position, etc.). This structure is stored in a file, that can be loaded from disk by the real-time applications (*Spécialiste*, *Conduite*), as needed by the operator. The real-time animation software allows to place and move such display panels in 6 virtual screens (thus defining 6 subtrees in the M.M.I. widget tree) that can be switched like TV channels. Each parameter value (and associated monitoring status) is passed to all active display panels (each of them knowing if the given parameter is used in this particular panel), ignoring whether the containing virtual screen is visible or not. This capability allows the display panels to be refreshed even when invisible, and kept up-to-date when the operator switches from a virtual screen to another.

6. Implementation & Tools

6.1. HOOD vs. Ada Concepts

As any other design method, HOOD provides high-level concepts. For most of them, Ada implementation is self-evident, for some others it is not, or may be discussed. For instance, ASER constraint has no "built-in" implementation, since Ada does not provide asynchronous rendezvous.

We have simulated it, by the way of relay-tasks (dynamically allocated on a task type, and thus, always ready), that take the calling task arguments, leave the rendezvous, wait for the called task to be ready, pass the arguments to the called task, and die after the deferred rendezvous is completed. Although it limits the task call profile to *in-mode* arguments (or none, i.e. signal-only), this mechanism smoothes overload peaks, and can be (actually is, in CCNT) implemented as generic units, including some extra features like on-purpose rendezvous loss.

Nevertheless, there is no evidence how much the design must tell about the implementation. This kind of mechanism may be as well represented by an unconstrained operation, implemented by an op-control calling on active object. In this case, the ASER label disappears and the parallel activity is only relevant of the object internals. We made no definitive decision on this subject (i.e. showing or not the ASER constraint), and we use the more pertinent for the reader's understanding, at the right abstraction level.

On the opposite, the semantics of some Ada features cannot be represented in a HOOD design, such as task types. This mechanism allows the representation of duplicable objects, in any number, which is quite different from classes : there is no specialisation when a task is allocated (all allocated tasks are identical to each other, and to the original one, defined by the type[13]), unlike generic unit instantiation. In the waiting of a possible change in the HOOD method, we merely represented this mechanism by a unique object, with a brief comment pointing out its multiplication ability.

---

[13] in an early version of our real-time display software, each active display panel was implemented by an allocated task, using its own panel descriptor.

6.2. Development Tools

Design tool

At the beginning of CCNT development, no HOOD design tool was available on PC. So we started the design with STOOD[14]. We used it on a workstation lent by another C.N.E.S. department, far from our platform and without any network communication with our PCs.

Such a poor integration level between design tool and compiler was not a good solution, so we used a newly released PC C.A.S.E. tool (*Select Case*), including a HOOD module, which is helpful for HOOD graphics, but lacks of ODS and Ada code generator. Moreover, it is not entirely compliant with HOOD method : some checks are not done, some others are not based on any HOOD rule, some features (such as links between HDTs[15]) are not correctly implemented.

As far as we know, this tool (or at least its HOOD module) is no more supported by its author. Thus, for maintenance purpose, we have ported back our design on STOOD, for we can, since a few months, access UNIX workstations running it via C.N.E.S. local network.

Compilation system

Only two native Ada compilers were available on PC : *Alsys* and *Meridian*. After a quick benchmark, it became obvious that only one was able to bear a complex, operational software application.

Meridian, like many PC tools, was a "toy compiler" : some loose checking on limited types, representation clauses not fully implemented, running out of memory when compiling large compilation units or many generic instantiations, memory and execution models limited to 286 real mode.

On the other hand, *Alsys* compiler implements the whole Ada 83 standard (including the whole chapter 13), and generates compact and efficient code. At the time we bought it, it was an expensive compiler (compared to other PC tools), but provided an optional toolset composed of a *make* tool, a debugger, a source code reformatter, and various other utilities like a cross-reference generator. Nevertheless, the development was rather uncomfortable for the following reasons :

- the user environment is old fashioned : command-driven shell, no integrated edition/compilation/test environment (the most recent release provides these features under *MS-Windows*, but has some other bugs);

- the toolset is immature : we waited more than one year for a *make* that runs without hanging, the debugger cannot handle graphic applications (unable to switch the screen from graphic to text mode and *vice versa*), nor real-time ones (it slows so much the application that the execution is no more real-time, and it

---

[14] HOOD tool from TNI running on Unix and VMS workstations

[15] Hood Design Tree

cannot debug tasks), and still has several bugs (incoherent values given for variables computed by generic units);

- although it provides some interesting features (such as interrupt buffering) the runtime executive has many serious bugs : erroneous pointer returned by task allocation, *delay* statements becoming non-preemptive when there is no user-defined idle task, partial memory reclaim after termination of an allocated task[16], nested interrupt stack allocations causes the application and/or the PC to hang;

- no efficient support was given by Alsys to help us finding workarounds, or to provide releases fixing the reported problems (we found workarounds for all the above problems, except the 'running out of stack buffers' hang, that still have serious operational consequences).

Obviously, PC is the poor relation for software development tools, and the few existing C.A.S.E. tools are not correctly maintained by their authors. PC's decreasing price and increasing power make it an interesting solution, compared to UNIX workstations, to develop cheap operational application, but the user is prevented to do it by the lack of operational development tools.

6.3. Test : HOOD and Ada Consequences

First, HOOD brings methodological particularities : object-driven breakdown makes easier interface management, unit testing (it is easy to built package-level batch tests) and assembly tests (by the use of stubs, having the same specification but not the same body), but increases the number of intermediate data formats, which are not easy to generate as test inputs.

Other test constraints are brought by Ada runtime : the encapsulation of tasks and memory management prevents observability of real-time activity and control of memory and CPU consumption.

In the first case, it seems necessary to add tests topics (especially assembly tests) to HOOD design process.

The second problem cannot be solved by other than compiler builders, who should provide instrumented runtimes, with such capabilities as real-time tracing (task activity, synchronisation), statistics on memory and CPU usage. This kind of solution has proved feasible and useful : an example is LICE[17] tool [CAR 92], developed by

---

[16] note that such a behaviour is partly caused by Ada standard's silence on said implementation-dependant capabilities in object deallocation and memory reclaim. Thus, some validated Ada implementations prevent the user to develop certain kinds of real-time applications, such as geostationary satellite ground control centers that run 24h a day during 10 years, unless he prohibits the usage of dynamic allocation (back to Stone Age!). Ada95's answer to this problem - replace the predefined allocator by your own - still does not satisfy me : if the memory allocation/reclaim manager provided with the compiler is bad or lazy, there are 99 chances on 100 that the one I will be bound to write will be much worse, because writing runtime executives is not my job.

[17] *Light In-Circuit Evaluator* : this tool is based on a permanent software instrumentation of ASTRES (a real-time kernel developed by C.N.E.S. for various targets such as i8086, MIL-STD-1750A, and obeying SCEPTRE standard), that sends to a hardware probe such events as task scheduling, kernel routine call,

C.N.E.S. and used during test phases of several on-board software applications (including PRONAOS on-board software).

7. The Lessons of this Experience

HOOD and Ada need to invest in training (even in education for Fortran addicts) : we had a 3-week Ada training course and we learned HOOD on the job in 1 week. But it was a profitable investment for a lot of reasons.

First, this approach leads to *methodological improvements* : both method and language improve the application reliability. Object oriented design reduces documentation effort (no need of interface control document, for instance) and Ada improves maintainability. Finally, the first step of unit tests (range control, caller/callees verifications, etc.) is no more necessary because of strong typing and profile strict-control.

Then, HOOD and Ada bring *new trends in software engineering* :

- "think reusable", in order to anticipate future needs and changes (you do not only work for the future generations since you can reuse software inside the same application),

- concentrate on architecture consistency and services definition, and relegate the implementation particularities in the deeps of package bodies,

- parallel processing is to be implemented at its right place (some use it to make a "spatial" parallelism, realising tree navigation by concurrent tasks running on each branch), no more at top-level of the software (so was it with traditional "out-of-the-language" real-time executives),

- design a clear, simple - even beautiful - software, and forget the optimisation obsession. Optimisation may come in a second step, and at the only places where it is needed and efficient. We never had to deny our religion of "whole Ada, nothing but Ada" for memory or CPU consumption considerations, though we never paid attention to the consequences of our design choices on those parameters, so fateful in the past. It should be never forgotten that nowadays, it is easier and cheaper to buy some extra megabytes of RAM than to develop, test and maintain an over-optimised software.

Finally, HOOD and Ada *increase productivity* : when comparing CCNT functions with those of satellite ground control centers, it becomes obvious that development time is shorter with HOOD and Ada, than with traditional methods and languages (such as functional breakdown and C). This can be explained by the following reasons : HOOD brings rapidly a sound and stable architecture; Ada is a powerful language that solves complex problems in a few lines of code; object-oriented design

---

signal raise, interrupts. These events are time-stamped by the probe with a precision of 1 μs, and sent to a micro controller, that manages data storage and user interface. Once post-processed, these data give such useful information as runtime activity charts, CPU load statistics, etc. Specific markers may be placed in the application software, so that it can use LICE event tracing.

and Ada makes the definition of reusable software easier, that can be reused in the application itself (for instance, adding to CCNT the software needed to process TM_EDE telemetry, took 2 days).

Size	source	38000 instructions[18], 250 package specifications (20% for M.M.I., 15% for general purpose software)
	applications	4 operational executable files (800 Ko to 2 Mo), 40 Ada tasks, plus 5 task types
Effort	M.M.I. mock-ups	1 person during 6 months
	design & coding	2 persons during 18 months
	test	2 persons during 8 months

Fig. 4. CCNT size and efforts

However, it should be untrue to say that PRONAOS CCNT is a completely positive experience, since we had - as said above - some problems with development tools. These problems are only relevant of tools, not of the method nor the language, even if some are caused by a lack of implementation constraints in the Ada standard : the success of an operational real-time application is still only based on the capability of an implementation to hold correctly such features as memory an task management, hardware interface, or interrupt handling. Ada95 brings no remedy to this problem, since it introduces no supplementary constraint and only gives you the mean of replacing a predefined feature by your own. Moreover, Ada is still felt as a language for big computers, as well because PC operational applications are very few, as because Ada compilers are expensive, compared to those of others languages.

Nevertheless, we still think HOOD and Ada were a good choice, and can be used in various space on-board or ground applications (why not a unique telemetry description package *with*-ed by either on-board and ground software?). Finally, one may hope that the next Ada95 compilers (as well because of OOP and distributed computing features, as because of some low-level features like pointers), will break the last mental blocks of using Ada for complex real-time software applications.

---

[18] I got this size by issuing `grep -c ";" *.ad?`, that is, each line containing ';' is considered as a statement. This is much different than counting source lines, that gives some 70000 lines.

References

[CAR 92]   *Le test des applications temps réel embarquées (la méthode LICE)* -
             J.L. CARAYON - *in* Actes du colloque "Systèmes Informatiques
             Temps Réel pour les Applications Spatiales" - Cépadues Editions,
             Toulouse, France, 1992

[LAU 92]   *PRONAOS Flight Software : a Real-Time Application for a
             Balloonborne Scientific Gondola* - A. LAURENS - *in* Actes du
             colloque "Systèmes Informatiques Temps Réel pour les Applications
             Spatiales" - Cépadues Editions, Toulouse, France, 1992

ASIS for GNAT:
Goals, Problems and Implementation Strategy

Sergey Rybin[1], Alfred Strohmeier[2], Eugene Zueff[1]

[1] *Scientific Research Computer Center*
Moscow State University
Vorob'evi Gori
Moscow 119899, Russia

[2] *Swiss Fed Inst of Technology in Lausanne*
Software Engineering Lab
CH-1015 Lausanne, Switzerland

e-mail: rybin@alex.srcc.msu.su,
zueff@such.srcc.msu.su

e-mail: alfred.strohmeier@di.epfl.ch

Abstract. This article describes the approach taken to implement the Ada Semantic Interface Specification (ASIS) for the GNAT Ada compiler. The paper discusses the main implementation problems and and their solution. It also describes the current state of the implementation.

Keywords. Ada, ASIS, Compilation, Software Engineering Environment.

1 Introduction

1.1 ASIS

The Ada Semantic Interface Specification (ASIS) [1] is an interface between an Ada environment, as defined by the Ada language definition [4], and any tool or application requiring information from this environment. ASIS is organized as a set of self-documented Ada package specifications providing abstractions and related queries which allow to obtain all statically-determinable information from any compilable unit contained in the Ada environment. Examples of tools which may benefit from ASIS include pretty-printers, cross-references, browsers, static code analyzers and derived measurement tools, etc.

ASIS is based on four main abstractions, represented by private types having the same names:

- Library - retrieval of state information about the Ada program library (for Ada 83) or the Ada compilation environment (for Ada 95);
- Compilation_Unit - retrieval of information related to the external view of a compilation unit such as its kind (subprogram, package, generic unit, specification or body, etc.) and of semantic dependencies between compilation units, including those defined by with clauses, and navigating between compilation units;
- Element - retrieval of information about syntactical components of a compilation unit, provided by its structural decomposition and the semantic links between related elements; as an example, the list of parameters can be retrieved for a sub-

program declaration, and then for each parameter specification, the name of the parameter, its type, and its default value, if any, can be obtained;

- Id - provides external images for items of type Element for storing to and retrieving from disk; can be used to implement persistent ASIS-based applications.

1.2 The ongoing revision of ASIS

The final ASIS specification defined for Ada 83 [5] is version 1.1.1 [1]; we will call it ASIS 83. The revision of ASIS for the new Ada language standard [4], sometimes called Ada 95 to avoid confusion, is in progress now; we will call it ASIS 95.There are plans to make ASIS an international standard. But already now, the ASIS 95 draft series [1] contains enough information to implement a working prototype for Ada 95.

The main changes in the new ASIS definition are changes in functionality and a new library/environment model.

1.2.1 Changes in functionality

Proposed changes in the functionality of ASIS can be subdivided in two groups.

The first group contains additions for new Ada 95 entities, such as child units and protected types.

With the aim of reducing the number of queries, many of the ASIS 83 queries have been aggregated in ASIS 95. Theses queries form the second group of changes.

For about half of the ASIS 83 queries, changes are proposed; therefore implementing ASIS 83 for an Ada 95 compiler would be a waste of resources.

1.2.2 The new library/environment model

The notion of the ASIS library, one of the fundamental ASIS abstractions, was revised to take into account the changes in the library model and compilation process definitions of Ada 95. Indeed, the new standard gives much more freedom to a compiler implementer than the old standard did. This issue is of special importance for the GNAT compiler which provides only a basic library facility.

The latest ASIS 95 draft (ASIS 2.0.C) contains the first version of the revised ASIS library model, which would be better called environment model to conform to Ada 95 terminology. The main points of this revision are:

- The notions of library, compilation/recompilation order and obsolete unit of Ada 83 are replaced by the notions of environment, semantic dependencies and consistency of a compilation unit of Ada 95; e.g., the consistency of a compilation unit as defined by ASIS 2.0.C is the consistency, in the sense of Ada 95, of the set of compilation units including the given unit and all other units on which it depends;
- The queries defined for the private type Compilation_Unit is revised in accordance with these changes. All queries reflecting the history of library creation and modifi-

cations (such as the test for a compilation unit to be obsolete or the query asking for the order of compilation/recompilation for a given set of units) are either removed or reformulated in terms of semantic dependencies and library units consistency;

- In the latest ASIS 95 documents, ASIS is defined as an interface to the Ada environment (not the Ada library), and the term ASIS library is for ASIS specific uses only; it really means an Ada environment for an ASIS application;

- ASIS 83 was really defined as being an interface to an Ada library linked to and managed by some Ada compilation system. But now for Ada 95, a stand-alone ASIS implementation, i.e. having no special connection to any Ada compiler and being able to process any consistent set of Ada sources, is considered to be very useful.

1.3 Implementing ASIS for GNAT

GNAT [6] is an Ada 95 compiler publicly available for many platforms under the copyright rules of the Free Software Foundation. Our project is aimed at the development of an ASIS 95 implementation for GNAT, called ASIS-for-GNAT. It is performed by the Scientific Research Computer Center of Moscow State University in cooperation with the Swiss Federal Institute of Technology in Lausanne. The project is supported by the Swiss EST funding programme.

The initial analysis and design efforts started with ASIS 83 in September 1994, but from the very beginning of the project (January 1995) we have been using the latest available ASIS 95 drafts as the basis for ASIS-for-GNAT. Ada 95 is used as an implementation language and GNAT itself is used as a compiler.

In a first stage we are building a partial prototype; the goal is to validate design and implementation decisions that can be used for further developments.

This prototype will be available at the end of 1995. Its main limitation will be that it can open only one ASIS library, that it processes only one compilation unit at a time, and that it provides only so-called structural queries.

2 Implementation strategy

2.1 The GNAT compiler

The GNAT compiler [2] is part of the multi-language GCC compilation system which includes front-end processors for several languages and code generators (back-ends) for various hardware platforms and software environments. GNAT is a Ada 95 compiler, consisting of a specific Ada 95 front-end, written mostly in Ada 95, combined with any standard GCC back-end.

GNAT uses the traditional scheme of the compilation process. It contains phases of syntax analysis, semantic analysis and code generation, which communicate through a common intermediate internal representation of Ada program units, the Abstract Syntax Tree (AST) [2]. The AST reflects the syntax structure of an Ada program unit (including symbol information) and also contains semantic attributes for all entities contained in the unit. GNAT has internal high-level procedure interfaces to this tree.

GNAT uses a so-called "source-based" compilation model requiring the source text of a program unit in the environment to be processed every time GNAT needs information about it [3]. For its operation, GNAT does not need to produce, store, or retrieve any centralized or distributed "library information".

However, the contents of the so-called .ali files could be used to determine dependencies between compilation units. An .ali file is created together with the object file when a unit is successfully compiled, and must be considered as being conceptually part of the object file. Such an .ali file contains the list of names and time stamps of the source files of all the units upon which the given unit depends.

On the other side, an AST contains information not only about the represented program unit, but also about all its supporters, i.e. the specifications of the units on which it depends, directly or indirectly.

Thus, the AST decorated by various semantic annotations is the main and only data structure built and handled by the GNAT front-end. Conceptually, the AST contains all information needed to answer almost all ASIS queries. 2.2 The fundamental implementation decision

The general background for the ASIS implementation for the GNAT compiler is:

- there is no specific library information;
- the AST is the high-level data structure containing all statically determinable information about the unit having been compiled by GNAT;
- there is a high-level procedural interface to the AST;
- the AST is the only data structure produced and maintained by GNAT;
- the AST is only internal to GNAT.

The main implementation decision is to use the AST as the basis for the internal representations of ASIS abstractions: the ASIS Compilation_Unit type is basically represented by the top node of the AST, which is constructed by the front-end for the corresponding Ada unit, and the ASIS Element type is basically represented by the tree node which is created for the corresponding (explicit or implicit) construct. The direct consequence of this decision is to implement ASIS-for-GNAT on top of the GNAT AST interfaces.

2.2 Some implementation problems

The GNAT front-end is a procedure which builds and handles only one AST during its invocation. The AST is kept in hidden data structures and the functional interface to the AST is rigidly bound to these structures. On the contrary, the ASIS interface is provided as a set of packages, and its implementation must be able to provide information about multiple compilation units, and, consequently, must be able to handle multiple ASTs.

So the main implementation problems are:

- how to access an AST from within ASIS queries; this problem is of primary importance for the prototype;
- how to access several ASTs at the same time when running an ASIS-based application; the solution of this problem has been postponed, and the prototype will process only one compilation unit.

3 Architecturing the interaction with GNAT

There are two possible ways to solve the problem of accessing the AST from inside the ASIS implementation - embedding the prototype just in the context of the GNAT compiler or adding special ASIS-related capabilities to GNAT.

3.1 First approach: building a modified GNAT

The first approach is to completely embed the ASIS implementation into the GNAT compiler. We modified the main GNAT driver Gnat1drv by replacing the call to the Back_End procedure by a call to an ASIS-based application. This application can make calls to our prototype, which in turn is built on top of the GNAT AST interfaces. Thus, the ASIS-based application starts in the dynamic context created by invoking the GNAT Front_End procedure. Launching the modified GNAT compiler with some compilation unit as a parameter corresponds to launching the ASIS-based application for this compilation unit.

In this approach all the compiler's internal data structures can be naturally accessed by the AST interfaces, and therefore by ASIS queries, without any additional transformations.

3.2 Second approach: adding special capabilities to GNAT

The second approach uses the extra functionalities in GNAT for storing to and retrieving from files its internal data structures making up the AST. This feature has been implemented as a special compiler option which provides dumping of the AST into a disk file, and a special interface for reading such files. This interface allows to reuse the trees already created during previous invocations of GNAT. As a result, the external images of the AST-related data structures become independent objects and can be processed by the prototype. Therefore, as long as the external images exist, GNAT has not to be called again.

We performed some preliminary work on this approach, and plan to adopt it in the future.

This second approach could also provide a natural way to access several ASTs at a time by means of re-retrieving them from disk, but the performance penalty may be too high.

3.3 Comparing the two approaches

The advantage of both of these approaches is to conform with the current GNAT philosophy: a single set of sources is used to make both GNAT and additional tools (binder, cross-reference utility, etc.), and the same source modules are included into various programs.

It is impossible to adapt the first approach for dealing with several compilation units at a time. As already stated, the second approach would probably show poor performance when an ASIS-based application needs to process multiple compilation units. The real cause of this disadvantage is the nature of the GNAT AST interfaces - they are not parametrized by the tree to which they provide access. But this problem can hardly be solved without serious modification of the compiler itself.

As stated above, the GNAT source-based compilation model requires to compile with a unit all its direct and indirect supporters. The AST of a unit contains hence full information not only about the unit itself, but also about all its supporters. ASIS queries about these supporters can therefore be satisfied without building their own AST and without recalling GNAT.

4 Architecture and capabilities of the prototype

4.1 Packaging the prototype and accessing the internal ASIS data structures

ASIS 95, in its draft ASIS 2.0.C, defines the following Sample Implementation Structure:

The main ASIS private types (Library, Compilation_Unit, Element, Id) are declared in subpackages of the package Asis_Vendor_Primitives, which should not be "withed" by ASIS-based applications:

```
package Asis_Vendor_Primitives is
   package Elements is
      type Element is private;
      ...
   private
      type Element is ...; -- implementation-defined
      ...
   end Elements;
   subtype Expression is Asis.Element;
      subtype Statement is Asis.Element;
...
end Asis_Vendor_Primitives;
```

Then operations for these types are defined in various packages making up the portable ASIS interface, for example:

```ada
with Asis_Vendor_Primitives;
package Asis_Statements is
   package Local_Renames is
      package Asis renames Asis_Vendor_Primitives;
   end Local_Renames;
   use Local_Renames;
   function Assignment_Expression
      (Statement : in Asis.Statement)
         return Asis.Expression;
   ...
end Asis_Statements;
```

And finally, the umbrella package ASIS provides uniform renaming for all ASIS resources which are available, by definition of the ASIS specification, to portable ASIS-based applications:

```ada
with Asis_Statements;
with Asis_Vendor_Primitives;
   ...
   package Asis is
      package Statements renames Asis_Statements;
      subtype Element is Asis_Vendor_Primitives.Element;
      ...
end ASIS;
```

This structure cannot be implemented in a clean way (e.g. without using unchecked conversions), because the package bodies implementing operations for ASIS types cannot access the details of their representations, and the package Asis_Vendor_Primitives does not provide any "interface" to those types.

In ASIS-for-GNAT, the packaging structure was enhanced by using child units together with library level renaming, as shown below.

ASIS types are defined immediately within the Asis_Vendor_Primitives package and enclosed subpackages are removed:

```ada
package Asis_Vendor_Primitives is -- ASIS-for-GNAT
   type Element is private;
   subtype Expression is Asis.Element;
   subtype Statement is Asis.Element;
   ...
private
   type Element is record
      ...
   end record;
   ...
end Asis_Vendor_Primitives;
```

For each of the ASIS packages mentioned as making up the portable ASIS interface and defining operations for ASIS types a corresponding counterpart package is implemented as a child of Asis_Vendor_Primitives. All these child packages contain the same specifications as the corresponding ASIS packages (with only a minor technical change which has no impact on a portable ASIS-based application: they do not any longer contain the Local_Renames packages):

```
package Asis_Vendor_Primitives.Asis_Statements is
   function Assignment_Expression
      (Statement : in Asis.Statement)
        return Asis.Expression;
   ...
end Asis_Vendor_Primitives.Asis_Statements;
```

This new structure provides direct access to all implementation details of the ASIS private types in the bodies of the child units.

And finally, the child packages are renamed at the library level as the corresponding ASIS packages to form the required interface and to provide the top-level Asis package, yielding as a result the semantics of the original ASIS specification:

```
with Asis_Vendor_Primitives.Asis_Statements;
package Asis_Statements
   renames Asis_Vendor_Primitives.Asis_Statements;
```

The proposed packaging structure solves in a natural way the problem of accessing the implementations of the ASIS types in package bodies. It can be considered as an alternative to the Sample Implementation Structure.

4.2 Selecting a subset of ASIS to be implemented in the prototype

Besides the main limitation of the prototype, which is only able to deal with one compilation unit at a time, the following principles were used for subsetting ASIS:

- It was decided to implement the operations for initializing a single library and a single compilation unit for an ASIS-based application; these operations are defined in the packages:
- Asis.Libraries Asis.Compilation_Units Asis.Environment The full implementation of these package was postponed.
- The implementation of the Asis.Text and Asis.Ids packages was postponed as a relatively independent part;
- The implementation of the structural ASIS queries, i.e. queries providing step-by-step top-down decomposition of a compilation unit was selected as being of first priority.

5 Implementation of the structural queries

The ASIS structural queries provide the top-down decomposition of an ASIS Compilation Unit according to its syntax structure. As a rule, a structural query yields a child element (or a list of child elements) for its argument element.

Implementing the ASIS structural queries on the base of the GNAT AST thus requires two main problems to be solved: defining and implementing the mapping between AST nodes and ASIS elements of various kinds, and traversing the AST, with operations provided by GNAT, with the purpose of yielding the decomposition as defined by ASIS.

5.1 The representation of the ASIS Element type

The ASIS Element type is implemented by an undiscriminated record type. This record contains the reference to the AST node corresponding to the given Element in its Node field, and the reference to the position of this Element in the ASIS Element classification hierarchy in its Internal_Kind field (i.e. we use a "flat" image of the hierarchy, where each kind having the subordinate classification is replaced by its subordinate kinds).

5.2 Mapping between tree node kinds and Element kinds

To implement an ASIS structural query, we can use the Node field of its argument Element to jump into the AST context exactly to the place of the corresponding node. The AST operations provided by GNAT are used for traversing the tree in order to find the node corresponding to the child element to be returned by the query (or to find several nodes if the query returns list of Elements). As a rule, this tree traversal is rather straightforward, but to build the result, we have to set its Internal_Kind field. In the remaining part of this subsection we will describe what is the problem.

The kind of an element returned by an ASIS query can vary. Moreover, when a query returns a list of elements (e.g. a list of statements, a list of declarations), each element of such a list can belong to another kind. So, we have to map the kinds of nodes in the AST onto Element kinds. This mapping problem is of special interest among the technical implementation problems; it arises from differences between the two approaches taken by GNAT and ASIS to represent an Ada program unit.

For two thirds of the more than 200 Node_Kinds values, the mapping is a rather trivial one-to-one mapping between a Node_Kinds value and an Internal_Element_Kinds value, for example:

```
N_Defining_Character_Literal <=> A_Defining_Character_Literal
N_Case_Statement             <=> A_Case_Statement,
```

but for other Node_Kinds values, the mapping is not one-to-one, as shown below.

Sometimes, a Node_Kinds value maps onto several Internal_Element_Kinds depending on the context (one-to-many mapping):

```
N_Subprogram_Declaration => A_Procedure_Declaration
N_Subprogram_Declaration => A_Function_Declaration
```

Sometimes, several Node_Kinds values merge into one Internal_Element_Kinds value (many-to-one mapping). For example, A_Procedure_Declaration Element can be associated with a tree node either of kind N_Abstract_Subprogram_Declaration or of kind N_Subprogram_Declaration:

```
N_Subprogram_Declaration          => A_Procedure_Declaration
N_Abstract_Subprogram_Declaration => A_Procedure_Declaration
```

The last two examples also show that the same Node_Kind value, i.e. N_Subprogram_Declaration, may participate in a one-to-many and in a many-to-one mapping.

There are even holes in the mapping.

Firstly, there are some nodes in the AST having no Element counterpart. Sometimes they are for internal use for the compiler only and must be ignored, e.g. the node N_Freeze_Entity, but sometimes they are the hook of a subtree which must be traversed. For example, there is an AST N_Mod_Clause node for record representation clauses, whereas ASIS simply yields the expression part of this clause.

Secondly, some Element values do not have a node counterpart in the AST. For example, the tree contains no single node corresponding to An_Else_Path Element, representing the last structural part of a composite control statement. Instead, the tree stores in the node of the enclosing control statement (i.e. N_If_Statement, N_Selective_Accept or N_Conditional_Entry_Call) a pointer to the list of nodes corresponding to the statement sequence.

5.3 Reconstructing the original unit structure from the tree

GNAT makes various tree transformations during semantic analysis, when performing compile-time optimization (for example, to replace a static expression by its value) and when preparing the tree for the code generation phase.

During these transformations, some nodes are replaced by newly generated subtrees.

Code generation related transformations can be suppressed by invoking GNAT with the compile-only flag: -gnatc.

For detecting the other transformations, we have to examine the Rewrite_Sub and Rewrite_Ins node flags to recognize the nodes which have been replaced by a subtree and to detect the nodes inserted during semantic analysis.

Fortunately, GNAT keeps the "replaced" nodes of the original tree, and they can be retrieved by the function Original_Node. Unfortunately, the "original" node does no longer contain a reference to the parent node in the tree, and this reference must therefore be retrieved from the "replacing" node, i.e. the root of the replacing subtree.

Inserted nodes can be skipped for structural queries, but they may be of use for some semantic queries, especially for element representing implicit constructs.

5.4 Too many case statements?

The code of our ASIS implementation contains a lot of case statements, sometimes replaced by look-up tables. It's well known, that this style of "variant" programming is best replaced by "incremental" programming, i.e. an object-oriented approach. Unfortunately, neither GNAT, e.g. its tree retrieval operations, nor ASIS make use of such an approach.

5.5 Is there enough information in the AST?

From the very beginning of our project the question whether there was enough information stored in the AST that could be retrieved by GNAT-provided operations was of prime importance. Now we can say that the features provided by GNAT are sufficient for implementing all structural queries about ASIS Elements corresponding to explicit constructs in the program unit. There is just one exception: GNAT does not care during tree creation whether or not a unit name is repeated after the last "end" of the unit specification or body; it simply assumes that the name is always repeated.

We have to say, however, that we have not yet thoroughly tested the use of the Original_Node function for recreating the original tree, and further investigations must be performed as GNAT relies heavily on rewriting for generic units.

As a last escape, when some information is definitely missing in the AST, it would be possible to retrieve it from the source buffer, which is part of the GNAT data structures. Indeed, every node in the AST contains a reference to the position in the source buffer where it originates from, and this reference could be used to jump from the node to right place in the buffer.

6 Designing the ASIS library model for the GNAT environment

Structural queries cannot cross compilation unit boundaries, and therefore don't really need the ASIS library model to be implemented. On the contrary, semantic queries usually express the properties of an element in terms of other elements: for example, the defining occurrence can be retrieved for a direct name. As shown by this example, that often means we have to jump to another compilation unit. Implementation of the ASIS library model is hence needed for semantic queries.

GNAT provides a simple "lightweight" Ada compilation model [3]. It sometimes looks very strange to Ada 83 programmers, but it is completely in conformance with Ada 95 rules: it contains no compilation/recompilation order requirement and no explicit notion of a library.

Our design for the ASIS library model is based on the following points:

- The starting point for an ASIS library is a set of directories of the file system.

- An object of type ASIS.Library is initialized by calling the procedure Librar-ies.Associate with all the directories belonging to the library as an actual.

- Searching in these directories will be performed in the order of their appearance in the actual parameter.

- Only compilable .ads and .adb files, i.e. files containing sources of the specifica-tions and bodies of Ada compilation units, in these directories are considered as belonging to the ASIS library. ASIS-for-GNAT will not require or assume anything about the presence or absence of any other files in the set of directories making up the ASIS library.

- The contents of all the directories making up the ASIS library must remain frozen between the initialization and finalization of the ASIS environment (otherwise the corresponding ASIS application could have erroneous behavior). "Frozen" means that .ads and .adb files cannot be changed, cannot be removed from the library, can-not be moved to another directory, and it's forbidden to create new ones.

7 Current state of the prototype

In mid-September 1995, the prototype supported most of the ASIS 2.0.C structural queries. The most difficult queries that remain to be implemented are the Enclosing_Element query and the generic procedure Traverse_Element.

The Enclosing_Element query returns the parent Element for its argument. It can be implemented by using the reference to the parent node kept in tree nodes, but a lot of technical problems related to differences in the ways of traversing Ada code in ASIS and in the GNAT AST operations must be solved.

The Traverse_Element generic procedure provides the recursive top-down and left-to-right traversal of the element passed as an argument while performing some pre-opera-tion and post-operation (provided by the corresponding generic parameters) for each subcomponent. It can be implemented on the base of all the other ASIS structural que-ries.

Let's recall that the prototype can process only one library and only one compilation unit during its invocation.

When writing this article, the prototype was composed of nearly 1.7 MBytes self-doc-umented Ada source code, including the 575 kBytes of the initial self-documented ASIS 2.0.C specification. It depends on most of the GNAT front-end components.

Systematic testing have not been performed so far. In order to avoid time-consuming rebuilding of the ASIS test applications when debugging, we implemented a debug-ging monitor allowing to call ASIS queries interactively and to view the result through debugging variables.

This monitor itself has become an additional branch of the project. Although it was originally seen as a mere secondary debugging and testing tool, it was found out that it opens several new avenues. First of all, being a conventional ASIS application, it appears to be portable between various ASIS implementations.

8 Conclusion

The project goal is to implement ASIS for the GNAT Ada 95 compiler; a prototype will be available at the end of 1995, with features as described in section 7. For fall 1996, we hope to implement the full ASIS library model and all semantic queries. The Ids and Text packages would then be the only missing parts for completing ASIS-for-GNAT.

9 References

1. ASIS 1.1.1, ASIS 2.0.A, etc. - ASIS documents are available electronically: on World Wide Web: http://www.acm.org/sigada/WG/asiswg/asiswg.html or by anonymous ftp: sw-eng.falls-church.va.us/public/AdaIC/work-grp/asiswg

2. E. Schonberg, B. Banner: The GNAT Project: A GNU-Ada 9X Compiler. Ada Europe News, No 20, pp. 10-19 (March 1995)

3. R. Dewar: The GNAT Compilation Model. Ada Europe News, No 20, pp. 20-23 (March 1995)

4. —: Ada 95 Reference Manual. Intermetrics, Inc., Feb. 15, 1995 (ISO/IEC 8652:1995)

5. —: Reference Manual of the Ada Programming Language. Washington, D.C.: Department of Defense, Ada Joint Program Office, Feb. 1983 (ISO/IEC 8652:1987)

6. GNAT Compiler: can be get by anonymous ftp: cs.nyu.edu/pub/gnat

KBSE and Ada: Object and Enabling Technology

Paul A. Bailes, Paul Burnim, Murray Chapman and Eric Salzman

Centre for Software Maintenance, Department of Computer Science
The University of Queensland QLD 4072, AUSTRALIA

Abstract. "Layering" is a visualisation technique that enables basic relationships between software system components to be overlaid with the results of more sophisticated design recovery analyses. Layering can be implemented via a simple presentation tool, to which the results of different analysers can be coupled. Knowledge-based analysis technology can be extended to support Ada83-Ada95 conversion. Taking advantage of the self-implementation of the enabling technology, the conversion tool can be involuted so that the enabling technology itself is able to be represented in Ada95.

1 Introduction

This paper shows how the introduction of Knowledge-Based Software Engineering (KBSE) technologies and techniques can enhance the maintainability of Ada programs, with respect to the actual characteristics of a prototype knowledge-based Ada reengineering tool "Know-Ada", and with respect to the prospects for further development indicated by the prototype.

2 Visualisation

The prime requirement-setting context for this application of KBSE is the visualisation of design information as follows.

2.1 Visualisation in SEE-Ada

Know-Ada builds upon the earlier Software Evaluation Environment for Ada (SEE-Ada) [1] which was developed by the Australian Defence Science and Technology Organisation (DSTO) to provide an Ada design visualisation tool that would cope with software systems on a realistic scale of defence/aerospace applications (e.g. over 100KSLOC). A selection of the information presented by SEE-Ada is as follows.

Layers: the basic SEE-Ada presentation is the graph of Ada compilation units comprising a software system of interest related according to the Ada "with" dependency. Relationships between nodes are not explicit: rather nodes are located in a window where they would have been located had the "with" relationship been explicated by arcs uniformly oriented left-right. This provides a user with a general idea of the role of each unit that is surprisingly effective in practice, and moreover an identifiable visual fingerprint of a software system that allows significant change to be identified. Different kinds of unit have different shapes e.g. package specifications are elongated hexagons, bodies are trapeziums, subprograms are rectangles.

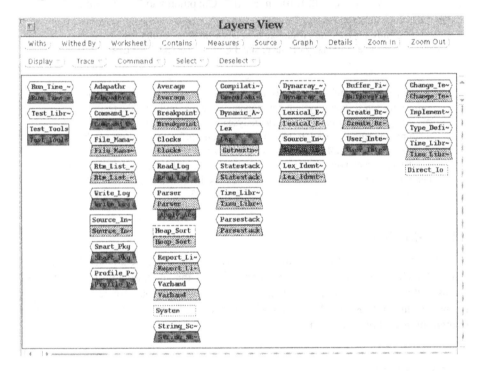

Fig. 1. SEE-Ada Layers/Measures

Measures: the layers view can be qualified by marking nodes subject to certain criteria. For example, Figure 1 depicts an Ada software system, where the level of shading indicates the number of executable statements in each unit. Thus, at a glance the project manager can see e.g. that the package bodies have all been substantially implemented.

Traces: Direct connections between nodes can be included to reflect specific relationships, such as the actual "with" relationships to and from selected compilation units.

Subsystems: one way of eliding extraneous detail is to define subsystems of compilation units, and to then work from a layers view including only the members of the subsisted.

Contains: another elision is to give a layers view of the units (packages, procedures etc.) contained by another unit.

2.2 Know-Ada Visualisation: Generic Graph Viewing

An implicit limitation of SEE-Ada is that the basic visualisation (layers) is in terms of concrete Ada program constructs. Higher-level views (e.g. in terms of abstract constructs such as abstract data types, libraries, classes etc., or in terms of software architectures) are conceivably discernible via measures and traces, but only inconveniently indirectly.

In order to prepare for the recovery of such sophisticated design information (see Design Recovery below) we have developed a "Generic (program) Graph Viewer" (GGV) which generalises the SEE-Ada presentation with user-definable symbolism, so that no longer are views restricted to the concrete Ada constructs envisaged by the developers of SEE-Ada, or to any Ada concrete constructs at all. Now we can apply the layers visualisation to recovered Ada abstract design information, or even other languages.

For example, see Figure 2 below which is the GGV layers view of an Ada system, and showing not just compilation units but also information about the variables and types found inside packages etc.

2.3 Future Developments

The following additional visualisation requirements have been identified to date, for which the GGV prototype provides its most important contribution: a suitably open development basis by comparison with the SEE-Ada product.

Linkage: now that several layers views are conceivable (Ada compilation units, as in SEE-Ada, plus abstract constructs layers and software architectures layers), relationships between these layers need to be presented. For example, operations that cause a package in the Ada compilation units layer to be highlighted would also cause the abstract objects recovered from that package to be highlighted in their layers view.

Scaling: a strength of the SEE-Ada approach is that a user is able to develop a good appreciation of the overall architecture of a software system at a visual glance, but large software systems cannot be displayed on a single screen. "Fisheye" views are conceptually attractive, but inefficient on stock hardware. Instead, a reference layer view is to be added, which compresses detail until it can be accommodated on a screen, and which shadows cursor movement, highlighting etc. in actual layers (e.g. much like a virtual desktop manager).

Detailing: graph nodes may be expanded to several levels of detail. Starting with the SEE-Ada presentation of a graph's node and type, GGV will allow expansion e.g. of concrete code objects to windows showing complete source text, or to nested layers views.

3 Design Recovery

What are the benefits of applying KBSE tools and techniques to this task?

3.1 Design Recovery in SEE-Ada

The strength of SEE-Ada is that it is a generic presentation tool, up to the limits of its assumptions about what the underlying layers view represents (i.e. Ada compilation units). It possesses little native design recovery capability, but there are couplings to a number of analysis tools. Current functionality is as follows.

AdaMAT[TM]: a vast range of metrics (from e.g. general reliability metrics to the use of specific Ada constructs) can be imported and displayed via SEE-Ada measures.

SCCS: enables display of measures metrics about library unit access: by whom, how often, etc.

Structure Measures: native SEE-Ada capability to measure further details of the basic "with" relationship: how often a unit is used elsewhere, directly or indirectly, how much use a unit makes of others.

Clustering: which units belong to a common cluster (defined by internal couplings).

"Simtel" Complexity Measures: measures for Halstead and McCabe metrics, line counts, etc. as produced by public-domain tools.

3.2 Know-Ada Design Recovery

We have already seen how it is possible to progress beyond SEE-Ada in the visualisation dimension. In the orthogonal dimension of the quality of recovered design information, progress is possible with knowledge-based analysis tools. Our choice of the Software Refinery [2] and its Ada instantiation "Refine/Ada" is made for the following reasons:

- appropriate *domain modelling* capability exists through an object-oriented data definition and manipulation sublanguage;

- this is further integrated with a concrete syntax specification subsystem ("Dialect") to provide a comprehensive *language modelling* capability;

- *analysis* is facilitated by the availability of very-high-level declarative formulations of transformation rules.

Moreover:

- Refine/Ada provides a comprehensive, extensible and so *reusable* Ada83 language model and basic analysis framework.

Know-Ada's Knowledge-Based Design Recovery has so far been implemented in two dimensions: long-range analyses of transitive relationships; and finer classification of source code into abstract categories.

Entity Non-Use: Know-Ada generates separate SEE-Ada numeric measures for the numbers of entities in each of the classes - subprogram, type, variable, task - that are exported by a unit but not used elsewhere.

Entity Reach: For each separate entity, Know-Ada generates a binary measure showing what units each entity is used in. For types, there are separate measures for direct and indirect (e.g. subtypes, access types, record components) uses.

Package Classification: Know-Ada generates SEE-Ada symbolic measure data to describe the kind of abstraction represented by a compilation unit, as a first step toward lifting the level of understanding of an Ada system from the concrete code level to an abstract design level. For example, figure 2 shows in GGV form the package classification measures for the previous system: abstract data structures (ADS); abstract data type (ADT); concrete data structures; libraries; and unknown.

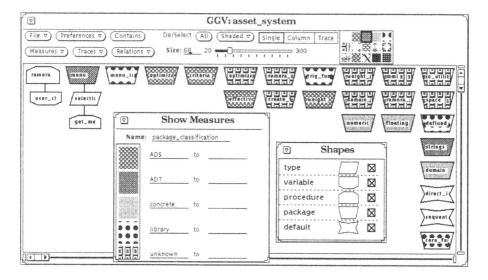

Fig.2. Know-Ada Design Visualisation in GGV

3.3 Future Developments

Work currently under way is concentrating upon the classification of Ada constructs into the higher-level design-oriented taxonomies foreshadowed with respect to the capabilities of the GGV component above. Progress to date is in areas as follows.

Abstract Constructs: Package classification is being extended so that a lifted view of an Ada system at a level that deals entirely with abstract constructs (ADTs, ADSs, tasks, libraries, monitors, generics) will be possible. GGV already provides an appropriate visualisation facility, so that the main task being to ensure that the design space chosen is complete and consistent.

Our approach in this direction to date has been to posit [4] a five-dimensional Abstract Program Space, where the value of each dimension signifies the extent to which some abstract attribute is discernible:

- *executability:* is an abstraction code, or data

- *typicality:* is an abstraction a class, or an instance

- *encapsulation:* are an abstraction's components accessible to its clients

- *activity:* can an abstraction initiate events, or is it passive

- *genericity:* can an abstraction accept parameters?

The binary nature of these attributes therefore gives rise two a thirty-two element space, exemplary elements of which are as follows:

	Executable	*Typical*	*Encapsulated*	*Active*	*Generic*
subprogram	yes	no	no	no	yes
concrete type	no	yes	no	no	no
process	yes	no	no	yes	no
process type	yes	yes	no	yes	no
block	yes	no	no	no	no
library	yes	no	yes	no	yes
generic ADT	no	yes	yes	no	yes

Object Hierarchies: The next stage on recovery of abstract constructs will be discernment of class and object hierarchies. There is already a substantial literature on class and object recovery from Ada source code in particular, which will be feasible to implement in Refine/Ada as a Know-Ada extension.

4 Ada83 - Ada95 Conversion

A further orthogonal dimension of enhancement to the SEE-Ada functionality is possible with the detailed knowledge of an Ada83 program that Refine/Ada provides, either directly through the abstract syntactic structures created as language model instances, or indirectly through the extra analyses that are relatively easily programmable. Specifically, this knowledge can be used in the process of converting Ada83 code to Ada95, either passively in the detection of Ada83 code that is Ada95-incompatible, or actively in the translation of Ada83 to Ada95 taking into account those incompatibilites that are capable of automatic resolution.

4.1 Ada95 Language Modelling

The obvious development path would have been to extend the Ada83 language model provided by Refine/Ada using the open interfaces provided to abstract and concrete syntax specifications. Unfortunately, the further language modelling component of static semantic analysis does not have a sufficiently open interface in Refine/Ada at the same time that Ada95 has a static semantics that is not upward compatible with Ada83.

Consequently it proves necessary to use (or manufacture) another Ada95 language model. In order to retain the benefits of operating with the Software Refinery toolset, we have reengineered the GNAT Ada95 domain model into Refine as follows:

1. exploit the self-implementation of GNAT to generate a dump of the internal representation of the GNAT Ada95 domain model;

2. at the same time, modify the dump format for compatibility with a language neutral object-oriented data modelling interface language [5];

3. employ the binding from that interface to Refine in order to generate a Refine Ada95 domain model;

4. attach unparsing Ada95 concrete syntax rules (which can assume the existence of correct static semantics) to the abstract syntax definition.

4.2 Ada83-95 Translation

The essence of the converter is the translation system, which accounts for the differences between Ada83 and Ada95 that are capable of automatic resolution. As the capacity of the design recovery component of Know-Ada improves, so will the sophistication. For example, it will be possible to exploit the object-oriented features of Ada95 to express object hierarchies only implicitly-represented in Ada83.

Ada83 programs are parsed and represented as abstract syntax following the existing facilities of Refine/Ada. The Ada95 AST to which translation is made is the result of reengineering the GNAT AST structure into Refine.

4.3 Ada83-95 Compatibility Validation

As part of the detailed analysis of Ada83 code that is necessary when converting to Ada95, it is easy to stop short of an actual conversion and merely to report on apparent changes that would (need to) be made to the Ada83 for it to be valid Ada95. The following types of incompatibility are detected.

Artificial Changes: because of some differences in internals between the Ada83 and Ada95 ASTs (due to their different provenances), details such as redundant parentheses are lost in translation. Likewise comments and white space.

Ada95 Translatable Changes: differences between Ada83 and Ada95 that are handled automatically by the translator are indicated - identifier-keyword clashes, CHARACTER type enumeration, scalar type representation clauses, unnecessary package bodies.

GNAT Untranslatable Changes: remaining deficiencies in GNAT that make the translator output incompatible with it.

Ada95 Untranslatable Changes: a surprisingly large number of detailed Ada83-Ada95 differences are too difficult or impossible to automate - e.g. ambiguities arising from extended character sets, collision between Ada83 implementation-specific and Ada95 language extensions, removal of pragmas and attributes. Machine assistance to help a programmer determine the "real meaning" of the Ada83 may be possible, but attempted full automation involving sophisticated design recovery would be unreliable.

Converter Limitations: the converter is unable to handle Ada systems with re-used source file names spread over different directories.

4.4 Further Work

It remains to be noted that with superior design recovery, more sensible exploitation of Ada95's ability directly to express design paradigms is possible. The notable example is of course with regard to class hierarchies, but there are numerous relatively minor difficulties. For example, when Ada95 predefines an Ada83 user identifier, when does an Ada83 use of that identifier "really mean" what the Ada95 predefinition intends, so permitting am identity translation as opposed to a comprehensive alpha-conversion?

5 Ada95 as KBSE Enabling Technology

Involution is a notable design validation technique. Applied to programming language processors, the possibility of self-implementation at once improves the prospects of portability, even if possibly requiring a bootstrapping stage. Applied to KBSE and Ada, it raises the question of using Ada itself as the implementation tool for knowledge-based design recovery from Ada source code.

5.1 KBSE Tool Criteria

What are the criteria to which any development of Ada for KBSE, or software re- and reverse engineering must aspire? We have previously identified [3] the following canonical criteria that need to be satisfied by reengineering environments (such as Software Refinery, and possibly Ada).

Expressive Programming Language: the embedded "Refine" programming language supports a wide variety of programming paradigms, complemented by the "Dialect" language processing system.

Persistent Storage: because reengineering is as difficult as natural language understanding, theorem-proving, etc., semi-automation must be facilitated, which by definition means that object data structures must be stored persistently.

Extensible Environment: reengineering tools can be expected to be enhanced as domain knowledge grows through semi-automatic processing.

5.2 Refine - Ada95 Conversion

An immediate practical possibility is a Refine-Ada converter.

Meta^2-Programming: inherent in the above characterisation of KBSE is that KBSE tools are suited to language processing i.e. metaprogramming. Because self-implementation is a prominent feature of Software Refinery, it supports an even higher order of meta-meta- (or meta^2-) programming in which the constructs of the metalanguage are themselves manipulated. It is in support of meta^2-programming that the more pathological features of the Refine language (e.g. class names as values) find use. We believe that support for simple "first-order" meta-programming will suffice for a sufficient number of KBSE applications for a Refine - Ada converter to be of genuine usefulness.

Interaction: in view of the emphasis placed on persistence in the KBSE requirements analysis, it is surprising to see that it is absent from the result. There is actually a sound practical reason for this omission: industrial demand for KBSE tools (e.g. for software reengineering) that can be used by application-domain as opposed to KBSE technology experts. Interaction with a KBSE tool has considerable negative appeal, while the appearance of a fully-automated processor has the opposite. Our experience leads us to suspect that persistence is of most use during KBSE tool development. In this context, the above Refine - Ada95 conversion establishes Ada95 as an execution, but not a development environment for KBSE tools.

5.3 Generic Conversion Architecture

Our technical foci within the specification of Refine-Ada95 conversion relate to an overall language conversion model with components as follows [3].

Specification: this initial phase corresponds to Analysis in conventional applications development.

1. Concept Mapping: Specify relationships between Origin and Target language constructs in general.

2. Idiom Analysis: Further determine Target forms corresponding to Origin forms representing particular design paradigms/idioms.

3. Target Lifting: Implement Target language extensions/libraries as required by Mappings.

Implementation: the next phase is to implement the specifications yielded by analysis.

Execution: the final phase applies the implemented tools.

5.4 Refine-Ada95 Concept Mapping

The essence of language conversion is how the constructs of the origin (Refine in this case) relate to the target (Ada95 in this case). Target Lifting is dealt with implicitly, and because the conversion is intended to be general, Idiom Analysis is irrelevant.

Data and Types: Refine has Lisp-based atomic data types, which are trivially expressed in Ada (Lisp "symbol"s are represented as strings). Refine structures (sequences and tuples) are similarly easily expressible by Ada ADTs. Refine's view of function ("map") types is a little more complex: a map can be one either a computationally-define function, or an explicit sequence of (domain, range) element pairs, or a class attribute in which a computation rule may in cases be superseded by an explicit (domain, range) pair. Ada95 implementation is straightforward, with advantages over Ada83 in achieving this as follows:

- inheritance, so that e.g. a computationally- and an explicitly-defined Refine function are both recognisable as "map"s

- functions as values, e.g. so that the computation rule may be stored alongside a pair-sequence in the representation of a class attribute.

The other challenge posed by Refine is the universal "any-type", which is widely-used in Refine programs to simulate polymorphism. Aside from a general reverse-engineering to determine the genuine polymorphism that might be expressed in Ada, our solution is to represent all Refine entities as Ada95 objects, which are themselves instances of the appropriate subclasses of a "refine-anytype" class. For example, the inheritance chain to computationally-defined functions is "refine-anytype", "refine-map", "refine-function".

Objects and Classes: Refine's object-orientation is not integrated with the type system, so that e.g. a class name is actually a data value that tags objects belonging to that class. Checking that operations apply to appropriate objects is at best dynamic. Because Ada95 has native inheritance integrated into the type system, and because the Refine operations that define and use classes are notationally well-delineated, it is straightforward to translate occurrences of them into the equivalent Ada95 type and class definitions and instantiations. Refine objects are members of "any-type", so that the corresponding Ada95 classes must be subclasses of the representation "refine-anytype".

Operators: because Refine entities are represented as instances of Ada abstractions, operations on Refine entities are simply implemented as methods on the abstractions and invoked as such.

Control Constructs: there is a close correspondence between Refine and Ada control constructs, the major difference being that Refine is an expression language where statements may yield values. The transformation that allows expression-language statements to be implemented in a non-expression language like Ada is straightforward.

Patterns and Transforms: standard techniques for implementing logic programming may even be simplified because the Refine structures over which logic patterns may be defined and instantiated are all constrained to be finite.

5.5 Ada95 to Refine Target Lifting Extended

We have referred in the above to the Ada95 support ADTs and libraries required to match the mapping output. Conceivably, these could be used to support direct Ada95 programming of KBSE applications, without a Refine preprocessing component. The following preconditions would however need to be satisfied.

Persistent Storage: while we have discounted persistence as an Execution-phase necessity, to supplant Software Refinery with Ada95 would require satisfaction of Implementation-phase requirements, for which persistence is necessary, certainly for incremental development of prototype reengineering applications, and possibly for incremental compilation. For this role, implementation-phase persistence would usefully be at a level of granularity comparable with Refine's incremental development environment, which may be difficult to achieve outside a self-implemented system such as Software Refinery.

Syntactic Considerations: first, it would be necessary to allow Ada95 programmers to define coupled abstract-concrete language models just as in Dialect (which has every appearance of plausibility, as Dialect deal with context-free productions and class hierarchies in general i.e. non-Refine-specific terms); second, a great deal of the excitement of Refine metaprogramming derives from being able to embed Origin and Target syntactic patterns in the Refine code that translates between them - extra levels of domain syntax could be accommodated in Ada programs with appropriate preprocessing, but preprocessing seems against the sprit of an exercise designed to avoid the Refine - Ada95 preprocessor already specified.

6 Conclusions

Previously-existing design recovery facilities for Ada are doubly limited: analysis was unable to make some of the sorts of connections between source code components that are needed to provide useful information; visualisation was limited in conception by the low expectations for the sorts of information that would need to be visualised. Experience in Know-Ada development to date demonstrates that better analyses and presentations may reasonably be expected by Ada developers. Ultimate involution seems potentially very feasible.

7 Acknowledgments

This work is sponsored by and proceeds in close collaboration with the Australian Defence Science and Technology Organisation, the developers of SEE-Ada. We are grateful to numerous DSTO personnel for their contributions to the Know-Ada development, in particular Gina Kingston, Stefan Landherr and Rudi Vernik.

8 References

1. Vernik, R.J. and Burke, M.M., "Perspective-oriented Description: Integrating and Tailoring Information for Software Engineering", Proc. 6th International Conference on Software Engineering and its Applications (1993).

2. Newcomb, P. and Markosian, L., "Automating the Modularisation of Large COBOL Programs: Application of an Enabling Technology for Reengineering", Proc. Working Conference on Reverse Engineering, pp. 222-230, IEEE (1993).

3. Atkinson, S., Bailes, P.A., Chapman, M., Chilvers, M. and Peake, I., "A Re-Engineering Evaluation of Software Refinery^{TM}: Architecture, Process and Technology", Proceedings of 3rd Symposium on Assessment of Quality Software Development Tools, 1994, pp. 191-200, IEEE (1994).

4. Bailes, P.A, Burnim, P. and Johnston, D. "Knowledge-based Requirements Analysis for Ada Design Recovery: Design Entity Identification and Representation", University of Queensland Department of Computer Science Technical Report no. 333, Brisbane (1995).

5. Bailes, P.A., Atkinson, S., Chapman, M., Johnston, D. and Peake, I., "Proprietary vs. "Open Systems" Options in the Construction of Knowledge-Based Software Re-Engineering Environments", Proceedings 1994 Asia-Pacific Software Engineering Conference, Tokyo, pp. 60-69, IEEE (1994).

Extending the Ada 95 Initial Conditions for Preelaboration for use in Real-Time Systems

Tim Birus, Paul Knueven, Ed Kuzemchak, Jack Rosenzweig, Joyce Tokar

Tartan, Inc.
Monroeville, PA 15146
USA
Tel: 1.412.856.3600
Fax: 1.412.856.3636
tokar@tartan.com

Abstract. The needs of the embedded systems community for program units which can be burned into Read-Only Memory (ROM) to be used in applications have been addressed in Ada 95 with the introduction of the preelaborable units. In addition, preelaborated program units can be easily restarted. This capability enables the development of efficient embedded applications. Tartan has extended this feature to support additional preelaboration conditions which satisfy the requirements of the embedded community for the ability to use ROM.

1. INTRODUCTION

Real-time applications need to be able to use Read-Only Memory (ROM) for both code and data. In the case of the latter, for example, large constant tables would be a typical usage. Code units might be initialization or restart routines, or simply fixed algorithms. For these units to be burned into ROM, they must contain no elaboration code.

Ada 95 [2] addresses the needs of the real-time community with the introduction of preelaborable library units through the use of *pragma Preelaborate* and with enhancements to the definition of *static*. Further refinements are made to the requirements for preelaboration in the Systems Programming Annex to offer additional support for real-time applications. These extensions to the requirements of preelaborable objects guarantee that there will be no writes to memory after load time for the elaboration of constant objects declared immediately within the declarative region of a preelaborated library package.

The rules specified in Ada 95 address the minimal requirements for preelaboration needed in real-time applications. Many real-time applications place further demands on the support environment to enable the preelaboration of objects that are determined to be constant at compile time or link time. This paper examines the Ada 95 preelaboration model. It then presents three common programming paradigms that allow more objects to be preelaborable. Finally, results demonstrating how these enhancements improve the performance of real-time applications are discussed.

2. PREELABORABLE OBJECTS IN ADA 95

The Ada 95 model for preelaboration is based on the concept of static values and static expressions, where static means determinable at compile time. A static value is a value which is specified by a static expression. Only scalars and string expressions are static.

Ada 95 defines the initial values of preelaborable objects to be static expressions. The Systems Programming Annex extends this definition to include allocators for an access-to-constant type and the attributes Address and Access as initial values.

The Ada 95 rules for preelaboration are designed to support the initialization of large blocks of data from information that is known at compile and link time; no run-time information is necessary for the initialization of these values. Preelaborable objects may be initialized with aggregates, string literals, and concatenations of string literals. These objects may also be initialized with values which are known at link time including expressions involving the First, Last, and Length attributes [1]. In summary, the rules for preelaboration are that all constructs within a preelaborated library unit will not require any run-time elaboration. These rules are designed to offer portability across implementations.

3. EXTENDING THE INITIAL CONDITIONS FOR PREELABORABLE OBJECTS

Real-time applications which have limited dynamic memory require additional objects to be preelaborated. The objective is to place all statically (compile-time or link-time) determinable data into ROM to allow units to be restarted without elaboration.

The initial condition of these real-time applications is the Ada 95 definition of preelaborable objects. The compiler and linker can determine the static values of some additional objects. The increased scope of values which may be placed in ROM is available due to the late binding of values to objects; post optimization and at link time. The extended definition includes pure functions, link-time known expressions involving the use of the Address or Access attribute and some composite objects, and propagated constant objects.

3.1. Pure Functions

The example in figure 1 contains two packages from a real time application which contain objects which are candidates for preelaboration. The package Global_Constant_Data includes the declaration of a constant table named Jump_Table. This table is an array of records which contain the address of a routine, Proc, and the parameters for this routine, Int_Value and Parameter. The package also includes the definition of a constant record, Default_Value.

The package Math_Support defines a function, F, which computes an equation which uses the floating-point parameter and returns the integer result. This is a pure function in that it has no side-effects and it will return the same result every time it is called with the same value. The formula to be computed has been encapsulated into a function to allow it to be modified during development without disrupting the full system.

```
package Math_Support is
   function F(X : in Float) return Integer;
   pragma Inline(F);
end Math_Support;

package body Math_Support is
   PI : constant := 3.14;
   function F(X : in Float) return Integer is
   begin
      return Integer(X + 180.0 / PI);
   end F;
end Math_Support;

with System;
with Math_Support; use Math_Support;
package Global_Constant_Data is

   procedure P1(X : Integer; Y : System.Address);
   procedure P2(X : Integer; Y : System.Address);

   type Integer_Array is array (1..10) of Integer;

   type Dispatch_Record is record
      Int_Value : Integer;
      Parameter : System.Address;
      Proc      : System.Address;
   end record;

   type Jump_Array is array (1..10) of Dispatch_Record;


   Param_Array : Integer_Array;

   Default_Value : constant Dispatch_Record :=
                        (Int_Value => F(45.0),
                         Parameter => Param_Array'Address,
                         Proc      => P1'Address);

   Jump_Table : constant Jump_Array := Jump_Array'
         (1 => (Int_Value => F(10.25),
                Parameter => Param_Array'Address - 16#1000#,
                Proc      => P2'Address),
          5 => (Int_Value => F(2.348),
                Parameter => Param_Array(5)'Address,
                Proc      => P2'Address),
       others =>  Default_Value);

end Global_Constant_Data;
```

Figure 1: Packages with Preelaborable Objects

The function F is used to initialize the Int_Value component of the Default_Value structure. The Default_Value object is to be preelaborated in the final system. Hence, the function F must be expanded before run time to initialize the Int_Value component. This is achieved through the use of the pragma Inline and the compiler's inline expansion optimization. The compiler will replace the call to F with the encapsulated formula, replacing all occurrences of the formal parameter with the actual parameter. The result is a static expression that can be preelaborated.

The inline expansion optimization allows the definition of preelaborable objects to be extended to include initial values which may be a function call provided that:

- The function adheres to the rules of pragma Pure as described in section 10.2.1 of [2].

- The function has a pragma Inline applied to it and the body of the function is available at compile-time.

- The function only contains declaration of constants and named numbers.

- The function only contains null, return, and if statements.

- Expressions within the if statements and return statements can only be references to the formal parameters, other Link-Time Known values (see Section 3.2), or other pure function calls.

- The return type is an elementary return type.

- The actual parameters are static scalars or Link-Time Known expressions.

If the function call satisfies these requirements, then the inline expansion optimization will produce a static result which may be used as a preelaboration value.

3.2. Link-Time Known Expressions

Often real-time applications need to perform some arithmetic on a base address to obtain the required address of an object. In the example in figure 1, the Address attribute is used in expressions to initialize the Parameter components of the records in the Jump_Table. It is possible to treat these expressions as compile time constant values because the values of the expressions will not change during run time. These expressions are an example of Link-Time Known (LTK) expressions.

A LTK expression is an expression which can be determined to have a constant value by the compiler or linker through optimizations and link-time expressions. LTK values will have a constant static value at the point at which the executable program image is created. No elaboration code is generated for these expressions.

The compiler can recognize LTK expressions as constants to be used as initial values for preelaborable constant objects. The compiler must inform the linker of LTK expressions to have the linker generate the appropriate values for the LTK expressions. The linker will see the LTK representations and will calculate the appropriate static values after it has allocated objects to memory.

Preelaborable objects may be initialized with LTK expressions, where an LTK expression:

- is of type System.Address
- contains only primary values that are either:
    - an integer literal,
    - a named number,
    - the result of the Address attribute applied to:

- a variable declared in a package specification or a package body,

- an indexed component of a statically constrained array declared in a package specification or a package body,

- a statically constrained composite object or a component of such an object,

- a subprogram or task,

- an object with an address clause.

  - the result of the Position, First_Bit, or Last_Bit attribute for a component of a statically constrained record,

  - the result of the Size attribute for a statically constrained composite object, or

  - the result of other LTK expressions.

- includes only the predefined operators on type System.Address

- does not raise an exception.

3.3. Propagation and Preelaboration of Constant Objects

The preelaborable constant record Default_Value is used as the initial value for some of the components of the Jump_Table array. This method of initialization is very common as it espouses good software engineering principles. For example, if the default initialization value needs to be changed, it must only be changed in one place, the definition of Default_Value.

The compiler can propagate the preelaborable values in much the same way as named numbers. The preelaborable values derived from LTK expressions and pure functions may be used as initial values for other preelaborable constant objects. The resulting code will not include any run-time code for the initialization of the objects declared with these preelaborable values as initial expressions. Hence, all of the constant objects declared in the package Global_Constant_Data are preelaborable.

4. EMPIRICAL RESULTS

Tartan has implemented these extensions to the definition of preelaboration in its 1750A Ada compiler. This entailed first modifying the compiler to recognize the Ada 95 definition of static. Then the compiler was revised to accept initial values of preelaborable constant objects as defined in Ada 95. Finally, the compiler was modified to support the three extensions to the definition of preelaborable objects described above: pure functions, link-time known expressions, and the propagation of constant values.

Table 1 shows the results of implementing this extended definition of preelaborable objects. The data shows the code sizes of three real-time applications compiled with the Ada 95 definition and with the extended definition. In addition to the reduction in code size, the elaboration time for these modules, using the preelaboration enhancements, was reduced.

	Ada 95 Preelaboration	**Enhanced Ada 95 Preelaboration**	**Scaling Factor**
APP1	58613	42643	1.37
APP2	66009	65046	1.01
APP3	6912	6654	1.04

Table 1: Preliminary Preelaboration Results

Note that the results of these enhancements may not produce modules that are significantly different from those produced with the Ada 95 system. This is primarily due to the fact that the Ada 95 features address the issues most common to real-time applications. Also recognize that there is a large improvement in size and time for those real-time applications which contain large constant tables or fixed code segments.

5. REFERENCES

[1]   *Annotated Ada 95 Reference Manual*
      ANSI/ISO/IEC-8652:1995 International Standard, 1994.

[2]   *Ada 95 Reference Manual*
      ANSI/ISO/IEC-8652:1995 International Standard, 1994.

The Use of Ada for the ENVISAT-1 Simulator

B.Davies, D.A.Rothwell

Science Systems (Space) Limited, Chippenham,
Wiltshire SN15 1BN

Abstract. The ENVISAT-1 simulator is a real-time software tool that is designed to 'look and behave' exactly as the spacecraft does when viewed by the Operations Control Centre. The software is being developed with the aid of a CASE tool using the Shlaer-Mellor Object-Oriented Methodology and will be implemented in Ada on a DEC Alpha AXP workstation running OpenVMS. The feasibility of automatic Ada code generation from the CASE tool database is being investigated.

1 Introduction

The primary role of the European Space Operations Centre (ESOC) is the monitoring and control of spacecraft and one of the most crucial phases of any mission is the Launch and Early Orbit Phase (LEOP) when complex operations have to be performed in a time critical environment. It is no surprise therefore that considerable effort is expended in the years prior to a launch to ensure its success. ESOC's record in spacecraft launches is exemplary.

One of the key tools used by ESOC to facilitate pre-launch preparations is a real-time spacecraft simulator. This is a software tool that is designed to 'look and behave' exactly as the spacecraft does when viewed by the Operations Control Centre (OCC), that is in terms of the telecommands it accepts and the telemetry that it generates. In order to achieve this the simulator must model the spacecraft environment and all spacecraft interfaces and internal features exhibiting both nominal and non-nominal behaviour. By satisfying these requirements fully, the simulator can be used for:

- training flight control personnel
- verifying and validating both nominal and contingency Flight Operations Procedures (FOPs)
- verifying and validating the ground support system.

Some of these activities will be ongoing even after launch, particularly training new staff and verifying and validating contingency FOPs.

In recent years it has been the practice to emulate the spacecraft on-board processor(s) so that executable images of the flight software (complete with 'quirks') can be readily incorporated within the simulator. This has resulted in a more realistic simulation of the spacecraft as well as enabling the simulator to provide flight software validation support following on-board software maintenance activities.

2 The ENVISAT-1 Mission

A simulator currently required by ESOC is that of the ENVISAT-1 spacecraft, an environmental satellite that will be launched into a low polar orbit during 1999. The spacecraft will monitor the oceans and atmosphere using a variety of payload instruments. It is part of the Polar Platform program and will exploit the capabilities of data relay satellites for data transmission. These will allow high rate data coverage and real time commanding and control over significant portions of the globe.

The spacecraft has an anticipated mission duration of four years.

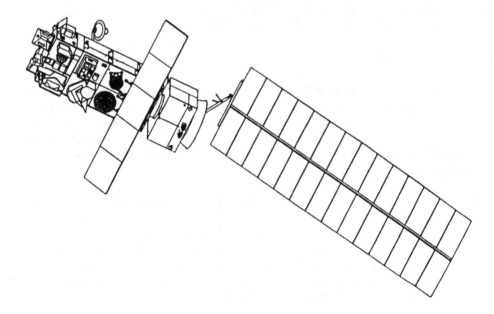

Figure 1 Envisat Spacecraft

3 The ENVISAT-1 Simulator

Responsibility for the design and development of the ENVISAT-1 simulator has been awarded to a consortium composed of Science Systems (Space) Limited and CRI. They have decomposed the development into three distinct stages.

The first stage is to develop the simulation of the spacecraft Service Module (SM) comprising the Central Computer Unit (CCU), Data Handling System (DHS), Attitude and Orbit Control System (AOCS), Propulsion System, Power Generation and Distribution System and Thermal Control System (TCS).

The second stage is to develop the simulation of the Payload Electronics Bay (PEB) and the Payload Data Management System (PL/DMS) - comprising the tape recorders, encoding and switching unit and high speed multiplexer.

The third stage is to develop the Payload Module simulation comprising the payload instrument models.

This staged approach has been adopted following experience gained on the ERS-1 simulator project where some early effort was used modelling payload instruments whose designs later turned out to be unstable.

The simulator is being developed on Alpha AXP workstations within the common framework of all current simulator projects at ESOC, that is:

- re-use of a simulator kernel written in Ada called the Software Infrastructure for Modelling SATellites (SIMSAT) which provides real-time scheduling facilities, user command handling and certain models such as the Ground Stations Model and the Position and Environment Model (PEM);
- analysis and design using Object Oriented (OO) techniques (in this case Shlaer-Mellor) and a Computer Aided Software Engineering (CASE) tool giving the possibility for automatic code generation and more re-use in subsequent simulators;
- implementation in Ada under OpenVMS.

The simulator schedule is tightly constrained by the spacecraft launch schedule and the System Validation Tests (SVT) that need to be performed prior to launch. The SVTs are used for closed loop testing of the spacecraft and ground support system whilst the spacecraft is still on the ground. The simulator is used to prepare the SVT procedures in advance of their actual usage. By inference, a successful SVT is a successful test of the simulator.

A formal delivery of the simulator is required before each SVT, the first one in January 1997 with subsequent deliveries currently planned between then and the launch in 1999.

4 On-Board Processor Emulation

The ENVISAT-1 spacecraft contains over 20 on-board processors. The key ones are: the CCU, which handles all telemetry/telecommanding and SM monitoring and control, and the Payload Management Computer (PMC), which handles the interfaces between the SM and the 10 payload instruments. Both are 1750A processors.

In addition, within the Sensor and Safe Mode Electronics unit of the AOCS hardware there is a standby processor which controls the spacecraft attitude during Survival Mode i.e. when main CCU processing is unavailable.

The activities of these three processors are sufficiently important to warrant the inclusion of their flight software in the simulation to ensure absolute fidelity. The need to support and regulate the operation of these software images within the simulation domain leads to the requirement to emulate the hardware of the on-board 1750A processors.

5 Architectural Features

The Envisat simulator architecture is heavily influenced by the architecture of the SIMSAT package. SIMSAT was designed to incorporate the best features of a previous package (written in FORTRAN) yet take advantage of the benefits provided by Ada.

From the start, the package was designed to be distributed across several nodes of a computer network.

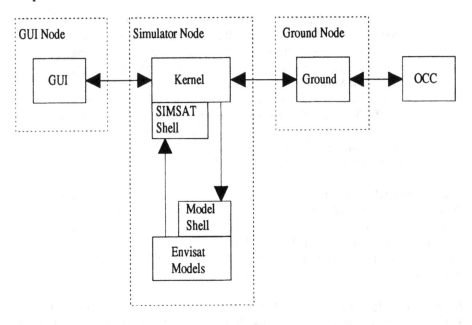

Figure 2 Basic SIMSAT Architecture

The OCC in figure 2 refers to the Operation Control Centre which is outside the scope of this paper.

The GUI and the Ground models in figure 2 are part of SIMSAT and only require project specific configuration. They will not be discussed further in this paper.

As shown in figure 2, the SIMSAT Kernel and the Envisat models co-exist on the simulator node; the interface between them is considered further in the following sections of this paper.

The architectural aspects of SIMSAT, embodying features and rules for the design of spacecraft elements, are driven by 3 main considerations: performance requirements, runtime user facilities and design constraints.

5.1 Performance Requirements

Realtime execution is mandatory - the simulator is part of a closed loop system in which the Operational Control Centre software rigorously monitors the rate of arrival, the time-tags and the content of all incoming spacecraft telemetry and compares this with the outgoing commands. The simulator includes a model of the ground stations, landlines and radio frequency links and provides facilities to model the time delays in all of these.

Each of the SIMSAT ground model elements and link handlers is a separate Ada task.

Simulations are typically run for 8 hour sessions and then the State Vector is saved; the following day, it is reloaded and run for another 8 hours. Thus, the duration is additive and errors can be additive although session specifics, such as log files, can be sized for 8 hours only. Accuracy requirements have to be maintained over 72 hour simulations.

There must be no memory leakage - which obliges designers to minimise the creation or deletion of objects at run time. Objects were selected to represent spacecraft hardware objects and properties rather than message types.

5.2 Runtime User Facilities

Two types of user are foreseen, and they tend to use the simulator in different ways:

- spacecraft operations analyst/engineers
- simulation operators.

The spacecraft operations analyst/engineer uses the simulator in standalone mode to test and modify his flight operations procedures. He needs to be able to send telecommands and watch their detailed effect on the modelled system. He may want to 'fast-forward' to the next period of interest;

The simulation operator 'drives' the simulator during simulations when the simulator is receiving telecommands from the control centre and generating telemetry in response. He needs to be able to set up a particular mode of operation for the tests being performed or introduce failures to practise recovery procedures and train spacecraft operators.

The SIMSAT GUI is designed to support both types of user. It provides rapid cyclic display of runtime parameters, the ability to set up new display groups at run time, and the ability to run prepared command sequences. In addition, telecommands can be 'sent' to the simulator either from the keyboard or from command procedures - although this facility is not used when linked to a control centre.

Spacecraft object specific user commands can be added to the set of SIMSAT commands.

As mentioned above, the ability to save and restore the simulator State Vector is essential. The files are known as Breakpoints, and contain all attributes of all objects plus dumps of all flight software images. SIMSAT maps all object attributes into a dedicated area of memory and reads or writes this area to file. In general, any object can be called to perform its individual breakpointing actions and flight software dumps are handled separately by the individual emulators when called by SIMSAT.

5.3 Design Constraints

The following design constraints are made by the SIMSAT package.

The spacecraft simulator will be designed to run in a single processor. The spacecraft models will be designed for single thread execution - ie. no parallel execution and no use of Ada tasking. Thus, there is no requirement for the use of rendezvous. The knowledge that every model will run to completion before another starts execution brings a significant reduction in debugging problems.

Apart from the filing system, the spacecraft models will make no use of VAX system services: SIMSAT services satisfy virtually all needs. The only models currently expected to make use of the filing system are the onboard processor emulations which need access to the disk files containing the flight software binary images.

The interface between the spacecraft models which are being developed using Shlaer-Mellor and the SIMSAT package (which was not) is characterised by a Model Shell which provides a focal point and is cognisant of all the services provided by all the models. At this level, the services fall into 2 categories:

event services
: by which individual models service events from the Realtime Scheduler in the SIMSAT Kernel;

user command services
: by which individual models service user commands received from the simulator GUI.

At least one model service shall be provided per object state transition (eg. initialization). User commands are queued by SIMSAT until the currently scheduled event has completed.

All spacecraft object models execute as part of the SIMSAT Nucleus process (which includes the Kernel): thus, all Scheduler events are communicated as procedure calls.

6 Code Generation

In the Shlaer-Mellor OOA method there are two distinct phases of software development - analysis and design. One of the key issues of this method is that analysis is kept separate from design so that it is independent of the implementation architecture. In this manner a problem can be analysed and then, using an architectural domain representative of the implementation architecture, it can be mapped into a design. In theory it should be possible to map an analysis into different designs on different architectures and conversely, it should be possible to re-use an architectural domain for a particular type of implementation to map analyses of different systems into their different designs (e.g. several simulators using SIMSAT could all use the same architectural domain).

The architectural domain can be viewed as a set of rules for translating analysis into design and then into code. By encapsulating these rules in a piece of software it is possible to automate and re-use this mapping process.

We are currently evaluating the feasibility of the following OOA to Ada implementation rules:

1. Each OOA object template will be implemented as an Ada package having separate specification and body files for individual compilation.
2. Objects will be instantiated through creation events by passing the name/id of the instance to be created, for example:
      %generate MASSP1: Initialise_Mass_Properties ("Mass_1")
    would create and initialise an instance of object Mass_Properties with id "Mass_1".
3. Instances of dynamic objects will be managed by a linked list package for each object type so that creation and deletion at run-time can be more easily handled.
4. Instances of static objects will be handled by an array package for each object type. This is more efficient at run time than a linked list since it will be unnecessary to search through the list to see if an instance exists.
5. Events will be implemented as synchronous procedure calls.
6. 'High-level' control code is written on the State Transition Diagrams (STDs) directly in Ada syntax apart from generation and deletion events which retain their original CASE tool (Teamwork) syntax.
7. 'Lower-level' detail is written in the body of Transformation and Tester process-specifications (p-specs), again, directly as Ada code. The Ada code in the STDs references the functions/procedures of the p-specs.
8. Required specification files are referenced through use of "BodyIncludes" and "SpecIncludes" fields within the Teamwork object descriptions. Some of these specification files may have to be defined outside of the Teamwork database.
9. Code generation philosophies for Inheritance and Associative objects are currently under review.

Potential benefits of Ada code generation are:

1. Time saving - particularly in the generation of package specifications and implementation of event handling routines.
2. Consistency of Ada package structures produced by different programmers thus facilitating readability and maintainability.

3.   The use of a CASE tool for analysis has provided a database that the OOA to Ada software can work upon thus making it possible to access the entire knowledge base created during earlier project phases.
4.   All of the system knowledge is contained in a single location. Changes and/or modifications to the system can be implemented at this location and the work products that depend upon these changes can be automatically updated.
5.   Re-use of the developed architectural domain for future synchronous systems implemented on single processor architectures.

7 Benefits of Using Ada

As mentioned above, all current and future ESOC simulators are to be developed using Ada. Ada was chosen for its support of data encapsulation and information hiding and because it provides a powerful method for software engineering as opposed to being just another programming language. Previous simulators were implemented in FORTRAN and, compared to FORTRAN, the sort of benefits expected from Ada include:

•   reduced debugging problems, time and effort
•   increased resilience of the delivered code
•   enhanced re-use possibilities in future simulators.

Hitherto, re-use of models has only tended to occur when a designer re-used parts of his 'own' code from a previous simulator.

Portability across hardware platforms is also an important consideration given the potential lifetime of the ENVISAT-1 (or indeed any other spacecraft) simulator code. The mission duration is four years and the simulator code which will start to exist quite soon will be in use until the end of the mission in 2003. Just as the ERS-1 simulator code has been re-used for the ERS-2 spacecraft it is expected that the ENVISAT-1 simulator code will be re-used for ENVISAT-2 and so it is easy to foresee a potential lifetime of 15 years for the simulator code. As hardware platforms change, and commercial trends evolve over this time, the code will almost certainly have to be ported.

8 Conclusions

The ENVISAT-1 simulator is the next in a long line of real-time spacecraft simulators that have been developed for ESOC. It brings together the latest techniques in software engineering including OOA, Ada, CASE tools and automatic code generation.

We anticipate that all these features will combine to enhance reliability, readability and efficiency thereby reducing the longer term maintenance costs generally associated with spacecraft simulators. As these technologiers are applied to more simulator projects, there will be greater scope for reuse of models - leading to further reduction in development costs.

Objects at Use in Nautical Simulators

Kor Molenmaker

MSCN
Maritime Simulation Centre the Netherlands
P.O. Box 90, 6700 AB Wageningen,
The Netherlands.

Abstract. The department "Development and Supply of nautical simulators" designs simulator systems to meet the requirements of ship's officers, pilots, ship engineers and nautical students. Currently three simulators have been designed; the manoeuvring simulator, the engineroom simulator, and the cargo handling simulator. To achieve maximum flexibility for the three simulators the object oriented design method is used for the design and implementation of the simulator. This abstract describes the way objects are used in the simulators to achieve this maximum flexibility.

1. Company Profile

The Maritime Simulation Centre the Netherlands, MSCN B.V. located in Wageningen, has been operational since January 1992. MSCN is an unique nautical centre: not only does it provide nautical training, research and consultancy, it also designs and develops advanced simulator systems in various applications for clients all over the world.

The department "Development and Supply of Nautical simulators", designs simulator systems to meet the requirements of ship's officers, pilots, ship engineers and nautical students. Currently three simulators have been designed and are fully operational; *The Manoeuvering Simulator, the Engineroom Simulator and the Cargo handling Simulator.*

The requirements for the Manoeuvering Simulator are specially designed in order to acquire or augment the knowledge of the behaviour of ships, the effect of external conditions such as wind, waves, current tidal streams and shallow water, how to deal with tugs, how to control computerized systems and how to act in case of emergency. The Manoeuvering simulator is capable of simulating up to 10 fully controllable ships, each equipped with a sophisticated Computer Graphics Image system covering up to 360 degrees horizontal angle view and a "real world" bridge with instruments including radar and navigational aids.

The Engineroom simulator provides a realistic environment in which trainee ship's engineers can take control of an engineroom without the risk of damaging the equipment. The Engineroom simulator has the capability to run up to six main engines and eight auxiliary engines, and off course may use new engine models (e.g. steam turbine or medium speed diesel main engine), which may be connected up to four shafts. Each of these shafts may use variable pitch propellers and so shall come complete with a pitch control system. The simulator uses high quality, digitized, images of various engineroom components, combines them with computer generated Local Operation Panels appropriate to the components displayed, and projects the resulting images onto a large scale screen. The resulting scene will provide a more realistic view from the point of view of the trainees. In addition to emphasize the fact that there are many low-level operations that must be performed manually, outside the control room, this projection screen is fitted with a movement detection system that allows the trainees to interact with the manual controls of the image.

The Cargohandling simulator offers the trainees the possibility to load various ship configurations with cargo. The loading of the ship can be monitored and controlled. The cargo which is loaded can be of various liquid types, oil, gas, water, etc. The loading with cargo has a direct impact on the ship behaviour. Due to the high grade of flexibility of the design of the simulator various ship and cargo configurations are possible. Through database resource file the instructor and trainer can design their own ship and cargo configuration.

As on many modern ships, the control room for the three simulators provide a computer-based graphical control system knows as Mimics. Each Mimic screen is a schematic diagram of (part of) a ship's subsystem. Objects on the Mimic screen may have their current state displayed, and may offer the trainee the possibility of altering this state. Included in each simulator is the possibility for an instructor to create abnormal conditions or to introduce special environment conditions.

2. Overview

The purpose of this paper is not to describe details about each of those simulators, or to describe one simulator in particular, but to describe the way objects are used in the design and implementation of the simulators.

In the case of the three simulators mentioned above we want to achieve maximum flexibility in the configurability of the simulators. You need to be able to use the manoeuvering simulator with many types of ships, many harbor or sea environments, without recompilation of the software. The design of the manoeuvering simulator is based on this concept. The ship for example, can have different implementations for the rudder mathematical model. The actual rudder model which is used during the simulation is read in through a parameter file. By changing the implementation number in this parameter file, you change the actual rudder model. You need not to recompile the ship software to establish another rudder behaviour.

A different approach with the design of the engineroom and the cargo handling was needed. One aspect was, as with the manoeuvering simulator to make the simulator very flexible. But with the manoeuvering simulator this mend that you can create various ships, harbor conditions and environmental conditions. The requirement for configurability with the engineroom and cargohandling simulator was more focused on the configurability of all the simulator components, not with the fact that you can use the engineroom with different engines models or shaft component models in various configurations. The individual configuration of each component of the engineroom or cargo handling was required because then the users could tune the system to the real world behaviour, and are able to configure components for different training purposes. The mathematical models in the engineroom and cargo are fixed, the static data which makes the mathematical models work is configurable.

3. System Design

3.1 Class Specification

The configurability of the simulators is a very important aspect in the design of the simulators. During the design of the simulators the question came up "How do we achieve this configurability for each individual component of the simulator?". The answer to this question was relative simple, for each individual component in the system you use an object. At creation of the object, the object reads its own configuration data. The result is that each component of the system is an object with its own configuration data. Realizing that this approach could cause the creation of hundreds of objects we also needed to design a way to handle all these objects.

The programming language for the simulators is Ada and C++. All the code handles the graphical part of the simulator is written in C++, and the code for all the mathematical models is written in Ada. Ada is an object-based language. It does not have "class" features, and does not support full scale inheritance nor polymorphism. However it contains very powerful abstraction, modularization, and data encapsulation features, with the concepts of package, generic unit, private type, and the clear separation it makes between specification and implementation. There are several ways to implement the major concepts of object-oriented design in Ada, a class maps to a package offering a private type, or a class being a generic package. In the design of our simulators the best solution for us was the class which maps to a package offering a private type. By declaring a variable of this private type, you have an object, an instantiation of the class.

The Ada specification for the class is as follows:

```
package AUX_BOILER_CLASS_PACKAGE is
    type AUX_BOILER_CLASS is private ;
    NULL_CLASS : constant AUX_BOILER_CLASS ;

    procedure CREATE (
                OBJECT_ID : in  OBJECT_ID_TYPE ;
                OBJECT : out AUX_BOILER_CLASS ;
                STATUS : out STATUS_TYPE ) ;
    procedure INITIALISE ( OBJECT : in out AUX_BOILER_CLASS ;
                STATUS : out STATUS_TYPE ) ;
    procedure PUBLISH( OBJECT : in AUX_BOILER_CLASS ;
                STATUS : out STATUS_TYPE ) ;
    procedure LINK ( OBJECT : in out AUX_BOILER_CLASS ;
                STATUS : out STATUS_TYPE ) ;
    procedure UPDATE ( OBJECT : in out AUX_BOILER_CLASS ;
                STATUS : out STATUS_TYPE ) ;
    procedure SHUTDOWN( OBJECT : in out AUX_BOILER_CLASS ;
                STATUS : out STATUS_TYPE ) ;

    function GET_WATER_VOLUME
            ( OBJECT : in AUX_BOILER_CLASS )
            return DECIMETRES3 ;

    function GET_PRESSURE ( OBJECT: in AUX_BOILER_CLASS )
            return PASCALS ;

private

    type AUX_BOILER_CLASS_DATA ;
    type AUX_BOILER_CLASS is access AUX_BOILER_CLASS_DATA ;
    NULL_CLASS : constant AUX_BOILER_CLASS :=  null ;
end AUX_BOILER_CLASS_PACKAGE ;
```

The procedures Create, Initialise, Link, Update, and Shutdown are to control the object. The functions are to get specific data from the object. Note that the private data of the class is a pointer to a data structure. The pointer structure is chosen to keep the data items hidden in the package body.

3.2 Class Instantiation

The engineroom simulator consists of several large system parts, like the Power Supply Switch board model, the Main Engine model, the Steam System model. In total there are about 15 of these large system parts. Each model can consist of many packages with private types, and thus each model can consist of many objects. To maintain full configurability, even within each model we decided that all objects should have a unique object id, each model has its own object manager to control the requests from other model objects to its own model objects, and that all data and control is done from object to object, even within a model.

With each object having an unique id, you can have parameter files, or resource files on a per object base. Once the object is instantiated, the resources files can be processed to find the configuration data for that specific object. Within the object itself the configuration or parameter file is read in and processed.

Example:

```
procedure CREATE( OBJECT_ID : in OBJECT_ID_TYPE ;
                  OBJECT    : out AUX_BOILER_CLASS ;
                  STATUS    : out STATUS_TYPE ) is
   LOCAL_OBJECT : AUX_BOILER_CLASS ;
   LOCAL_STATUS : STATUS_TYPE ;
   LOCAL_OBJECT_ID : OBJECT_ID_TYPE ;

begin
   LOCAL_OBJECT := new AUX_BOILER_CLASS_DATA ;
   LOCAL_OBJECT.STATIC_DATA :=
     AUX_BOILER_PREP_SERVICES.GET(OBJECT_ID) ;
   LOCAL_STATUS := NORMAL ;

   OBJECT := LOCAL_OBJECT ;
   STATUS := LOCAL_STATUS ;

end CREATE ;
```

3.3 Object hierarchy

Each object, once its is created, has been configured, using the Prep_Services package. The configuration data contains not only models behaviour data, like temperatures, velocities or constant values, but also the id of other objects, used for interface. This object id is needed to get the desired object with the desired behaviour. To get the object, one needs to know in which system part is it created. One then uses the object manager for this system part, to get the desired object data.

Example:

In the AuxBoiler object you need a feedwater connection which is created in the Component Library system part, and a steam valve which is created in the steam System system part.

```
procedure LINK ( OBJECT : in out AUX_BOILER_CLASS ;
                 STATUS : out STATUS_TYPE ) is
   begin

      OBJECT.LOCAL_DATA.FEEDWATER_CONNECTION :=
   COMPONENT_LIBRARY_LINKER.GET_CONNECTION_OBJECT
      (OBJECT_ID= > OBJECT.STATIC_DATA.FEEDWATER_ID);

      OBJECT.LOCAL_DATA.STEAM_VALVE_CONNECTION :=
   STEAM_LINKER.GET_VALVE_OBJECT ( OBJECT_ID = >
         OBJECT.STATIC_DATA.STEAM_VALVE_ID_NUMBER ) ;

      STATUS := NORMAL ;

   end LINK ;
```

3.4 Object Management

Each system part has its own object manager, like the Component Library Linker or the Steam Linker. This package takes care of the objects within the model, the child objects, it retrieves the object data of the child objects. In fact we have created an object hierarchy. The overall system software, responsible for the simulator sequence of events, needs to know only the main system parts, the parent objects. Each parent object takes care of its own child objects. Adding this object hierarchy hides away the complexity of handling all the simulator objects.

The functionality for the object manager is generic for each object. The object must be created, it must be initialised, linked, synchronized and destroyed. The manager is therefor implemented as a generic package:

generic

    type OBJECT_TYPE is private ;
    IDENTIFICATION : in VSTRING.VSTRING ;

package MANAGER_TEMPLATE is

    generic

    with procedure GET_SUMMARY_DATA
      (NUMBER_OF_OBJECTS : out NATURAL ;
      LIST_OF_OBJECTS   : out LIST_OF_OBJECT_IDS_TYPE) ;

    with procedure CREATE_OBJECT (
        OBJECT_ID : in OBJECT_ID_TYPE ;
        OBJECT : out OBJECT_TYPE ;
        STATUS : out STATUS_TYPE) ;

    procedure CREATE (STATUS : out STATUS_TYPE) ;

    ....

end MANAGER_TEMPLATE ;

package STEAM_SYSTEM_MANAGER is new MANAGER_TEMPLATE
    (OBJECT_TYPE => STEAM_SYSTEM_CLASS,
    IDENTIFICATION => "STEAM SYSTEM") ;

To illustrate the creation of an object I have removed the other procedures from the specification. The Steam System Manager package is an instatiation of the Manager Template generic. Thus the Steam System Manager package has the generic procedure Create to create a steam system object with its initial data.

procedure STEAM_SYSTEM_CREATE is new
    STEAM_SYSTEM_MANAGER.CREATE (
  CREATE_OBJECT=>STEAM_SYSTEM_CLASS_PACKAGE.CREATE,
  GET_SUMMARY_DATA=>GET_STEAM_SYSTEM_SUMMARY_DATA);

The Steam System Create package is an instantiation of the Steam System Manager package generic procedure Create. When calling this Steam System Create the actual steam system object is created, using the Get Summary Data to retrieve data for the steam system object. The steam system object will then create its own child objects. This same concept applies to the Initialise, Link, Sync and Shutdown state of the simulator.

The sequence of events in the simulator is that the overall system software, creates the main system parts. When these system parts are created they create their children. During creation the objects get there initial configuration data. Objects can be linked to each other, again the overall system software issues the link to the main system parts, these themselves issue a link to their children objects. Once the create and the link sequence has been performed, the simulator is ready to operate. If the simulator is operational all the main system parts are called to perform an update of their mathematical models. These main system parts call their own child object to perform an update of their mathematical models. During each timestep of the simulation all the objects are updated, causing the simulation state to change. The simulation is underway!

3.5 Communication

The above applies to objects which are created in one main program, and run on one CPU. How do objects on one CPU interface with objects on a different CPU? Each object has an object data store. In this data store, called dynamic object data, the object stores the data which must be available to other objects in the simulator, on different CPU's. This dynamic object data is distributed over the network. Each CPU in the network can receive this data, and the local objects can read from it. The distribution of the dynamic object data store is done by COMMS, which hides away the complexity of distributing the dynamic object data in the simulator network. This dynamic object data is used by the screen display software, called MIMICS, to display the simulation processes. The hardware panels available in the simulator fill dynamic object data, to be processed by the models on different CPU's.

Example:

To put and get data from the dynamic object data the COMMS interface is used.

    -- Get dynamic data for a valve.
    VALVE_COMMS.GET (OBJECT_ID, VALVE_DATA) ;
    -- Put dynamic data for a valve
    VALVE_COMMS.PUT (OBJECT_ID, VALVE_DATA) ;

By using the COMMS software, a local object can retrieve and store object dynamic data without knowing were the object it interfaces with is located. COMMS hides away the complexity of the transmit and receive of these dynamic object data. This concept of each object having its own dynamic object data, which is distributed by the COMMS software is also used to transmit and receive data among object of a different programming language, like Ada objects, C and C++ objects. The COMMS software can handle procedure calls from more programming languages. In general one object owns the dynamic data, and write changes into this data. Other objects can read and use this data.

Don't forget however that there are more components in the total simulator, like the large display screens, the hardware control panels, and the startup, communication and distributing software to run the simulator over several CPU's. These components are mostly written in C+ +. It would be too much detail for this paper to describe in more detail the interaction between these objects and the objects of the main system parts of the simulator. The object communication for all the objects in the simulator is based on the above concepts.

4. Conclusion

One of the requirements for the nautical simulator was the high level of configurability. To meet this requirement the concept of configurable objects was used. Each individual object could be configured using the resource file. Using the Ada package and private type concept to model OO behaviour in Ada we managed to create configurable objects. By adding an object hierarchy for the main system parts and their child objects we hide away the complexity of handling over hundred objects in the simulator software. Objects need not to be aware of where the objects which are used for interface, are located. The COMMS interface hides away the complexity of the object communication over the network.

5. References

1. Object-Oriented Analyses and Design with Applications
    Grady Booch, Second edition.
    ISBN 0-8053-5340-2
2. Programming in Ada
    J.G.P. Barnes, Third Edition.
    ISBN 0-201-17566-5
3. Designing Object-Oriented Software
    Rebecca Wirfs-Brock
    Brian Wilkerson
    Lauren Wiener
    ISBN 0-13-629825-7

DIS - An Interface to Distributed Interactive Simulation

Peter E. Obermayer, Georg Schüer, Rudolf Landwehr

Competence Center Informatik GmbH
Lohberg 10
D-49716 Meppen, Germany

Abstract. The implementation of a software interface in Ada according to the standard 'Protocol for Distributed Interactive Simulation Applications' is described. The interface covers the levels 5 to 7 of the ISO-OSI reference model by providing services for receiving, transmitting, and managing Protocol Data Units from a simulation application to a network and vice versa as well as additional services defined in the standard. The implementation runs on single- and multi-processor environments. Using Ada as implementation language a high readability of the code as well as a very high traceability to the requirements and the standard was achieved, portability and maintainability proved to be excellent.

1   Introduction

Distributed Interactive Simulation (DIS) is a time and space coherent synthetic representation of world environments designed for linking the interactive, free play activities of people in operational exercises. The synthetic environment is created through real time exchange of data units between distributed, computationally autonomous nodes comprised of entities in the form of simulations, simulators and instrumented equipment interconnected through standard computer communication services.

'DIS-Standard' stands for a set of standards [1-7], of which some are still in the standardization phase. The 'Protocol for Distributed Interactive Simulation Applications' (IEEE-1278) is currently reworked and in the stage of Draft Version 2.1.1 [8].

For an implementation project software providing an interface between the application software and the network software according to the 'Protocol for Distributed Interactive Simulation Applications' was needed.

2   Requirements for the Implementation

The project required Ada to be the implementation language of the DIS-layer. For this purpose Ada 83 was used, since at the time of development Ada 95 was not yet available. Furthermore, the DIS-layer had to be developed independently of hardware and of additional software. It should be possible to run this interface on systems with one as well as with two or more processors. The operations of the DIS-layer should possibly be distributed on two processors in order to provide efficient usage of resources on multi-processor systems.

The DIS-layer is sandwiched between the simulation and the network layer. The network layer was required to be a separate layer between the DIS-layer and the TCP/IP or UDP/IP protocols, effectively being able to replace these network protocols with different protocols.

3   Architecture of the Implementation

The DIS-layer has two external interfaces, the interface between the simulation and the DIS-layer and the interface between the DIS-layer and the network. The simulation process and the network process are both active processes while the DIS-layer provides services passively through its interfaces to both. In order to support efficient usage of multi-processor-systems the simulation and the DIS-layer can run on different CPUs. Therefore the data exchange between the simulation process and the network process is performed via shared memory.

The information exchange between the simulations is performed by sending and receiving Protocol Data Units (PDUs). The PDUs can be grouped in three groups. The members of each group are handled similarly by the DIS-layer. These groups are the object-PDUs, the effect-PDUs and the control-PDUs.

Three buffers are provided in the shared memory for each group of PDUs, a send buffer, a receive buffer and a playback buffer. Through the buffering the simulation process and the network process are loosely coupled in time.

4   Simulation Interface

For the simulation process the simulation interface of the DIS-layer provides the constants, types and operations necessary to communicate with other simulation processes. The simulation interface is wrapped in three packages.

4.1   PDU-Recordspecification

Since the PDU-layout is defined by the DIS-standards, this definition was used for record specification. The package LNDSDISINT provides the records specified for the PDUs.

4.2   Procedural Interface

The procedures and functions to access the DIS-interface are provided in the package LNDSSIMDIS.

4.3   Error constants declaration

The error constants used by the DIS-interface are defined in the package LNDSERRORS.

5 Services of the DIS-Interface

5.1 Dead Reckoning

'Dead reckoning' stands for algorithms extrapolating the values of the dynamic variables of a given object from the current values. Dead reckoning can be applied to the object's position, its velocity, its orientation and its articulation. Dead reckoning may be applied in the case that PDUs required from the network for updating are missing.

5.2 Smoothing

Extrapolations may lead to deviations of the extrapolated values from the actual ones once a valid PDU is received again. This difference may lead to noticeable 'jumps' in the display of these values in the simulation. Therefore smoothing is applied, i.e. an adjustment of the actual values received to those previously used in the simulation. This adjustment is consecutively reduced for every subsequently arriving PDU.

5.2 Coordinate Transforms

Coordinates of the PDUs have to be transformed, if the coordinate systems used in the simulator differ from those specified in the DIS-Standard. The implementation provides a transformation between the coordinate system specified in the DIS-Standard and the simulator coordinate system.

5.3 Playback

The playback facility allows the simulation to record the information exchange. With the recorded PDUs the simulation can be reconstructed and replayed. Any missing PDUs can be reconstructed using 'dead reckoning'.

6 Management Issues

As standard for the software development lifecycle the 'V-Modell' software development standard of the German authorities [9] was used. Requirements for the interface, the architecture, the implementation, test plan, test specification and test procedure were derived and in the test protocol documented.

In the development a major effort was put in direct translation of the DIS-standards' requirements into the architecture and into the code in order to reach high traceability. Together with the high readability of the code through the use of appropriate naming and the advantages of the naming possibilities in Ada this lead to an easily maintainable software.

Since the code was fully written in Ada and since implementation dependencies were localized in few packages the code is highly portable and was ported to the customers' target system, the SUN environment with SunOS or SOLARIS on single- and multi-processor-machines, the PC environment and other targets.

7 Conclusion

Since the standards for DIS are continuously further developed and new PDUs are added [2] an object oriented approach is taken in analysis and design for new versions of implementations of the DIS-layer. For this implementation Ada 95 will be used. It is anticipated, that the properties of Ada 95 will lead to a straightforward translation of the design into code.

References

1. Standard for Information Technology - Protocol for Distributed Interactive Simulation Applications (IEEE-1278)
2. Standard for Distributed Interactive Simulation - Application Protocols, Version 2.0, Fourth Draft, March 16, 1994 (IST CR-93-40)
3. Draft Standard for Information Technology - Protocol for Distributed Interactive Simulation Applications, Version 2.0.4, February 2, 1994 (IST-CR-93-40)
4. Enumeration and Bit Encoded Values for Use with Protocols for Distributed Interactive Simulation Applications, March 22, 1993 (IST CR-93-02)
5. Draft Standard for Fidelity Description Requirements for Distributed Interactive Simulation Applications, March 22, 1993 (IST CR-93-04)
6. Draft Standard for Exercise Control and Performance measures Feedback Requirements for Distributed Interactive Simulation, March 22, 1993 (IST CR 93 05)
7. Final Draft Standard Communication Architecture for Distributed Interactive Simulation (CADIS), November 8, 1993
8. Standard For Distributed Interactive Simulation - Application Protocols, Version 2.1.1 (Working Draft), February 14, 1995 (IST-CR-95-06)
9. A.-P. Bröhl, W. Dröschel (Hrsg.), „Das V-Modell", R. Oldenbourg Verlag, München, 1993

PARIS - Partitioned Ada for Remotely Invoked Services

Anthony Gargaro[1], Yvon Kermarrec[2], Laurent Pautet[3] and Samuel Tardieu[3]

[1] Computer Sciences Corporation
Moorestown, New Jersey 08057
USA
agargaro@isd.csc.com
[2] Télécom Bretagne
Département Informatique
Technopôle de l'Iroise
29 285 Brest Cedex
France
yvon@enstb.enst-bretagne.fr
[3] Télécom Paris
Département Informatique
46, Rue Barrault
75 013 Paris
France
(pautet,tardieu)@inf.enst.fr

Abstract. This paper presents our experience implementing the Ada 95 Annex E to support distributed systems using the GNAT compiler[6]. The work has been performed by a multinational team from France and the USA. The paper describes the implementation of the Partition Communication System and the required support from the GNAT compiler. In addition, extensions beyond Annex E are described that facilitate programming the next generation of distributed applications in Ada 95.

1   Introduction

A distributed system architecture comprises a network of computers and the software components that execute on the computers. Such architectures are commonly used to improve the performance, reliability, and reusability of complex applications. Typically, when there is no shared address space available to remotely-located components, components must communicate using some form of message-passing abstraction or the remote procedure call paradigm. In both instances, the corresponding support to the application is not included within the disciplined semantics of a standard language that supports type-safe object-oriented programming.

Recently academic and industrial initiatives have attempted to compensate for this lack of support by providing a variety of different solutions. These solutions range from standardizing various message-passing interfaces to language mappings for client/server interfaces. Unfortunately, these solutions often fail to balance the desirability of raising the level of distributed programming abstractions with the predictability of application performance. For example, the use of a message-passing interface may provide predictable performance but its level of abstraction is not conducive to developing reusable components. Conversely, a client/server interface, that promotes a more abstract and transparent view of remote communication, is unlikely to meet the predictable performance required by many applications.

The Ada Distributed Systems Annex, Annex E, provides a solution to programming distributed systems that balances abstraction with predictable performance. An Ada application may be partitioned for execution across a network of computers such that typed objects may be referenced through remotely-called subprograms. The remotely-called subprograms may be either statically or dynamically bound, thereby allowing applications to use either the classical remote procedure call paradigm or the increasingly popular distributed object paradigm. In this paper, the implementation of both paradigms is explained.

1.1 Objectives

Ada incorporates facilities for programming distributed systems as a consistent and systematic extension to those provided for programming non-distributed systems. Thus, the benefits of a type-safe object-oriented programming language that supports both data access synchronization and concurrency are made available for programming distributed systems. Furthermore, the language-defined interface between the compiler and the Partition Communication Subsystem (PCS) makes it possible to use different PCS implementations so as to achieve specific application performance requirements.

A principal objective of our implementation is to provide a timely demonstration of these benefits using the NYU GNU Ada 95 compiler (GNAT). Since the GNAT compiler is readily available for numerous architectures our implementation is designed to be portable. This portability is achieved by secondary objectives to conform, where possible, to the POSIX standards and to structure the PCS as reusable components. In this way, we hope to promote further contributions and refinements to our implementation so that Ada will become a dominant distributed programming language for both academic and industrial applications.

1.2 Contributors

International teams are involved in this project and they have backgrounds in Ada, compilers and distributed systems: New York University, Texas A&M University, Computer Sciences Corporation and France Telecom Universities in Brest and in Paris.

1.3 Paper outline

In the first section, we present the distribution model of Ada 95 and its relations with other efforts in both academia and industry. The second section presents the extensions that have been integrated in the GNAT front-end in order to deal with the Distributed System Annex. Next, we present the interface that Ada 95 defines between the application and the communication facilities and its interests. In the remaining section, we present the global architecture of the system we have implemented. In our conclusion, we present the status of our developments and the research in progress.

2 Design Overview

2.1 Related Work

The increasing use of workstations connected to network servers has popularized distributed systems outside of the application domains that have traditionally employed distributed system architectures to meet high performance and reliability requirements. As a consequence, various approaches for programming distributed systems have emerged to support the message-passing, remote procedure call, and distributed object paradigms.

The message-passing paradigm continues to dominate in applications where improved performance is required. Recent work in developing standard message-passing interfaces such as Message Passing Interface (MPI)[11], and POSIX 1003.12/1003.21 are indicative of the interest to increase application portability without compromising performance. For example, MPI unifies various schemes and defines both the syntax and semantics of a message-passing library. In those applications where performance is not critical, approaches such as the Parallel Virtual Machine (PVM) [1] have become attractive alternatives.

The remote procedure call (RPC) paradigm[3] is a proven approach that has been embodied in the OSF Distributed Computing Environment (DCE) architecture[12]. DCE provides a collection of services similar to RPCs that are to be integrated directly in the OS. This approach is a significant step towards facilitating programming distributed systems, but still concentrates on services that are separate from the programming language.

In contrast to these two approaches, the distributed object paradigm provides a more object-oriented approach to programming distributed systems. The notion of a distributed object is an extension to the abstract data type that permits the services provided in the type interface to be called independently of where the actual service is executed. When combined with object-oriented features such as inheritance and polymorphism, distributed objects promote a more dynamic and structured computational environment for distributed applications. The OMG Common Object Broker Request Architecture (CORBA)[5] is an industrial-sponsored effort to standardize the distributed object paradigm via the CORBA Interface Definition Language (IDL). Mappings between the IDL and different programming languages allow for the paradigm to be expressed directly in the programming language. Currently, several implementations of CORBA implementations exist that map the IDL to C++.

2.2 Definitions

The distribution of an Ada program is achieved through the Ada partition model. Library units may be included in partitions and each partition may be elaborated and executed independently. Partitions may be active or passive. An active partition comprises one or more tasks, whereas a passive partition must be preelaborated and may not perform any action that requires runtime execution. Typically, a passive partition is configured to represent a shared address space accessible to one or more active partitions. The annex requires the construction and configuration of partitions for a distributed systems architecture to be specified by the implementation; our approach is discussed in section 5 of this paper.

The annex defines package categorization pragmas that allow packages to be explicitly assigned to partitions. The categorization pragmas place restrictions on the declarations in a package; in this way inter-partition references, namely invoking remote services, can be checked to ensure that they are permissible.

There are three categorization pragmas to facilitate inter-partition references:

- Shared_Passive which support the shared objects paradigm,
- Remote_Control_Interface which support the statically bound remote subprogram (procedure) call paradigm.
- Remote_Types which support the dynamically bound remote subprogram (procedure) call paradigm; i.e., distributed objects.

In addition, the annex specifies the interface between the compiler and the Partition Communication Subsystem (PCS) in package System.RPC. Apart from this interface and the pragma, the implementor has a large degree of freedom. This presents an immediate benefit as the annex does not prevent the extension of the partition model; e.g., dynamically replacing failed partitions.

The Ada partition model presents several advantages which include:

- Consistency of the distributed application is preserved since all the partitions are subject to the same rules as a non-distributed application
- Strong typing is enforced on all inter-partition references
- Clear compiler and PCS independence is maintained
- Difference between the paradigms for distributed and non-distributed programming is minimized
- Applications may be partitioned for different distributed systems architectures without recompilation

2.3 Design Principles

The integration of the annex in the GNAT system has been done with the following criteria:

- Modularity. We have not mixed low level communication features with the high level communication interface so that our system can be adapted for different distributed system architectures. Our approach exploits the development of reusable software components.
- Portability. GNAT targets a wide range of architectures and operating systems with the help of the gcc back-ends. Therefore, we must deal with various network interfaces and operating systems. In this context we have designed a common interface called GARLIC (Generic Ada Reusable Library for Interpartition Communication).
- Efficiency. For obvious performance purposes, we want to make direct calls to the run time low level libraries and to implement efficient algorithms. Moreover, we use protected types and requeue to reduce the cost of race-free data synchronization.
- Availability. We want to make limited modifications in the GNAT system so that it is readily available. Therefore, we have chosen an approach where code transformation (carried out by the expander) is the major issue. This approach makes it possible for other compilers to be readily adapted to make our implementation available.
- Evolution. The implementation is intended to be used in production-quality applications and to fulfill the needs of distributed system architects, designers, and programmers. What we have implemented is a compliant open implementation that may be extended to meet future requirements.

2.4 Inter-Partition Communication

The RPC paradigm implies the notion of servers and clients. The server offers its services to its environment (it can execute some code for someone else) and the clients call these services. This raises the issue of server localization: i.e., how one client determines the address of a required server. We have discarded the static solutions which are the easiest to implement but which do not fit the programmer's need. We have a dynamic approach which involves a name server that we call the partition server. When a server has terminated its elaboration, it registers itself to this partition server: i.e., it transmits its name and information to reach its services. When a client wants to reach a server for the first time, it queries the partition server and retrieves the localization information.

The above scheme is straightforward and facilitates reconfiguring distributed applications. We depict the various elements of an RPC in Figure 1. In the context of Ada, the Partition Server is also responsible for checking that the library unit consistency of the distributed application is not compromised. It is a requirement of the annex that such inconsistencies in a distributed application are detected prior to execution.

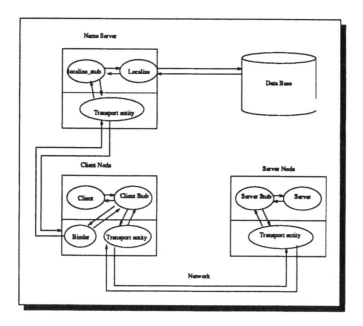

Fig. 1. Remote communication architecture

3 Stub Generation

The distribution directives are provided through categorization pragmas. Using these pragmas, the compiler determines which subprogram calls and which memory accesses may involve remote accesses. Thus, the compiler generates specific code to handle these situations and this is performed at expansion time.

The stub generation is performed by the GNAT compiler and is based on our previous work as described in [10] and [9]. The code expansion involves the generation of stubs as depicted in figure 2. A similar treatment would apply in the case of programs written in IDL (interface definition language) for Sun RPC and CORBA. The code expansion performs the following steps:

- On the client side. The expanded code locates the required server, sends a request with the parameters of the RPC and waits for the result.
- On the server side. The expanded code registers the new server and makes it available to its environment, accepts requests, decodes them and executes the corresponding subprogram and then returns the result.

The complete scenario can be depicted as in figure 3.

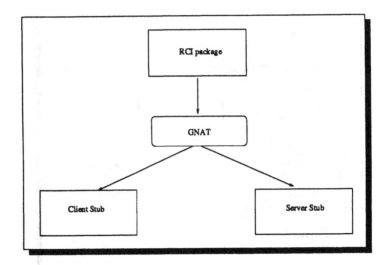

Fig. 2. Code expansion in the front end of GNAT

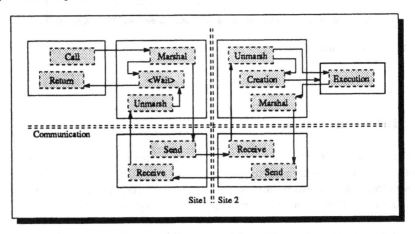

Fig. 3. Involved interactions during an RPC

3.1 Statically Bound Calls

This is the classical RPC operation, and presents no particular difficulties. The compiler is able to resolve the nature of the call statically and to determine the implied RCI package and the requested service.

3.2 Dynamically Bound Calls

Dynamically bound calls are integrated with Ada capabilities to dereference subprograms and to dispatch on access-to-class-wide operands. Thus their compilation requires some additional code expansion activity, beyond that required for statically bound RCI stubs.

Remote Access to Subprograms

For statically bound calls, the location of the service can be determined at compile time; this is not the case for remote access to subprograms. The application during execution may obtain an access value of a remote subprogram, and this access value can then be dereferenced. The previous scheme (the static one) cannot be used as neither the server partition nor the location of the service are known. Therefore, access values to remote subprograms must incorporate all the necessary information to reach their corresponding subprogram. This is accomplished by introducing the notion of a fat pointer.

The annex specifies rules that restrict the use of remote access to subprograms so as to avoid illicit usages. These rules enforce semantics that may be used by the annex implementor. We indicate the principles of the code expansion:

1. The value of an access to a remote subprogram is represented by a fat pointer, i.e., a value that includes partition and server information.
2. All operations on the original access type are replaced with operations that expect a fat pointer value. There are very few cases to consider because accesses to remote subprograms can appear only in three contexts: in calls, in assignment statements and as the expected type of the 'Access attribute. Assignments are straightforward, while the evaluation of the 'Access attribute must construct the fat pointer.
3. Any dereference of such a remote access value (in the context of a call) is expanded to become a remote call to the appropriate partition.

Remote Access to Class-wide Types

Remote access-to-class-wide types (henceforth RAC) appear at first sight to be a complex mechanism because they involve both remote operations and object-oriented features with dispatching. In that respect we introduce the notion of remote dispatching.

RAC types are introduced in the following steps. A remote types package declares an abstract type and abstract subprograms on the type, together with a RAC type designating the abstract type. The abstract type or "5 keywords" type (i.e., is abstract tagged limited private) is the root type of a class that will be used by both clients and servers. Then, an RCI server declares a set of remotely callable subprograms that allow values of the RAC type to travel among partitions. A server extends the "5 keywords" type, declares objects of that type and passes references to these objects to other partitions via the RCI server. Such references can then be used as controlling operands to call the abstract subprograms. This involves remote dispatching since the code to be executed is located on the server partition that has extended the designated type. (A complete but terse example can be found in the Ada Reference Manual.) First, a remote call is performed and then once the server partition is reached a normal dispatching call is performed.

To simplify the implementation, it is convenient to handle occurrences of RAC types as regular access types as much as possible, in order to minimize the changes to the compiled code. The technique is to define the fat pointer in an extension of the original abstract type, and to use a reference to objects of the extended type to designate occurrences of the RAC type in the client partition. In this way, the server code uses a local access type which references a local object, whereas the client code accesses a local object containing a fat pointer that references a remote object. Some of the details follow:

1. A fat pointer is defined in the client partition. The fat pointer stores information on a remote object, that is to say its server partition and its location on that partition, in addition to other components that we do not discuss here.
2. Given that the fat pointer is contained in an extension of the original abstract type, the subprograms for this type must be replaced in the client partition.
3. Given that fat pointers are transferred from one partition to another by means of remote subprograms declared in the RCI server, 'Read and 'Write attributes must be provided for them. The 'Write operation constructs the fat pointer for the access value to the object in the server partition and the 'Read attribute recovers the fat pointer for use in the client partition.

4 System.RPC

As mentioned earlier, System.RPC is the interface to the PCS and is defined as part of the annex. The interface provides only those facilities needed to support minimal implementations; therefore, more advanced implementations are expected to provide additional facilities as child packages of System.RPC.

4.1 Read and Write

The attributes 'Read and 'Write convert values of objects into a stream of elements suitable for transmission across a communications network. Calls to these attributes are located in the client and server stubs by the expander phase of the compiler. Before sending a request to perform a remote call, the subprogram identity and parameter values must be converted by 'Write (marshaled) into a stream. This sending stream is then sent as one or more messages that are recovered into a receiving stream at the receiving partition. The receiving stream is converted by 'Read (unmarshaled) into values that are used to reconstruct a call to the subprogram with the same parameter values.

Before the stream is transformed to or from a message format, any necessary encoding or decoding of stream elements to support heterogeneous communication may be performed. For example, the stream may be encoded into a neutral network representation such as ASN.1. In this way partitions executing on different computer systems may be supported since the Read and Write subprograms implemented by System.RPC in each system may recognize the neutral network representation. Currently, we do not support such a representation in our implementation.

4.2 Do_RPC and Do_APC

These two interfaces are both related to calling a remote service. The client stub calls them and supplies three parameters: the partition identity of the server, and two streams. The first stream includes information to reach the requested service and the parameters of the call; the second stream provides a location for returning the parameters (or result) of the call, or an exception occurrence.

Both interfaces require support from communication services that are provided through other lower level interfaces within the PCS. Since Do_RPC is a blocking operation, it is necessary to ensure that only the calling task is suspended while the remote subprogram is executed. This is achieved by queuing the calling task to wait for the subprogram to complete and for the corresponding notification to be returned. Immediately the notification is returned, the calling task is dequeued and the Do_RPC completes its execution.

4.3 Establish_Rpc_Receiver

The annex leaves the role of this procedure open to interpretation by implementations. It must be called once the partition has completed its elaboration so that a connection between the PCS and the stubs of the RCI servers is established. Unfortunately, this means that it is impossible to call a server before its partition has elaborated completely. This is a potential inconvenience since mutual dependencies between RCI servers that are placed on distinct partitions are subject to deadlock condition.

Our approach is more flexible and interprets the annex to allow mutual dependencies. As soon as a RCI server completes its elaboration, it registers itself to the partition server; i.e., it may be called from other partitions. (To comply with the annex, we may still call Establish_Rpc_Receiver when the elaboration is completed.)

4.4 Partition ID

Type Partition_Id is an integer type defined in System.RPC. A value of this type is used to identify and access a partition. Do_RPC uses a value of this type as its first parameter to locate the RCI server that will execute the remote subprogram.

This implies that partitions have unique values: i.e., the location of a partition can be determined from only its partition id value. This raises the problem of making partition ids unique throughout the distributed system. For this we have at least two schemes:

- A specific partition server maintains a counter. The counter is a logical number that contains no implicit information. The matching between the logical number and a physical partition location (e.g., process number and port number) can be computed through a table look-up; this is a common situation for distributed systems.

- External facilities are used requiring integration of the port number and the process number to create a partition_id value. This information is sufficient if the same OS and the same data representation are used throughout the distributed system; however, this presents a problem in the context of heterogeneous systems. For example, in PVM [1], such identifiers (TIDs) are intended to be opaque to the application; thereby, disallowing attempts to modify or predict their values by the application. This is consistent with the objectives that lead to the design of the System.RPC interface. Another potential drawback with this approach is that it requires arbitrary long integers that would compromise portability.

4.5 Implementation Dependencies

System.RPC is the required minimal interface to the PCS. It offers the operations to marshal and unmarshal the subprogram parameters and to execute the remote call. Nevertheless, this interface is not complete and extensions are required. We indicate additional facilities that we need to implement the annex based upon the experience we have gained.

- Numbering the partition. In the previous section, we have outlined schemes for identifying partitions. In the first scheme a partition server is required together with elaboration code of a partition that requests a number. In the second scheme, we require explicit calls to the operating system to construct a composite value of the partition location. Therefore, both schemes have a dependency that prevents interchanging PCSs.
- Localizing an RCI server. This operation makes possible for a client to determine where the server it needs is. We have at least two approaches: a static and a dynamic one. The static one involves the replacement of the server reference by its physical address as soon as this information is known (at configuration time). Whereas the dynamic one requires the help of a server. In both cases, we have the notion of server information and there is a system dependency to fetch this information or to modify it.
- Establishing a correspondence between a partition number and a network address. In the previous section, we have mentioned two approaches to build partition id in a distributed system. These partition ids appear as logical values and the PCS needs to interpret them to reach the server with physical information (e.g., a network address, a port number and a processes number). We also have here a system dependency.

The above considerations indicate that there exist system dependencies in our implementation but also in any implementation. This is due in part to the limited interface given by System.RPC. When dealing with partition numbers, we need specific services to build a partition id and to interpret it and this is linked to the fact that there is no constructor-selector for type partition id: it is just an integer type.

We consider it as an illusion to build a universal PCS and in this respect the use of System.RPC might appear of limited interest. This interface is restricted since the programmer is not supposed to access it. We can find interests and benefits of System.RPC for the future. For example, in CORBA we have the notion of dynamically built requests to an object. With System.RPC, the system programmer is guaranteed to find the same interface on any implementation and then its extension is portable.

5 The System Architecture

5.1 Configuration tool and language

5.2 The partition server

We have already presented the partition server in figure 1. We have selected this name in order to avoid confusion with what we can find in other systems. We can compare it to the portmap (SUN RPC) or to the Cell Directory Service of DCE. This database forms a kind of a clearinghouse where all the information on RCI servers is stored. The data can be retrieved with the key which is the name of the RCI package.

This server is centralized and it is known by all the partitions. Nevertheless, a client contacts the partition server only once. The information that is obtained from the partition server is stored locally and we have here a notion which is similar to the delegate of DCE.

5.3 The agent task on the server side

We maintain a pool of anonymous tasks that are responsible for RPC-receiver execution as depicted in figure 4. They receive a request from their environment and they execute a service. They also receive a handle so that the client is reactivated at the end of the RPC. The number of these tasks is defined by our implementation and it can be increased to fit the needs of parallelism for some applications.

5.4 The environment task

This task is present on each partition and is waiting for incoming messages from the network. On the reception of a message, the environment task extracts the header of the message. We have two possibilities here:

- the header indicates that the message is a request for a remote service. The environment task selects an anonymous task in the pool, keeps track of it since the execution of the service might be cancelled by the client.
- the header indicates that the message carries the results of a RPC. This message is sent by the server which has completed the remote execution and now the client has to be reactivated. The header contains information so that the environment task knows which client is to be reactivated. The results of the RPC are then placed in the context of the client.

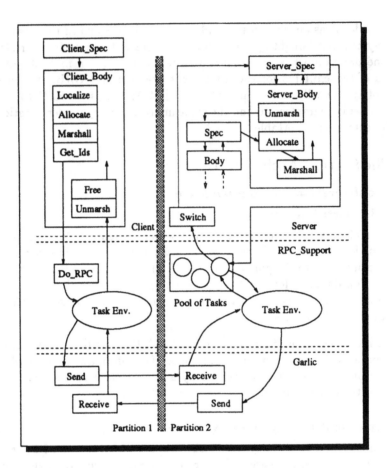

Fig. 4. Our global architecture

6 Implementation Experience

6.1 Target Systems

Network programming depends on the architecture and on the underlying operating system. They constitute critical points in any implementation as they are tedious and also very low level. That is the reason why we have isolated them in the structure of the PCS. Moreover by selecting PARADISE as the low level communication and POSIX-compliant interfaces, we benefit from several implementations of PARADISE on a wide range of platforms.

6.2 Work in progress and planned extensions

For the last few years, we have been working on environments for distributed system programming. Our major target was the design and the implementation of a repository of software reusable components. These components address and implement distributed control algorithms and programmers can tailor them to their needs [7]. In that context, we have been developing components for mutual exclusion, deadlock and termination detection, message-passing for real time applications and the Linda paradigm. We consider reusability as a major issue as distributed applications are complex and modularity is a way to manage their complexity.

Our current implementation targets immediate result and we have selected the most critical elements to be implemented as a demonstration of the annex. That is the reason we have not yet addressed the shared variables in the context of GNAT. The shared memory paradigm presents several benefits even in a distributed system where we have the notion of virtual distributed memory. In [8], we have proposed a new algorithm which implements such a memory and which is suitable for embedded applications. One of our aims is to incorporate this algorithm inside the GNAT system.

Fault tolerance is another concern and we have already integrated in GNAT the recovery block mechanism. This backward error recovery support has been implemented only in the context of sequential programs and we believe that its extension to distributed system would be of interest for the programmer.

The annex leaves any implementor free to add other paradigm. The RPC is of high interest but other paradigms (like Linda [4], Orca [2]) may fulfil the programmer's specific needs. Our objective is to offer several paradigms and to incorporate them in GNAT so that the programmer can select the most appropriate one to its requirements.

6.3 Conclusions

Our implementation forms the basic core for distributed system programming. We have started to investigate fault tolerance issues, reconfiguration and virtual shared memory but numerous subjects can also be investigated by other individuals and teams.

7 Acknowledgements

The authors are very grateful to the GNAT team at New York University and specially to Prof. E. Schonberg and Prof. R. Dewar. L. Nana has implemented the stub generation in the GNAT compiler. The authors are also grateful to Prof. R. Volz from Texas A&M University who leads and manages the ADEPT project.

References

1. Al Geist et al. *PVM : Parallel virtual Machine*. The MIT Press, 1994.
2. H. Bal and A. Tannenbaum. Orca : a language for distributed object-based programming. Technical Report IR 140, Vrije University, Amsterdam, December 1987.
3. A. Birrell and B. Nelson. Implementing remote procedure calls. *ACM Trans. Computer Systems*, 2(1):39–59, 1984.
4. N. Carriero and D. Gelernter. *How to write parallel programs : a first course*. The MIT Press, Cambridge, Massachussetts, 1991.
5. DEC, HP, and et al. The common object request broker : architecture and specification. Technical Report OMG 91-12-1, Object Management Group and X Open, December 1991.
6. E. Schonberg et al. GNAT: the GNU - NYU Ada translator, a compiler for everyone. In *Proceedings of the TRI Ada conference*, Baltimore, Maryland, november 1994. ACM.
7. Y. Kermarrec and L. Pautet. Ada reusable software components for education in distributed systems and applications. In J.L. Diaz-Herrera, editor, *Proceedings of the 7th SEI conference on Software Engineering Education*, number 750 in Lectures Notes in Computer Science, pages 77–96, San Antonio, Texas, 1994. ACM IEEE, Springer Verlag.
8. Y. Kermarrec and L. Pautet. Integrating page replacement in a distributed shared virtual memory. In *Proceedings of the 14th international conference on distributed computing systems*, Poznan, Poland, June 1994. IEEE.
9. Y. Kermarrec, L. Pautet, and E. Schonberg. Design document for the implementation of distributed system annex of Ada 9X in GNAT. Technical report, New York University, Courant Institute, 715 Broadway, New York NY 10012, March 1995. (to be published).
10. Yvon Kermarrec and Laurent Pautet. Evaluation of the distributed systems annex of Ada 9X and its implementation in GNAT. Technical report, Courant Institute of Mathematical Sciences, New York University, 715 Broadway, New York NY 10012, 1994. to be published.
11. Message Passing Interface Forum. Mpi : a message passing interface standard. Technical Report 230, CS Department, University of Tenessee, Knoxville, April 1994.
12. Ward Rosenberry, David Kenney, and Gerry Fisher. *Understanding DCE*. O'Reilly and associates, inc, 1993.

Programming Distributed Systems with Both Ada 95 and PVM

Yvon Kermarrec[1] and Laurent Pautet[2]

[1] ENST de Bretagne
Technopole de l'Iroise
F 29 285 Brest Cedex
France
kermarrec@enstb.enst-bretagne.fr
[2] Télécom Paris
Département Informatique
46, Rue Barrault
75 013 Paris
France
pautet@inf.enst.fr

Abstract. This short paper aims at describing our experience [11] in implementing the distributed features of Ada 95 in GNAT. Our approach was to validate our proposals as quickly as possible by providing the communication architecture and the low level facilities for dealing with distributed aspects. In this context, we have selected PVM (Parallel Virtual Machine) [2], [1] and [7] as our foundation. This early experience was invaluable for our implementation of the distributed system annex of Ada 95 into the GNAT system ([6] and [16]).

1 Introduction

Network and distributed system programming is an area in which software development is often more difficult than it should be [8]. The programmers have to face the daunting issues of synchronization, communication and termination of the distributed application and to deal with low level details (e.g., operating system and network interface). This situation is error prone and time consuming. Ada 95 proposes two high level paradigms for distributed system programmings: the remote procedure call (RPC) and the shared variables. As members of the GNAT team, we want to implement the distributed system annex of Ada 95 in a short time and be able to run applications with a set of workstations as a target. Therefore, our approach is to reuse existing software and to concentrate our activities at a higher level. We have been experimenting in two distinct ways:

- The PVM approach as this software integrates all we need and even more what we really need.
- The approach of reusable software components which aims at interfacing the communication issues.

In this paper, we shall present the PVM approach and our software developments on top of PVM. In a first section, we shall present the PVM system as a tool for distributed programming. The presentation is intended to be very succinct and the interested reader will find more information with the given bibliography. In the second section, we shall describe how we have built our system on top of PVM and how we have been able to test our approach before integrating it into the GNAT system. The third section presents the potential dangers of relying on the PVM system for the communication support between the various processing elements. As a conclusion, we present the status of our current activities and the work in progress.

2 PVM and Ada 95

2.1 Presentation of PVM

PVM is a software package that permits a heterogeneous collection of machines and workstations to appear as a unique computing resource. PVM was publicly released in march 1991 and, over the years, this software has been widely used in numerous domains. In fact, PVM appears as the mostly chosen solution as far as distributed computing is concerned. PVM makes it possible to exploit the aggregate power of processing elements and thus the system can be used as a supercomputer for intensive scientific computations. Other software packages are of interest for distributed programming and now the programmer can select among P4, MPI [13], Express, Linda [4] [3] or DCE [14].

The PVM system is composed of two main elements. The first element is a daemon (pvmd) which runs on each processing element of the virtual machine. This daemon is in charge of PVM process management and catches system signals. The second element of PVM is the library. Basically, this library is composed of user-callable routines which are intended to configure the virtual machine (e.g., adding or removing processing elements of the virtual machine), to spawn processes (i.e., to start a new activity on one of the processing element), to make them communicate and synchronize. Applications programs just need to be linked with this library.

Moreover, PVM benefits from a wide interest of the scientific and education communities and this leads to the development of numerous tools and extensions of the original system. For example, XPVM is a graphical tool which assists the programmer during the configuration of the distributed system and during the execution of the application by monitoring the distributed computation.

2.2 Ada 95 and distributed systems

The distributed features of Ada do not belong to the core language but are placed in the annex. Implementors may or may not offer the facilities of annexes since they are optional. The distribution of an Ada program is achieved through the Ada partition model. Library units may be included in partitions and each partition may be elaborated and executed independently. Partitions may be active or passive.

The distribution of an Ada program is achieved through the Ada partition model. Library units may be included in partitions and each partition may be elaborated and executed independently.

The interactions between partitions can be of two kinds:

- Remote calls. They can be either statically or dynamically bound and they requite the categorization of the library unit with pragma RCI (remote call interface).
- Shared variables. This paradigm is made available with pragma Shared_-Passive and the categorized unit is to be assigned to a passive partition.

In addition, the annex specifies the interface between the compiler and the Partition Communication Subsystem (PCS) in package System.RPC. The interested reader can find in [12] and [10] a more detailed description of the distributed system annex.

2.3   Linking PVM and Ada95

Our work is targeted at the three following levels:

- Binding level,
- Pedagogical purposes,
- Support for the distributed system annex.

Binding level

Up until recently, the Ada community was isolationist and very reluctant to the outside world: Ada was is the universal language and thus the programmer did not need to go beyond the language. An excursion outside te Ada language was considered as a non sense. In fact this attitude made prejudice to Ada itself and thanks to many groups and individuals, several bindings have appeared (SQL, Unix, CORBA, POSIX, for example). Our work around Ada 95 and PVM aims at the same target: to make the Ada community benefit of the PVM system and make the PVM community benefit of the Ada language. Let us now detail how PVM and Ada 95 can benefit to each other.

PVM is mainly intended for the C / C++ community (the target of Unix) and also for the Fortran community (PVM aims at intensive scientific computations). Ada can bring all its merits for software enginnering issues: reusability, strong typing and its numerics facilities. The software engineering issues are of major interest as they can reduce the debugging time of distributed systems (which is quite complex) at execution time by ensuring several checks at compilation time.

Pedagogical purposes

Our students are trained with Ada as the support for programming. Parts of their curriculum integrate distributed system and our research activities target distributed systems and Ada [9]. Our major concern was to design and implement several reusable software components that the Ada programmer can use to build his complete distributed system. Our components repository includes other paradigms for distributed system programming.

The PVM component can be considered as another tool in our repository and this tool offers message-based communication even in heterogeneous systems. Or, the PVM component can be viewed as an interface and thus its users do not need switching to C for their experimentation.

Support for the distributed system annex

PVM with all its extensions are an interesting solution because they form a complete system: from the design of a parallel application, to its execution onto a distributed machine and its monitoring. PVM is also available on several architectures and this makes possible to investigate the issue of running distributed Ada applications on heterogeneous networks. Nevertheless, we have to note that that Ada limits the scope of the distributed system annex to homogeneous systems. The availability of PVM on numerous platforms and systems is very appealing since this may avoid complex software developments by using PVM communication support. This is particularly interesting for multi-processors.

3 Implementing the distributed features of Ada 95 with PVM

3.1 Why using PVM as a foundation

J. Dongarra in [5] wrote : "PVM can be used on its own or as foundation upon which other heterogeneous network software can be built".

We have selected PVM for several reasons. We indicate here only the major ones and their order is not significant:

- PVM exists and has been widely appreciated even outside the computer science community. Simplicity of its concepts, efficiency and also abstraction are its properties.
- All the low level details can be completely ignored by the user: e.g., communication protocol, group handling, Unix process management.
- Debugging facilities do exist and we all know that they are of major interest for the programmer. Also, in this domain, PVM can generate traces of the program execution.

- Tools (e.g., Xpvm, Xab, HeNCE) can monitor the current status of the processing elements and they give interesting feedback to the programmer during trace analyzing.
- PVM presents several similarities with MPI (Message Passing Interface) which is supposed to be the next standard for message based communication. Thus, our initial investigation and experiment with PVM could be reused in the context of MPI.
- PVM is available on numerous platforms and this presents numerous benefits for GNAT, based on gcc, which will be available on several targets.

3.2 Configuration of the virtual machine

The first two primitives of PVM we need are **Pvm_Addhosts** and **Pvm_Delhosts**. These primitives add new processing elements if the virtual machine (resp. remove them). **Pvm_Addhosts** starts a pvmd daemon on the indicated machines. The info parameter is a returned code which can help the PVM user determine why the machine could not be added.

```
-- dynamic configuration

procedure Pvm_Addhosts
        (Host   : in out List_Dyn_String.List;
         Info   : System.Address;
         Result : out Integer);

procedure Pvm_Delhosts
        (Host   : in out List_Dyn_String.List;
         Info   : System.Address;
         Result : out Integer);
```

Ada 95 related issues

These primitives are of interest in our context as they are used to set the distributed system. PVM offers facilities that are beyond our requirements as heterogeneous machines may appear in the same virtual machine. We also have to note that these primitives are called from a running program and therefore we can envision fault tolerance and also reconfiguration.

3.3 Process identification

All registered PVM process are given a number. This number is a a unique identifier of the PVM process for the whole virtual machine. This number is given when the process registers itself to the daemon and they cannot be selected by the programmer. PVM primitives do exist to access these identifiers:

e.g., PVM_Mytid registers the calling process to the local daemon and also returns a unique identifier.

Ada 95 related issues

We shall present the issue of partition identification later in this document. For the moment, we can stretch the similarity between PVM and Ada 95. In both cases, the partitions (and the PVM processes) are represented by integer. In the PVM user's guide [7], we can find the detailed information about coding.

3.4 Process launching

This primitive starts a new PVM activity (or task according to the terminology). The code of the PVM activity can be either a generic code (e.g., the activity is a "slave" and several "slaves" work together) or a dedicated code which is to be executed on a given machine (e.g., the activity uses a resource which is only available on a given processing element). **Pvm_Spawn** is the primitive to be used in either situation. In fact, this primitive supports three levels according to the value of a flag:

- the transparent mode : PVM selects the most appropriate processing element to start the new activity. We suppose here that the virtual machine is homogeneous.
- the machine specific node : PVM selects the most appropriate processing element of a given type to start the new activity (e.g., any Sun4 machine).
- the machine specific mode : the programmers indicates where the activity has to be started.

Other flags can be indicated: e.g., debug mode, trace mode. As a result, this primitive returns a way to access the new created activity (known as task id in the PVM terminology).

```
-- PVM task creation

function Pvm_Spawn (Nom   : Dyn_String;
                    Flag  : Integer;
                    Where : Dyn_String;
                    Ntask : Integer;
                    Pt    : System.Address)
                    return Integer;
```

Ada 95 related issues

This PVM primitive has been used to start partitions onto the processing elements of the virtual machine. We have supposed that for each partition we have an associated executable file. With the help of this primitive we have a way to introduce a form of dynamism and this presents interesting features for dynamic reconfiguration and for expressing the master/ worker paradigm.

3.5 Communication

Sending a message to a PVM task requires three successive operations:

- The programmer prepares a buffer at first. He can either reinitialize an existing buffer (and each PVM task has an implicit buffer) or ask for a new buffer. Also, the programmer can specify the way of coding the data to be transferred and this is mandatory in the case of heterogeneous systems.
- The message to be sent is then inserted in the buffer. For this operation, the programmer uses a set of primitives which insert the various components of the message into the buffer.
- The buffer is then sent to a specific PVM task and a tag is also provided. This tag is used on the receiver side to discriminate the flow of messages.

```
-- communication packing for integer

function Pvm_Pkint (Data          : Integer;
                    Nitem, Stride : Integer)
                    return Integer;

-- communication unpacking for integer

procedure Pvm_Upkint (Data          : out Integer;
                      Nitem, Stride : Integer;
                      Result        : out Integer);
```

Ada 95 related issues

These two operations are not essential in the context of Ada 95 since we have attributes which flatten the data in a stream of bytes (resp. unflatten the data of a stream). Nevertheless, we have used this primitives as the attributes 'Read and 'Write have not been incorporated in GNAT.

Sending Data

The data to be sent are stored in a buffer (the current one) and the data are coded according to the user's specification. The data are sent to a task and a tag is also added. This primitive is asynchronous: i.e., the sender does not block until the receiver has received the message.

```
-- send
function Pvm_Initsend (Mode : Integer)
                       return Integer;

function Pvm_Send (Tid     : T_Tids;
```

```
                    Msgtag : Integer)
                    return Integer;
```

Ada 95 related issues

This communication primitive has been used directly in our implementation. The asynchronous send is very interesting as we can program the RPC.

Receiving Data

Two primitives are of interest. They allow the reception of the data synchronously or asynchronously, from a specific sender or from whoever, with a specific tag or whichever tag is carried by the message. Other primitive exist to get more information on the tag or on the sender.

```
  -- receive

function Pvm_Nrecv return Integer;
function Pvm_Nrecv (Tid     : T_Tids;
                    Msgtag : Integer)
                    return Integer;

function Pvm_Recv (Tid     : T_Tids;
                   Msgtag : Integer)
          return Integer;
```

Ada 95 - GNAT related issues

The translation of a RPC, with an asynchronous send followed by a synchronous wait is the best. Unfortunately, it does not work in conjunction with the GNAT system. The reason is linked to some Unix signals that the PVM system is waiting for unlocking the blocked tasks and those signals are already being used by the Ada run time system. We shall describe those points more precisely later on.

3.6   Group management and communication

The related primitives allow dynamic groups of PVM tasks. Tasks can join or leave a group, communication can be broadcast to all the members of a group. The PVM system handles this management with the help of another daemon which can be compared to a name server. In PVM, a group is referenced with its name (a string).

```
-- primitives which operate on group membership

-- function to join a group with a specific name
function Pvm_Joingroup (Name : Dyn_String)
return Integer;

-- function to leave a group with a specific name
function Pvm_Lvgroup (Name : Dyn_String)
return Integer;

-- returns the pvm task id of  the inum
-- the member  of the given group
function Pvm_Gettid (Name : Dyn_String;
                        Inum : Integer)
return T_Tids;

function Pvm_Getinst (Name : Dyn_String;
                        Id   : T_Tids)
return Integer;

-- returns the numbers of task in a given group
function Pvm_Gsize (Name : Dyn_String)
return Integer;
```

Ada 95 related issues

Group primitives are used in a peculiar way in our implementation. Our idea is to use the name server and discard the notion of group itself. In fact, the groups we manage are composed of only one element. For each RCI package, the partition where the package body resides joins a new group and the name of the group is set to the name of the RCI package (which is unique in the distributed Ada application). The same partition can therefore belongs to many groups.

On the client side, when it needs to make a RPC, the client uses the broadcast facility and thus sends its message to the adequate server. This feature presents potential benefits as no localization of the servers is needed. In fact, this approach delegates the work to the group daemon of PVM.

4   Troubles with PVM and GNAT

We shall indicate here a few points which complicate the integration of the distribution annex of Ada 95 in GNAT and on top of PVM.

- PVM is intented for C where we have no notion of tasks. The Ada programmer has to be aware that only one buffer is allocated to one PVM task. Therefore, concurrent operations on the buffer (e.g., two concurrent tasks want to send data) are troublesome and induce abnormal behavior like message mixing. The programmer has to implement some mechanism for protecting the buffer. We can think about the traditional approaches for mutual exclusion.

- PVM uses signals as GNAT and the intersection is not null as both systems use the same signals. Therefore, signals may be lost. This leads to the impossibility of using synchronous PVM communication and also the group synchronization operation. One way to avoid this is to introduce busy waiting but we know all the drawbacks of this approach.

- PVM supports only the basic C types when preparing a message or extracting data from a buffer. This leads to major difficulty in the context of Ada 95 as the programmer disposes of a wide range of type constructors. One way to cope with this situation would be to consider the 'Read and 'Write attributes.

5 Conclusions

With PVM, we have been able to experiment some distributed Ada 95 features in a very short time. All the code has been compiled with GNAT and no major problem were encountered. This experiment with PVM and GNAT has been successful and also we have isolated the required functionalities we need for implementing the distributed system annex of Ada 95:

- The ability to configure a virtual machine.
- The ability to start new activities on any processing elements of the virtual machine. The dynamism of PVM presents interesting potential that we can investigate more. Nevertheless, this form of dynamism is not necessary at the early stage of our GNAT implementation.
- The ability to communicate with an activity like an Ada partition. The point here is to investigate activity naming [15].
- The ability to handle group and to localize members of the group.

Our PVM work formed the basic components for a group of demonstrations we did in the last Tri Ada conference in Baltimore with the GNAT team: a distributed computation of a Mandelbrot set on a heterogeneous network and the computation of prime numbers. They make it possible to validate our approach and strategy for integrating the distributed system features of Ada 95 into the GNAT system. We are also working on an MPI bindings.

Our work in the distributed system area is going on in collaboration with New York University and Texas A&M University and we have just released the communication components. The complete system is described in [16] and should be integrated in the GNAT distribution at the beginning of next year.

References

1. Al Geist et al. *PVM : Parallel virtual Machine*. The MIT Press, 1994. also available from ftp netlib2.cs.utk.edu.
2. A. Beguelin, J. Dongarra, R. Manchek, and V. Sunderam. A users' guide to PVM parallel virtual machine. Technical Report ORNL/TM-11826, Oak Ridge NAtional Laboratory, July 1991.
3. N. Carriero and D. Gelernter. How to write parallel programs : a guide to the perplexed. *ACM Computing Surveys*, 21(3):323–358, 1989.
4. N. Carriero and D. Gelernter. Linda in context. *Communications of the ACM*, 32(4):444–458, April 1989.
5. J Dongarra, G. Geist, R. Manchek, and V Sunderam. Integrated PVM framework supports heterogeneous network computing, January 1993. available with ftp from netlib.
6. A. Gargaro, Y. Kermarrec, L. Pautet, and S. Tardieu. PARIS : Partitionned Ada for Remotely Invoked Services. In Eurospace, editor, *Ada Europe Conference, Franckfurt Germany*, Heidelberg, October 1995. CNES and European Space Agency, Lectures Notes in Computer Sciences.
7. A. Geist, A. Beguelin, J. Dongarra, and W. Jiang et al. PVM 3 user's guide and reference manual. Technical Report ORNL/TM-12187, Oak Ridge National Laboratory, May 1993.
8. M. Hillman. A network programming package in Eiffel. In Jean Bezivin et al., editor, *TOOLS 2 Proceedings of the Second International Conference*, pages 541–551, Paris, France, 1990.
9. Y. Kermarrec and L. Pautet. Ada reusable software components for education in distributed systems and applications. In J.L. Diaz-Herrera, editor, *Proceedings of the 7th SEI conference on Software Engineering Education*, number 750 in Lectures Notes in Computer Science, pages 77–96, San Antonio, Texas, 1994. ACM IEEE, Springer Verlag.
10. Y. Kermarrec and L. Pautet. Evaluation of the distributed systems annex of Ada 9X and its implementation in GNAT. Technical report, Courant Institute of Mathematical Sciences, New York University, 715 Broadway, New York NY 10012, 1994.
11. Y. Kermarrec and L. Pautet. Implementing the distributed features of Ada 9X with PVM. In *EuroPVM conference*, Rome, Italy, October 1994. ENS Lyon, Universita di Roma and IBM.
12. Y. Kermarrec, L. Pautet, and E. Schonberg. Design document for the implementation of distributed system annex of Ada 9X in GNAT. Technical report, New York University, Courant Institute, 715 Broadway, New York NY 10012, March 1995.
13. Message Passing Interface Forum. MPI : a message passing interface standard. Technical Report 230, CS Department, University of Tenessee, Knoxville, April 1994.
14. John Shirley. *Guide to writing DCE applications*. O'Reilly & Associates, Inc, June 1992.
15. A. Tannenbaum. *Modern operating systems*. Prentice Hall.
16. R. Volz, R. Thierault, Y. Kermarrec, L. Pautet, S. Tardieu, and G. Smith. Ada 95 distribution annex implementation for GNAT. Technical report, Texas A&M University, College Station, Texas, November 1995. to be published.

Distributed Object Oriented Programming and Interoperability for Ada 95: An OMG/CORBA Approach

Zièd Choukair[1] and Yvon Kermarrec[1]

Télécom Bretagne
Département Informatique
Technopôle de l'Iroise
29 285 Brest Cedex
France
(choukair,yvon)@enstb.enst-bretagne.fr

Abstract. This paper presents an implementation in the Ada 95 [10] language of an object oriented architecture in order to communicate requests to remote objects in a common way. Our purpose is to provide the Ada language with interoperability between heterogeneous systems and also with distribution transparency. In this context, we have selected CORBA (Common Object Request Broker Architecture and Specifications) [7]. Different approaches will be discussed before the presentation of the designed model. The mapping of the model is under construction. This work constitutes a pedagogical opportunity to experiment and implement CORBA in order to understand it better.

1 Introduction

In the client/server computing era, the upcoming wave is based upon applications centered on a distributed-object paradigms [8]. The latter helps to break large monolithic applications into more manageable pluggable and reusable components. Due to [8], it seems that the object oriented technology will subsume in the future other forms of client/server computing.

CORBA is a well-defined publicly available specification released by the OMG (Object Management Group) which federates a consortium of almost 500 member companies. It is based upon an ORB (Object Request Broker) core [1] interfaced with clients and servers supplying services from objects. Its purpose is to make remote objects look for the client like local ones. In other words, remote object service invocations will look like local object invocations, the whole distribution mechanism being transparent to the user. In addition, whether the interacting systems be homogeneous or heterogeneous, requests must be processed. This is defined by the OMG as an explicit goal and is called interoperability between heterogeneous systems. The interoperability between two or more systems expresses their ability to cooperate and to deliver requests to the adequate object.

The integration of the CORBA mechanism is fundamental for open systems as it eases the collaboration of object oriented systems with no drawbacks for the user's ease of programming. The new system can act as a server and offers its services to its environment.

The following section is devoted to the merits and interests of CORBA in more details. The third section presents CORBA in the context of Ada 95 and the inherent benefits of this association. The fourth and fifth sections discuss some implementation approaches and present our model and the advantages we find in implementing CORBA on Ada 95. A conclusion and some perspectives will end this paper.

2 CORBA model

2.1 An overall presentation

CORBA is an architecture aimed at specifying an ORB (Object Request Broker) for open distributed object systems. The ORB is an object bus (object oriented client/server middleware) and provides interoperability between applications on different machines in an heterogeneous distributed environment by interconnecting multiple object systems. It is the object interconnection bus and constitutes the cornerstone of OMG's architecture.
Historically, when introduced in 1991, CORBA 1.1 [7] defined an Interface Definition Language (IDL) and Applications Programmers Interfaces (API) to allow interaction between clients and server objects within a specific implementation of an ORB. More recently, the version 2.0 specified how heterogeneous ORBs will actually interoperate.

The architecture is based upon a model which describes an application as a set of objects in mutual interaction but refrains from making assumptions on the object location, the communication protocol or the execution infrastructure.

Each object interacts with its environment by sending or receiving requests. From the client's point of view, each request is sent to the local stub representing the remote object services as if it was a local procedure call. The stub is then in charge to make the request progress in the distributed system and to make it reach its final destination: the requested server. So, the client does not care about how this stub handles the request. Nevertheless, the request must contain a reference to the targeted object-server and the required service in addition to its parameters. Adequate mechanisms must ensure those implicit links and they are referred to as distribution transparency mechanisms. They are composed of:
- the localization transparency which guarantees that the access to the external view of the object is not subject to the knowledge of the localization of the object itself.
- the access transparency which guarantees an identical access form to operations whether the operation interface is local or not.

2.2 Interface based language

Having briefly described the CORBA concept, a basic analysis shows that it is oriented towards an interface paradigm. An object interface forms an external view of the object and describes the set of operations callable on the object from its environment.

The specifications of the interfaces are supported by IDL, a purely descriptive language. IDL was released by the OMG as a part of CORBA and has lexical and syntactic rules close to those of C++. An IDL specification can be implemented in any language providing the means to support IDL data types, to encapsulate services inside objects, to reference objects, to call operations and to provide exception mechanisms. Ada 95 fulfills those requirements.

2.3 CORBA mechanism

The following is a presentation of the mechanism which is in charge of processing client requests on an object server. To be part of the CORBA system, each object should export its IDL interface to all the other sites in order to be visible from outside. This interface constitutes a basis to generate skeletons for server sites and stubs for client sites.

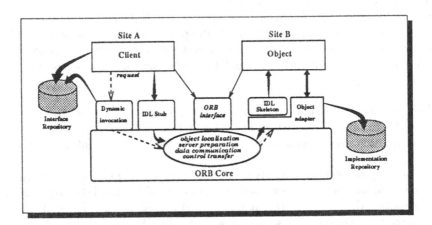

Fig. 1. CORBA architecture

Stubs, used in the client side, are down-call interfaces which make calls to the available ORB cores (see figure 1). Skeletons are used in the server side to pass requests to the object methods and then play a binding role between CORBA and the object implementation. The profiles of stubs and skeletons are identical to those of their corresponding IDL interfaces: the inclosed services and their signatures are the same.

The stub, on the client side, transmits the request to an appropriate ORB in a synchronous or asynchronous manner and this choice depends on the programmer. It is in charge of preparing the remote call (by integrating the information contained inside the object reference and by marshalling the data) and getting the result (result unmarshalling, type controlling and possibly dealing with exceptions).

The ORB-core is in charge of broking requests between objects of different systems using one or a sequence of ORBs. When a client calls an ORB by invoking an operation, the ORB localizes the object server and prepares the request. Then it communicates the data of the request and the control to the skeleton via the Basic Object Adaptor. The latter is an interface above the ORB's core. It supports the particular object implementation, assigns references to the objects and adapts the requests; it also registers the classes it supports and their run-time instances with the implementation repository. The implementation repository is a database that lists the classes a server supports, the objects that are instanciated, and their references. It can also contain debugging information, security and other administrative data.
The skeleton unmarshalls the parameters, calls the targeted object service and then marshalls the result (or the returned exception) to send it back to the ORB core. The latter forwards the result to the calling stub and then back to the client. Figure 1 illustrates the different stages.

From the architectural point of view, we distinguish two main levels: the ORB core and the invocation level. The latter lies on the first and constitutes a user interface access to the ORB's services.

3   Why CORBA for Ada 95

Our objective is to allow Ada 95 users to make use of CORBA programming paradigm. It should be remembered that the effort to bind Ada to "standards" and especially, in our case, to open object systems is supported by the ABWG (Ada Binding Working Group), a subgroup of SIGAda.
Our motivation is due to the following reasons: software engineering techniques encourage reusability of generic and specific software components. The buildings of a complete system can be obtained by plugging software components and by composing them to form more abstract and more complex components. Ada 95 stretches this reuse strategy and CORBA approach appears as an interesting solution to the ever increasing problem of composing and interacting with already existing systems. In other words, Ada 95 needs to be interoperable with heterogeneous systems to meet the challenges of openness and CORBA is a widely accepted support for interoperability. Still, since Ada 95 already proposes schemes for dealing with large and distributed systems, the integration of CORBA into Ada 95 is to be considered as a complement and not as a substitute.

CORBA provides an interface layer so that the user does not have to deal with low level features but only with the application level (see figure 1). Implementing this architecture in Ada 95 provides the programmer with a wide range of facilities to produce portable, interoperable object oriented software and makes it possible for the user to have access to services on heterogeneous systems. As far as we know, there is no such implementation yet.

4 Implementation approaches

The immediate approach is to provide a thick or thin binding from a C++ implementation of CORBA towards an Ada 95 one. The interest in wrapping existing components written in C++ is to benefit from some available software and from the efforts of the CORBA community towards C++. The main drawbacks are that we need to have the use of the code of a convenient available public domain C++ implementation of CORBA. Besides, this wrapping is still totally reliant on C++ features without any opportunity to take advantage of Ada 95 facilities.

So we discarded these approaches to consider the direct implementation in Ada 95 of the CORBA mechanisms. The increase in value is the independence from any other language and the benefit desired from the suitable features of the language such as the Ada 95 object oriented and distributed systems features. In addition, we have at our disposal the free portable GNAT (GNU NYU Ada Translator) [2] compiler; since we have its source code, we will extend it so that it can generate our stubs and skeletons modules. The BOAS (Basic Object Adaptors) and ORBS have to be developed independently of the compiler.

5 Our model

The design criteria are focused on openness, modularity and reconfigurability of the set of involved machines in the CORBA application. Openness is guaranteed by the interoperability requirement, the portability of GNAT and by the will to provide many communication protocols whereas the modularity is inherent to the CORBA architecture and Ada 95 use.

5.1 Compilation and stub generation

Each CORBA object should have its interface specified in IDL to externalize it. First of all, each IDL module is translated into a corresponding Ada 95 package [6] categorized with a new pragma *Idl_Interface*. This pragma indicates to the compiler that the package is to be considered as an "IDL interface". Restrictions on the use of this pragma ensures that only IDL compliant declarations [7] are inside the categorized package.

We are modifying the GNAT compiler so that each such categorized package will undergo the following actions:

- a type verification: since Ada 95 is a strongly typed language, we verify that the only types declared and used are those allowed by the IDL language (see figure 2); all the types used in a package specification categorized by this pragma must be declared inside the system-level package (System.Corba) where we declared the exhaustive allowed IDL types and otherwise inside another Idl_Interface categorized package.
- an expansion code stage: from the Idl_Interface categorized packages, we generate skeletons and stubs. Concretely, files containing the skeletons specifications and bodies as well as files containing the stubs specifications and bodies will be created and inserted into the working directory.
- a binding stage: the ORBs and BOAs modules are developed (based on the Garlic Library common facilities) [5] and bound to the CORBA interfaces (see figure 4).

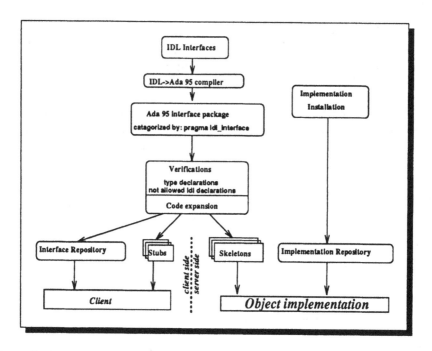

Fig. 2. Stubs and skeletons generation.

For the moment, the translation from Idl written modules towards Ada 95 categorized packages has not engaged our efforts as it seems long and fastidious and does not constitute an immediate necessity for the implementation of the Corba architecture. So we made the choice to edit the IDL/Ada 95 packages directly so that we stay exclusively in an Ada 95 world. Nevertheless, the type verification is done and the stub and skeleton generation is in progress.

5.2 Initialization of the CVM

A CORBA application involves a cluster of machines that constitute what we call the CORBA Virtual Machine CVM. At configuration time, the user enters the names of all the machines belonging to the CVM. The CVM_Names file containing the names of the different involved machines is used to start a cvmd (CVM daemon) on each site.

Each site of the CVM should have the use of a range of skeletons (resp. stubs) corresponding to the services it provides (resp. requests) to (resp. from) another site of the CVM. The signatures of the operations inside stubs and skeletons are composed of the external object reference, the requested service, the parameters (in mode in, out or in out for results) and the context environment if present.

5.3 Object-Server binding

We chose to implement a shared server policy where multiple active objects of a given implementation share the same server. The activation of an object will correspond to the creation of a new thread of control. Each active partition launches its own servers and each server binds with its corresponding skeleton through the Basic Object Adaptor; this server approach helps to satisfy the needs for dynamic creation and deletion of objects. Let us remind that from a client's point of view, there is no special mechanism for creating or destroying an object [7]: objects are created and destroyed as an outcome of issuing requests. The outcome of object creation should be revealed to the client in the form of an object reference that denotes the new object. When the Basic Object Adaptor is notified of the creation of an object, it generates an object reference that should contain enough information to localize and access the object.

Our proposal is to use fat pointers for the object references. They reference information such as site location, Idl_skeleton address and object local address in purpose to reach the object. In the case of the object being local, the fat pointer will contain only its address. The advantage is that we deal with dynamic object localization by avoiding accesses to static tables through the network to determine the object localization. Operations to marshall and unmarshall those object references are provided all over the system.

5.4 Distribution transparency

The object referencing by using fat pointers leads to the following object request broker mechanism (see figure 3):

- When a client wants to make a request on an object, knowing its object reference, it calls the desired service on the local object stub and transmits the object reference and the operation parameters.

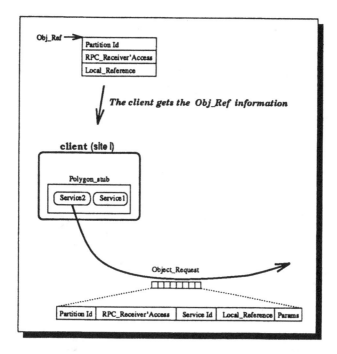

Fig. 3. Client side scenario

— The stub processes the request by unpacking the object reference so that it gets the partition_id of the object server. Then it marshalls the idl_skeleton local address, the targeted object local address and the parameters to send the stream to the ORB.

— Having the partition_id of the server site, the ORB establishes the connection with the server site daemon and transfers the data and the control.

— When a BOA receives an RPC, the first item of the stream gives the local address of the IDL_skeleton. It then processes a call to this local address value (see figure 4).

— Finally, when an Idl_skeleton receives an RPC request, the first item of the stream helds the required service_id.

— The skeleton can execute the corresponding code of the selected service since the object server is already bound to it and the object reference is contained inside the request.

The case of the dynamic invocation on services discovered at run-time is supported by the Corba DII (Dynamic Invocation Interface); the latter makes it possible for a client to determine at run-time whether there are suitable object services available for use. The client can then invoke services on the fly using dynamic invocation APIs. Parameters supplied to a dynamicly created and invoked requests are subject to run-time type checking. The interface repository is useful to obtain a definition of the service so we can construct the request. A

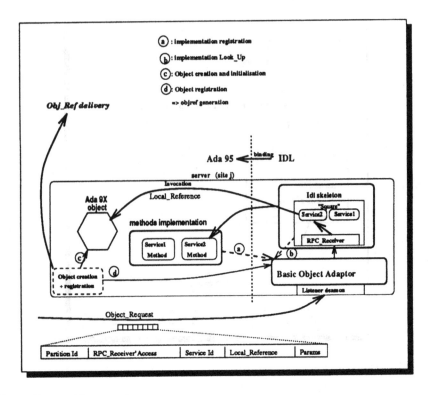

Fig. 4. Server side scenario

parameterized call is then issued to the service and a reply or an exception is received from it.

For the servers, there is no difference between static and dynamic invocations. The same message semantics applies in both cases.

We can imagine the duplication of the object servers, so that the object system becomes fault tolerant. In the case of a server failure, the duplicate should automatically replace the original. For the moment, we have not investigated this issue into the detail, but two policies are to be evaluated. The first alternative consists on broadcasting each request to the original as well as to the clone. The request queues being identical, the clone is able, in case of original server failure, to continue to process requests. It processes the first request, removes an eventual duplicate answer and go through the next requests. The other alternative consists on establishing roll back mechanisms so that we can restart the execution from the last coherent stage. This supposes the registration of data relative to the server entry queues and the object attributes.

5.5 Communication issues

The ORB core is based upon the communication layer. Our first concern is to choose a communication protocol. We will provide the TCP protocol to tackle

RPCS weak performances, but the Ada 95 RPCS will be also available. We chose also PVM (Parallel Virtual Machine) [11] which is a software system that enables a heterogeneous collection of computers to be programmed as a single machine. It provides the user with process control and message passing calls for communication between tasks running on different hosts. The advantage of using PVM is the quick prototyping and also its availability on a wide range of platforms. At the CVM launching stage, the user will have to chose between those communication protocols.

Our second concern consists of dealing with the data representation so that they are correctly interpreted by heterogeneous platforms. Byte organization, data representation as well as the filling mode to extend data differ from one system to another; so before sending data, the client side implementation should translate them into an Xdr or other format and on the other side unserialize them to the corresponding type. Another point to deal with is the standardization of the requests composition and the organization of their items to help different systems understand the items contained inside the requests. This constitutes the Achille's heel of the CORBA 1.2 model for the interoperability requirements.

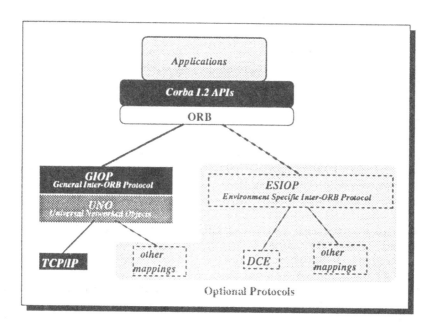

Fig. 5. Corba 2.0 inter-ORB protocols

Corba 2.0 tackle the interoperability requirement (see figure 5) by specifying the IIOP (Internet Inter-ORB Protocol) UNO (Universal Networked Objects) which supports a TCP/IP protocol with exchanges of messages in a common format and a common data representation for all the IDL types. This IIOP is mandatory but optional ones like DCE, OSI, Netware should be considered to fulfill the requirements of a wide range of users.

Our policy is to keep the user free to choose between different communication protocols depending on his application needs (TCP/IP, Ada 95 RPCs, PVM, DCE [9] that is specified by the CORBA 2.0 as the first of many ESIOPs (Environment Specific Inter-ORB Protocol) [3]). The DCE ESIOP provides a more secure environment for critical ORBs that require facilities such as security, administrative partitionning, authentification and distributed time.

6 Conclusion

The implementation is still being worked on and is in its last stages. It constitutes a didactic work to widen its audience due to the simplicity of the implementation choices. We planned to use the future implementation for pedagogical purposes to help teach open heterogeneous distributed systems.

A prime application consists in carrying out a first interoperability experiment between the future product and the HP Distributed Smalltalk [4] which already implements CORBA as support for remote object invocation. The interest being that Ada 95 and Smalltalk are quite different languages.

An Ada 95 user will have the ability to use those new features to design distributed object oriented applications easily and profit by services from remote heterogeneous objects on other systems in various domains from which tasking management, real-time execution, fault tolerant applications, systems management, information management.

References

1. BNR Expertsoft IBM ICL IONA SunSoft consortium. *Universal Networked Objects (ORB 2.0 RFP Submission)*. OMG TC Document 94.9.32, September 1994.
2. E. Schonberg et al. GNAT: the GNU - NYU Ada translator, a compiler for everyone. In *Proceedings of the TRI Ada conference*, Baltimore, Maryland, 1994. ACM.
3. B. Orfali & D. Harkey. Client/Server with Distributed Objects. *Byte*, April 1995.
4. Hewlett Packard. *HP Distributed Smalltalk release 4.0*, November 1994.
5. Y. Kermarrec, L. Pautet, and S. Tardieu. GARLIC : Generic Ada Reusable Library for Interpartitions communication. *Tri Ada*, 1995.
6. Mitre Team. IDL to Ada Language Mapping Specification. Technical report, Mitre Corporation, Objective Interface Systems and OC Systems, May 1995.
7. OMG. *The Common Object Request Broker: Architecture and Specification*, December 1991.
8. Dan Harkey Robert Orfali and Jeri Edwards. Intergalactic Client/Server Computing. *Byte*, April 1995.
9. Ward Rosenberry, David Kenney, and Gerry Fisher. *Understanding DCE*. O'Reilly and associates, inc, 1993.
10. Ada 95 Mapping/Revision Team. *Programming language Ada: Language and standard librairies*. Intermetrics Inc, January 1995.
11. PVM Team. *PVM 3.3 User's Guide and Reference Manual*. University of Tennessee, Knoxville TN, May 1994.

Distributed and Parallel Systems and HOOD4

Rainer Gerlich, Mladen Kerep

Dornier Satellitensysteme GmbH
D-88039 Friedrichshafen, Germany
Phone +49/7545/8-2124   Fax +49/7545/8-5626

Abstract: For distributed and parallel computing the new version of HOOD, HOOD4 [1], brings a significant advantage: it decouples the logical design from the partitioning required to map software onto a net of processors. The HOOD Run-Time Support System (HRTS), introduced for HOOD4, will support an engineer to distribute the software. With the HOOD4 approach a software engineer can concentrate on the required functionality and has not to care about a certain hardware configuration which may have to be changed when he has finished the implementation. HOOD4 tackles the problem of software distribution in threefold manner: Firstly, it introduces clearly defined planes in a design where a cut can easily be done without impacting the logic of the software system. Secondly, the HRTS provides the means needed to establish the communication channels between the physically separated partitions. Thirdly, it allows to provide timing information from which a performance prediction can be derived. This allows to evaluate the performance of a hardware and software configuration already during the design phase. Based on the results of the performance prediction the optimum hardware configuration can be evaluated in advance. The HOOD4 concept for support of distributed systems was defined during the SOFTPAR project [2] by customising approaches for migration of software [3,4] and for real-time processing [5]. During the SOFTPAR project an exercise with this concept will be done for a high performance parallel C++ application [6,7] using tools of the project and a PowerPC network [8] and a workstation cluster.

Keywords: HOOD, Distributed Systems, Parallel Systems, Software Partitioning, Software Design

1. INTRODUCTION

Partitioning of software over a network of processors is a difficult task. Potential cuts must already be considered during design and the engineer must foresee the communication links. This makes the software rather inflexible for repartitioning. Usually, poor performance is detected when design and implementation is finished, unfortunately not before. Then much effort is needed to change partitioning of software.

The problem one is faced with here is well known, but difficult to solve if the following cyclic dependency between design, software partitioning and performance exists:

- the design fixes partitioning,
- partitioning impacts performance,
- performance constraints impact design.

If design and partitioning are not decoupled, one has to spend a lot of effort for another system configuration. Again, whether a change in design will solve the performance problem can only be analysed when one has done the code change. So one has to perform a maintenance cycle in addition, but still the risk not to meet the performance goals when starting the re-design.

A solution to break this cyclic dependency is (see Fig. 1)

1. to make the design invariant against partitioning by introducing a concept which allows to perform the cuts where and when needed,

2. to ensure that a cut has minimum impact on the overall software system,

3. to ensure automated insertion of communication interfaces at the cut planes.

This is the way HOOD4 supports partitioning of distributed and parallel systems. The chosen approach also satisfies (hard) real-time needs because the interface between operations is not changed when an operation is accessed remotely[1] [2].

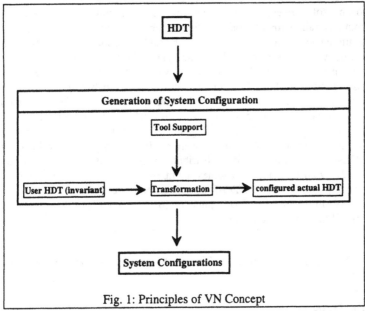

Fig. 1: Principles of VN Concept

Moreover, HOOD4 supports specification of real-time properties now. This information can be accessed via the HOOD SIF (Standard Interchange Format). In the SOFTPAR project a Performance Prediction Tool (PPT) will be established which allows early evaluation of performance of a distributed / parallel system already during the design phase based on this timing information.

The advantage of using the PPT is that one can get the performance figures in less time by simulation. Here the term "less time" is overloaded: firstly, one does not need to wait for completion of system development. Secondly, real runs may need more execution time. So

---

[1] HOOD4 will also cover hard-real time processing by introduction of related attributes for operations. A final decision will be made in near future.

[2] Of course, one has to pay in terms of performance for communication through the network. But by parallel execution several reporting ER's may be executed in parallel so that deadlines can really be met whilst they may be lost when the ER's are executed on a single processor.

one will get the performance figures faster. In consequence, more system configurations can be analysed for their performance.

2. GETTING DESIGN STABILITY BY OBJECTS AND STUBS

Object-oriented software engineering introduces objects as entities of high stability: they encapsulate operations and data, provide a well-defined interface and hide everything else. Consequently, in an object-oriented approach objects are the ideal units of distribution.

The software architecture of a HOOD design is represented by a HOOD Design Tree (HDT) consisting of objects. Fig. 2 shows a sample HDT. It comprises six objects: two non-terminal objects 1 and 4 (including the root object) and four terminal objects 2, 3, 5 and 6.

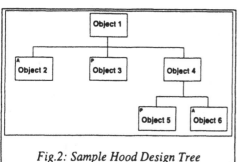

Fig.2: Sample Hood Design Tree

The letter in upper left corner indicates whether the object is an Active or Passive Object. However, in fact the nature of an object can be ignored when partitioning an HDT in HOOD4. So actually we do not care about these letters. In the HOOD4 approach a Passive Object has not to become an Active Object when it is migrated. This is an important step towards design stability: objects using a migrated object shall not recognise that an object is migrated. Design would become rather instable, if a Passive Object would have to become an Active Object when (re)-partitioning a HDT. The chosen VN approach is compatible with the CORBA concept.

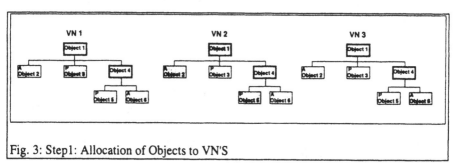

Fig. 3: Step1: Allocation of Objects to VN'S

Fig. 3 shows the partitioning of this sample HDT into three pieces: VN1, VN2 and VN3[3]. The shadowed (terminal) objects represent the real objects available on a certain node, the non-shadowed objects indicate that the corresponding software has been migrated to another node[4]. So we have the following situation for each Virtual Node:

---

[3] We will call these pieces "Virtual Nodes": these are the units of distribution. Seen from an HDT they look like software entities allocated to processor nodes. But they are independent of physical nodes. Therefore they are called "Virtual Nodes" to indicate partitioning of the HDT w.r.t. to units of distribution.

[4] The non-terminal objects have a special status: as empty shells they can exist on each Virtual Node.

VN1:   objects 2, 5 and 6 must be accessed via the network[5],

VN2:   objects 3 and 6 must be accessed via the network,

VN3:   objects 2, 3 and 5 must be accessed via the network.

As some objects are missing in each VN the resident objects cannot be executed. Therefore each VN needs a complementing functionality for handling of remote execution of missing operations. To build a specific environment for each of the VN's, this is one solution. However, this is a solution which makes the design heavily dependent on the allocation of objects to nodes. If a configuration is changed, then the complementing environment on each node has to be changed as well.

But one can easily see what is stable and identical for each of the nodes: this is the HDT which is still completely shown in Fig. 3. So the goal is to keep the full HDT on each node. The object-oriented design makes it easy: when keeping the interfaces of each of the missing objects, we will get identical HDT's on each node, although we do not have available the full functionality. Only by remote access we will get the needed functionality. But that is another problem, we will care about later.

The available objects in each VN cannot recognize the missing functionality of the migrated objects. So they can execute. In an object-oriented approach it is just sufficient to provide the interfaces in a VN. This ensures correct compilation and linking for each such HDT which is incomplete from a functional point of view. The missing functionality can be provided by remote execution, but this mechanism is hidden to the client objects.

The stability we aimed to get we have now achieved by means of stubs, which are (nearly) empty shells. They just keep the interface and a little bit more: the capability for communication and remote access of operations.

The task of a HOOD tool is now, to replace a real object (which shall be migrated to another VN) by such a stub (placeholder) which forwards messages to the remote object and returns its messages. This task is usually not too difficult and can be automated in most cases. What the tool has to do is:

1.   to provide remote access, and

2.   to convert pointers to values and vice versa and to pack/unpack values of parameters,

There may be some exceptions, when too complex types occur in the parameter list of operations. Then a user has to provide operations which do the transformation.

The HRTS specifies which support a HOOD4 toolset must provide for "Virtual Nodes". So a user just establishes a HOOD design, defines the allocation of objects to Virtual Nodes and then asks the tool to generate the code for the Virtual Nodes and adds - if needed - operations for parameter transformation. Finally, a user has to specify which VN's shall be loaded on which Physical Node.

3.   VIRTUAL AND PHYSICAL NODES

Having introduced the principal mechansim which ensures design stability we can now look on "Virtual Nodes" (VN) in more detail. Virtual Nodes consist of a subset of real

---

[5] The term "network" implies direct communication on the same physical node, e.g. by message passing.

objects of a HDT plus a set of stubs complementing this set towards the full HDT. VN's are heavy-weight processes which can be migrated. They include

- the full functionality of their real objects,

- the information visible via the interfaces of the migrated objects, and

- the capability for communication so that remote objects can be accessed.

A VN is executable under an operating system and the smallest unit of migration. By the size of a VN a user defines the granularity of load balancing.

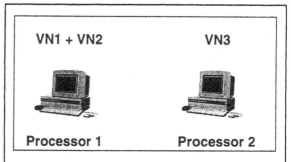

Fig. 4: Step2: Allocation of VN's to Processors)

The fact that VN's are heavy-weight processes is rather trivial. As they represent the full HDT (from a logical point of view), they represent the full system. As the full system is a heavy-weight process by definition, VN's are also heavy-weight processes. They may include Active Objects as light-weight processes if the operating system supports it[6].

VN's are allocated to "Physical Nodes" (PN) for execution. The mapping is not necessarily one to one[7]. More than one VN may be allocated to a PN (Fig. 4). Even all VN's may be allocated to one PN, only. This case is equivalent to a single processor system, but bears some communication overhead, of course. Also, a VN may contain only one object or it may contain all objects: these are the two extreme cases of partitioning a HDT into VN's.

Hence, distribution of a HDT across a network of processors is a *two-step* process:

1. a HDT is partitioned into VN's,
   i.e. objects are allocated to VN's

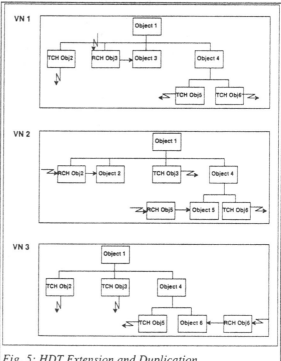

Fig. 5: HDT Extension and Duplication

---

[6] In the SOFTPAR project the operating systems MPI and PVM allow only one heavy-weight process per physical processor. Therefore only one Active Object is possible in a VN. This is the worst case.

[7] This is the reason why we distinguish between "Physical Nodes" and "Virtual Nodes".

2.   VN's are allocated to physical processors.

In HOOD4 the first step is performed at pre-run-time, the second step at pre-run-time or at run-time.

There is a high flexibility for selection of objects. Objects included in a VN may belong to different branches and different levels of the HDT hierarchy. There is no rule limiting the selection of objects. Passive Objects remain Passive Objects when they are migrated. Migration of other objects of an HDT is hidden for the objects inside a VN.

Fig. 5 shows what must be included in a VN: the remaining objects and communication handlers. "Transmitting Communication Handlers" (TCH) take the role of the migrated objects. For VN1 a TCH is needed for Object2, Object5 and Object6. They forward all execution requests to the real object and return output data. "Receiving Communication Handlers" (RCH) take the task to forward execution requests to the objects which shall be remotely accessed. In case of VN1 a RCH is needed for Object3. For VN2 and VN3 it is similar.

A TCH has to provide the following functionality (the numbers refer to Figs. 6-1 and 6-2 where the principal steps are shown in detail):

    T1.   ER service request (source: box 1, OP1 ER)

        a.   parameter transformation (box 2, OPCS_ER)

            Parameters have to be transformed to a single data stream attached to an execution request. Only "values" can be included in such a data stream. Therefore addresses (pointers) have to be replaced by their values. In case of data structures the full data structure has to be included in the data stream. Also for nested data structures all addresses have to be replaced. In case of linked lists or cyclic references this transformation becomes very complex. Therefore a user has to provide the operations for parameter transformation. In simpler cases the transformation process may be automated.

        b.   putting the ER on the network (box 3, Client_OBCS)

            The ER has to be transmitted to the VN and PN where the missing object has migrated to.

    T2.   Reception of results (destination: box 12, ER Termination)

        a.   getting results from network (box 10, Server_OBCS)

            Results must be returned to the calling operation when they are received from the network including identification of the object and operation which shall receive the results.

        b.   inverse parameter transformation (box 11, OPCS_SER)

            Now the received data stream has to be converted into a format which is equivalent for the normal direct access of an operation. Values which correspond to addresses or data structures have to be stored at the appropriate memory places. This step is inverse to step T1a.

A RCH has to include the following functionality:

    R1.   Reception of an ER (destination: box 6, OP1 OSTM)

        a.   getting parameters from network (box 4, Server_OBCS)

The object and operation to be executed must be identified. The data stream must be forwarded.

b.   inverse parameter transformation (box 5, OPCS_SER)

The data stream must be converted to a format which corresponds to the direct call (see step T2b above).

R2.   Transmission of results (source: box 7, OP1 Body)

a.   parameter transformation (box 8, OPCS_ER)

The return parameters must be converted to a data stream similat to step T1a.

b.   putting results onto the network (box 9, Client_OBCS)

The data stream including the results has to be sent to the requesting VN and PN .

Steps T1a, T2b, R1b, R2a, the parameter transformations, are depending on the actually called operation. Steps T1b, T2a, R1a and R2b are independent (or can be made independent) from the actually called operation.

In fact, box 3 and box 9 have to transmit data through the network. Their functionality is similar. So the same object Client_OBCS can be used. Also, boxes 4 and 10 receive information from the network and distribute it to dedicated objects. They can share the same object Server_OBCS, too. Similarly, parameter and result transformation can be allocated to one object OPCS_ER and the inverse transformation to object OPCS_SER.

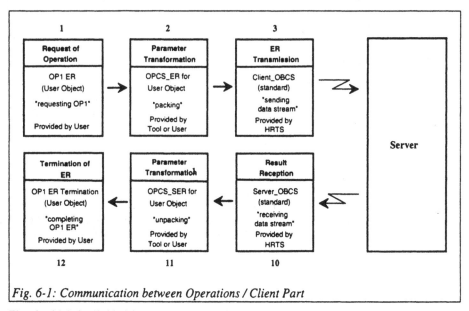

Fig. 6-1: Communication between Operations / Client Part

Fig. 6 which is divided into a client part (6-1) and a server part (6-2) shows in detail the communication and transformation steps.

Of course, network performance may impact real-time performance of a distributed system. However, this is unavoidable when one needs to use a set of processors. But the performance of a distributed / parallel system is surely better than the performance of a single processor system bearing all the load of the complete software system[8].

By introducing VN's as independent units of distribution one decouples partitioning of software from allocation of software to hardware. First comes design stability, then partitioning to VN's and then allocation of VN's to PN's. This leaves a high degree of freedom to the engineer to optimise the hardware and software configuration of distributed and parallel systems.

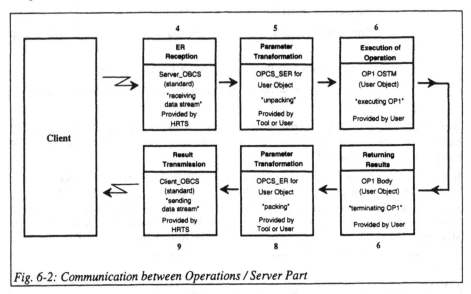

Fig. 6-2: Communication between Operations / Server Part

4.   PERFORMANCE PREDICTION

Performance of a distributed / parallel system depends on the overall processor and channel utilisation to which each processor contributes when it executes operations. High processor utilisation can only be achieved when distributed operations can execute in parallel. Due to the usually highly complex dependencies between operations one does not know if decoupling is good or bad. Therefore one needs to get sufficient knowledge on sequential dependencies.

Objects which use each other by unconstrained operations or by HSER's (Highly Synchronous Execution Requests) can share the same VN. There is no advantage if they are allocated to different processors, but there might be a disadvantage by communication overhead. Vice versa, higher utilisation can be achieved, when objects using each other by loosely coupled execution requests (e.g. ASER, LSER, RASER, RLSER)[9] are allocated to different VN's and different PN's.

---

[8] Communication overhead (at least) must be compensated by parallelisation: this requires sufficient degree of parallelisation and sufficient parallel computing resources.

[9] HOOD4 introduces new types of execution requests (RASER, RLSER) to allow parallelisation with return of results. Therefore we have: ASER = Asynchronous Execution Request, LSER = Loosely Synchronisation Request, RASER = Asynchronous Execution Request Returning Results, RLSER = Loosely Execution Request Returning Results

The problem is how shall we know which objects depend on each other and which do not depend on each other. Usually, the problem is so complex that it cannot be analysed theoretically. Therefore simulation is needed to provide the right information.

The degree of coupling between objects depends on the type the operations couple themselves via execution requests (ER). Several ER types are defined in HOOD4. Some new ER types have been added (compared with HOOD3) in order to meet the objectives of distributed and parallel systems. For derivation of processor utilisation we need knowledge on these dependencies. Also, we need information on the execution time.

The type of execution request, the timing information (e.g. time out, worst case execution time) can now be expressed in HOOD4[10]. Together with additional assumptions on the execution time profile of operations and performance of the network, a simulation can be executed which provides representative information of processor utilisation of the actual hardware and software configuration. This is the task of the Performance Prediction Tool (PPT) of the SOFTPAR project. The PPT shall provide information on the performance of a certain system configuration by simulation and modelling of operations, processors and network topology.

4.1 The User Interface

A user has to provide information on software design and configuration. This information comes from different sources and may have to be defined

- only once,
  -- e.g. the objects and operations during development,
- from application to application,
  -- e.g. the scheduling strategy, or
  -- network properties
     which depend on the chosen processor type
     (transputer, workstation)
- frequently for optimisation of object distribution over the processors.

In addition to above information which is precisely available by design or configuration a user has also to provide some estimations on the timing profile on the operations. This is necessary because the operations may not be implemented when the prediction is needed. If the operations are already implemented and there timing profile is available a user has also to characterise the timing profile by parameters.

The timing profile may impact the prediction significantly. This can be investigated by running several tests with different profiles in order to see what the performance is and if it depends critically on the profile or not.

The approach used for the PPT is that the body of an operation consists of a sequence of local processing in the operation itself (processor time consumption by the operation) and ER's. For better user support standard sequences can be defined and embedded in other sequences.

Fig. 7 shows the PPT interfaces and its principal components.

1. By HOOD information is provided on objects and their operations and the ER's issued inside an operation. This allows to provide information on scheduling, call of operations and operations' timing profile.

---

[10] The final decision on how the attributes look like is pending.

2.   A user has to selcect a certain scheduling strategy, e.g. for hard real-time processing. This impacts the scheduler included in the PPT.

3.   The properties of the actual hardware configuration especially of the network, influence transmission time of data. Data may be routed by a certain strategy through a network, e.g. by dedicated channels between the physical processors, by a bus to which all processors are connected or by another more complex connection like in a crystal frame work.

4.   Allocation of objects and operations to physical procesors impact degree of parallel execution as already mentionned above. This information is delivered from the HPC++[11] configuration files.

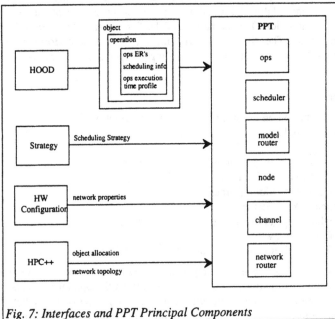

Fig. 7: Interfaces and PPT Principal Components

The components of the PPT are: the operations, the scheduler, the model router which forwards the ER's between the operations and returns the results, the nodes (physical processors) providing CPU power as shared resource for the operations, the channels of the network, and the network router which has the knowledge by which channels the data shall be transmitted between the processors.

For all the components model types are provided which can be instantiated for the desired number of elements. The behaviour of the instances can be customized by parameters.

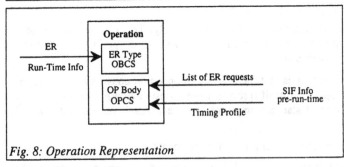

Fig. 8: Operation Representation

Fig. 8 shows how an operation is modeled for the simulation. In object-oriented manner it is divided into an interface and a body. The interface handles the protocol of the ER type

---

[11] High Performance C++

and receives and returns data. For simulation the length of the input and output data stream is relevant, only.

An operation body executes normal statements and issues ER's according to information received from a data file which may be derived from SIF information.

For each ER type a template is provided for protocol handling in an operation's interface and in an operation's body for execution of an ER.

Execution of an operation is performed by acceptance of an ER or its rejection by the OSTM[12] and the execution of the operation body. For the PPT an operation body is represented by a sequence of "Basic Operations" which can be reused by a number of operations. This allows to provide templates for certain timing profiles (Fig. 9).

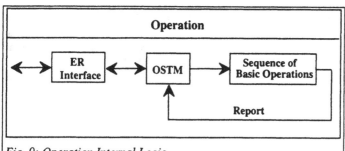

Fig. 9: Operation Internal Logic

A "Basic Operation Sequence" is shown in Fig. 10. The length of the input and output data is relevant only. Such a sequence is represented by "local" execution of code and ER's. The

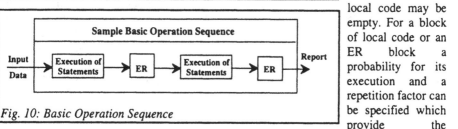

Fig. 10: Basic Operation Sequence

local code may be empty. For a block of local code or an ER block a probability for its execution and a repetition factor can be specified which provide the

capability to simulate IF's and LOOPs. For each block a type is provided: for representationn of pure code and of an ER type.

The PPT is based on the commerical tool SES/workbench [9] which is a tool for performance simulation.

4.2 Results

The sample configuration consists of eight processors and a set of objects and operations which are allocated to the processors. The results evaluate dependencies on network configuration and on ER type. Also, the capabilities for evaluation of communication between processors and channel length are shown. The graphical figures are derived with SES/graph. When the interfaces to other tools are implemented which specifically support graphical presentation of properties of parallel and distributed systems, the visualisation capabilities will become much better.

The system configuration consists of eight physical nodes (processors) connected by three different network configurations:

---

[12] Operation State Transtion Machine which is a Finite State Machine and decides according to the actual state of an operation wheter it accepts the request or not.

1. all processors are connected to a bus
   e.g. workstation cluster (Ethernet)

2. the processors are connected through a network described by a matrix
   e.g. transputer network

   We consider in the examples "virtual channels". A "virtual channel" between processors may consist of several physical channels which connect two physical processors directly with each other, i.e. another processor may be involved in data transmission between two processors.

3. all processors are connected directly by physical channels.

Operations were allocated to four of the eight processors only as a starting point.

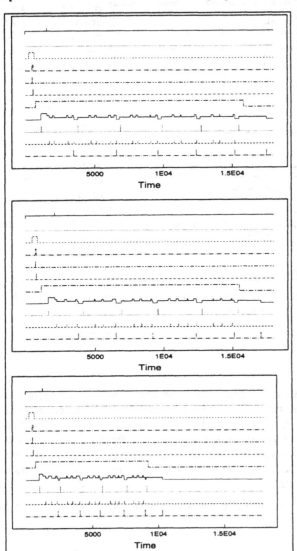

Fig. 11 shows the execution time of operations for the three network configurations and use of RLSER's. As far as an operation is active, the trace is at "high" level, when it is inactive, it is at "low" level. The top figure corresponds to the bus configuration, the middle figure to the matrix network and the bottom figure corresponds to the direct physical connection of processors. In the example the operations have a high amount of communication.

Between the bus and the matrix network there is nearly no difference in total execution time. The matrix network has a small advantage which is hardly to see. In case of direct processor connection the execution is significantly lower (10 000 compared to 18000). This means that the bus traffic is a performance bottleneck.

Fig. 11: Execution of

Operations at high bus traffic

for three different network

configurations

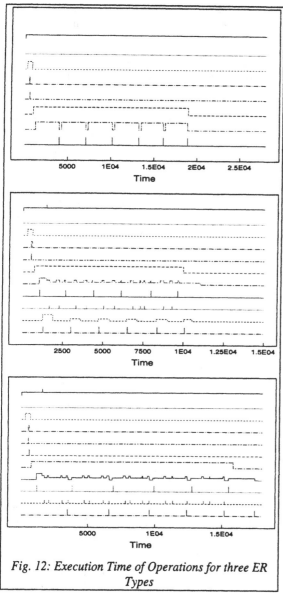

Fig. 12 evaluates the dependency on the ER types. In the example a sequence of ER calls for the same type of ER's (HSER, LSER, RLSER) is executed. The execution time for a HSER is shown by the top figure. The repetition of ER calls is clearly to see.

For LSER and RLSER the execution requests are issued one after the other in the predefined sequence when executing operation bodies in parallel. In case of an RLSER no synchronisation point for a report is inserted. The report is just received when it arrives.

The middle figure shows the results for a LSER. Now we have more traces due to the fact that acknowledges (ACK) and negative acknowledges (NAK) can occur. As LSER's can be executed in parallel an operation can be called more than once at a certain time. The y-axis shows not only that a certain operation is called, but it gives also information on the number of additional calls which are rejected in our case. The steps on the y-axis indicate how many accesses to an operation are performed at a certain time.

Fig. 12: Execution Time of Operations for three ER Types

The bottom figure gives the results for the RLSER. Of interest are traces 7, 8 and 9 (counted from top of each figure) and 9 and 10. Trace 7 shows the number of calls and operation execution (this operation shall be called "OPS1"), trace 8 shows the ACK'S and trace 9 the NAK's. Similarly it is for traces 9 and 10. Trace 9 represents number of accesses for another operation ("OPS2") and trace 10 shows the ACK's from that operation. One can see that the second operation does not reject any request because it has already finished when a new request arrives. For the first operation it is different. A lot of NAK's occur as the operation is frequently called and more CPU time is consumed.

The worst case in view of total execution time is obtained for a RLSER, of course, because more data and more CPU time are consumed for preparation and transmitting of the reports.

The execution state and protocol handling for OPS1 is given by traces 8 - 11. Trace 8 shows the execution state, trace 9 the ACK's, trace 10 the NAK's and trace 11 the reports. The report is extending the execution time sigificantly so that more NAK's occur. In case of reception of a NAK the request is repeated in a loop for a predefined number (user-defined parameter) of events. Between two following requests a delay (which is also a user defined parameter) is executed. As more NAK's occured the time until a succesful reply is higher. Therefore an operation has to wait a longer time and the total execution time is significantly increased.

These results are interesting for two reasons. Firstly, one sees that the report may extend the execution time at high network traffic and high data rates. Secondly, this is an example for a case where a small increase in an operation's execution time can dramatically impact the total execution time due to the number of additional NAK's and related wait delays.

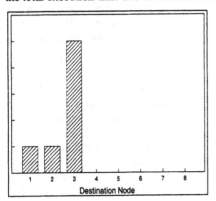
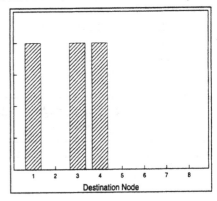

Fig. 13: Communication between Processors

Fig. 13 shows the number of communications from one processor to all other ones for two physical nodes. Such figures indicate how much the distributed operations depend on each other. If processor pairs create a high amount of messages compared to the other ones one should include the related objects into the same VN or allocate the VN's on the same processor at least in order to reduce the overhead for message exchange.

Fig. 14 gives the amount of input and output data exchanged between one processor and the other ones. This is another criterion for allocation of VN's to processors. The amount of data create loads on the data channels. If this load is too high it can be reduced by allocating objects with an high amount of data exchange on the same processor or in the same VN.

Fig. 14: Input - Output Data Transfer between Processors

Two processors may not be directly connected to each other by physical channels, but by virtual channels consisting of a number of physical channels which are used one after the other for transmission of data through the network. The transmission time of a

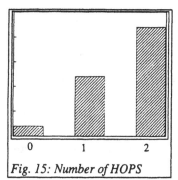

Fig. 15: Number of HOPS

virtual channel is the sum of the transmission time of its physical channels. As can be seen by Fig. 11 such a time delay can extend the execution significantly if transmission times are in the order of the normal processing times. Therfore it is important to know how long paths are really and how frequently they are used. Fig. 15 gives this information for the matrix network. The length of a virtual channel is also expressed in HOPS[13]. The number of HOPS is the number of physical channels a virtual channel consists of minus one, i.e. the number of transitions from one physical channel to the next one. For the bus configuration and the direct connection there is only one physical channel to be used, hence the maximum number of HOPS is one.

Above examples represent only a small percentage of information which can be derived on system performance by the PPT. E.g. response times, number of time-outs, number of ACK's and NAK's for each operation, each VN or each processor can also be derived and presented by histograms, statistics and graphical capabilities of other evaluation tools.

Each such performance information can be provided on an average level, e.g. per processor, per VN or per object, or more detailed for each operation, for each ER in an operation etc. An engineer gets a lot of possibilities to identify which component in the system consumes which amount of time. He can identify on a high level a global source of time consumption, e.g. a VN as a performance bottleneck, and can then look into this component to identify which of the subcomponents creates the load.

5. CONCLUSIONS

HOOD4 significantly improves the support for distributed and parallel (real-time) systems. It shows the way how to achieve stability of design without limiting the repartitioning capabilities and supports it by toolsets and HRTS. It further allows to define and to extract the information needed to predict performance from the design.

This information is taken as input for the PPT. The first results obtained from the Performance Prediction Tool prove that the essential performance bottelnecks can be identified.

The SOFTPAR project has introduced significant improvements to HOOD4: new types of execution requests, the new VN concept, and a proposal for harmonisation of HOOD and hard real-time needs. It has applied it to a C++ pilot application and provides a tool for optimisation of VN configuration.

In summary, much experience was gained in applying HOOD4 for parallel and distributed systems and for optimisation of system configuration. The VN concept of HOOD4 was validated for C++ in a parallel environment. Performance prediction will be validated by the pilot application by end of this year. This makes it easier for future users to apply the VN concept and to optimise their system configuration.

---

[13] A "HOP" is a transition from one physical channel to the next one.

REFERENCES

[1] HOOD4 Reference Manual, Draft,

[2] CEC ESPRIT Project 8451 "SOFTPAR" , *A Software Factory for the Development of Parallel Applications, November 1994*

[3] R.Gerlich: , 1st EUROSPACE Symposium "Ada in Aerospace", December 1990, Barcelona, Spain, pp. 254-272

[4] R.Gerlich: *Dynamic Configuration with Ada*, 10th National Conference on Ada Technology, February 1992, Washington D.C., pp.276-284

[5] Hard Real-Time System Kernal Operating System, ESTEC contract no. 9198/90/NL/SF, Final Report 1993, Noordwjk, The Netherlands

[6] J.M.Letteron, J.Bancroft, K.Wolf, A.Holtz, M.Lang, R.Gerlich, V.Debus: *HOOD and Parallelism in the SOFTPAR Project, HPCN95, Milano, Italy*

[7] K.Wolf, A.Holtz, M.Lang: *High Performance C++*, HPCN95, Milano, Italy

[8] PowerExplorer, Parsytec Computer GmbH, Juelicher Strasse 338, D-52070 Aachen

[9] SES/workbench, Scientific and Engineering Software Inc., Building A, 4301 Westbank Drive, Austin, Texas, 78746-6564, USA

ReverseNICE: A Re-Engineering Methodology And Supporting Tool

Marco Battaglia, Giancarlo Savoia

Intecs Sistemi s.p.a.
Via Gereschi 32, 56127 Pisa, Italy
Phone: +39 50 545111, Fax: +39 50 545200

E-mail: batmar@pisa.intecs.it, savoia@pisa.intecs.it

Abstract. Software systems are often re-engineered for better maintainability, to migrate into newer computers, databases or languages, and to be in tune with an evolving environment. Such re-engineering can extend the life-time of programs in the short term, and in the long term it allows to fully exploit the advantages of new technologies and to fit companies' strategic plans. This paper describes ReverseNICE[1], a re-engineering toolset which supports the process of reverse-engineering existing systems in a HOOD (Hierarchical Object Oriented Design) design. The recovered design, including both source code and documentation, is built according to the HOOD notation, and it can be maintained (both restructured and forward-engineered) by HoodNICE, the Intecs CASE toolset which supports the HOOD method. The current version of ReverseNICE supports only the analysis of the C language.

1. Introduction

Software systems, independently of their application domain or technological basis, must be constantly upgraded to be in tune with an evolving environment; each implemented change could erode the structure of the system and make the following change more expensive to be implemented. As time passes, the cost to implement a change could become too high, and the system could then be unable to support its intended task. In this context, the re-engineering process is a particular kind of maintenance intervention, with the aim of obtaining better maintainability and to facilitate both upgrading and migration to different platforms (databases, languages, machines).

If the system has become difficult to change, but it has a high business value, the best solution is probably to re-engineer such a system, that is to perform the three following activities:
- creating an abstract description of the system;
- reasoning about changes at the higher abstraction level;
- re-implementing the system.

The first activity, known as Reverse Engineering, involves extracting design artifacts out of the source code and building or synthesizing abstractions that are less implementation-dependent than the source code, while the overall process of re-engineering consists of a reverse-engineering phase followed by a forward-engineering or re-implementation phase. This presentation speaks about ReverseNICE, a tool developed by Intecs Sistemi to support the process of re-engineering existing system in a HOOD design. The ReverseNICE methodology is largely independent of the selected target

---

1. This work has been partially funded by the European Commission in the context of the ESPRIT project N. 8156 - AMES.

language, but, since the C-systems market is wide and manyfolded, it represents the best candidate for approaching the maintenance problem by using reverse-engineering technology.

2. The Reverse Engineering Process

Re-engineering techniques, presented in this paper, are specific for the C language and the HOOD method. However, the Re-Engineering process implemented by ReverseNICE is of wider applicability, and independent both of the target programming language and the target notation, and, we think, can constitute the basis for a more general Re-Engineering methodology.

In the context of this paper, the term "Re-Engineering" has been used to mean the overall process of re-designing, restructuring and evolving a system. In other terms, we consider the Re-Engineering process to be composed of three main processes: Reverse Engineering, Restructuring and Forward Engineering.

However, the re-engineering process is not the simple sequential composition of these three processes. Reverse Engineering activities and Restructuring activities, in particular, have to be executed in an iterative way to recover a good design of the system.

A comprehensive re-engineering process, shown in Figure 1 as a typical V-cycle maintenance intervention, is composed of the following tasks:

- *System Analysis*. The main purpose of this task is to identify the components (parts of the system) which will be re-engineered.
- *Component Interfaces specification*. This task is aimed at identifying and specifying the interfaces between the components to be re-engineered and the rest of the system, in order to assure that the re-engineered components will fit again in the system.
- *Component Information Gathering*. In this task, for each component to re-engineer, all the relevant information sources are identified and collected.
- *System Adaptation*. This is an optional task which has to be executed if changes in the interfaces of the components to re-engineer are necessary. In this case the rest of the system must be adapted to maintain the consistency with the modified interfaces.
- *Component Reverse Engineering and Restructuring*. This task is concerned with the restructuring of the code and the recovery of the component desig. It is composed of two sub-tasks, which are usually executed iteratively:
    - *Component Analysis*, and
    - *Component Design Building*.
- *Component Forward Engineering*. This is an optional task, which may be executed for some of the Reverse Engineered components. During this task pending Problem Reports are analyzed and solved.
- *Component Testing*. During this task each re-engineered component is tested before its re-insertion into the system.
- *Component Insertion*. During this task the complete system is re-built by re-inserting the re-engineered components.

The first phase of the Re-Engineering process (reverse-engineering) is language-dependent and essentially involves the parsing of the source code and the storing of the artifacts in a repository. The definition of specific techniques for reverse-engineering components coded in C to the corresponding HOOD design requires the identification of proper code analysis techniques and the definition of the mapping between code entities and design entities. Code Analysis plays a fundamental role in the Component Reverse Engineering activity. The aim of the Code Analysis task is to identify the set of C-entities forming the component to be reverse-engineered, the set of attributes specifying each entity and the set of relationships among the identified entities. The entities-relationships model for each component to be reversed can be automatically built by performing a deep static analysis of the corresponding C source code, and it is the basis to derive the lowest level of the HOOD design for the considered component. According to the HOOD terminology this layer of the design is named the level of the terminal HOOD objects.

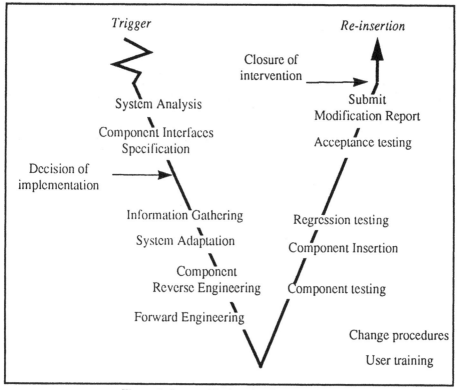

Figure 1: Reverse Engineering Process Model

The logical structure, leading to a design with a multi level hierarchy, can be built from this first design by using both heuristic techniques to group sub-components quite isolated from the other ones, and all the documentation gathered for the component. In fact, both grouping techniques and information available can be used to replace a subgraph with an imaginary new non-terminal object that implements the hidden subgraph and fits in the design. Measures, like i.e. a sort of a coupling degree, will be taken into account to suggest how to collect groups of objects. The aim is to have low coupling among subsystems and high cohesion within subsystems either to minimize the number of paths through which changes and errors can be propagated throughout the system, and to facilitate impact analyses and changes. The final HOOD design is thus obtained by an iterative process of successive refinements.

The last step of the Component Design Building activity is an optional one and it consists in the restructuring of the resulted design to minimize the use-relationships among objects or to adapt it to a new *logical* view of the component.

It has to be noted that the proposed re-engineering process suggests an incremental approach to the re-engineering of a system. A single re-engineering intervention should focus on a subset of the system in order to reduce the risks and the costs. It is generally unrealistic to replace an old system by a completely new system: such a change requires too much resources. A more realistic process of re-engineering a system must be performed gradually replacing older system parts without completely losing the investment made so far: incremental re-engineering is the answer to the need of having old systems with a high degree of understanding,, that represents the basis for long lifetime systems.

3. The HOOD Method

HOOD is a method of hierarchical decomposition of the design in the solution domain into software units, based on identification of objects and operations reflecting problem domain entities or more abstract objects related to design entities.
The HOOD method comprises textual and associated diagrammatic representation allowing formal refinement, automated checking, user customizable documentation generation and target language source code generation.
HOOD has been initially concerned for supporting the Ada language, and subsequently extended for supporting other programming languages, such as C and C++.

4. ReverseNICE Architecture

The ReverseNICE architecture is shown in Figure 2.

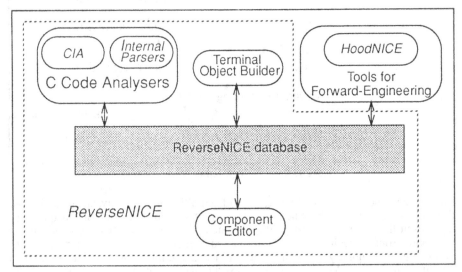

Figure 2: ReverseNICE Architecture

ReverseNICE approaches the re-engineering of C systems as an iterative process of successive refinements. It supports:
• the identification of the components (C subsystems) to be recovered in a HOOD design;
• the analysis of the components to be recovered, both from the documentation and the source code point of view;
• the recovering of each component in a HOOD design, which involves the translation from C to HOOD entities without losing information (neither code nor documents); and the optional Restructuring and Forward Engineering activities.

The global architecture, shown in the figure below, reflects the previous discussion:

- the *Component Editor* supports the description of the components to be re-engineered (sets of .c and .h source files, libraries and other "environment" files);
- *C Code Analyzer tools* access the database, analyze the source code associated to the selected component, identify the set of C-entities forming the component, the set of attributes specifying each entity and the set of relationships among them, and store the result in the repository, refining the initial component database;
- the *Terminal Object Builder* accesses the database and builds the (one level) HOOD design for the component, including both documentation and information about how to re-compile the code re-extracted from the design

Once the design (which can be built in an incremental way, by interrupting the process, saving the state, and then re-reading the last saved state and continuing the process) has been created, *HoodNICE* provides support both for the restructuring and forward engineering activities, including the ability to re-extract code and re-generate the system from the design.

The commercial code analyzer tool we have selected to use is an AT&T product named C Information Abstractor (CIA). CIA abstracts C-language programs into a (textual) relational database and allows both to build new C analysis tools, and to download its database to user-defined repositories; other information abstractors (*Internal Parsers*) have been built to answer specific needs.

Translating Shlaer/Mellor Object-Oriented Analysis Models into Ada 95

Heinz Schneeweiss
Cadre Technologies GmbH
Arnikastraße 2
85635 Höhenkirchen

V. Amiot (Thompson Software Products,Inc)
O. Vix   (Thompson Software Products,SA)
Dr.Peter.Dencker
Thompson Software Products
Kleinoberfeld 7
76135 Karlsruhe

Abstract: This paper introduces the Shlaer/Mellor Object-Oriented Analysis(OOA) and Recursive Design (RD) Method together with a possible translation of Shlaer&Mellor Models into Ada 95. Because of the rigourous and formal approach and of the work-partitioning possibilities, the Shlaer/Mellor Method is suitable for large Ada-Projects.

1 The Shlaer/Mellor Method - An Introduction

The Shlaer/Mellor Method has developed over the last couple of years. The Method has been used in many real-world project of all types.(including Space and Aircraft Projects in Europe and USA)
The Method requires to specify a tightly integrated set of models in a complete, consistent and unambigous way.

The major steps of the Shlaer/Mellor Method are:

1) Partition into Domains
2) Analyze the Application Domain
3) Extract requirements for the Server Domains
4) Analyze the Server Domains
5) Specify the Architectural Domain Components
6) Build the architectural components (Templates)
7) Populate the Templates by translating the models of each domain

Ste· 1: Partition into Domains

This step is the first step in the method. Purpose of this step is to separate the System to be developed into several Domains. A Domain is a distinct, independent subject matter of the System to be built. Domains can be classified

> as **Application Domain** (the system from the user's perspective)
> as **Service Domains** (more or less generic services),
> as **Architectural Domain** (defines Control/Data aspects of the System- the System Architecture)
> as **Implementation Domain** (Operating_System, Database, Programming Language)

The Domains are organized in a Client-Server-Relationship, so that a Domain acting as client can rely on a server Domain to provide commonly-needed mechanisms and services. The result of this step is the Domain-Chart, showing all identified Domains plus the Client-Server Relationships between these Domains, the so-called "Bridges".
A textual description of Domains and Bridges completes the Work-Products for this step.

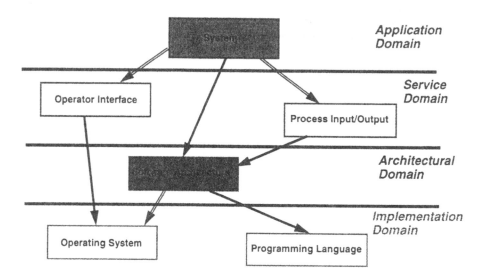

FIGURE 1: Domain Chart

If a Domain is too large, the Domain could be further partitioned into Subsystems. Subsystems should be small enough to be analyzed by a small team of analysts. The relationship between all Subsystems within one Domain is shown by the following set of diagrams:

- *Subsystem Relationship Diagram*
  This diagram shows the data relationship between the subsystems.
- *Subsystem Communication Diagram*
  This diagram shows the event communication between the subsystems.
- *Subsystem Access Model*
  This diagram shows the data access between the subsystems.

Ste₁ 2: Analyze the Application Domain

In this step the **Application Domain** is being analyzed. The result of this step is an **Information Model, State Models and Process Models,** i.e. three separate but fully integrated OOA Models.

There is only **one Application Domain.**

1) The Information Model

This model defines the objects of the Domain including the object attributes and the relationship between the objects in the Domain. Attributes are either *Ordinary Attributes* (i.e. descriptive or naming attributes) or *Referential Attributes*, which are used to tie instances of objects together.

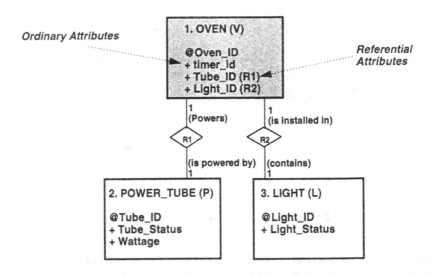

FIGURE 2 : **Example of an Information Model**

The Shlaer/Mellor-Method defines one special predefined object, the so-called **TIMER**-Object, whose *attributes* are:

- *Timer ID:* An identifier for the Timer itself
- *Time remaining:* The amount of time that must pass before the Timer fires
- *Event Label:* Label of an *Event* to be generated when the Timer fires
- *Instance ID:* An identifier to be passed with the generated *event*

2) The State Models

A State Model is defined for each object **on the Information Model** showing the behavior of the object (the object lifecycle).
State Models are finite state machines (MOORE Machines)

3) The Process Model

This Model specifies the processing required **by the State Models**. There is one **Action Data Flow Diagram** for each state of each **object`s lifecycle.**
There are the following fundamental types of processes:

- Accessors
- *Create Accessor*   *(creates a new instance of an object)*
- *Read Accessor*   *(reads attributes of a single object)*
- *Write Accessor*   *(writes attributes of a single object)*
- *Delete Accessor* *(deletes an instance)*

- Event Generators *(produces one event, the event generator is assigned to the object to which the output event is directed)*

- Transformations *(a computation, e.g. convert a temperature)*

-Tests   *(tests a condition)*

An Object may also have an *Assigner State Model* similar to its regular *instance state model:*
some rules exist as to where the fundamental processes should be assigned (either to the *instance state model* or to the *assigner state model)*
The *Accessors* are assigned to the *instance state model. Transformations* and *Tests* are assigned to the state model in which they occur (*instance or assigner state model*). *Event Generators* are assigned to the state model that receives the generated event.

According to Shlaer/Mellor, the Analysis is finished, if the model executes properly. Thus after applying external stimulis to the Model, e.g. events, a proper reaction of all involved State Machines and Process Models must be guaranteed.

Two kind of Diagrams, the **Object Communication Diagram** (asynchronous event communication) and the **Object Access Diagram** (synchronous data access between objects) are „derived", i.e. the information in the 3 basic models - the *Information Model*, the *State Model* and the *Process Model* - is extracted to form these Diagrams to give an important, additional view of the communication between the individual objects.
An additional **Event List** is used to show all events being sent within and/or between State Models .
CASE-Tools supporting the Shlaer/Mellor Method should be able to generate these diagrams plus the Event List automatically, after the user has entered the basic models.

Step 3: Extract re uirements for the Server Domains

In this step the requirements for the server Domains (one or several) are extracted from the analysis models of the Application Domain. Server Domains are usually highly reuseable. Examples are User Interface, I/O-Handling, Mathematical Routines, a.s.o.

Step 4: Analyze the Server Domains

This step finalizes the analysis of the remaining Domains, i.e. generating the appropriate models (Information Model, State Model, Process Model).

Step 5: Specify the Architectural Domain

This is usually the final Domain to be treated. The Architectural Domain should

  - specify generic mechanisms and structures for managing data, function
    and control for the system as a whole and
  - defines the translation of the OOA Models into these mechanisms and
    structures

In specifying this Domain, issues such as available combinations of languages, operating system aspects, performance requirements for data access and event transmission, multitasking and synchronization requirements must be considered.
The Architecture must not be necessarily an object-oriented one. The Method has been used already for several projects with non OO - Architectures. (e.g. Ada Projects in Europe and USA, Implementation in C, a.s.o.)

Ste⋅ 6: Build the Mechanisms and Templates (the Architectural Components)

In this step, two separate types of components, mechanisms and structures, are specified. Mechanisms define architecture specific capabilities such as Classes for Finite State Machine Implementation, Object Communication Events and Timers. (for a typical Object-Oriented Design). These Mechanisms are built in traditional manner by designing and implementing code.

Structures define how OOA-Models of the client Domains (Application, Server) will be translated into the Architectural Components.

Step 7: Populate the Templates

Translate the models into the templates, i.e. populate the **"Architectural Templates"** with the analysis results of the individual Domains.

2 Object Oriented Features in Ada95

The object-oriented features of Ada95 revolve around the notion of tagged types[1] (necessarily record types).

An example of such types is

```
package Foo is

    type Rec is tagged record
        Name := String (1..8);
    end record;

    procedure Method (On : Rec);

end  Foo;
```

the type Rec can be further extended in components and operations as follows:

```
with Foo;
package My_Foo is

    type Colors is (Red, Green, Blue);

    type Rec is new Foo.Rec with  record
```

---

[1] Note: underlines are used in this document to denote Ada technical terms.

```
      Color : Colors;
   end record;

   procedure Method (On : Rec);

end My_Foo;
```

Since My_Foo.Rec is <u>derived</u> from Foo.Rec, it inherits from it all the Operations (Methods) defined for Foo.Rec. Conceptually it may be convenient - for the use of the Object-Oriented features of Ada95 for the mapping of Shlaer & Mellor Method - to merge the notion of <u>package</u> and (<u>tagged</u>) <u>type</u> to give birth to an *Object*. In Ada95 - this is a legacy of Ada83 - there is no notion <u>package</u> 'Object' - a weak form of this may however be <u>generic</u> <u>packages</u> (with or without parameters) ; hence, it is useful to adopt the following convention:

```
package Foo is

   type Foo is tagged record
      Name := String (1..8);
   end record;

   procedure Method (On : Foo);

end  Foo;
```

whereby the name of the <u>tagged type</u> is the same as the one of the package.

Some other Ada95 feature that would prove useful is the availability of a new <u>attribute</u> for subprograms namely 'Access for the implementation of the automaton/transition table. Whereby an event may toggle the state of an object and trigger some action.

```
package Door is
   type Door_States is (Opened, Closed);
   type Door is tagged ...;
      ...
end Door;

package Light is
   type Illumination is (On, Off);
   type Light is tagged ...;
      ...
end Light;


package body Light is
   -- Action prototype
   procedure Action (Object : in out Light) is
```

```
begin
    ...;
end Action;
type AA is access procedure (Object : in out Light);
type Action_List;
type Action_Node is record
    Action :  AA;
    Next   :  Action_List;
end record;
type Action_List is access  Action_Node;
type Actioned_States is record
    State : Illumination;
    Action :  Action_List;
end record;

State_Model : constant array (Event_Index, Action_Index)
of  Actioned_States           := (...);
end Light;
```

3 Mapping of Shlaer & Mellor onto Ada95

To discriminate the technical terms of Shlaer and Mellor from those of Ada the following convention was used: italics to denote OOA/Shlaer & Mellor technical terms to distinguish them from Ada technical terms, underlines to mark Ada technical terms.

The translation of the mechanism of the Shlaer & Mellor-Method hinges around the translation of the following **key elements**:

- *Objects*
- *Attributes*
    - Ordinary Attributes
    - Referential Attributes
- *Events*
    - Creation Events
    - Received Instance Events
    - Received Assigner Events
- *State Models*

3.1 Objects

The following mapping is performed:

Object ⇒ Ada package containing tagged private type with the same name

Each OOA object is mapped to an Ada package (containing tagged private type with the same name).
e.g.

> **package** Foo **is**
>
> > **type** Foo (D : Data_Items) **is tagged private**;
> > **type** All_Foos **is access all** Foo'Class;

3.2 Attributes

The *attributes* are usually either

> - Ordinary attributes   (i.e. Descriptive Attributes or Naming Attributes)
> or
> - Referential attributes   (to tie an instance of one object to the instance of
>   another object)

3.2.1 Ordinary Attributes

The following mapping is performed:

Ordinary Attributes ⇒ Component of the tagged private type

Each ordinary attribute is mapped to a component in the corresponding tagged private type (remember a tagged type is always a record type). The name of the component is the same as the *attribute* name. The type of the component is the same as the Domain property of the *attribute*, except for the domain Id. Domain Id corresponds to a system-defined arbitrary identifier that carries no user distinguishable data, and that can be used during recursive design in any manner appropriate to the target architecture and implementation language. Ordinary *attributes* of Domain Id are ignored in this mapping, an access to the object is implied.

Attributes of Domain 'same as object.attribute' are converted to the Domain of object.attribute.

3.2.2 Referential Attributes

The following mapping is performed:

> **Referential Attributes ⇒**   **Component of the tagged private type,
>   itself an access to another tagged private
>   type**

Each *referential attribute* is mapped to a <u>component</u> of the corresponding <u>tagged type</u>. The name of the <u>record</u> <u>component</u> is the same as the *attribute* name. The type of the <u>component</u> is <u>access</u> to referenced object. Although the Domain property of the referential attribute is ignored, it should be 'same as referenced_object.preferred_identifier'. A consequence of using <u>accesses</u> to implement *referential attributes* is that the *attribute* cannot be used to formalize more than one relationship (an access cannot designate more than one object at a time), and referential attributes cannot be composite. This is easily achieved by using attributes of Domain Id as preferred identifiers, and using these preferred identifiers in formalizing relationships.

3.3 Events

The *events* come in three flavors:

- ***Creation events*** (trigger the creation of a new object)
- ***Received instance events*** (affect the state of a previously created object, triggers an action)
- ***Assigner events*** (modify a state model)

3.3.1 Creation Events

The fundamental mapping is the following:

Creation Event ⇒ Package/Tagged type elaboration

Each creation event received by an object is implemented via the evaluation of an <u>allocator</u> returning an access to a <u>tagged private type</u> of the corresponding Ada package whose name is the same as the event label. The event data items may be passed as <u>constraint</u> to a <u>discriminated tagged private (record) type</u> in full Ada95.

The implementation of the creation event allocates an object. Dispatching to the creation state as specified on the object's state model is performed explicitly by the user main program.

e.g.,

New_Instance : All_Foos;

New_Instance := **new** Foo.Foo'(D => Data_Item);

further initialization may follow.

3.3.2 Received Instance Event

The following mapping is performed:

Received Instance Event ⇒ visible procedure of the Ada package

Each non-creation, non-assigner *event* received by an object is mapped to a public procedure of the corresponding Ada package whose name is the same as the event label, and whose parameters are the same as the event data items, except for the first parameters.

The implementation of the received event determines the next state given the current state and event number, then calls the corresponding state action function.

3.3.3 Received Assigner Event

The following mapping is proposed:

Received Assigner Event ⇒ visible procedure of the Ada package

The corresponding 'Access may be used in the implementation of the package body for the object on which the event applies.

3.4 State Model

The automation/Transition table is mapped as follows:

State Model ⇒ Data structures in Ada package body

The state model for an object is mapped to the package body data containing states, events, and state transition arrays. This allows the state model to be shared by all objects of the package tagged private type, and eliminates the need for initialization functions to set up the state model. Each object has its own component for its current state.

The *states* are implemented as members of an enumeration type, tracing upon switching to a state is determined by the value of a Boolean, these Booleans are stored in an array indexed by the state; the association with the action subprogram is achieved through accesses to procedures (should this feature not be present in a particular implementation, a dispatcher subprogram implementing the association with the action subprograms can be automatically generated).

The *events* are implemented as members of an enumeration type, tracing of this event is made according to the value of a Boolean stored in an array indexed by the event; the association with the event subprogram is achieved through accesses to procedures (and again a dispatcher subprogram can be generated if need be).

The *state transitions* are stored in a two dimensional array indexed by the state and the event containing the next state. Using an array for the state transitions wastes some space due to ignored or undefined transitions, but eliminates the need for searching lists for the next state and is much more efficient. The amount of space wasted is usually small considering the size of most state models, the number of undefined or ignored transitions, and the size of the index type used to represent the state.

Assigner state models are handled exactly the same way, except the current state is also part of the Ada package body data. This is because there is only *one assigner state model* for all the declared objects. An object that has both an active state model and an assigner state model has two sets of arrays for defining the active state model and assigner state model.

3.5 Actions

The mapping for actions is performed as follows:

Actions ⇒ Package Body Procedure

Each state of the state model for an active object is translated into a package body level procedure of the corresponding Ada package, whose name is the same as the state name, and whose parameters are the same as the event data items. This procedure represents the actions that are to be performed when the object transitions into this state. The dispatching is done either using the stored accesses to procedures or explicitly through a dispatching procedure. Assigner state model actions are translated similarly, as package body level procedure.

Note: In the model version, the implementation of the state action function is generated by copying the contents of the state action from the OOA model into the body.

4 Conclusion

Shlaer/Mellor is a very strict OO-Method with strong formal aspects and many guidelines.
In addition, Domain and Subsystem Concepts are offered making the Method suitable for medium to large-sized projects.
A translation to Ada95, according to the defined mapping rules, is possible and shows an ideal implementation of Object-Oriented Design and Analysis Models. The process of translating OOA-Models can be performed by Tools.

References

1 Shlaer/Mellor
   Object-Lifecycles - Modelling the World in States
   Prentice Hall

2 Shlaer/Mellor
   Object-Oriented Systems Analysis - Modelling the World in Data
   Prentice Hall

3 Ada 95 Reference Manual: Language and Standard Libraries

Appendix

The excerpt of code below shows a partial application of the ideas developed in the current paper and are part of a complete working environment.

Several packages/procedures are listed:
- Oven package specification and body (**automatically generated by a translator**)
- RunOvenApplication (**the main program, manually written**)

Note, because of the lack of accesses to subprograms, a dispatching procedure is automatically created in Oven package body. (The same kind of technique could be used to emulate some other needed features in Ada83.)

```
----------------------------------------------------------------------
--
-- MODULE: OVEN
--
-- SYNOPSIS:
--    ADA95 Package specification for OOA Object OVEN
--    From domain: OOA_Microwave_SMcode.OvenApp
--
--    This file was generated by ooa2ada9x
----------------------------------------------------------------------


with ActiveInstance;
with Timer;
with Light;
with Power_Tube;


----------------------------------------------------------------------
--
-- PACKAGE: OVEN
--
-- SYNOPSIS:
--    A Microwave Oven
--
----------------------------------------------------------------------

package OVEN is

    Name : constant String := "Oven";

    type Oven_State_Set is    (NONEXISTANT, Idle_With_Door_Closed,
                               Initial_Cooking_Period, Cooking_Period_Extended,
```

Cooking_Complete, Idle_With_Door_Open,
Cooking_Interrupted, IGNORE);

   subtype OvenStatus **is** Oven_State_Set **range** Idle_With_Door_Closed ..
Cooking_Interrupted;

   type Oven_Event_Set **is** (V1,V4,V2,V3);

   package Oven_Instance **is new** ActiveInstance (Object_Name   => Name,
                                                         State_Set   => Oven_State_Set,
                                                         Event_Set   => Oven_Event_Set);

   package Oven_Timer **is new** Oven_Instance.CallableInstance (Caller => Timer.Timer);

--
-- Type: OVEN
--
----

   type OVEN **is new** Oven_Instance.ActiveInstance **with private**;

   type All_OVEN **is** access **all** OVEN;
   type All_Timer **is** access **all** Oven_TIMER.CallableInstance;

   -- Default Accessor Functions

   function GetTimer_ID (O : OVEN) **return** All_Timer;

   procedure allocate_Timer_ID(O : **access** OVEN);

   function GetTube_ID (O: OVEN) **return** Power_Tube.ALL_Power_Tube;
   procedure SetTube_ID (O: **in out** OVEN; value: Power_Tube.ALL_Power_Tube);

   function GetLight_ID (O: OVEN) **return** Light.ALL_Light;
   procedure SetLight_ID (O: **in out** OVEN; value: Light.ALL_Light);

   -- Received Instance Events

   procedure V1 (O: **in out** OVEN);
   procedure V4 (O: **in out** OVEN);
   procedure V2 (O: **in out** OVEN);
   procedure V3 (O: **in out** OVEN);

```
    procedure event_dispatch    (O      : in out OVEN;
                                 Event  : Oven_Event_Set);

private

    type OVEN is new Oven_Instance.ActiveInstance with
        record
            -- Object attributes (referential)
            timer_acc    : All_Timer;
            Tube_ID      : Power_Tube.All_POWER_TUBE;
            Light_ID     : Light.ALL_LIGHT;
        end record;

end OVEN;
```

```
-----------------------------------------------------------------------
--
-- MODULE: OVEN
--
-- SYNOPSIS:
--    Implementation of OOA Object OVEN
--    From domain: OOA_Microwave_SMcode.OvenApp
--
--    This file was generated by ooa2ada9x
-----------------------------------------------------------------------


with POWER_TUBE;
with LIGHT;
with Timer;

package body OVEN is

     subtype Oven_State_Width is Positive range 1 .. Oven_State_Set'Width;
     subtype Oven_Event_Width is Positive range 1 .. Oven_Event_Set'Width;

     type Oven_State_String is new String (Oven_State_Width);
     type Oven_Event_String is new String (Oven_Event_Width);

     State_Model: Oven_Instance.StateTransitionTable := (

     NONEXISTANT              => (IGNORE,                    IGNORE,           IGNORE,
     IGNORE),
     Idle_With_Door_Closed    => (Initial_Cooking_Period,    IGNORE,           IGNORE,
     Idle_With_Door_Open),
     Initial_Cooking_Period   => (Cooking_Period_Extended,   IGNORE,           Cooking_Complete,
     Cooking_Interrupted),
     Cooking_Period_Extended  => (Cooking_Period_Extended,   IGNORE,           Cooking_Complete,
     Cooking_Interrupted),
     Cooking_Complete         => (IGNORE,                    IGNORE,                  IGNORE,
     Idle_With_Door_Open),
     Idle_With_Door_Open      => (IGNORE,                    Idle_With_Door_Closed,   IGNORE,
     IGNORE),
     Cooking_Interrupted      => (IGNORE,                    Idle_With_Door_Closed,   IGNORE,
     IGNORE),
     IGNORE                   => (NONEXISTANT,               NONEXISTANT,      NONEXISTANT,
     NONEXISTANT));

     -- Forward declarations for dispatchers

     procedure action_dispatch (O: in out OVEN);

     -----------------------------------------------------------------
     function GetTimer_ID (O : OVEN) return All_Timer is
     begin
          return O.timer_acc;
     end GetTimer_ID;
```

```
procedure allocate_Timer_ID(O : access OVEN) is
begin
    O.Timer_acc := new Oven_Timer.CallableInstance;
    Oven_Timer.Instance(Oven_Timer.CallableInstance(O.Timer_acc.all),
    Oven_Instance.Access_Instance(O));
    Oven_Timer.currentState(O.timer_acc.all,Timer.ReSet);
    Oven_Timer.settimeRemaining(getTimer_ID(O.all).all,0);
end allocate_Timer_ID;

function GetTube_ID (O: OVEN) return Power_Tube.ALL_Power_Tube is
begin
    return O.Tube_ID;
end GetTube_ID;

procedure SetTube_ID (O: in out OVEN; value: Power_Tube.ALL_Power_Tube) is
begin
    O.Tube_ID := value;
end SetTube_ID;

function GetLight_ID (O: OVEN) return Light.ALL_Light is
begin
return O.Light_ID;
end GetLight_ID;

procedure SetLight_ID (O: in out OVEN; value: Light.ALL_Light) is
begin
    O.Light_ID := value;
end SetLight_ID;
```

-- State Action Function Implementations for embedded Oven State
-- Machinery : Oven_instance.

-- state 1

```
procedure Idle_With_Door_Closed (O: in out OVEN) is
begin
    -- Turn Oven light off.
    Light.L2(O.Light_ID.all);
end Idle_With_Door_Closed;
```

-- state 5

```
procedure Idle_With_Door_Open (O: in out OVEN) is
begin
    -- Turn Oven light on.
    Light.L1(O.Light_ID.all);
end Idle_With_Door_Open;
```

```
-- state 3

   procedure Cooking_Period_Extended (O: in out OVEN) is
   begin
      -- Add 5 seconds to Oven timer.
      Oven_Timer.settimeRemaining(getTimer_ID(O).all,
      Oven_Timer.gettimeRemaining(getTimer_ID(O).all) + 5);
   end Cooking_Period_Extended;


-- state 4

   procedure Cooking_Complete (O: in out OVEN) is
      beepingInterval: constant := 10;
   begin
      -- Turn off Oven power & Oven light.
      Power_Tube.P2(O.Tube_ID.all);
      Light.L2(O.Light_ID.all);
      -- Sound Warning Beep.
      -- soundWarningBeep( beepingInterval );
   end Cooking_Complete;

-- state 6

   procedure Cooking_Interrupted(O: in out OVEN) is
   begin
      -- Get power tube for Oven & de-energize.
      Power_Tube.P2(O.Tube_ID.all);
      Oven_Timer.TIM(getTimer_ID(O). all,Timer.TIM2);
   end Cooking_Interrupted;

-- state 2

   procedure Initial_Cooking_Period(O: in out OVEN) is
   begin
      -- Set the timer to 5 seconds.
      Oven_Timer.TIM1(getTimer_ID(O).all,5);
      Oven_Timer.Arm_Callback(Oven_Timer.CallableInstance(O.timer_acc.all),V2);
      -- Turn on light.
      Light.L1(O.Light_ID.all);
      -- Start up power.
      Power_Tube.P1(O.Tube_ID.all);
   end Initial_Cooking_Period;

----------------------------------------------------------------------
```

```
procedure V1(O: in out OVEN) is
    from_state: Oven_State_Set := CurrentState (O);
    to_state:  Oven_State_Set := nextState (O,V1);
begin
    if to_state = IGNORE then
        return;
    end if;
    currentState(O,to_state);
    action_dispatch(O);
end V1;
```

```
procedure V4(O: in out OVEN) is
    from_state: Oven_State_Set := CurrentState (O);
    to_state:  Oven_State_Set := nextState (O,V4);
begin
    if to_state = IGNORE then
        return;
    end if;
    CurrentState(O,to_state);
    Action_dispatch(O);
end V4;
```

```
procedure V2(O: in out OVEN) is
    from_state: Oven_State_Set := CurrentState (O);
    to_state:  Oven_State_Set := nextState (O,V2);
begin
    if to_state = IGNORE then
        return;
    end if;
    currentState(O,to_state);
    action_dispatch(O);
end V2;
```

```
procedure V3(O: in out OVEN) is
    from_state: Oven_State_Set := CurrentState (O);
    to_state:  Oven_State_Set := nextState (O,V3);
begin
    if to_state = IGNORE then
        return;
    end if;
    currentState(O,to_state);
    action_dispatch(O);
end V3;
```

```
procedure action_dispatch (O: in out OVEN) is
begin
    case CurrentState(O) is

        when NONEXISTANT I IGNORE =>  null;
        when Idle_With_Door_Closed      => Idle_With_Door_Closed(O);
        when Initial_Cooking_Period  => Initial_Cooking_Period(O);
        when Cooking_Period_Extended  => Cooking_Period_Extended(O);
        when Cooking_Complete            => Cooking_Complete(O);
        when Idle_With_Door_Open         => Idle_With_Door_Open(O);
        when Cooking_Interrupted          => Cooking_Interrupted(O);
    end case;
end action_dispatch;
```

```
procedure event_dispatch    (O      : in out OVEN;
                             Event  : Oven_Event_Set) is
begin
    case Event is
        when V1  => V1(O);
        when V4  => V4(O);
        when V2  => V2(O);
        when V3  => V3(O);
    end case;
end event_dispatch;
```

```
begin
   Oven_Instance.stateModel(state_model);
end Oven;
```

```
--------------------------------------------------------------------------
-- runOvenApp.adb
--------------------------------------------------------------------------
--
-------------------------------------------------------------------------
--
-- Module: main
--
-- Synopsys:
--    Template main program for executing an OOA model.
--    This program creates initial instances of objects
--    corresponding to a particular test scenario, and
--    then sends some external events to these instances
--     to start the model executing.
--
--------------------------------------------------------------------------


with Timer;
with OVEN;
with LIGHT;
with POWER_TUBE;

with User_Action_Pkg;


-------------------------------------------------------------------------

procedure main is

    package User renames User_Action_pkg;

    -- decalare pre-existing instances of objects
    the_oven:       Oven.All_Oven := new OVEN.OVEN ;
    the_light:      Light.All_Light := new LIGHT.LIGHT;
    the_power_tube: POWER_TUBE.All_POWER_TUBE := new
    POWER_TUBE.POWER_TUBE ;

begin

    -- create the oven, its light and power tube
    -- and Set their initial states

    -- off
    LIGHT.currentState(the_light.all,LIGHT.Off);
    LIGHT.setLight_Status(the_light.all,LIGHT.Off);

    -- de-energized
    POWER_TUBE.currentState(the_power_tube.all,POWER_TUBE.Deenergized);
```

```
    POWER_TUBE.setTube_Status(the_power_tube.all,POWER_TU
BE.Deenergized);
    POWER_TUBE.setWattage(the_power_tube.all,500);

    -- Set the Oven in Idle_With_Door_Closed
    OVEN.currentState(the_oven. all,OVEN.Idle_With_Door_Closed);

    -- Set the Timer
    OVEN.allocate_timer_ID(the_oven);

    -- Establish the necessary relationships with the oven
    -- idle with door closed

    OVEN.setLight_ID(the_oven.all,the_light);
    OVEN.setTube_ID (the_oven. all,the_power_tube);

    ------------------------------------------------------------------------

    -- Now the test case scenario

    User.display_prompt;

    loop
    -- map the UI event to the OvenApp domain
        case User.get_user_action is
            when User.Increase_Cooking => -- turn the oven on for 5 seconds
                OVEN.V1(the_oven.all);
            when User.Open_Door => -- open the oven door
                OVEN.V3(the_oven.all);
            when User.Close_Door => -- close the oven door
                OVEN.V4(the_oven.all);
            when User.Quit => -- exit
                exit;
            when User.No_Action => -- ignore all others
                null;
        end case;

        -- send a timer tick

        delay 1.0;

        if
OVEN.Oven_Timer.gettimeRemaining(OVEN.getTimer_ID(the_oven.
all).all)      /= 0 then
            OVEN.Oven_Timer.TIM(OVEN.getTimer_ID(the_oven. all).all,Timer.TIM6);
        end if;
    end loop;
end Main;
```

The Introduction of An Object Oriented Analysis/Design Method and Object Oriented Metrics in the Software Development Life-Cycle

Rik Simoens

Eurocontrol - DEI3, Rue de la Fusée 96, B-1130-Brussels, Belgium
E-mail: simoens.rik@eurocontrol.be

1. Introduction

Eurocontrol is the European Organisation for the Safety of Air Navigation. One of its tasks is the Air Traffic Control in the Upper Airspace of Benelux and parts of Germany.

For this task, Eurocontrol uses an automated real-time system (Maastricht Automated Dataprocessor, MADAP). The system was developed in the late 60's and was first used in 1972. The system will undergo a stepwise re-engineering and modernisation programme lasting until the year 2000.

One of the first activities in this re-engineering programme was the establishment of a Quality System and the definition of a Software Development Environment that supports the complete development life-cycle [BLUM].

This paper first describes the introduction of Object Oriented Analysis and Design Techniques in the Software Development Life-Cycle. Next it describes the definition of a set of Object Oriented Metrics.

2. Context

Both the organisational and the technological context of the re-engineering programme introduced radical changes in the way Eurocontrol staff in the Maastricht Centre operates. It changed the organisation from maintenance oriented using (software engineering) techniques of the 70's to development oriented using modern software engineering practices.

Systems developed under the re-engineering programme are procured from industry. Eurocontrol intends to perform the long-term maintenance. Eurocontrol staff perform three major roles during the procurement. They act as requirements engineers before the contract, and as domain specialists or reviewers during the contract execution. Eurocontrol staff will maintain the systems after final acceptance.

Eurocontrol defined and introduced a quality system that covers the complete re-engineering programme. This quality system is imposed on the contractor during the development. For software, the development life-cycle is based on the ESA-PSS-05 model. In simplified terms this implies that the requirements for a (software) product are established during the User Requirements Phase. They are documented in the User Requirements Document (URD). The analysis of the User Requirements is performed during the Software Requirements Phase. The results of this analysis are documented in an Object Oriented Analysis model that is included in the Software Requirements Document (SRD). The architecture of the software product is defined during the Architectural Design Phase. It is documented in the Object Oriented Architectural Design Model and included in the Architectural Design Document (ADD). The design is further detailed during the detailed design phase and the product is finally implemented during the coding and unit test phase [PSS05].

This paper discusses the introduction of the Object Oriented Methods and Metrics in the Software Requirements Phase and Architectural Design Phase.

3. The Introduction of the Object Oriented Analysis Method

3.1 The Introduction Process

Eurocontrol selected the Coad-Yourdon Object Oriented Analysis method for the re-engineering programme. The selection of this method was largely based on previous experiences in its experimental centre in Bretigny [LOTT]. The method is used during the Software Requirements Phase.

A training programme was set up to train Eurocontrol staff in Object Oriented Techniques. The goal of the training programme was to train the staff who would use the method on the (pilot) projects and the domain experts who would review the deliverables of the upcoming projects.

At the same time, a small group of people was charged to establish a set of guidelines to apply the Coad-Yourdon method (January 1993) [BUCK][JOST]. The guidelines were first issued in May 1993.

Next a pilot project was conducted to validate the guidelines. The staff involved in the pilot project included following persons:

Staff Member	Involvement in Drafting Guidelines	Training	Role
Technical Manager	None	Yes	Review/Approval
Analyst 1	Review	Yes	Produce Model (site 1)
Analyst 2	Review	Yes	Produce Model (site 1)
Analyst 3	None	Yes	Produce Model (site 2)
Analyst 4	Author	No	Produce Model/Feedback (site 3)
Quality Assurance	Review	Yes	Review/Feedback (site 1)

Table 1: Staff on the Pilot Project.

As can be seen from the table, the pilot project involved persons working on three sites and executing all roles played on a typical project.

The guidelines were reviewed after the pilot project in October 1993. They were approved in December 1993 and introduced into projects at the same time.

3.2 The Object Oriented Analysis Guidelines

The goals of the guidelines are to elaborate the method where it revealed weaknesses (e.g. modelling of dynamics, requirements traceability, management of the model) and to define the application of the method within the selected tool. The guidelines focus on a set of 'Rules' that thoroughly define the method. They define the organisation of the model for large scale projects and the naming and drawing conventions. They also define in process requirements traceability [POHL] and in process model documentation. As a result, models developed by different teams, perhaps different contractors, at different sites deliver analysis models with a consistent notation and organisation.

All (textual) documentation of the model is organised in 'annotations'. An annotation is a key-worded piece information attached to an item in the model (Class, Service, Attribute and relations between them) and stored into the repository. Constraints and Requirements Traceability are specified in the model as annotations. To prevent the modelling activity from degrading into a drawing activity, all items to which annotations must be attached are identified in the rules of the guidelines. An object is undefined as long as its annotations are not specified. The guidelines left some freedom to the teams to define own 'annotations' but they specify that a full set of key-worded annotations must be defined before the modelling starts.

[COAD] suggests "flat" Object Models in which subjects are used to guide a reader through the model or to control visibility. In spite of his strong arguments against hierarchy we have introduced leveling in our approach because flat models are not very practical for large models. The solution we adopted uses a concept of leveled subjects. At the lowest level, classes are grouped into subjects. Classes may be shown on any subject diagram, giving the impression of a flat model, but each class is associated to just one subject. These lowest level subjects are then grouped into higher level subjects to form a subject hierarchy. The major reason behind this decision was to provide better means to manage a large model and to navigate through it and to enable document generation. The approach suggested by [COAD] could not be applied for very practical reasons. He suggests the use of a tool that supports "layers" that can be switched on or off at wish. At the time of introduction, such a tool was not available. On the other hand, [COAD] suggests the use of "a double-size sheet of paper" to represent the lowest level diagrams. We did not apply this method as not every user had access to an A3 printer and we felt that this format was difficult to review.

Modelling the dynamics of a system is an area where we found the method revealed serious weaknesses. We therefore introduced the concept of 'Object Interaction Diagrams'. They document the interactions between the Class-&-Objects in the model. The approach is based on Event Traces as defined in OMT [RUM].

3.3 The Tool Support for the Analysis Process

Tool support was a hot issue and the source of harsh debates during the introduction process. Eurocontrol had selected StP/OOSD from IDE as a *design* tool prior to the establishment of the development life-cycle and the drafting of the guidelines. The OOSD tool provides customisation facilities. They may be used to adapt the pre-defined annotations, some built in rules and the document generation templates. A decision was taken to customise the StP/OOSD tool to mimic the Coad-Yourdon Method and to provide documentation templates to produce an extensive set of reports for the models. The set of pre-defined annotations was adapted to the type of information that is captured during the analysis phase. The full responsibility for tool customisation and configuration was given in the hands of the software engineering team. No single project team has the right to adapt any of the pre-defined settings or documentation templates. All settings of the tool are under configuration management and subject to change control procedures.

3.4 The Results

The learning curve was one of the key elements when the method was introduced. The Eurocontrol domain specialists followed the courses but never used the methods and concepts as 'modellers'. The contractors were responsible for their own training. We had to make trade-offs in the complexity of the method so that it was usable and understandable by everyone. The scale of the projects necessitate bigger teams in which not every engineer has the same skills or experiences. This means that in some cases we had to disappoint analysts with (subjective) preferences for other methods, or analysts with a degree of knowledge that was too extensive for general introduction.

The guidelines are a critical success factor. They are essential to define the goals of the activity and are required to limit the support requirements of the project teams. No matter which method is selected, or tool is used, guidelines must be defined. They should at least guide the users in the selection of the right level of abstraction and the balancing of various parts of the model (for example dynamic versus static models). They should clearly identify the goals and define when the modelling is complete.

As a result of the thorough definition of the method, walkthrough and review meetings concentrate on the contents of the model. We feel this is extremely beneficial since no time is lost on academic discussions whether the model follows the 'true' method or not.

Eurocontrol found itself in a weak position with respect to the introduction of the selected tool, especially as it had to be imposed on the contractors. However, we feel that the selection of the tool is not as important as to know what one wants to achieve with the tool (guidelines). One team refused to use the tool and the associated guidelines. Instead they opted for a 'real' Coad/Yourdon tool and the 'real' method. During the course of the project they spent an enormous amount of effort in defining what the model should look like and what 'Object-Oriented' was after all.

Eurocontrol underestimated the effort to draft the guidelines. One year elapsed between the start of the introduction and the full scale application of the method. We also underestimated the effort to support the project teams. In part, this was due to the use of an imperfect tool. On the other hand, the support for both the method and the tool was concentrated in the hands of a small team. This allowed us to keep the application of the method consistent across various projects and to prevent users of loosing time on configuring the tool and its associated templates.

4. The Introduction of the Object Oriented Design Method

4.1 The Introduction Process

The introduction process for the Design Method was similar to the process followed for the Analysis Method. There were some important deviations:

1. There was no training programme. The programme that was set up in 1993 covered both the analysis and design phases.
2. The method further deviates from the Coad-Yourdon Object Oriented Design method and borrows a lot from Booch [BOOCH] and OMT [RUM].
3. Better use was made of the in-house experts to draft the guidelines.
4. The process to define the guidelines was devised in a sub-process that dealt with method issues and a sub-process that dealt with tool issues.

The result is two sets of guidelines. The first set is a process and method oriented standard. The second set is a 'Rules' oriented documentation and tools standard. The advantage of this approach is that the tool can be replaced without an impact on the process or the method. The first standard was written by the in-house design experts. The second standard concentrates on the introduction and management of the methods and tools. This approach allowed us to keep the learning curve acceptable, the method applicable and the support requirements to a minimum. The drafting of the method standard must be well managed to avoid the re-invention of the wheel.

The establishment process was started in August 1994 and terminated in February 1995.

4.2 The Results

The result of the guidelines activity is an analysis and design method that uses the same notation in both phases. The difference in the information to be captured or defined in an analysis model or a design model are well defined in the guidelines. The tool support guides the user to gather and specify the information relevant to the phase in which she is working.

The marriage of a waterfall model with object-oriented techniques still leaves us with some unanswered questions.

The analysis model is carried forward from the Software Requirements phase into the Architectural Design phase. The model is then 'enhanced' with design specific information. This has an impact on the configuration management of the baselines created after the Software Requirements phase. In a traditional waterfall approach, modifications to these baselines are managed under change control. In our approach, the deliverables of one phase are modified (enhanced) in the next phase. In concrete terms this means that the baseline is modified.

In the approach that we adopted, Software Requirements are implicitly expressed in the model. They are not explicitly written down in plain text. User requirements are expressed in plain text. In terms of traceability, this means that we trace back from classes, attributes, services or relations between them to user requirements. The traceability between the analysis phase and design phase must be expressed as traces between a model and an enhanced model. We do not have a clear solution for this issue yet. We will either define traceability between models, or trace back from the design to the user requirements. It is important to us that the traceability can be specified 'in process', or as the designer goes progresses[POHL].

One could observe that a solution for these problems could be the adoption of an incremental or spiral life-cycle model for the development. This decision however does not only have a technical impact but also a managerial impact. It would mean that Eurocontrol had to redefine its tendering policy (turn key products) and that the contractual status of analysis and design models should be defined.

5. The Introduction of Object Oriented Metrics

5.1 Context

The above sections described how Object Oriented Analysis and Design Methods were introduced for the re-engineering programme. The method has now been applied on five projects:

1. A Radar Tracker and Server.
2. A User Interface and Database application for an Initial Flight Plan System.
3. A User Interface and Database application for a Training Simulator.
4. A real time Data Driver for a Training Simulator.
5. A Display System for the real time display of the current Air Situation Picture. This project was split into eight sub-projects after the user requirements phase.

Although the method was defined in detail, it left sufficient freedom to the development teams to adopt a 'way of modelling' that best fitted their application. The degrees of freedom lay in the domain of the complexity of the model:

1. The size of the model (which is driven by the size of the application).
2. The relative weight of static modelling and dynamic modelling.
3. The degree in which inheritance is used.
4. The granularity of the traceability to the User Requirements.
5. The amount of descriptive text added to the annotations.

The software engineering group observed that depending on how the freedom in modelling was used, some projects delivered 'better' models than others. Some projects were 'more' successful than others. We also observed that some groups made false progress during the early modelling stages. They identified large sets of classes but did not define them. Other groups abused the Object Interaction Diagrams to use Data Flow Modelling instead of Object Oriented Modelling. Finally, some groups were more support intensive than others. We therefore attempted to define a set of metrics that assess the complexity and completeness of the Object Oriented models.

We were also confronted with the literature that tells us *'You can't control what you can't measure'* [DEMARCO]. Other authors suggest that the collection can be used for software process improvement [GRADY]. This we felt is important, as the methods and tools we are using are not perfect but allow us to achieve our goals. Before taking a decision on the future of the methods, processes and the associated tools, we need to have a better view on the achieved results.

5.2 Metrics Introduction: The Process

The process followed to introduce the metrics is based on [GRADY]. The author suggests ten steps to success. We did not follow all steps, neither did we execute them in sequence. The steps we executed are 'Assign Responsibility', 'Do Research', 'Define Initial Metrics', 'Sell the Initial Metrics', 'Get tools for automatic data collection and analysis' and 'Create a metrics database'.

The steps we did not (yet) execute are 'Define company/project objectives for program', 'Establish a training class in software metrics', 'Publicise success stories and encourage exchange of ideas', 'Establish a mechanism for changing the standard in an orderly way'.

Currently we do not have a real metrics introduction program. This is why steps that require management support are not executed. We describe the steps we executed below.

5.3 Metrics for Object Oriented Models: The initial metrics.

This section will define the data collected for each class and how it was summarised on the level of a model. In the definition of the metrics, we should bear in mind that the metrics are collected in the Software Requirements and Architectural Design Phase. Detailed information such as 'lines of code', 'complexity measurements' are not yet available in these phases. The metrics collected are based on the information available in the repository of the Object Oriented Model. Since the notation for both the Analysis and Design method is the same, definitions apply for both types of models.

5.3.1 Class Metrics

Class Metrics are data collected on a class per class basis. They include (per class):

1. The number of Services and Attributes.
2. The number of Relations (Whole-Part, Instance-Connections) [COAD].
3. The number of Sub-Classes and Parent-Classes.
4. The number of Inherited Services and Attributes.
5. The number of paragraphs of text specified for the class and its services and attributes.
6. The depth of the class in the inheritance tree.

5.3.2 Absolute Model Metrics

The models produced under the various projects vary in absolute size. We therefore introduced a set of *Absolute Metrics*. These metrics count the number of items in a model. They include:

1. Total number of Classes
2. Total number of Services
3. Total number of Attributes
4. Total number of Relations between Classes
5. Total number of Traces made to the User Requirements Document
6. Total number of Scenarios documented on the Object Interaction Diagrams

	Project 1	Project 2	Project 3
Number of Classes	216.00	45.00	90.00
Number of Services	426.00	117.00	82.00
Number of Attributes	137.00	223.00	332.00
Number of Parts	184	22	58
Number of Traced Items	626	551	122

Table 2: An example of some Absolute Metrics.

5.3.3 Relative Model Metrics

Relative Metrics are introduced to allow the comparison the apparent complexity of the models. They represent average measures. They are defined as the averages of the *Class Metrics*.

	Project 1	Project 2	Project 3
Services/Class	1.97	2.60	0.91
Attributes/Class	0.63	4.96	3.69
Parts/Class	0.85	0.49	0.64
References/Traced Item	2.23	2.42	2.38

Table 3: An example of some Relative Metrics.

Relative Model Metrics allow us to assess the use of inheritance and the relative weight of the static and dynamic models. They also allow us to assess the relative size of textual information stored in their data repository.

5.3.4 Partial Metrics for the Model

The collection of the metrics for various models revealed that some models contained rather large sets of classes that did not define either services or attributes, or even neither of them. We therefore decided to collect the above defined metrics for various sub-sets of classes (*Partial Metrics*):

1. All Classes.
2. Classes with defined Services.
3. Classes with defined Attributes.
4. Classes with Services. They could have inherited Services.
5. Classes without defined Attributes. They could have inherited Attributes.
6. Classes without defined Services or Attributes.

This classification revealed that larger models (in absolute size) contained a rather large number of obsolete classes in some cases. We could observe that in some projects, classes without defined services or attributes were indeed located deeper in the inheritance tree and did indeed inherit more services and attributes from their parent classes. However, other projects identified groups of classes without clearly defined responsibilities or contained data. We suggest that Partial Metrics are collected during the modelling process. The results could provide a good overview of the real progress of the team.

Figure 1 provides an example of a typical project. The data presented in the chart is the Average Depth of a Class in the Inheritance tree, the Average Number of Inherited Services and the Average Number of Inherited Attributes. This information is included for the set of All Classes, a sub-set containing only Classes without defined Services and a sub-set containing only Classes without defined Attributes.

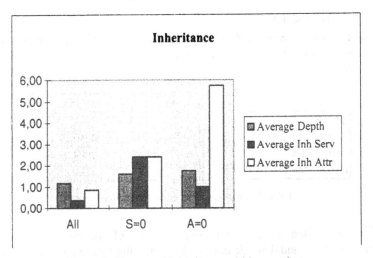

Figure 1: The use of Inheritance within a project.

Table 4 contains an example of a project that contains an un-acceptable number of classes without services and attributes. Investigation of the result lead to the observation that attributes of classes had been modelled as a sub-classes for each allowed value of these attributes.

	All	S>0	A>0	S>0,A>0	S=0	A=0	S=0 A=0
# Classes	216	148	76	63	68	140	55
# Services	426	426	209	209	0	217	0
# Attributes	137	113	137	113	24	0	0

Table 4: Partial Metrics for Project 1.

5.4 Selling the Metrics

We found ourselves in a specific position with respect to the selling of the metrics. In the first place we collected the metrics on work performed by our contractors. On the other hand, metrics were collected for models produced by various companies.

We invited the contractors to presentations to present the initial metrics. We announced that only data would be presented, questions would be raised but no conclusions would be formulated. We observed that although anonymous data was presented, most participants were able to identify the models on which the data were based and made conclusions for themselves.

The report produced at the occasion of these presentations was sent to the management. This report contained, on the first page, a warning that it was for information only.

Further selling of the metrics has not yet taken place. Once we have a better understanding of the metrics and their role in a quality model, we intend to make their collection mandatory. The metrics report would then be a deliverable together with the Software Requirements and Architectural Design Document.

5.5 Automatic Data Collection and Analysis

The collection of the metrics is automated. As mentioned above, all projects use the same method and the same tools. The data repository contains the same information and has the same structure. We decided to extract the metrics using the interface to the data repository and to manage the results using a spreadsheet.

The following has now been made available to the project teams

1. A script that accesses the repository to produce the Class Metrics.
2. A spreadsheet that imports the Class Metrics and produces the Absolute and Relative Model Metrics for both the complete and partial models.
3. A summary spreadsheet that contains the Complete and Partial Model Metrics of other projects.
4. A manual which describes the complete system.

The system only collects the data. Analysis is still performed as 'an observation'. We intend to use a statistical package to further define the analysis of the results. This automated analysis should then allow us to define a quality model and to assess the models on a class per class basis.

5.6 The results and future work

5.6.1 What we learned

We adopted the 'how can we learn?' mindset during the selling meetings. The facts we learned so far will probably have an impact on the guidelines. They are:

1. Small models are better documented than large models. Models with 10 to 20 classes are 'over' documented. Models with 20-100 classes are 'well' documented. Models with a higher number of classes are 'poorly' documented. The 'over' documentation of small models could be explained by observing that in general these models are produced to clarify a specific high risk area, or an area with vague requirements.
2. Classes without services and attributes must be assessed.
3. The importance of the dynamics modelling must be carefully managed. In some cases, we observed that large dynamics models were produced to document algorithmic descriptions contained in the User Requirements Document. In these cases the dynamic models of the interactions between classes can be large but bring very little added value. The project teams with large dynamic models are more support intensive.

5.6.2 Future Work

The results obtained so far permit us to assess the models on an ad-hoc basis. They permit us to compare the models produced by various projects and to identify areas of concern. The results do not yet allow us to make qualitative statements such as 'simple' or 'complex', or 'good' or 'bad'. They do not yet allow the identification of outliers both on class level and on model level.

We have not yet produced a complete quality model that appraises the obtained results. Considering the data collected we started to define some affected criteria as described in [COUT].

We observed that *Annotations Per Class + Annotations Per Service + Annotations Per Attribute* is a good measure for the *self descriptiveness* of a class. For *simplicity* we used *#Attributes + #Services + #Inherited Attributes + #Inherited Services + #Whole-Part Connections*2 + #Parent Classes*2*. We observed that complex classes are *key classes*. [LOREN] defines key classes as classes central to the business domain being developed.

6. Conclusion

The process to introduce new technology was critical to its success. In a sense, the process to introduce the technology was as important the technology itself. Other methods or other tools could have solved some problem areas but would not have had a drastic impact on the effort needed to introduce the methodology.

User support is essential too. Our attitude is that users are always right but cannot have everything. Organisation productivity is more important than personal productivity. Organise tool configuration and tool customisation on an organisational level. Make changes to the method and the tools subject to change control procedures. Finally, avoid discussions with 'tooligans', who do not accept any method or tool that is not invented by them.

7. References

[BLUM] Blume, et al., *'New Generation of Software Engineering Environment in place at EUROCONTROL and DFS'*, Proceedings of the Fourth Symposium 'Ada in Aerospace', 1994.

[BOOCH] Booch, Grady, *'Object Oriented Design with Applications'*, The Benjamin/Cummings Publishing Company, ISBN 0-8053-0091-0.

[BUCK] Buckley, Fletcher J. *'Establishing Software Engineering Standards In an Industrial Organisation'*, IEEE, Software Engineering, Project Management, ISBN 0-8186-0751-3, 1988.

[COAD] Coad, Peter, Yourdon, Edward, *'Object-Oriented Analisys'*, Yourdon Press, ISBN 0-13-629981-4.

[COAD] Coad, Peter, Yourdon, Edward, *'Object-Oriented Design'*, Yourdon Press, ISBN 0-13-630070-7.

[COUT] Coutand, Thierry, *'Assessing the Maintainability of the On-Board Software of the Hermes Shuttle'*, Proceedings of the Fourth Symposium 'Ada in Aerospace', 1994.

[DEM] DeMarco, T., *'Controlling Software Projects, Management Measurement and Estimation'*, Yourdon Press, ISBN 0-13-171711-1.

[GRADY] Grady, Robert B., Caswell, Deborah L., *'Software Metrics: Establishing A Company-Wide Program'*, Prentice-Hall, ISBN 0-13-821844-7.

[JOST] Jost, Jim, Chambers, Tim, *'Lessons learned while implementing a sofware lifecycle'*, Hewlett-Packard, Ltd., 1988

[LOREN] Lorenz, M., Kidd, J., *'Object-Oriented Software Metrics'*, Prentice Hall, ISBN 0-13-179292-X.

[LOTT] Lott, M., Burr, M., *'EEC Standard for the Coad and Yourdon Method'*, Eurocontrol (Not Published), 1992.

[POHL] Pohl, K. et al., *'Workshop Summary First International Workshop on Requirements Engineering: Foundation for Software Quality'*, Software Engineering Notes vol. 20. no. 1.

[PSS05] European Space Agency / Agence Spatiale Européenne, *'ESA PSS-05-0 Issue 2, ESA software engineering standards'*, 1991.

[RUM]   Rumbaugh, J. et al., *'Object-Oriented Modeling and Design'*, Prentice Hall, ISBN 0-13-110439.

[SHAR]   Sharble, Cohen, *'The Object-Oriented Brewery: A comparison of Two Object-Oriented Development Methods'*, ACM SIGSOFT, Software Engineering Notes vol 18 no 2, 1993.

Modelling and validation of tasks with algebraic structured nets

D. Buchs C. Buffard P. Racloz
e-mail {buchs, buffard, racloz}@di.epfl.ch

Swiss Federal Institute of Technology in Lausanne
Software Engineering Laboratory
EPFL-DI-LGL
CH-1015 Lausanne
Switzerland

Abstract. Ada offers several mechanisms for expressing concurrency, like tasks and protected types. The use of concurrency can introduce significant problems which are inherent in the program's interactions or can require some particular properties. Amongst these problems or necessary properties, we can mention deadlocks, fairness and particular temporal characteristics. The modelling of concurrency behavior with tools can help prevent these problems. For this purpose, we show in this paper that programs written in Ada can be modelled using the formalism CO-OPN, based on Petri nets and algebraic specifications, which offers the possibility to select the level of abstraction of the modelling. These modelling can be used to detect the program anomalies.

Keywords: Ada, protected type, task, abstract data type, concurrency, CO-OPN, Petri net.

1 Introduction

Concurrent programs execute faster the same work than sequential programs on the same resource. Nevertheless, their complexity imply that they must be carefully designed using well defined software engineering principles such as modularity, composition techniques and behaviourally predictable properties. We mean by predictable behavior the fact that it is possible to decide some interesting properties of the considered software system and this is only possible if a formal semantics is given to the analysed program. We will see latter that our approach can be used to prove properties such as deadlock, fairness or temporal properties by modelling Ada programs using a well defined formal model called CO-OPN (Concurrent Objected Oriented Petri Nets).

Ada tasking and rendez-vous based communication provide a mechanism to implement both concurrent and distributed software. The interaction between tasks give rise to issues such as avoiding deadlocks and guaranteeing fairness of tasks scheduling. Moreover, the design of concurrent programs is much more difficult and mastering the interactions between tasks can be quite complex.

The problems inherent in concurrency are not simple to detect, thus we are interested in the modelling of Ada programs, in particular the task parts, in order to perform simulation and analysis as a mean of detecting problems. The goal of our project is to develop a concurrent object model for Ada, based on Petri nets and abstract data types, within the CO-OPN framework. Our idea is that the main aspects dealing with concurrency must be modelled through the use of Petri nets while depending on the focus of attention, particular aspects of data structures and procedures can either be modelled using Petri nets or algebraic abstract data types.

Other authors treat the transition from Ada code to an analysis model such as [DNC] and [MSS 89]. Our approach introduces the possibility to model both the communication and the data structures that are not present in the other studies.

The goal of the software engineering is the production of quality software that is delivered on time and within budget and which satisfies all its requirements [SE 90]. An important aspect of software engineering is that software production should be helped by tools. The formalism CO-OPN is supported by a computer tool including a graphical editor, a compiler, a simulator and a temporal verifier. We plan to implement in the near future a tool supporting the user guided translation of Ada programs into CO-OPN specifications. Another domain of application is the Software re-engineering which improves the understanding of the software, prepares or improves the software itself, usually for increased maintainability, reusabilty or evoluability [Arnold 93]. The software re-engineering, sometimes called in the literature software-renewal or software-renovation, is also a term applied to software development where an existing system is undergoing some degree of redevelopment.

This paper is structured as follows. Section 2 describes the CO-OPN formalism and Section 3 gives a brief overview of tasking in Ada (95). We examine the transition from Ada code to the CO-OPN model in Section 4. A short description of the different forms of analysis that may be performed on the model is presented in Section 5. Finally, concluding remarks are given in Section 6.

2   CO-OPN Model

2.1   The CO-OPN Approach

CO-OPN (Concurrent Oriented Object Petri Net) is a specification language used for the specification and the design of large concurrent systems. The last version called CO-OPN/2 extends the CO-OPN language by means of some object-oriented features such as class, inheritance and sub-typing. The object paradigm is introduced into CO-OPN in order to solve the problem of large specification management. *Encapsulation* and *abstraction* are key notions included in the model. Each class or template can be used to instantiate the objects which compose the modelled system. A CO-OPN object can be viewed as a set of *encapsulated* state variables or attributes which can be used for implementing accessible its methods. Moreover, autonomous object reaction is implemented by means of internal transitions. According to the common intuition, each object has its own behavior and evolves in concurrence with other objects. As the purpose of CO-OPN is to capture the abstract concurrent behavior of each modelling entity, the concurrency granularity is not found in the objects but rather in the methods. Intra object concurrency can be obtained by expressing the causality relation between the behavior of the different methods. The relations between objects, such as object synchronization, must also be captured using method synchronization schemes allowing for the building of hierarchies of *abstraction*.

CO-OPN uses Petri nets, which are an elegant model of true concurrency (true in opposition to interleaving semantics). Unfortunately, Petri nets have very weak modelling capabilities in term of the functional aspects and structuring capabilities. CO-OPN adds to Petri nets a synchronization scheme for each method of the objects. This approach generalizes other approaches such as, the transition fusion [DHP 91] and the hierarchical nets [Kie 89].

Real systems must include other features such as data structures with the associated operations acting upon these data. This is the reason why data structures are incorporated into Petri nets. This class is formed of Petri net specifically called high-level nets i.e. Petri net with tokens modelling by data structures instead of anonymous entities. We need an abstract formalism to describe structured tokens. In our case we chose algebraic abstract data types which combine abstraction through functions with a simple system of properties notation derived from the equality relation and the first order logic.

2.2 Petri Nets

The first component on which CO-OPN is based are the Petri nets [Reisig 85]. These nets are used to model and analyse discrete systems in which notions such as interacting components, concurrency and synchronisation play a key role. A Petri net modelling embeds both the structural aspect of the system and its evolution. Among the pleasant features embodied in Petri nets we can mention:

- the distribution of state and the change-of-state in the net,
- the common synchronization schemes such as sequentiality, non-determinism, concurrency and conflict naturally handled,
- the existence of graphical representation.

The states of a system are represented through *places*, these one can contain a varying number of *tokens*. A given distribution of tokens in the places represents a state. The events of the system are represented by transitions and the occurrence of an event corresponds to the firing of a transition which depends on the existence of a minimal number of tokens in some places of the net.

When a transition is fired, a new state is reached. This state is given by a new distribution of tokens. Informally, the tokens can be considered as resources needed to the occurrence of events. The firing of a transition consumes some resources and generates new ones. The semantics of Petri nets can be expressed by a transition system.

2.3 Abstract Data Types

The second component on which CO-OPN is based, are the abstract data types (ADT). An ADT is a representation of a data structure coupled with a set of operations which manipulate this data structure (data type) independently of any particular implementation (abstract).

The algebraic approach [EM 85] to specification considers a system in terms of abstract data types represented, in a mathematical discourse, by many-sorted algebras in combination with axioms or equations. An algebra is simply a domain provided with a set of operations. An algebraic specification $Spec = <S, F, X, Ax>$ consists of a set S of sort names, a set F of operation names including their profile, a set X of variables and a set Ax of positive conditional axioms (Horn clauses). With an algebraic approach the terms sort and type are distinguished. A type represents a domain and a set of operations whereas a sort is simply the name of a type. The axioms embody the operations properties and they are described as conditional equalities, as follows: $Condition \Rightarrow term = term'$ where $Condition$ is the conjunction of equalities $t_1 = t_1' \wedge \ldots \wedge t_n = t_n'$.

3 Ada Tasks

Ada 95 offers several mechanisms for expressing the concurrency: tasks, which are active entities, and protected types, which can be considered as passive tasks. Tasks express concurrency and their execution can take place on one or more processors depending on the run-time implementation. Tasks allow simultaneous execution and the order of execution is undefined except when two tasks are participating in a rendez-vous, which is the only form of direct communication between tasks. A rendez-vous is asymmetric: the caller must know the called task while the called task is unaware of the identity of the caller.

Calling an entry of a task is very similar to call a procedure with the exception that the called task can decide when and how to accept the call. If the called task is not ready to accept the entry then the execution of the calling task is suspended until the called task is ready to accept the entry call. Once the called task accepts the entry the rendez-vous begins. The duration of the rendez-vous is controlled by the called task, and is equal to the duration of the accept statement.

The general mechanisms studies in the concurrency for the cooperation between tasks are either based on message passing where a task communicate with another by sending a message through the tasking kernel, or based on the explicit use of synchronisations between the involved parties.

Ada provides a concurrency model based on the asynchronous execution of each task as if each task had its own processor. In contrast to the asynchronous model of execution, a communication between two tasks takes place through a rendez-vous, which is synchronous.

4   Construction of CO-OPN Model

We can represent Ada code in the CO-OPN model with varying levels of abstraction depending upon the point of view adopted. For example we can stay very close to the code or take a much more abstract view. A program is a sequence of statements and only the necessary statements with respect to synchronisation will be considered in the model. The principal objective is the detection of errors such as deadlocks. The deadlocks do not depend only on the synchronisation skeleton of the communicating entities, but also on the data structures exchanged. Our approach is to model intertask communication while conserving the structures of the exchanged data. Data are modelled with the necessary abstract level depending on the analysis point of view. The novelty of our approach, as compared to others in this domain, is the modelling of both the communication and the data structures involved. The correspondences between Ada data structures and the CO-OPN components are shown in figure 1. For intertask communication we have retained two categories of streams. The first stream which can alter the control flow, is defined by the Ada reserved words **if, loop, requeue** and **select**, while the second constitute the rendez-vous defined by the Ada reserved word **accept** and the *entry calls*.

Ada	CO-OPN	
	Petri net	Algebraic Spec
Abstract Data Type inclusion of types		●
procedures	●	
tasks protected types	●	
functions(pure)		●
Exceptions	?	?

Fig. 1. Correspondence between Ada data structures and CO-OPN components

As we said above the main goal is to anticipate errors due to concurrency in programs. We choose to retain only the functions and procedures that are directly linked with statements expressing concurrency in Ada. We have two ways for modelling a function or a procedure, calling a task or accepting an entry call: either by a Petri net or with a transition defined in a object specification.

In this way, we keep only the necessary representation of concurrence and data. Tasks are modelled with CO-OPN objects, and the task's functions are modelled in the same way as other functions. Protected types are modelled like tasks.

The **requeue** statement can be use to complete an **accept** statement or entry body, while redirecting the corresponding entry call to a new entry queue. The requeue statement is modelled in CO-OPN a Fifo ADT (cf. figure 5). Methods must be added on the interface in order to be complete. These methods can be called by clients, they are not implemented yet. The Fifo ADT is also used to model the waiting line of entries and tasks priorities and provides functions for manipulating this waiting line.

Exceptions are not modelled in the present work, we plan to study this complicated problem in the near future.

```
Adt Standard;
Signature
  Sorts integer, boolean;
  Sorts character, float;
  Generators
  0 : → integer;
  succ : integer → integer;
  Operations
  _+_ : integer integer → integer;
  _=_ : integer integer → boolean;
    ⋮

Body
  Axioms
  0+n = n;
  (succ n)+m = succ(n+m);

    ⋮

  0=0 = true;
  0=(succ n) = false;
  (succ n)=0 = false;
  (succ n)=(succ m) = n=m;

    ⋮

  Where
  n, m : integer;
End Standard;
```

```
Adt Stack_Of_Item
Signature
  Use Standard;
  Use Item_Spec;
  Sorts Stack;
  Generators
  Assign : Stack, Stack → Stack;
  Pop : Stack → Stack;
  Push : Stack, Item → Stack;
  Operations
  TopValue : Stack → Item;
Body
  Axioms
    ⋮

End Stack_Of_Item;
```

Fig. 2. Ada Standard package and an Ada Package specification

4.1 Data Type Model

A CO-OPN data specification is built using an ADT. An ADT include a *Signature* and a *body*. All the components accessible from the outside are given in module's signature. The signature of a formal specification is composed of the *sort* and *function*. The signature contains informations similar to those found in an Ada specification, where a type is called a *sort* and a subprogram an *operation*. The *axioms* and the *variables* do not appear in Ada specifications because Ada specifications do not carry information regarding the behavior of the component. On the contrary the CO-OPN body part includes all the local aspect such as the properties of operations or the operational description of the object.

We can find, as in Ada, two different types of specification, a generic and non-generic ones. Contrary to non-generic specifications, generic ones takes a formal parameter which specify the properties of the acceptable parameters. figure 2 illustrates a part of the package Ada Standard, some operations and axioms are missing.

Figure 2 gives an overview of a package specification, the Ada package is presented in figure 3. It is also possible to model a procedure which return more than one parameter, by mean of a Cartesian product.

```
type Stack_Type is limited private;

Empty_Structure_Error: exception;

- CONSTRUCTORS:

 procedure Assign (Destination: in out Stack_Type;
                   Source: in Stack_Type );
- OVERVIEW:
- Begins by a call to DESTROY(DESTINATION) and
- then copies SOURCE into
- DESTINATION. Note the "in out" mode of the formal
- parameter DESTINATION.

 procedure Pop (Stack:  in out Stack_Type);
- ERROR:
-  If the STACK is empty, then EMPTY_STRUCTURE_ERROR is raised.

 procedure Push (Stack:  in out Stack_Type;  Item:  in Item_Type);

- QUERIES:

 function Top_Value (Stack:  in Stack_Type)  return Item_Type;
```

Fig. 3. An Ada Package

4.2 Model of the Constructions

In this section we give an example of the way an Ada rendez-vous and protected type is handled in our framework. As we mentioned in Section 4, the package module can be included in either of the parts of the CO-OPN model (Petri nets and Abstract Data Types). When a package contains a type description, it is owned by the ADT part of the model, otherwise when a package contains a procedure, a function or a task body related to synchronisation aspects, it is represented with Petri nets. This correspondence is depicted in figure 1 while the dependences of the models are suggested in figure 4.

Overview of an Ada rendez-vous: an example We take the Ada program of figure 5 to illustrate our approach.

Ada's Entities

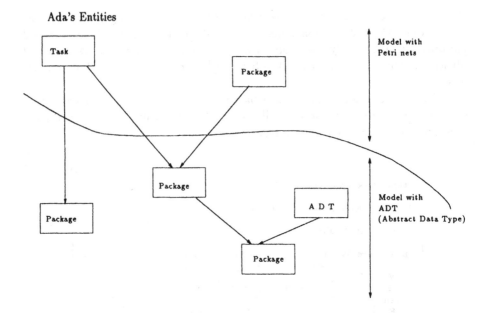

Fig. 4. Petri nets and ADT model of Ada's module

As we have seen, a calling task is suspended until the other task is ready to accept the call. We model this example with two tasks: the client and the server. A rendez-vous can be modelled as a temporary association between client and server task with a CO-OPN object. This temporary association can be in either of the following two states:

- the client task is suspended and the tasks are not yet synchronised.
- the client and server tasks are synchronised and the rendez-vous is taking place.

A rendez-vous binds two tasks during the time that they need to exchange information. We call this temporary association an *interface* in order to facilitate the translation from Ada code to the CO-OPN model.

We also assume a hierarchical (cf. figure 7) order in the representation of the model. Hierarchical means that the direction of the arrows are oriented from the interface to tasks. CO-OPN synchronisation arrows do not represent the data flow but the dependencies.

When the client task is calling there are two possibilities(cf. figure 7).

- the server task is busy. In this case, the data are stored in place *p1* and the client is waiting for the server.
- the server task is free. The internal transition *t1* is fired and the data are sent to the server task via *p2*.

```
task body Task1 is
begin
   while Cond1 loop
      Task2.Entry1;
   end loop;
end Task1;

task Task2 is;
   entry Entry1;
end Task2;

task body Task2 is
begin
   accept Entry1;
end Task2;
```

```
Adt Generic Fifo(Item);
Signature
   Use Item, bool;
   Sorts fifo;
   Generators
   empty : → fifo;
   insert _ _ : item fifo → fifo;
   Operations
   first _ : fifo → item;
   extract _ : fifo → fifo;
Body
   Axioms
   extract(empty) = empty;
   extract(insert(item),f)) = f;
   first(insert(item,f)) = item;
   Where
   item : Item;
   f : Fifo;
End Fifo;
```

Fig. 5. Code example and The Fifo ADT

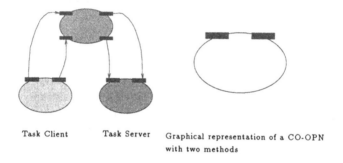

Task Client   Task Server   Graphical representation of a CO-OPN
                                     with two methods

Fig. 6. CO-OPN model of Ada's module

The data structure that the place can contain are:

- *p1*: contains an instantiation of the generic Fifo waiting line for the structure that must be sent to the server task,
- *p2*: black token, (as in usual Petri nets, i.e. without any structure), and an internal data structure,
- *p3*: black token,
- *p4*: contains an instantiation of the generic Fifo waiting line for the structure that must be sent to the server task.

Places *p2* and *p3* keep the mutual exclusion of two calling task for the same server. The place *p1* and the place *p4* contain a stack of the user's data. The place *p1* contains a stack data structure which allows to store data sent by the client. The place *p4* contain a stack data structure which allows to store data sent by the entry that must be sent back to the client. The transition *m* model the task body.

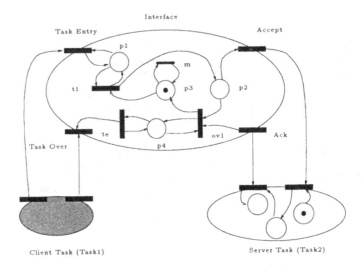

Fig. 7. Representation of the temporary association

Multiple Clients, Single Server: In figure 8 we show an example of the possibility for multiple clients to communicate with a server from the code given in figure 9. The data structure exchanged between a client and a server contains communication data (the data processed by the entry) and model data (model data contain information about client and functions used to extract, eg. its ID, useful data for the client).

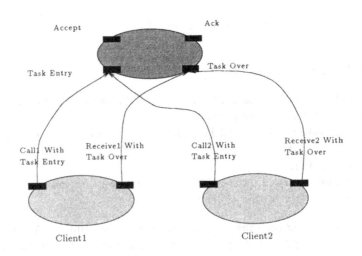

Fig. 8. Multiple Clients and one Server

```
with Text_IO; use Text_IO;
procedure Main is

task Task1;

task Task2 is

task Task3 is
  entry Entry1;
end Task3;

task body Task1 is
begin
if Cond  then
    .
    .
  Task3.Entry1;
end if;
    .
    .
end Task1;
```

```
task body Task2 is
begin
if cond  then
    .
    .
    Task3.Entry1;
end if;
    .
    .
end Task2;

task body Task3 is
begin
loop
    accept Entry1 do
    .
    .
    end Entry1;
end loop;
end Task3;

begin
null;
end Main;
```

Fig. 9. Multiple Clients, Single Server Ada program

Multiple Servers, Single Client: The code given figure in 11, gives the
model of figure 10 and the code given figure in 13, gives the model figure 12.
These examples show the possibility for a single client to send request to multiple
servers or multiple entries. The server selects requests that are addressed to it
by reading a server ID contained in the structure exchanged between servers and
clients. The structure exchanged between tasks is hidden from the user.

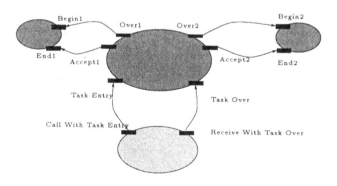

Fig. 10. Multiple entries and one client

```
with Text_IO; use Text_IO;
procedure Main is

task Task1;

task Task2 is
   entry Entry1;
   entry Entry2;
end Task2;

task body Task1 is
begin
if cond then
   :

   Task2.Entry1;
else
   :

   Task2.Entry2;
end if;
end Task1;
```

```
task body Task2 is
begin
select
   accept Entry1 do

   :

   end Entry1;
or
   accept Entry2 do

   :

   end Entry2;
end select;
end Task2;

begin
null;
end Main;
```

Fig. 11. Multiple entries and one client Ada program

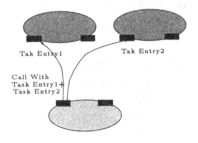

Tak Entry1   Tak Entry2

Call With
Task Entry1
Task Entry2

Fig. 12. Multiple servers and one client

Protected Types: Ada language specifies protected types, they formalize and expand on the use of passive tasks of Ada 83. Protected types give the possibility of defining a passive object, such as a monitor. A protected type consists of functions, procedures and entries. Which are mutually exclusive. It can also be defined entries that are different from the functions or procedures that define a barrier condition. We model this protected type in CO-OPN with a waiting line, which is defined using the same abstract data type Fifo ADT. Protected Types are modelled like tasks, except that Protected Types are active only when a rendez-vous is called.

5 Model Analysis

The analysis of the system can be roughly devised into two cases: the verification of whether the system is bounded or not (in terms of the amount of data needed

```
task Task1;

task Task2 is
    entry Entry1;
end Task2;

task Task3 is
    entry Entry1;
end Task3;

task body Task1 is
begin
if cond  then
    .
    .
    Task2.Entry1;
else
    .
    .
    Task3.Entry1;
end if;
end Task1;
```

```
task body Task2 is
begin
accept Entry1  do
    .
    .
end Entry1;
end Task2;

task body Task3 is
begin
accept Entry1  do
    .
    .
end Entry1;
end Task3;
```

Fig. 13. Multiple servers and one client Ada program

for its evolution) and whether parts of the system or the entire system has the possibility to evolve. The checking of these properties, well developed for the usual Petri nets is difficult in our framework because of the use of the structured tokens and the modularity. Currently, the means we investigate cover the different techniques. In some cases, from the underlying structure of the Petri nets (projection of the data to unstructured tokens) some properties can be deduced. The simulation [BFR 93] is very useful to give a first impression about the intended behaviour of the system. Lastly, we study the use of the temporal logic as a tool to the specification and verification of the system in terms of the occurrence of its events over the course of the time [RB 93] and [BFR 93].

6 Conclusion

We have presented an overview of modelling Ada code by mean of the CO-OPN formalism. The advantage of this model is that it allows us both to model the data structures and to preserve the oriented object paradigm across CO-OPN. Much work remains in order to model all of Ada features particularly the exceptions and requeue statements that are still under study. The way Ada 95 components are represented, either by Petri nets or algebraic specifications, as proposed in figure 1 is still subject to be modified. Up to now, this correspondence is intuitive in that dynamic items are handled by Petri nets and data structures by ADT, but this correspondence can be re-evaluated by future examples. Our efforts bear also on the extensions of the verification techniques to the entire CO-OPN framework.

References

[Arnold 93] R. S. Arnold. *Software reengineering*, IEEE Computer society, Inc., 1993.

[BFR 93] D. Buchs, J. Flumet, P. Racloz. *SANDS: Structured Algebraic Net Development* System 14th Int. Conf. on Application and Theory of Petri Nets, Tool presentation abstract (Ugo Buy ed.) page. 25-29, Chicago, USA, 1993.

[BG 91] D. Buchs, N. Guelfi. *CO-OPN: a Concurrent Object Oriented Petri Net approach* 12th Int. Conf. on Application and Theory of Petri Nets, page 432-454, Aahrus,1991.

[DHP 91] C. Dimitrovici, U. Hummert, and L. Petrucci. *Semantics, composition, and properties of algebraic high-level nets.*In Advances in Petri nets, volume 524 of LNCS, page 93-117. Springer Verlag, 1991.

[DNC] M. B. Dwyer, K. A. Nies et L. A. Clarke. *A compact Petri net representation for Ada tasking programs* University of Massachusetts.

[EM 85] H. Ehrig and B. Mahr. *Fundamentals of algebraic Specification 1: Equations and Initial Semantics*, volume 6 EATC Monographs. Springer-Verlag, 1985.

[Kie 89] A. Kiehn. *Petri net systems and their closure properties*. In Grzegorz Rozenberg, editor, Advances in Petri nets, volume 424 of LNCS, pages 306-328, Berlin, 1989.

[MSS 89] T. Murata, B. Shenker et M. Shatz. *Detection of Ada static deadlocks using Petri net invariants,*IEEE Transaction on software Engineering volume 15 number 3, 1989.

[RB 93] P. Racloz, D. Buchs. *Symbolic Proof of CTL formulae over Petri Nets* 8th Int. Symp. on Computer and Information Sciences pp. 189-196, Istanbul, 1993.

[Reisig 85] W. Reisig. *Petri nets: an introduction*. EATCS Monograph on Theoretical computer Science, Vol 4, Springer Verlag 1985.

[SE 90] S. R. Schach *Software engineering*, Irwin, Aksen associates, 1990.

Design of Concurrent Software Based on Problem Concurrency

Bo I. Sandén

George Mason University, Fairfax, VA 22030-4444, USA

Abstract. Two main approaches to the design of concurrent real-time software exist. One approach looks at how input data is transformed into output. The transformations essentially become the tasks. The other approach models the concurrency of the software on concurrency inherent in the problem. One example of this approach, *entity-life modeling*, starts by partitioning the events in the problem into concurrent *threads*, where each thread consists of a sequence of events with a minimum interval between each. Such a *thread model* is *minimal* if there is a time when all the threads occur simultaneously. A thread can often be seen as the "life" of some *entity* in the problem. Essentially, each thread gives rise to a task in the software. As an example, three different thread models of a flexible manufacturing system (FMS) are given. The FMS is essentially about resource contention. This can be made explicit by choosing a thread model where the entities contend for simultaneous, exclusive access to multiple resources.

1 Introduction

Generally speaking, there are two main, systematic approaches to the design of concurrent real-time software. One approach starts with a *data-flow* model that captures the successive *transformations* of system input into system output. These transformations essentially become the tasks. With the other design approach, the concurrency in the software is modeled directly on concurrent processes that are inherent in the problem. In the following paragraphs, these two approaches are further discussed and compared. The paper then describes in depth one approach to software design based on problem concurrency called *entity-life modeling* or *ELM*, and applies it to a flexible-manufacturing problem.

Data-flow approach. The data-flow approach [14, 3, 7] considers each input to the system and the successive computations that transform the input into output or some external action. Each such transformation is regarded as a potential task. To reduce the number of tasks, heuristics are given for consolidating the transformations before implementing them as tasks. The tasks communicate via some form of shared data, often envisioned as a queue of messages between the tasks. Each task either executes on a periodic basis or pends on its input queue.

Variations of the data-flow approach include control transformations and control flow in addition to the data transformations and the data flow. Some variations target distributed systems, where the tasks execute on different nodes, and the data flow relies on some form of inter-node message communication rather than shared memory. In other variations, the transformations contain persistent state information and are sometimes referred to as objects [3]. But the concept of data flowing between the transformations remains the same.

Although the data-flow approach is systematic and may result in viable designs, the development process tends to be lengthy and may involve a variety of different notations. This makes the design even of a small and straight-forward real-time system into a large undertaking. (In [3], a 40-page case study is devoted to a simplified cruise-control system.) The thesis [6] illustrates the complexity of the rules necessary to convert transformations to tasks. The data-flow approach may be criticized for producing many tasks, which often execute not concurrently but one after the other [8]. It is also difficult to determine the system's end-to-end response time to a stimulus since its reaction is not spelled out in one place but may consist of a cascade of task activations [4].

Approach based on problem concurrency. The second approach tries to overcome these disadvantages by modeling the concurrency in the software on concurrency inherent in the problem. This typically leads to a less fragmented solution with fewer tasks, where the system's reaction to a given stimulus appears in one place, and the handling of related, successive stimuli appears together in the text of one task. That task can in turn reference various objects. The philosophy is similar to the *use-case* approach taken in object-oriented analysis [5]. A use case is the sequence of object accesses necessary for a particular purpose, usually a transaction that a human operator wants to complete. In a real-time system, various inanimate entities in the problem domain take the role of the operator and define sequences of operations. As a rule, each such entity is mapped onto a task.

Entity-life modeling is an example of this approach. It starts by identifying *threads of events* in the problem domain. A thread is a set of events that occur sequentially, with a certain minimum time between events. ELM is discussed in a number of earlier publications [9, 8, 11, 12, 13, 1]. This paper adds a new way to identify threads by partitioning the set of all events that a software system has to deal with. It also introduces the concept of thread models. This is described in Sect. 2. Sect. 3 discusses the flexible-manufacturing example. Sect. 4 lists a number of problem categories where ELM has been successfully applied.

2 Entity-life modeling

Sect. 2.1 is an informal description of entity-life modeling. Sect. 2.2 includes formal definitions of concepts such as events, threads and thread models. These formal definitions are not required for the understanding of the rest of the paper.

2.1 Informal description

Problem analysis. The assumption is that a real-time system must react to (or create) *events* in the problem environment, where each event is without duration in time but requires a finite amount of processing time. For example, an elevator control system may react to the event that a particular elevator arrives at a particular floor in a particular building at a particular time. The analyst's concern is to attribute the events in a given problem to different *threads*. To do this,

- create an imaginary *trace* by laying out all events that the software has to deal with along a time line. (Include both external stimuli and actions that the software must take spontaneously at particular times.)
- partition the trace into *threads*, where a thread is a set of events such that
  1. each event belongs to exactly one thread
  2. the events within each thread are separated by sufficient time for the processing of each event
- capture each thread in a state-transition diagram or some other notation suitable for a sequential structure

The set of threads resulting from this partitioning is called a *thread model* of the problem. A thread model is called *minimal* if there is a point in time where every thread has an event. All minimal thread models of a given problem have the the same number of threads. This number is the *concurrency level* of the problem and equal to the maximum number of simultaneous events.

Example: In a simplified elevator control problem with two elevators, we may form a trace by noting each time an elevator arrives at or leaves a floor and each time a door opens or closes. A part of such a trace might be as follows:

```
time-1: elevator A arrives at floor 2
time-2: door A opens at floor 2
time-3: elevator B arrives at floor 3
time-4: door B opens at floor 3
time-5: door B closes at floor 3
```

The events associated with each elevator and its doors form a thread. Together, these threads form a minimal thread model.

Threads and tasks. Each thread model for a given problem is potentially the basis for a software design for that problem. As a rule, each thread maps onto a task. By basing the tasks on a thread model of the problem, we make sure that each event is handled by one task, and that no task is inundated with simultaneous events. Such simultaneous events are taken care of by different tasks, which may execute on different processors. The designer may choose between the different thread models, and may opt to minimize the number of tasks. This can be done by choosing a minimal thread model. As shown in Sect. 3, there may also be reasons to choose a non-minimal model.

Sometimes, additional tasks are needed to those based on the thread model. An example is when a stimulus cannot be attributed to a thread without further analysis of its associated data. In other cases, less than one task per thread is needed, as when the probability of simultaneous events is small, and the loss of an event is acceptable. There are also cases where it is sufficient for a certain action to be taken within an interval. An example is the sampling of a condition with a known minimum extent in time. In that case, the sampling can be timed so as not to occur simultaneously with some other event.

A thread model suggests a concurrent software architecture. In addition to the tasks, the design will contain objects that may or may not be shared between tasks. The thread analysis does not identify objects. We shall see in the Sect. 3 how a designer may complement a given thread model with objects as necessary.

Threads map smoothly onto tasks in Ada and particularly Ada 95. This is because tasks are integrated with the Ada syntax. Shared resources may be represented as protected units.

Threads and entities. Threads can usually be associated with *entities* that are intuitively prominent in the problem, such as an elevator, a robot, etc. The thread is then the "life" of the entity. In the multi-elevator system, we can attribute threads to elevators since the events associated with each elevator are spaced in time. It is impossible to include *all* events in the multi-elevator system in one thread, since several events associated with different elevators can occur simultaneously. For the same reason, it is impossible to associate a thread with each floor, since several elevators can arrive at or depart from a given floor at the same time.

It is particularly useful to look for entities that are either *delayable* or *queuable*:

- A *delayable* entity has events that are triggered by time. This is easily modeled in the software since tasks can reschedule themselves for later execution by means of a `delay` statement. The elevator entities are delayable if, for instance, we want the doors to close automatically after they have been open for a certain period of time.
- *Queuable* entities are *resource users* competing for simultaneous exclusive access to shared resources. Situations where entities wait for access to shared resources are easily modeled in software based on a task's ability to suspend its activity and queue for access to a resource.

To avoid excessive task creation at run-time it is also suitable to choose *long-lived* entities.

2.2 Formal description

A formal definition of threads and thread models can be found in [10] and is recapitulated here for completeness. The first part of the definitions is concerned with describing problems, which are defined in terms of timed traces. The second part has to do with thread analysis of problems.

Problem descriptions. Each individual interaction between the software system and the problem domain is referred to as an *event*. An event is a concrete, unique occurrence at a particular point in time. As a starting point for the analysis, the analyst/designer envisions those possible *traces* of events in which the software system might be engaged. A trace is an ordered set of events that describes one possible unfolding of events in a given problem. Each trace extends in time to infinity; there is no notion of one trace following another. The distance in time is defined for each pair of events in each trace.

A *problem* is defined as a set of traces, which may be mutually inconsistent. For example, in the elevator problem one trace may have elevator A arriving at floor 4 at a certain time on a certain day, while in another, elevator A arrives at floor 5 at the same time and day. The set of all events in a problem, P, is referred to as $Eventset(P)$.

Thread analysis. It is necessary to distinguish between an event that happens once at a particular time, and a *class* of events. We will define a class as all events that have a common *property* such as "Elevator A arrives at floor 3". This class has any number of instances in a given elevator system. "Elevator A arrives at floor 3 during rush hour" is another property that defines a class of events (assuming that "rush hour" is well defined).

Given a trace, S, and a property, e, $eventset(e, S)$ is the set of all events in S with the property e. Given a problem, P, $eventset(e, P)$ is the set of events with the property e in any trace in P.

In the elevator problem, we may define the following properties:

e_A = "Elevator A arrives or leaves"

e_B = "Elevator B arrives or leaves"

d_A = "The door of elevator A opens or closes"[1]

d_B = "The door of elevator B opens or closes"

f_k = "An elevator arrives or leaves, or a door opens or closes on floor k"

We use connectives such as $\vee, \wedge$ and $\neg$ to define new properties from existing ones. For example, we may define the property

$daytime$ = "This event occurs between 6 A.M. and 6 P.M"

and construct new properties such as $e_A \wedge daytime$ or $f_3 \wedge \neg daytime$.

Threads and thread models. The concepts *thread* and *co-occurrence* are used to separate what is sequential from what is concurrent.

A property, h, defines a *thread* in a problem, P, if all the events with the property h in every trace in P are separated in time by some $\delta_h > 0$. Of the

---

[1] For simplicity we let the property d_A include any movement of any door of elevator A irrespective of floor, and assume that only one of these doors can move in either direction at a given point in time.

properties define above, e_A, e_B, d_A and d_B each defines a thread since an elevator cannot arrive or leave more than one floor at a time, and a door cannot open or close more than once at a time. f_k does not define a thread for any k, since for example, elevators A and B can arrive at or leave floor k at the same time.

A *thread model* of a problem, P, is a set of properties, $\{h_1 \ldots h_n\}$, such that each event in each trace in P has exactly one of the properties $h_1 \ldots h_n$. Otherwise put, $eventset(h_1, P) \ldots eventset(h_n, P)$ partition $Eventset(P)$. As an example, $\{e_A, e_B, d_A, d_B\}$ is a thread model of the elevator problem.

Concurrency exists when different threads occur simultaneously by coincidence. Since an event has no extension in time, the probability that two real events will coincide is zero. For this reason, such coincidental simultaneity is formalized by the concept of *co-occurrence*:

A set of threads *co-occur* in a problem, P, if for any $\delta > 0$ there is a trace in P where all the threads in the set occur[2] within an interval of δ time units. In the example, $\{e_A, e_B\}$ co-occurs but $\{e_A, d_A\}$ does not, since the safe operation of the elevator system imposes precedence constraints on the movements of each elevator and its doors.

A thread model $\{h_1 \ldots h_n\}$ is *minimal* if $\{h_1 \ldots h_n\}$ co-occurs. In the example, neither $\{e_A, d_A\}$ nor $\{e_B, d_B\}$ co-occurs, so it follows that $\{e_A, e_B, d_A, d_B\}$ is not a minimal thread model of the elevator problem. If we combine the elevator events and the door events for each elevator by defining the threads

$$g_A = e_A \vee d_A \text{ and } g_B = e_B \vee d_B$$

then we can form the minimal thread model $\{g_A, g_B\}$ of the elevator problem.

3 Example: The FMS Problem

In this section, entity-life modeling is applied to a flexible manufacturing system (FMS), which essentially is a problem of resource allocation.

3.1 Problem description

The FMS controls the jobs in an automated factory [2, 11, 13]. Each job is concerned with the development of one part, which starts out as a piece of raw material and is then milled, lathed and drilled in a series of steps at different

---

[2] We say that a thread, h, occurs at a given time in a given trace if an event with the property h occurs at that time in that trace.

workstations. The series of such job steps is defined in a process plan associated with each job.

The layout of a simple FMS is shown in Fig. 1. Parts are moved between workstations on automated guided vehicles (AGVs). There are A independently traveling AGVs. The system includes an automated storage and retrieval system (ASRS) for raw material and finished parts, which is also used to stage parts that must be taken off the factory floor between job steps. Each job has its own dedicated ASRS bin. F forklift trucks carry parts between their bins and S storage stands, where they are accessible to the AGVs.

There may be several workstations of each type (mill, lathe or drill) for a total of W workstations. Each includes an in-stand, a tool, an out-stand and a robot that moves a part from in-stand to tool to out-stand. (We shall refer to the components of workstation n as $instand_n$, $outstand_n$, etc.)

The FMS is supervised from a terminal. Once a raw part, $part_p$, say, is present in its bin, the supervisor creates a job by associating the bin with a process plan. The job is scheduled for a workstation of a type appropriate for its first job step. If no such workstation is available, the job is queued on that workstation type. $part_p$ remains in its bin until the in-stand of a suitable workstation, $instand_1$, becomes available. It is then moved by a forklift from bin to storage stand, and by an AGV from storage stand to $instand_1$.

The part remains on $instand_1$ until $tool_1$ becomes available and is then moved by the robot into the tool. When the tool has finished its operation, the robot moves the part onto $outstand_1$, and the job is scheduled for a workstation appropriate for its next job step.

The part remains on $outstand_1$ until the in-stand of a suitable workstation ($instand_2$) becomes available or $outstand_1$ is needed by another job. If $instand_2$ becomes available, the part is transported there by an AGV. But if $part_p$ is still on $outstand_1$ by the time $part_q$ is finished in $tool_1$, $part_p$ is bumped and staged in the ASRS. For this, it is removed from the workstation-type queue, then taken by an AGV to a storage stand, then by a forklift to its bin. The job is then scheduled for an appropriate workstation and possibly queued on that workstation type. This continues until the job has completed its process plan. It is then placed in its bin until removed by some mechanism not included in this problem.

The FMS software is distributed. Each workstation has a microcomputer that runs the numerically controlled machinery and coordinates the robot and the

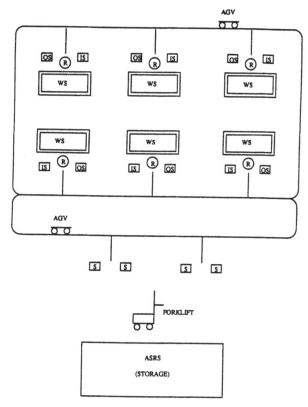

Fig. 1. Layout of a small FMS showing 6 workstations (WS) with in- and out-stands (IS, OS) and robots (R), 2 AGVs and one forklift.

tool. The bulk of the software, which is concerned with resource allocation, runs on a central mini-computer. We shall concentrate on this part, which presents a challenging design problem.

3.2 Thread models of the FMS problem

Some examples of relevant events occurring in the FMS are: "part loaded on an AGV", "part loaded onto a forklift", "forklift starts moving", "part moved from tool to out-stand", etc., and also "forklift assigned to a part", etc. We now define three different thread models of the FMS problem by partitioning the events into threads.

- *Model 1.* Each event in the FMS problem happens to a specific part. No event involves two parts, and no two events in the life of a part are simultaneous. We can therefore partition the events into a thread Job_p per part p.

Intuitively, the jobs "drive" this model by pursuing their own process plans to completion. State-transition models of the Job thread appear in [11, 13]. *Model 1* is not minimal unless the number of jobs in progress is unusually small. (Normally, many jobs are idle in storage.) On the other hand, jobs are queuable entities that need simultaneous exclusive access to multiple resources in different combinations such as workstation in-stand, storage stand and forklift, and the model makes the resource allocation explicit and shows why bumping is necessary to prevent deadlock[3].

– *Model 2.* The intuition of this model is that each in-stand "drives" the system by successively moving one part after the other onto itself as it becomes vacated by a part moving into the tool. *Model 2* has three threads per workstation: *input, tool* and *output*. The *input* thread is concerned with the movement of a part to the in-stand and into the tool, *tool* is concerned with movement from tool to out-stand, and *output* with movement from out-stand to storage when the part is finished or must be staged. In a sense, this model breaks the *Job* thread of *Model 1* into three parts: movement toward a workstation (*input*), movement within a workstation (*tool*), and movement from workstation to storage (*output*). For this reason, *input* and *output* are queuable entities that need roughly the same combinations of resources as *Job*, such as storage stands and AGVs. The model has the advantage over *Model 1* that no threads are associated with jobs in storage. Its entities are also more long-lived than the Job entities. *Model 2* is minimal for certain values of W, A and F.

– *Model 3.* The rationale for this model is that everything that happens in the FMS needs either an AGV, a forklift or a workstation. In this view, a job is handed over from one instance of these three to another, usually via some queueing. There is one thread per workstation, one thread per AGV, and one thread per forklift. *Model 3* is minimal for certain values of W, A and F since it is clear that, given optimum values for W, A and F, there will be a time when all AGVs, forklifts and workstations are busy.

In this solution, the *AGV, forklift* and *workstation* entities may be queued up waiting for jobs. But the entities are not queuable since they do not use

---

[3] To see that bumping is necessary regardless of thread model, assume that there is only one workstation of each type. Without bumping, we can then construct a circular chain involving two workstations with a part on the in-stand, tool and out-stand of each, where the part on each out-stand is waiting for the in-stand of the other workstation.

multiple, shared resources simultaneously. Thus, the solution violates the heuristic that favors resource users as entities. Consequently, the potential resource conflicts are obscured in this solution: for example, some jobs in the AGV queue have exclusive access to a storage stand or a workstation in-stand, while others do not. Thus the model is not immediately conducive to deadlock analysis.

3.3 FMS software designs

Each thread model corresponds to a possible, concurrent design of the FMS software, where each thread maps onto a task.

- *Model 1* results in one queuable task per job, which explicitly describes the successive steps taken to move the job from storage to workstation to either storage or another workstation, until job completion. This implementation is discussed in detail in [11]. As indicated above, a new task is created for each job and remains while the job is idle in storage.
- In an implementation of *Model 2*, *input* and *output* are queuable task types that contend for access to storage stands, AGVs and forklifts. (In addition to the bumping problem, *Model 2* contains a particular resource conflict where an *input* and an *output* task may compete for access to the part on an out-stand.) This implementation is discussed in [11, 13].
- *Model 3* results in an implementation with a queue of job records waiting for an AGV, another queue waiting for a forklift, etc. (These queues are implemented as data structures.) There is one task per AGV, forklift and workstation. Each task removes a part from a queue, moves it or operates on it, then puts it in another queue.
  In *Model 3*, each job may be represented by an instance of an abstract data type that hides the current state of the job and allows the tasks to perform state-changing operations such as putting the job on a queue.

4 Problem categories

Entity-life modeling has been successfully applied to many realistic problems, albeit in a laboratory scale. The examples often fall into the following, not necessarily disjoint categories:

- Periodic problems. These problems rely on delayability. Examples include:

- Automobile cruise control: A *regulator task* periodically compares the current and desired speeds and adjusts the throttle according to a control law [3, 11].
- The remote temperature sensor: A number of *sampler tasks* sense the temperature of different furnaces [7, 8, 11].

- User-thread systems. These problems are largely structured around a thread that represents the behavior of a human operator. Examples include a supermarket checkout system and various automatic vending systems [11].

- Assembly-line systems. In these systems, the entities are typically stations between which material or parts flow. Each station–entity operates on the part when it arrives. A good example is a baggage control system for an airport, where the stations are way-points where a piece of luggage may be routed off the main conveyor onto a baggage pick-up or loading area.

  An alternative model of the baggage control system would include one thread per piece of luggage. This model is not minimal unless the number of pieces of luggage to be accommodated is unusually small.

- Resource contention. The FMS is an example of this problem category, where multiple entities vie for resources. Additional examples are:

  - An automated switchyard [11], where the switch engines are entities contending for exclusive access to track segments or switches.
  - An automated parking garage, where cars contend for parking spaces and trolleys to travel on, and either the cars or the trolleys vie for exclusive access to segments of roadway within the garage.

In the design, Ada task queues are used to represent problem-domain entities waiting for resources.

5 Conclusions

The design of concurrent, real-time software can rely on a problem-domain model that is either based on data flow or on problem-domain concurrency. While the data-flow approaches prescribe a step-wise development procedure with intermediate models, entity-life modeling, which is based on problem concurrency, is more direct. It emphasizes the relationship between the problem and the solution rather than the series of steps necessary to get from one to the other. The directness is also important for reuse, where design does not start from a functional view of requirements alone but must take into account existing pieces of software. A recent study indicates that reuse is most successful when designs are built around such preferred parts [15].

It may be noted that a discrete-event simulation program of a system such as the FMS might have the structure suggested here for the control system itself. This is no coincidence. The real-time control system and the simulation program need not be differently structured only because the events are simulated in one case and come from the external environment in the other. A simulation captures the mechanism that makes the real system works. The ELM principle is to base the software that controls the real system on the same mechanism.

References

1. A. Q. Dinh. *A Development Method for Real-time Software in a Parallel Environment*. PhD thesis, George Mason University, Fairfax, VA, 1994.
2. H. Gomaa. A software design method for distributed real-time applications. *Journal of Systems and Software*, 9(2):81–94, February 1989.
3. H. Gomaa. *Software Design Methods for Concurrent and Real-time Systems*. Addison-Wesley, 1993.
4. N.R. Howes, J.D. Wood, and A. Goforth. The peer tasking design method. In *Proceedings, Third Workshop on Parallel and Distributed Real-Time Systems, Santa Barbara, CA*, pages 20–29, April 1995.
5. I. Jacobson. *Object-oriented software engineering*. Addison-Wesley, 1992.
6. K. L. Mills. *Automated Generation of Concurrent Designs for Real-Time Software*. PhD thesis, George Mason University, Fairfax, VA, 1995.
7. K. W. Nielsen and K. Shumate. Designing large real-time systems with Ada. *Communications of the ACM*, 30(8):695–715, August 1987.
8. B. I. Sandén. Entity-life modeling and structured analysis in real-time software design - a comparison. *Communications of the ACM*, 32(12):1458–1466, December 1989.
9. B. I. Sandén. An entity-life modeling approach to the design of concurrent software. *Communications of the ACM*, 32(3):330–343, March 1989.
10. B. I. Sandén. A restrictive definition of concurrency for discrete-event modeling. Technical Report ISSE-TR-94-114, Dept. of Information and Software Systems Engineering, George Mason University, Fairfax, VA, 1994.
11. B. I. Sandén. *Software Systems Construction with Examples in Ada*. Prentice-Hall, 1994.
12. B. I. Sandén. Design of concurrent software. In *Proceedings, Seventh Annual Software Technology Conference, Salt Lake City, Utah*, April 1995.
13. B. I. Sandén. Designing control systems with entity-life modeling. *Journal of Systems and Software*, 28:225–237, April 1995.
14. H. Simpson. The MASCOT method. *IEE/BCS Software Engineering Journal*, 1(3):103–120, 1986.
15. R. M. Sonnemann. *Exploratory Study of Software Reuse Success Factors*. PhD thesis, George Mason University, Fairfax, VA, 1995.

ECLIPS - A Successful Experiment Combining CCSDS SFDUs, X/Motif, HOOD and Ada

Andrew Matthewman

Space and Aeronautics Department
SYSECA
105, Ave. du Général Eisenhower - BP1228 - 31037 Toulouse cedex - France
Tel. (33) 61197841
Fax. (33) 61197959

Abstract. The ECLIPS research project conducted by SYSECA for the French space agency, CNES, has yielded some interesting results concerning the use of the HOOD design method and the Ada programming language, particularly in the area of Man-Machine Interfaces (MMIs).

The use of HOOD/Ada as a data modelling technique in the specification phase of the project proved extremely effective and a substantial saving in effort was achieved as the model was recovered directly for the design and coding phases. A report is given of the advantages offered by the XInAda all-Ada implementation of the X/Motif graphic MMI libraries, compared to the de facto standard implementation in C. A generic model for the design of MMI software in HOOD is presented, together with its translation to Ada. This model was developed with the aid of the DIADEM MMI engineering method.

1. Introduction

ECLIPS (Environnement de Construction par Logiciel Interactif de Produits SFDU) is the result of a research project conducted between 1990 and 1994 by SYSECA for the French space agency, CNES. The product is an application of the CCSDS SFDU concept [1, 2].

CCSDS (Consultative Committee for Space Data Systems) is an organisation that brings together the world's space agencies for the purpose of jointly developing solutions to common problems involving space information and data systems. These solutions are documented as CCSDS Recommendations, which become international standards through the standardisation process of each agency and of the International Organisation for Standardisation (ISO).

One such Recommendation [1] defines the SFDU (Standard-Formatted Data Unit). SFDUs are intended for exchanging data products between suppliers and users in the open, heterogeneous environment outside any agency or project structure, possibly with many years separating the two parties (use of archives). SFDUs are formed by "packaging" data in a standard manner. The format of the data is unchanged, but the package allows the recipient to delimit the different data objects in the product, understand the relationship between them and, for each, obtain detailed descriptions of the format and meaning from a CCSDS member agency or associated organisation.

ECLIPS consists of an SFDU Structure Editor utility, an SFDU Generator utility and sundry software components available to application programmers. With the SFDU Structure Editor, one can design templates for SFDU-formatted data products, including tokens to represent the application data. ECLIPS enforces the SFDU Structure and Construction Rules, ensuring that only legal products can be designed. The SFDU Generator, which is interfaced with the application, generates actual data products with the structure described by the templates, including application data at the specified places in the product and calculating all necessary delimitation information.

ECLIPS was designed and developed using HOOD and Ada, and has yielded some interesting results concerning this methodology.

2. Project Objectives

The development of ECLIPS took place in two phases. The first phase concentrated on the software functions as a method of validating reference [1], then in draft form. Because of portability and budget constraints, the Man-Machine Interface (MMI) of this first version was limited to the capabilities of TEXT_IO. The second phase built on the success of the first, endowing the software with a graphic MMI more attractive to potential users and more intuitive to use. The development of this graphic MMI required the solution of some known technological problems.

More specifically, the objectives were :

Phase 1 :

- Analyse the (then) future utilisation of certain CCSDS Recommendations in operational projects. Propose and specify software services to assist such operations.
- Develop some of these services, which should be :
    - of a quality consistent with future operational use,
    - highly portable,
    - independent of, but easily interfaced with, potential applications.
- Feed back the implementation experience to CCSDS.

The second of these objectives led to the choice of HOOD/Ada for the development. SADT was used to specify the software functions.

Phase 2 :

- Develop a graphic MMI for the Structure Editor while retaining the alphanumeric one to ensure portability.
- Determine the best method of designing graphic MMI software with HOOD; reputedly difficult.
- Determine the best method of interfacing an Ada application with X/Motif; known to be difficult.
- Provide experience of the benefits of HOOD/Ada in evolutive maintenance.

3. Technological Solutions

The objective of Phase 2 of the project included finding solutions to two problems related to the implementation technology :

- A number of projects known to CNES and SYSECA using HOOD had had difficulties with the MMI. HOOD had acquired a reputation of not being suitable for this type of software.

- Ada programs are difficult to interface with X and Motif, the de facto industry standard graphic MMI libraries. Principal problem areas are calls from C to Ada, dynamic binding and incompatibility with Ada tasking.

The HOOD problem was solved with the aid of DIADEM [3, 4]. This methodology for MMI development provides (amongst other things) methods for the Specification, Architectural Design and Detailed Design of MMI software. There is a direct mapping between the three levels of analysis.

The project employed DIADEM for the specification and design of the MMI, then reproduced the design in HOOD. However, there was not a complete overlap between the DIADEM and HOOD designs. The DIADEM design provided the software architecture, inspired and justified by the specification. The HOOD design reproduced the decomposition of the software without justification, but gave the precise definition of the interfaces, which had been left informal in DIADEM. The internal structure of the software components was detailed in the HOOD design, but no algorithm description was provided. This information was given graphically in the DIADEM design. Figure 1 illustrates the relationships between the two designs.

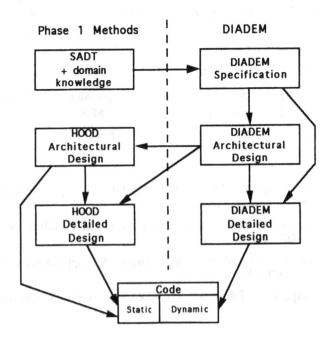

Figure 1. Information Flow Between the ECLIPS MMI Development Methods.

The problem of representing callbacks in HOOD was solved by a naming convention. Any operation name beginning with REQUEST_ is understood to be a callback. During the translation to code, these operations became generic formal subprograms of the package implementing the HOOD object.

The Ada-X/Motif problem was solved by using the XInAda library [5], which reimplements the X/Motif libraries entirely in Ada. XInAda implements the mechanisms of the X Toolkit in a manner more compatible both with the Ada language and with the Ada philosophy (strong typing) than those of the original C implementation. However, the model of the X/Motif API is maintained.

4. Results of the Study

4.1. The Use of HOOD/Ada as a Data Modelling Tool

The primary purpose of the ECLIPS project was to assist in the elaboration and validation of reference [1]. Despite its apparent simplicity, this standard can present some difficult problems resulting from a combination of simple options. To validate the draft standard required an extensive understanding of the logical relationships between the elements of an SFDU, which are not always apparent from the syntactic structures, chosen for their independence of specific data storage media and their ability to be simply transferred using the most common and often rudimentary techniques.

An early decision for the ECLIPS project was to develop an internal model of the structure of SFDUs. Actual SFDUs would be analysed on input or generated on output, but there would be no actual SFDUs within the software, only their logical properties. A similar project at NASA which chose the other option of using SFDUs as the internal format was later abandoned and redeveloped using this principle. HOOD/Ada, of course, is perfectly adapted to such an approach. Analysis of the draft standard led to the identification of a number of elementary types and a series of (mostly limited) private types of which the principal is AN_SFDU. Figure 2 shows the relationships between objects of these types. The relationships are represented in the software by the list of operations possible on the types. Most of the rules contained in reference [1] are implemented by the choice of types and operations, the remaining ones give rise to exceptions raised by the appropriate operations.

Thanks to the top-down approach inherent in HOOD, one of the early results of the Architectural Design was the (large) object STRUCTURES, whose PROVIDED_INTERFACE contains all the types, operations and exceptions constituting the logical model of the standard. Naturally, this object is not terminal and its decomposition was undertaken in due course. However, very early in the project, the project team had a detailed model of the data structures proposed by the draft standard and, with the software developer's eye, were able to spot the inconsistencies, ambiguities and implementation difficulties.

The final version of reference [1] differs significantly from the draft that was current at the start of the ECLIPS project and which contained important technical defects. The ECLIPS modelling experience was of capital importance in the contribution made by CNES to the development of this standard. The power of the techniques used is evident not only in the results achieved but also in the fact that this work was recovered in its entirety for the design and code of the ECLIPS software.

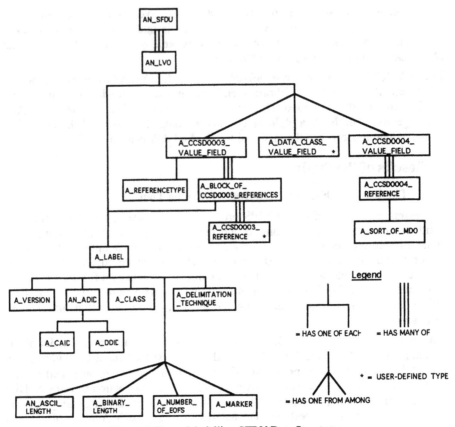

Figure 2. Types Modelling SFDU Data Structures.

4.2. An all-Ada Implementation of X/Motif

XInAda [5], is a proprietary product. It was used for ECLIPS principally because, being written entirely in Ada, it presents none of the many problems which are encountered when interfacing Ada programs with the MIT/OSF X/Motif libraries, written in C.

The designers of XInAda have conformed to the de facto X/Motif standard for the obvious reasons of compatibility with existing environments, software tools and human experience.

However, they also took as an objective to Ada-ise the Application Programming Interface (API), adopting the principle of rigorous typing as a means to detect application programming errors.

The X Toolkit and Motif which depends upon it, repose on the generalised notion of resources. The programmer manipulates objects known as widgets, setting the values of the resources they offer, which can be of two types : data resources (a value) and callback resources (an application routine to be called by the widget to signal an event). In the C implementation, all resources are passed as addresses; it is an implicit understanding between the application and the widget about the meaning of the address (data or routine, structure, argument list, ...). Obviously, this system provides many opportunities for trivial programming errors whose symptoms are random dysfunctions of the software. Such errors typically take some time to become apparent, their consequences can appear in functions entirely unrelated to the erroneous code and are not always repeatable.

XInAda avoids these pitfalls by typing all resources. When the widget designer defines a data resource, he assigns it a type; only values of the type can be assigned to the resource. Similarly, when the designer defines a callback resource, he assigns it a parameter profile. Only procedures with the correct parameter list can be assigned to the resource.

The typing of resources, while eliminating an important class of application coding errors cannot eliminate them all. However, the simple fact of using Ada to implement the Toolkit and widgets allows many errors to be detected at an early stage in development. With XInAda, an application bug generally results in an exception (usually CONSTRAINT_ERROR) being raised within the XInAda code; a call to product support may be necessary to interpret the diagnostic and pinpoint the error, but detection and diagnosis are rapid. Errors resulting in a dysfunction of the software, much more difficult to detect and diagnose, are relatively rare. The same cannot be said of the C implementation.

The same remarks about coding errors apply to the X/Motif libraries themselves. Apart from any bugs introduced during its own development, XInAda inherited many of the bugs present in the MIT/OSF software, which was transcoded from C to Ada without modification of the algorithms employed.

By way of illustration, ECLIPS encountered a Motif bug which results in widgets being only partially removed from the software context when they are destroyed. The problem was diagnosed within a matter of hours and a corrected library was delivered within a week. It turned out that another project in the same office at SYSECA had encountered the same bug in the C libraries. In this case, the diagnosis took weeks and the solution involved rewriting the application around the bug, a result of inadequate support by the computer platform supplier for what it essentially freeware distributed with the operating system.

4.3. The ECLIPS MMI Design

4.3.1. Relevant Features of DIADEM

While it is not the purpose of this paper to describe DIADEM, a brief summary of those aspects necessary for understanding the relationship with HOOD/Ada is given below.

An essential, though by no means unique, feature of DIADEM is conformance with the Seeheim model of interactive software structure, illustrated in Figure 3. The software is divided into three distinct parts :

- the Presentation permits the communication of events and information between the computer system and the user via the interactive peripherals,
- the Application performs all processing not directly related to the involvement of the user in the system,
- the Control conducts the dialogue between the computer system and the user, proposing possible actions, reacting to choices and to events notified by the application.

There is no direct link between the Application and the Presentation.

The combination of the Control and Presentation is named the Man-Machine Dialogue (MMD).

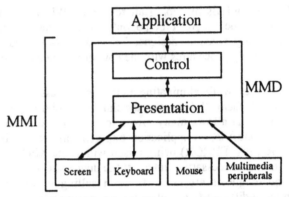

Figure 3. The Seeheim Model of Interactive Software Structure.

A DIADEM specification of an MMD begins with the identification of the objects perceived and manipulated by the user via the MMI (user objects). The next step is to develop the Task Graph, a hierarchical decomposition of the user's task into sub-tasks; Figure 4 shows the ECLIPS Task Graph. The arrows indicate the USE relationship between a task and its sub-tasks, which has the following semantics : "to accomplish the task, the user may need to accomplish the sub-task".

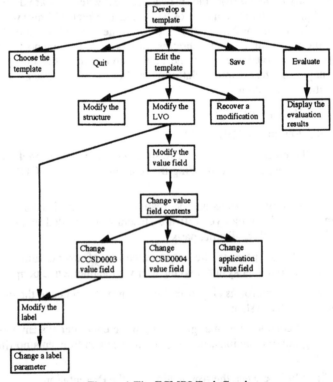

Figure 4. The ECLIPS Task Graph.

No indication of the conditions or the order in which the sub-tasks are accomplished is given in the Task Graph. This information is reserved for the task strategy, elaborated for each task in the graph and detailing the strategy offered to the user by the computer system for accomplishing his task.

Figures 5 and 6 are examples of ECLIPS task strategies, expressed with the DIADEM graphic formalism. The ovals on the left, right and top sides of the strategy are ports; respectively the activation port, the result port and the abandon port. As their names suggest, they represent the beginning of the task, the successful conclusion of the task and the abandon of the task. The activation and result ports transfer context information (parameters) from and to the parent task. The abandon port can be triggered from within the task or from the parent task.

Figure 5 is interpreted to mean "On beginning the task, the user must choose a template. If he abandons this sub-task, the task is abandoned. Once a template has been chosen, it is no longer possible to choose a template, but the user has a parallel choice of four sub-tasks : Quit, Evaluate, Save and Edit the template. When the sub-task Quit is accomplished, the task is abandoned."

Figure 6 is interpreted to mean "On beginning the task, the user has a parallel choice of two actions : Selecting a CANCEL button or entering a filename. If he chooses the former, the task is abandoned. If he chooses the latter, he has the possibility of selecting a button OK (note that the filename and the CANCEL button are still active). If the user selects OK, the application is instructed to load the template and the task is complete."

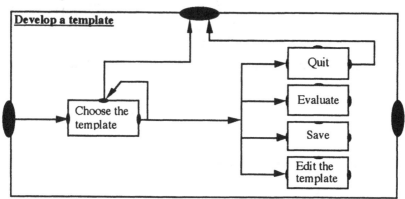

Figure 5. Strategy of the Task Develop a Template.

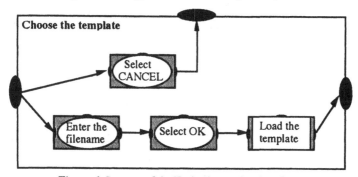

Figure 6. Strategy of the Task Choose the Template.

319

The strategies reveal the need for elementary interactions between the user and the software (CANCEL, filename, OK). The final steps in the specification are to assemble these into the Presentation Hierarchy, illustrated in Figure 7 and to establish the Presentation Constraints on the graphic layout. In the case of ECLIPS, a small application, the Presentation Constraints consisted in laying out the main window, shown in Figure 8.

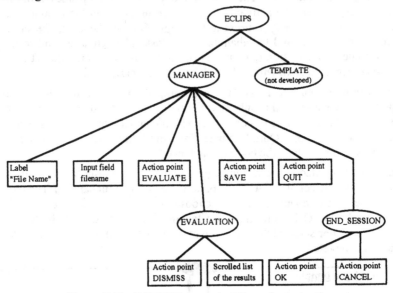

Figure 7. The ECLIPS Presentation Hierarchy (extract).

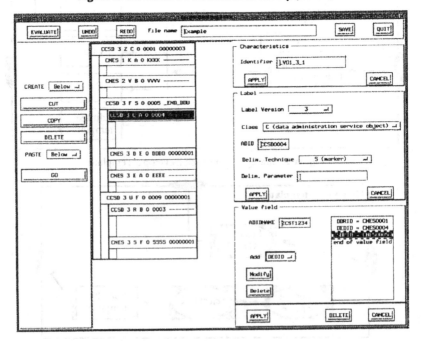

Figure 8. The ECLIPS Presentation Constraints.

As will be seen later, the techniques used in a DIADEM specification are re-used for the detailed design. The level of detail appropriate for the specification is thus a project-specific decision about how precise one must be in the early stages of the project in order to ensure a satisfactory result in the development phases. The small size of the ECLIPS application and the exploratory nature of the work meant that the specification was quite detailed. A larger project would typically halt the specification at a higher level.

For the Architectural Design, DIADEM divides components into three types : presentation components, control components and dialogue components (combining presentation and control). Dialogue components are similar to non-terminal objects in HOOD; "containers" for the other components, implementing the hierarchical structure of the software architecture. The hierarchy of components is that of the Task Graph. A task identified in the specification gives rise to either a dialogue component (non terminal task) or a control component (terminal task). A dialogue component contains its own principal control component, responsible for implementing the strategy of the task, plus the components corresponding to the sub-tasks and the Presentations used by the task. The structure of the Presentation components is similarly derived from the Presentation Hierarchy.

Within the dialogue components, a message-passing semantic is used for the communication between control components and the presentation components they use.

For the Detailed Design, the task strategies and presentation constraints from the specification are revisited and refined to a level suitable for coding. In the strategies, such aspects as user errors, rare application events, or maintaining the Presentation up to date with the context of the dialogue are dealt with. These aspects are generally left out of the specification, which concentrates on the essentials of the dialogue. As can be seen in Figure 9, what started as a description of the strategy offered to the user by the system has now become a detailed algorithm for the conduct of the dialogue. Similarly the Presentation Constraints are revisited and each display, window, etc. is designed in detail, ready for coding. For ECLIPS, the Presentation Constraints in the specification were already at a detailed design level.

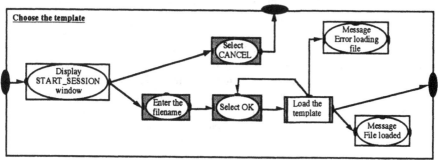

Figure 9. The Strategy of Figure 6 Developed in the Detailed Design.

4.3.2. The Transition from DIADEM to HOOD

As explained in section 3, the ECLIPS Architectural Design was first developed using DIADEM and then mapped to HOOD. Up to a certain point, each dialogue component mapped to a non-terminal HOOD object but, the DIADEM hierarchy going to a greater level of detail than is reasonable for a HOOD object hierarchy, the lower levels of each branch in the DIADEM hierarchy were grouped together in a terminal HOOD object. The DIADEM hierarchy was still maintained, however, by the use of OPERATION_SETS within the terminal objects to group together the operations implementing the remaining levels of decomposition.

The structure of the HOOD design is thus derived from the Task Graph via the concept of dialogue components. The first version of the ECLIPS HOOD design shown in Figure 10, disastrously flawed, based the design on the Task Graph *and* the Presentation Hierarchy.

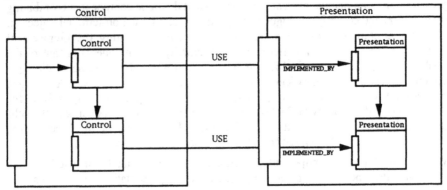

Figure 10. First Model for the ECLIPS MMI HOOD Design

The presentation components are visible to the control components because their PROVIDED_INTERFACEs are offered by their parent components. The complexity of the resulting Presentation PROVIDED_INTERFACE was managed using OPERATION_SETs and was not as laborious to develop as might be imagined, thanks to the HOOD tool. This model for the software design was seductive because it is a pure application of the Seeheim model. In particular, the relationships between the presentation components are entirely contained in the presentation part. The model is consistent with the DIADEM notion of dialogue components in the sense that the dialogue component does not contain the presentation component itself, but a projection of the component from its place within the Presentation Hierarchy.

The flaw in this model is that it has absolutely no modularity. It can be seen in Figure 4, for example, that the task Modify the label is used in two different contexts; Modify the LVO and Change CCSD0003 value field. In software terms, we must have a design model which allows for the development of a single piece of software for the task, called in two different contexts. The model of Figure 10 divides the software for a task into two widely separated but intimately related pieces. When these pieces must operate in two or more different contexts it is quickly apparent that this model is unreasonably difficult to implement because of the coordination to be maintained between the corresponding instances of the control and presentation components.

The ECLIPS design was thus restructured to follow the model illustrated in Figure 11. A terminal dialogue object (terminal in the hierarchy of dialogue objects, which are always non-terminal HOOD objects) contains two terminal (in the HOOD sense) child objects; the control and presentation. A non-terminal dialogue object has dialogue object children. One of these, the coordinator, serves to group together the control and presentation for this level of dialogue. At first sight, this model would seem to contravene the Seeheim model in that a presentation object USEs a dialogue object, which is a component derived from an analysis of the control of the MMD. In fact, the presentation object calls operations IMPLEMENTED_BY presentation objects within the dialogue object and the Seeheim model is respected.

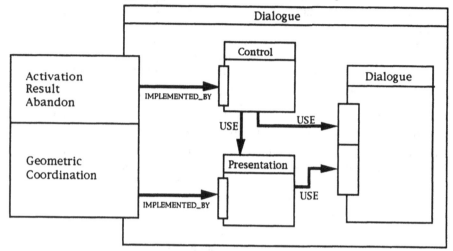

Figure 11. Final Model for the ECLIPS MMI HOOD Design.

So far we have only considered the structure of the design, but the other important aspect at the architectural level is the PROVIDED_INTERFACE of the objects.

The PROVIDED_INTERFACE of a control object consists of four operations corresponding to the three ports of the DIADEM task it implements (one port is bi-directional). Ports leaving the task use the REQUEST_ naming convention described in section 3.

The PROVIDED_INTERFACE of a presentation object is directly derived from the list of elementary interactions that it offers. Each gives rise to one or more of the following operations : set the value, get the value, activate, deactivate, notify user interaction. Additional operations are required to ensure the geometric coordination with other objects : where to display, display, un-display, activate, deactivate.

The PROVIDED_INTERFACE of a dialogue object consists of the four operations corresponding to task ports, IMPLEMENTED_BY the control object, plus the geometric coordination operations IMPLEMENTED_BY the presentation object.

This design model is highly modular and it performed extremely well in the case of ECLIPS. Each dialogue component is entirely independent and testable and this characteristic saved a major project objective. The objective in question was a demonstration at one of the CCSDS international meetings. Due to the problem of increasing compilation time described in section 4.4.1, ECLIPS was not completed as planned and, though the three major MMI components were developed and tested, it was proving difficult to integrate them. The demonstration was saved by integrating the three components at the presentation level only; the ECLIPS main window was complete, each of the three main areas in the window was fully functional, but they were not functionally interconnected. The result was sufficient to give a reasonably representative demonstration of the software, since complete use could be made of the three main areas corresponding to distinct sub-tasks.

4.3.3. The Coexistence of Two Presentation Technologies

As mentioned in section 2, the second phase of the ECLIPS project was to develop an X/Motif MMI while retaining the existing TEXT_IO MMI. The MMI was entirely contained in one (non-terminal) HOOD object. One approach would have been to entirely redevelop this object using X/Motif and maintain two parallel versions of the MMI software, containing many of the same functions but in two entirely separate implementations. The undesirable consequences of such an approach for the maintenance of the software are obvious. The approach adopted, inspired and enabled by DIADEM, was to have common control components between the two MMI versions and variants only of the presentation components. Thus, the differences between the two versions are limited to the INTERNALS of the presentation objects. The control objects and the PROVIDED_INTERFACEs of the presentation objects (the latter is a necessary condition of the former) are common.

This result is somewhat surprising considering the vastly different capabilities of TEXT_IO and Motif. Even more so when one considers that the TEXT_IO MMI has a menu-driven action-object style of interaction and the Motif MMI a graphic object-action style. This "victory" for the Seeheim model is perhaps one of the most significant results of the ECLIPS project.

Without going into too much detail, the secret lies in the use made of the activate operation in the geometric coordination operations offered by a presentation object. In the Motif version the level n presentation object activates all the level n+1 objects together, and the user selects which one will react by clicking one of the interactive items it offers. In the alphanumeric version, the same operation results in a menu choice being read from the input stream. The level-n object recognises all the choices of the level n+1 objects. It pushes the choice back into the input stream and activates the level n+1 object corresponding to the choice. In one of these two ways control flow arrives in the terminal presentation object responsible for detecting the user interaction and informing the corresponding control object.

4.4. Implementing the ECLIPS MMI in Ada

The preceding section described the ECLIPS MMI design in terms of a basic model, the dialogue object (Figure 11). We will now look at the mapping of this design to Ada code.

4.4.1 Declarative Part

As mentioned in section 3, the callback operations prefixed by REQUEST_ were implemented as generic formal parameters. Thus, the two terminal objects in Figure 11 lead to the following package specifications.

```
-- Example of a window with a text field and an option menu,
-- plus OK and Cancel buttons.
generic
    -- Presentation callbacks are very low-level.
    with procedure REQUEST_CHANGE_TEXT_FIELD
                        (TO : in STRING);
    with procedure REQUEST_CHANGE_OPTION
                        (TO : in ENUMERATED);
    with procedure REQUEST_CONFIRM_MODIFICATIONS;
    with procedure REQUEST_CANCEL_MODIFICATIONS;
package GEN_PRESENTATION is
    procedure SET_TEXT_FIELD (TO : in STRING);
    procedure ACTIVATE_TEXT_FIELD;
    procedure DEACTIVATE_TEXT_FIELD;
    procedure SET_OPTION (TO : in ENUMERATED);
    procedure ACTIVATE_OPTION;
    procedure DEACTIVATE_OPTION;
    procedure ACTIVATE_CONFIRM_BUTTON;
    procedure DEACTIVATE_CONFIRM_BUTTON;
    procedure ACTIVATE_CANCEL_BUTTON;
    procedure DEACTIVATE_CANCEL_BUTTON;
    -- Geometric coordination operations.
    procedure DISPLAY (USING : in out A_WIDGET);  -- Simple example.
    procedure UNDISPLAY;
end GEN_PRESENTATION;

generic
    with procedure REQUEST_RESULT (<result parameters>);
    with procedure REQUEST_ABANDON;
package GEN_CONTROL is
    procedure ACTIVATE (<activation parameters>);
    procedure ABANDON;
    procedure EXECUTE_CHANGE_TEXT_FIELD (TO : in STRING);
    procedure EXECUTE_CHANGE_OPTION (TO : in ENUMERATED);
    procedure EXECUTE_CONFIRM_MODIFICATIONS;
    procedure EXECUTE_CANCEL_MODIFICATIONS;
end GEN_CONTROL;
```

The prefix GEN_ (for generic) was used, reserving the unprefixed object name for the package which implements the object in the USE and IMPLEMENTED_BY relations. We will later see the INST_ prefix (for instance), too. We can note that for each callback offered by PRESENTATION (REQUEST_), CONTROL has a corresponding EXECUTE_ procedure, used to instantiate PRESENTATION in a plug-socket arrangement. In the HOOD design, these operation were considered as INTERNALS. In Ada, they appear necessarily in the package specification in order to be visible for instantiating PRESENTATION.

A chicken-and-egg problem is immediately apparent between these two packages : PRESENTATION is instantiated with generic actual parameters from CONTROL, but CONTROL must have visibility over PRESENTATION in order to USE it.

This problem is compounded by the fact that, since both objects implement operations offered by their parent, the instantiations must be made in the parent package specification (where restrictions apply), to allow the renaming corresponding to the HOOD IMPLEMENTED_BY relationship.

The solution consisted in developing dummy packages as seen in the generalised package structure given below. A simple text-processing program was written to generate the dummy package from the real package specification. Since, as shown below, these and other packages have to be declared in-line within the parent package and not as library units, an "include" preprocessor was used so that the source code for a child object is independent of its parent.

```
generic
   with procedure REQUEST_RESULT (<result parameters>);
   with procedure REQUEST_ABANDON;
package GEN_DIALOGUE is

   package CONTROL is
      procedure ACTIVATE (<activation parameters>);
      procedure ABANDON;
      -- The EXECUTE_ procedures are not necessary.
   end CONTROL;

   package PRESENTATION is
      <same declarations as GEN_PRESENTATION>
   end PRESENTATION;

   procedure ACTIVATE (<activation parameters>)
      renames CONTROL.ACTIVATE;
   procedure ABANDON renames CONTROL.ABANDON;

   procedure DISPLAY (USING : in out A_WIDGET)
      renames PRESENTATION.DISPLAY;
   procedure UNDISPLAY
      renames PRESENTATION.UNDISPLAY;

end GEN_DIALOGUE;
```

```
with GEN_PRESENTATION;
package body GEN_DIALOGUE is

    -- To avoid a chicken-and-egg visibility problem,
    -- GEN_CONTROL is declared here and USEs PRESENTATION
    -- declared in the package specification.
    <declaration of GEN_CONTROL as above>
    package body GEN_CONTROL is separate;

    -- The dialogue callbacks are IMPLEMENTED_BY
    -- the control callbacks.
    package INST_CONTROL is new GEN_CONTROL
       (REQUEST_RESULT => REQUEST_RESULT,
        REQUEST_ABANDON => REQUEST_ABANDON);

    package body CONTROL is

       procedure ACTIVATE (...) is
       begin
          INST_CONTROL.ACTIVATE (...);
       end ACTIVATE;

       etc.

    end CONTROL;

    package INST_PRESENTATION is new GEN_PRESENTATION
       (REQUEST_CHANGE_TEXT_FIELD =>
           INST_CONTROL.EXECUTE_CHANGE_TEXT_FIELD,
        REQUEST_CHANGE_OPTION =>
           INST_CONTROL.EXECUTE_CHANGE_OPTION,
        REQUEST_CONFIRM_MODIFICATIONS =>
           INST_CONTROL.EXECUTE_CONFIRM_MODIFICATIONS,
        REQUEST_CANCEL_MODIFICATIONS =>
           INST_CONTROL.EXECUTE_CANCEL_MODIFICATIONS);

    package body PRESENTATION is

       procedure SET_TEXT_FIELD (TO : in STRING) is
       begin
          INST_PRESENTATION.SET_TEXT_FIELD (TO => TO);
       end SET_TEXT_FIELD;

       etc.

    end PRESENTATION;

end GEN_DIALOGUE;
```

The above package structure represents a typical terminal dialogue object. Below is
the structure of a typical non-terminal dialogue object.

```
generic
   with procedure REQUEST_RESULT (<result parameters>);
   with procedure REQUEST_ABANDON;
package GEN_DIALOGUE is

   package COORDINATOR is
      <same declarations as GEN_COORDINATOR in the package body>
   end COORDINATOR;

   procedure ACTIVATE (<activation parameters>)
      renames COORDINATOR.ACTIVATE;

   etc.

end GEN_DIALOGUE;

with GEN_CHILD_DIALOGUE1;
with GEN_CHILD_DIALOGUE2;
package body GEN_DIALOGUE is

   package CHILD_DIALOGUE1 is new GEN_CHILD_DIALOGUE1
      (REQUEST_RESULT => COORDINATOR.EXECUTE_RESULT1,
       REQUEST_ABANDON => COORDINATOR.EXECUTE_ABANDON1);

   package CHILD_DIALOGUE2 is new GEN_CHILD_DIALOGUE2
      (REQUEST_RESULT => COORDINATOR.EXECUTE_RESULT2,
       REQUEST_ABANDON => COORDINATOR.EXECUTE_ABANDON2);

   generic
      with procedure REQUEST_RESULT (<result parameters>);
      with procedure REQUEST_ABANDON;
   package GEN_COORDINATOR is
      <typical declaration of a dialogue package, but including the
       EXECUTE_ procedures of CONTROL in the PROVIDED_INTERFACE>
   end GEN_COORDINATOR;

   package body GEN_COORDINATOR is separate;

   package INST_COORDINATOR is new GEN_COORDINATOR
      (REQUEST_RESULT => REQUEST_RESULT,
       REQUEST_ABANDON => REQUEST_ABANDON);

   package body COORDINATOR is

      procedure ACTIVATE (...) is
      begin
         INST_COORDINATOR.ACTIVATE (...);
      end ACTIVATE;

      etc.

   end COORDINATOR;

end GEN_DIALOGUE;
```

The non-terminal dialogue object model worked extremely well low down in the dialogue hierarchy but, as integration of the MMI software proceeded in a bottom-up fashion, a problem of rapidly increasing compilation times was encountered. No systematic investigation was undertaken, but the root cause is the nested use of generic units. Each dialogue package is instantiated within its parent dialogue package which is instantiated within....

For the alphanumeric version of the MMI, this nested structure was maintained, despite the compilation penalty, in order to stay within the Ada standard.

For the X/Motif MMI, XInAda callback technology was used to allow the instances of the dialogue objects to be library units and not subunits of their parent objects. With the scheme shown below, the parent object only instantiates the package DIALOGUE_CALLBACKS and not GEN_DIALOGUE.

```
with GEN_DIALOGUE;
package DIALOGUE is

   -- Instantiating this package connects the callbacks.
   generic
      with procedure REQUEST_RESULT (<result parameters>);
      with procedure REQUEST_ABANDON;
   package CALLBACKS is
      MUST_HAVE_A_DECLARATION_HERE : constant := 0;
   end CALLBACKS;

   procedure REQUEST_RESULT (<result parameters>);
   procedure REQUEST_ABANDON;

   package INST_DIALOGUE is new GEN_DIALOGUE
      (REQUEST_RESULT => REQUEST_RESULT,
       REQUEST_ABANDON => REQUEST_ABANDON);

   procedure ACTIVATE (...) renames INST_DIALOGUE.ACTIVATE;

   etc.

end DIALOGUE;


with X_Toolkit_Basics;
package body DIALOGUE is

   RESULT_CALLBACK : X_Toolkit_Basics.Callback;
   ABANDON_CALLBACK : X_Toolkit_Basics.Callback;

   package body CALLBACKS is
   begin
      <assign generic formal parameters to callback variables>
   end CALLBACKS;

   procedure REQUEST_RESULT (<result parameters>) is
   begin
      <call RESULT_CALLBACK>
   end REQUEST_RESULT;

   procedure REQUEST_ABANDON is
   begin
      <call ABANDON_CALLBACK>
   end REQUEST_RESULT;
end DIALOGUE;
```

4.4.2 Subprogram Bodies

The declarative part of the MMI code was derived from the HOOD design as described above. The procedural part was derived from the DIADEM design.

The code of the presentation objects was evident from the package specification and from the detailed design of the graphic layout. The operations are typically only a few lines long, accomplishing only very basic functions (set value, get value, activate, deactivate, etc.).

The code of the control objects was based on the detailed task strategies; each result port corresponds to an EXECUTE_ procedure and the transitions from the port correspond to the actions to be taken when the procedure is called. This powerful diagrammatic specification of the algorithm was extremely useful in mastering the complexity of the state transitions within the package.

5. ECLIPS Project Profile

Budget and Timescales

Phase 1 : 1.2 man-years over 2.5 years

Phase 2 : 0.9 man-year over 1.5 years

Team size : 1.5 people

Code volume :

Phase 1 : 8500 delivered source lines

Phase 2 : 15500 delivered source lines

Development Environment

Phase 1 : VAX/VMS, STOOD, VAX Ada Compiler

Phase 2 : SPARC/SunOS, STOOD, TSP/Alsys Compiler

6. Conclusions

ECLIPS is a software tool that works well and is in use at CNES to develop the use of SFDUs within the Agency. The fact that the project was run as an industrial development, despite its research objectives, has meant that the technological problems posed were resolved in a manner that can be repeated on larger projects.

The project experience indicates that HOOD/Ada can be used as a data modelling tool in the specification phase of a project, leading to a significant saving of effort when the results are reused to provide a foundation for the design and code.

The application of the Ada language and the Ada philosophy to the large and complex X/Motif libraries has been shown to bring benefits above and beyond simple compatibility with an Ada application. This is not to underestimate the importance of a truly satisfactory solution to the problem of X-Ada compatibility, which has plagued many projects.

A generic HOOD design model for MMI software has been derived which yields highly modular components, independently testable and highly maintainable.

This model was obtained via use of the DIADEM method of MMI engineering. With further work, it should be possible to develop a HOOD-only methodology for the Architectural Design. Though the use of DIADEM for the specification and detailed design brings important benefits, it is not an absolute prerequisite for the application of the results obtained concerning HOOD.

The ECLIPS MMI was developed in two versions, one using TEXT_IO for communicating with the user and one using X/Motif. Despite the considerable differences between these two technologies, much code is common between the two versions, leading to savings in the development and maintenance of the software.

The systematic way in which the design and development proceeded from the specification does demonstrate DIADEM's ability to accelerate and secure the MMI development process, and the ECLIPS results do suggest that automatic design and code generation are feasible, though substantial investigation is still required if this is to be achieved.

ECLIPS was developed by direct programming using the X/Motif libraries, however most projects now use one of the many MMI development tools available on the market. How HOOD might best be used in conjunction with such a tool is a subject for further research, where the results will probably depend upon the characteristics of the tool (or class of tools) in question.

7. References

[1]   Standard Formatted Data Units -- Structure and Construction Rules
       CCSDS 620.0-B-2, May 1992
       ISO 12175

[2]   Standard Formatted Data Units -- A Tutorial
       CCSDS 621.0-G-1, May 1992

[3]   DIADEM - Méthode Intégrée de Développement du Dialogue Homme-Machine
       P. Aknin, C-A. Poirier
       Proceedings, Le Génie Logiciel et ses Applications, 15-19/11/94

[4]   Egonomie et Méthodologie de Développement IHM : l'Exemple de DIADEM
       D. Tasset
       Proceedings, Ergonomie et Ingénierie, 21-23/9/94

[5]   Top Graph'X, 10 Allée de la Mare Jacob, 91290 La Norville, France.

Applying Teamwork/Ada and RAISE for Developing an Air Traffic Control Application

A.Alapide, S.Candia, M.Cinnella, S.Quaranta

Space Software Italia
Viale del Lavoro 101
Quartiere Paolo VI
74100 Taranto Italy
Tel: + 39 99 4701 619
Fax: + 39 99 4701 777
E-Mail: cinnella@ssi.it

Abstract. The paper illustrates the results of applying Teamwork/Ada and the RAISE Formal Method to develop an Air Traffic Control application. Two approaches have been applied for the development of the application: integrated-parallel and a-posteriori. After a quick description of Teamwork/Ada and RAISE, the paper illustrates how these two approaches have been adopted and discusses the costs, the benefits and the changes associated to each of them. Based on lessons learnt, the paper also provides recommendations on how to apply the two approaches effectively.

1 Introduction

As well known, the adoption of a new technology for software development always brings about risks that need to be carefully controlled especially when the software has to be delivered with a very tight schedule.

The Space Software Italia (SSI) has applied Teamwork/Ada and the RAISE Formal Method (FM) to develop an Ada software application, in the domain of the Air Traffic Control (ATC), for the Alenia Radar System Division. In order to facilitate the transition towards FMs, RAISE was not applied for the development of the whole application, but only to some critical sub-components and always in combination with Teamwork/Ada.

This combined approach, based on both formal and structured methods, allowed to learn some lessons that can facilitate a lower risk transition towards a larger scale adoption of FMs.

Two approaches have been followed for the application of FMs: *integrated - parallel* and *a-posteriori*. The paper briefly illustrates the two approaches and discusses the costs, the benefits and the changes associated to each of them. Moreover it provides some recommendations on how to apply them effectively.

Even if based on the results of applying the RAISE FM, most of the considerations in this paper are applicable to the adoption of any FM based on a toolset which supports automatic Ada code generation from a formal specification language.

2 Application Background

SSI developed the TCA (Traffic Conflicts Alert) Analyzer, a software application in the ATC domain. The Detector is the critical software component, of the Analyzer TCA, that was developed almost entirely applying RAISE. The Detector is in charge of processing radar data in order to predict potential air conflicts belonging to the following classes:

- STCA (Short Term Conflict Alert): conflicts between planes;
- MSAW (Minimum Safe Altitude Warning): planes going lower than the minimum safe altitude;
- DAIW (Dangerous Area Infringement Warning) : planes entering a restricted area.

The application was required to be implemented in Ada and C. It was developed in Unix and VMS environment, but had to be ported on the MARA operating system. Moreover it had stringent performance requirements in order to give the operator enough time to take corrective actions and high reliability requirements to minimize the number of nuisanse alarms and avoid to the maximum extent omitting alarms corresponding to real conflicts.

The development process followed the SSI Software Quality System (SQS) for projects having a medium criticality level. SSI SQS has been accredited by ESA (European Space Agency) for the PSS-05-0 and PSS-01 series and is also compliant with the 2167-A DoD standard (required by the customer) and the Nato standard.

RAISE was selected for the application development because SSI had a previous related experience on it and because the CEC (Commission of the European Communities) sponsored the application within the LaCoS ESPRIT (European Strategic PRogramme for the Information Technology) project.

3 Teamwork/Ada and RAISE

Formal Methods claim to provide advantages that are to a certain extent complementary to the ones provided by structured methods. The subject of integrating formal and structured methods is not new to literature. [6], [7] and [8] provide a good insight on the topic.

This article focuses on the integration of two specific software technologies: Teamwork/Ada and RAISE. The following subsections provide a brief description of the two technologies and make comparative analysis of the support provided by each in the design and implementation phases.

3.1 Teamwork/Ada

Teamwork/Ada [1] is based on the Ada Structure Graph (ASG) editor and on the Teamwork/Ada Source Builder. The former can be used for creating models of Ada application systems using graphic icons that map to the semantic of the Ada language. The latter can be used to automatically generate source code from analyzable sets of ASGs to which appropariate source code notes shall have previously been associated.

3.2 RAISE

The RAISE (Rigorous Approach to Industrial Software Engineering) FM is based on the formal language RSL (RAISE Specification Language), the RAISE method and a powerful toolset. The *RAISE Specification Language* (RSL) [2] is provided with structuring mechanisms that allow one to build layers of modularized specifications for complex systems. It includes constructs to model concurrency at different level of detail (from abstract to concrete). The *RAISE method* [3] allows two types of formal proofs: *inter-level* proofs and *intra-level* proofs. The former deal with proving that the specification of level i+1 is consistent with the specification of level i, while the latter deals with proving that the specification of level i is consistent and satisfies the stated critical requirements. The RAISE toolset [4] allows to edit RSL specifications with automatic correctness checks, supports the automatic generation of confidence conditions and the automatic verification of the static development relation. It provides support to edit and prove theories, confidence conditions and the dynamic development relations. Moreover it allows to automatically translate in Ada or C++ the RSL concrete specifications. The following table makes a comparison between Teamwork/Ada and RAISE.

Functionality	Teamwork/Ada	RAISE
Automatic inter phase consistency	no	partial
Automatic intra phase consistency	yes	yes
Support of a graphical notation	yes	no
Automatic code generation	only skeleton	yes

Fig. 1. Comparison between RAISE and Teamwork/Ada functionalities

4 Managerial and Technical Approach

The focus in the definition of the managerial approach for the TCA Analyzer project was on minimizing the risks of adopting RAISE, a new, somehow still in progress technology, to the development of a real application.

The adoption of RAISE for the TCA application has therefore had a very practical cut also because the application had to be developed starting from the design phase, with strict schedule requirements and emphasis also on portability aspects. As already said, the Detector was one of the three major software components of the TCA Analyzer application and was selected as the one to be implemented with RAISE, due to (a) its criticality, (b) a smaller interface towards the TCA environment. The team in charge of developing the Detector has interacted strictly and has sometimes been coincident with the team developing the two other main components of the TCA Analyzer: Gatherer and Tracker. The overall team had a strict communication with the customer technical representatives that provided feedback on requirements understanding and reviewed all the developed documentation.

Based on the RAISE background and the application requirements, the following decisions were taken in order to minimize the risks:

- *Integration of RAISE with Teamwork/Ada*, in order to (a) use the Teamwork/Ada graphical notation as a bridge towards the customer, facilitating the review of the Detector design, (b) guarantee an unique notation for the whole Analyzer-TCA documentation;
- *Minimum Level of formality*, starting with RSL at a very concrete level, because the project had to start from the detailed design phase;
- *Focus on Code Efficiency*, with the continuous need to monitor the resulting quality of the automatic code;
- *Tailoring of the design documentation outline* to produce the documentation on the parts developed with RAISE, compliant with the 2167-A DoD project standard.

The approaches followed for the TCA Detector development are illustrated in fig.2 and discussed in more detail in section 5. In the integrated approach the RSL specifications have substituted the PDL (Program Design Language).
In the a-posteriori approach some abstract RSL specifications have been derived from the more concrete RSL and have been used to formulate some algorihmic properties of the tracks' alignement.

5   Integrated Parallel Approach

The integrated-parallel approach has been applied to develop three main sub-components of the CSC Detector. Teamwork/Ada was adopted for creating the Ada Structure Graphs (ASGs), similarly to what was done for the rest of the TCA application, but rather than producing "informal" PDL (Programming Design Language), RSL concrete specifications were associated to each module. The RSL specifications reflected the structure of the ASGs and, in most cases, the Ada code could be automatically generated from them. It must be noted that the creation of the ASGs and RSL concrete specifications was made in parallel, with feedback from one method to the other.

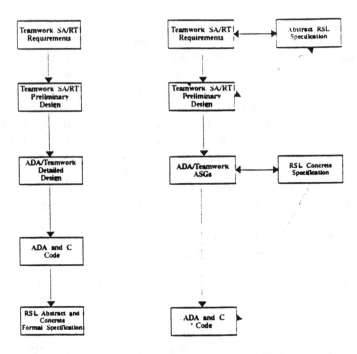

Fig. 2. A-posteriori(a) and Integrated-Parallel(b) approaches

Advantages The main advantages in integrating Teamwork/Ada and RAISE were:

- *(due to Teamwork/Ada)*: graphical representation of the detailed design, possibility to generate automatically skeleton Ada code consistent with its graphical representation;
- *(due to RAISE)*: automatic code generation, automatic consistency between unit detailed design and code, early error discovery.

Fig. 3 shows an example of ASGs, fig. 4 the mapping between ASG graphical entities and RSL constructs, and fig.5 the corresponding RSL specifications.

Costs Some extra costs must be associated to the adoption of the integrated approach because:

- Two methods, rather than one, shall be learnt by the developer;
- Writing RSL is more onerous than writing PDL;
- The Teamwork/Ada and RAISE documentation need to be integrated. For what concerns the design documentation it must be said that Teamwork/Ada

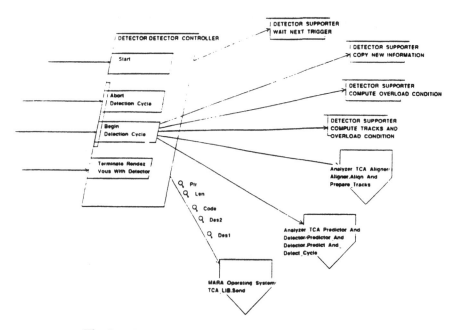

Fig. 3. Ada Structure Graph for the Detector task

allows to automatically generate Interleaf documentation based on a pred-
ifined model of the 2167-A documentation outline, while, so far, with RAISE
it is only possible to generate LaTex or Interleaf pretty printed specifications.
Therefore for documenting the parts developed with RAISE, two alternative
possibilities exist:

1. pretty printing of the specifications with LaTeX and definition of the outline for an appendix, compatible with the 2167-A standard, containing
   all the specifications referred to in the design document;
2. generation of the design documentation with Teamwork and inclusion
   of the Interleaf pretty printed RSL specifications in the Interleaf document. This inclusion would be manual and not automatic as it is from
   Teamwork to Interleaf.

In the TCA application, the first alternative was followed because the Interleaf conversion tool was not available in time. In any case this integration
requires an extra cost in the application development.

Changes The main changes to the process consequent to the adoption of the
integrated approach relate to:

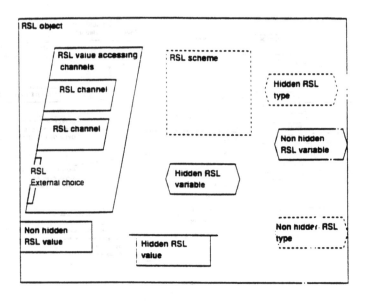

Fig. 4. ASG icons versus RSL constructs

- Lifecycle effort distribution;
- Need of a specific training on the specification language for the customer;
- Need of a specific training on the specification language for the test and quality assurance representatives.

Effort distribution Figures 6 and 7 show the effort distribution through the lifecycle for the CSC Detector and for the whole TCA Analyzer development. For what concerns the CSC Detector, it must be said that the effort for the design phase does not include the one required to define an approach for integrating RAISE with Teamwork/Ada. For the Analyzer TCA the requirements analysis and understanding was not a separate phase, but was done as part of the design phase, by reading the input documentation.

5.1 Guidelines to Integrate RAISE and Teamwork/Ada in the Design Phase

Based on lessons learnt, this section provides guidelines for applying the integrated-parallel approach and shows the applied mapping between ASG icons and RSL

```
1.0   context: DETECTOR_SUPPORTER. PREDICTOR_AND_DETECTOR.
1         ALIGNER. TCA_LIB
2
3     objectDETECTOR :
4       class
5         channel
6           Begin_Detection_Cycle. Abort_Detection_Cycle.
7           Terminate_Rendez_Vous_With_Detector. Start
8
9           Unit
10
11        value
12          Detector_Controller : Unit — in any out any write any Unit
13          Detector_Controller( ) ≡
14            local
15              variable
16                Ptr : TCA_LIB.BUFFER_REF_T.
17                Len : TCA_LIB.BUFFER_LEN_T.
18                Des1 : TCA_LIB.DES_CODE_T.
19                Des2 : TCA_LIB.DES_CODE_T
20            in
21              Start? :
22              DETECTOR_SUPPORTER.Initialize_State( ) :
23              while true do
24                DETECTOR_SUPPORTER.Wait_Next_Trigger( ) :
25                TCA_LIB.Send
26                  (Ptr. Len. TCA_LIB.MSG_RV_REQ_FROM_DET. Des1. Des2) :
27                  (
28                    (
29                      Begin_Detection_Cycle? :
30                      DETECTOR_SUPPORTER.Copy_New_Information( ) :
31                      Terminate_Rendez_Vous_With_Detector? :
32                      ALIGNER.Align_And_Prepare_Tracks( ) :
33                      PREDICTOR_AND_DETECTOR.Predict_And_Detect_Cycle( ) :
34                      DETECTOR_SUPPORTER.Compute_Overload_Condition( )
35                    )
36                  []
37                    Abort_Detection_Cycle?
38                  )
39            end
40        end
```

Fig. 5. RSL specifications

entities. The guidelines are presented in the style of the SSI SQS guidelines. They relate to factors that must be considered at the beginning of a FM project and include some recommendations that should be given to project managers and development teams that are going to start an Ada project adopting RAISE, or any FM supported by a toolset which allows automatic Ada code generation.

- Rather than developing the whole application with the selected FM, *identify one critical sub-component* of your application to develop formally.
- At the beginnning don't rely only on the FM for project success, but *exploit also the positive support of structured methods*, expecially from the graphical point of view. This can be valuable both for communication with the customer and for a quick analysis of modularity choices.
- Maintain *consistency among names in the structured graphs and in the concrete formal specification*, so that formal RSL specifications and ASGs can

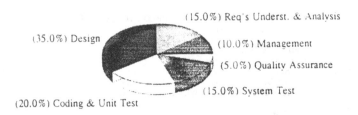

(15.0%) Req's Underst. & Analysis

(35.0%) Design

(10.0%) Management

(5.0%) Quality Assurance

(15.0%) System Test

(20.0%) Coding & Unit Test

Fig. 6. Effort through the lifecycle phases for the Detector CSC

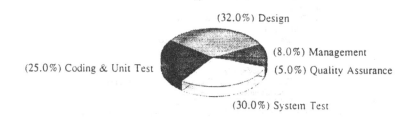

(32.0%) Design

(8.0%) Management

(25.0%) Coding & Unit Test

(5.0%) Quality Assurance

(30.0%) System Test

Fig. 7. Effort through the lifecycle phases for the whole Analyzer-TCA

be easily mapped. Note however that the correspondence ASG graphical entities, RSL constructs is not always immediate. For instance, using RAISE and Teamwork/Ada it was not possible to have a correspondence one to one between ASGs unit representations and RSL values (procedures/functions in Ada) because, in RSL, values cannot be edited in isolation, but shall be included in an object or scheme (respectively package and generic package in Ada).

– Try, to the maximum extent, to *isolate the automatically translatable specifications from the manual ones*. Consider that, for instance, concurrent RSL constructs are not automatically translatable into Ada tasks. An acceptable result would be no module needing further adaptions after automatic translation.

- *Analyze carefully the automatically generated code*, before the beginning of the design phase and make sure that the translation strategy for the specification language constructs that you are going to use is acceptable for the application purposes. If not, define some dummy modules and write the related code manually.

- If you are developing only part of your system with FMs, *specify the external interfaces* to the component developed with the FM, maintaining the same names of the corresponding Ada entities. With RAISE we had a problem because translator does not support procedure output parameters remember that each procedure shall be converted to a function. Consider, in your estimates that the interfaces specification is an extra.

- *Insert the unit prologue as a comment in the specifications* before the declaration of an RSL value after making sure that the automatic translator preserves the comments (the RAISE Ada translator version 1.7 does it). In this way you are not forced to reinclude the unit prologue each time you retranslate.

- Define in the specification language all the *basic constructs in the target programming language* (Ada and C++ for RAISE) that you need to use and are *not supported by your specification language* in a dummy module which must be translated manually. For example RSL does not support type conversion and does not have a delay construct as in Ada. These may be needed in the concrete specifications therefore define an RSL_ADA module dummy definitions for them and write the corresponding Ada code.

- *Generate confidence conditions* as soon as possible and justify them informally.

- Prepare *unit test plans based on RSL* rather than on the Ada code. The automatic translation will garantee that no additional path is in the code. Consider that the justification editor can provide support to for branches identification.

- Keep under *configuration control*, for the formal part, at least all the automatically translatable specifications and the handwritten code for the environment.

- If the standard for the PDL are not applicable to the specification language, *define appropriate standards* based on the specific formal language you are adopting. If using RSL, remember that it, as a substitution of the PDL, is very concrete and quite low-level becuase due to the synthax oriented editor you are forced to declare all the entities you use.

- Check the *standards and procedures* which need to be updated tailoring, as necessary, the contents of the *SDF (Software Development Folders)*.

- *Involve your customer in the process* as early as possible, asking him to describe some properties of the system, he/she would like to hold, and formulate them as theories, based on your concrete specification.

5.2   A-Posteriori Approach

The a-posteriori approach has been applied to the Aligner subcomponent of the Detector. This approach is illustrated in fig. 2. The main benefits arising from it consist in the possibility of detecting hidden undiscovered errors, hints for the production of more generic/reusable documentation and code, and a probably better communication with the customer. It requires an extra cost in terms of effort and implies a deep change in the mental attitude of the software developer. The main guideline that should be followed, in order to maximize the advantages arising from this approach, is to conceive it as an approach complementary to the project testing and validation activities. Without focusing on documentation, deliverables and reenginering aspects, an attempt to formalize the consistency properties of the system should be made. The experience made in TCA for instance, helped to gain a deep understanding of a specific subset of the Detector requirements. A deeper investigation on this approach was outside the scope of the TCA project, therefore the gained experience is not sufficient to state in this article if RAISE might have really helped in the a-posteriori formulation of the system consistency and correctness. In particular, the most interesting aspect in the TCA application, requiring a deeper investigation, would have been (a) to formulate and prove the consistency at each time of the TCA status information (tracks, flight plans, conflicts), (b) to define a concurrent model of the whole TCA software.

6   Conclusions

The RAISE FM has been applied to develop a a sub-component of an air traffic control application, the Detector. This article has illustrated the application results focusing on the obtained benefits, but also on the faced problems, on the application background constraints and on the perspectives of a future adoption of RAISE. However it must be said that this is not the first ATC application to be developed with FMs. Many formal approaches exists and the literature reports the results of at least two other applications developed with FMs in the ATC domain [5], [11].

In particular the article *Requirements Specification for Process-Control Systems* by N. G. Levenson and M. Heimdahl, [5] deals with an aircraft collision avoidance system and reports conclusions similar to the ones made by the Detector development team, outlining the criticality of the communication with the operator, the need of an adequate graphical user interface, and the necessity of using an integrated development approach complemented by reverse engineerin techniques.

Some useful lessons, overall conclusions and basic results derived from this experience are:

– The formal specification process cannot avoid taking into consideration the training and backgrounds of those who are to read and review the specification;

- The specifications should include graphical, symbolic, tabular and textual notation, depending on the type of information being conveyed, to facilitate the reviews from the customer;

- The integrated RAISE-Teamwork/Ada approach is advantageous because it allows to use different notational tecniques to communicate different types of information. This conclusion is confirmed by a tendency in the related literature to consider these kinds of approaches as the most appropriate for the introduction of FMs [5];

- Also the a-posteriori approach can result useful because it may help to discover hidden errors which might remain such even after the acceptance phases;

- If SSI had started the development of Analyzer-TCA from scratch, it would have been possible to derive a complete and suitable requirements specification, more implementation-independent and therefore more reusable.

- It might be very useful to follow a systematic process of requirements formulation, applying FMs from the requirements phase rather than from the design phase. When the specification language can be selected carefully basing on the specific application requirements, the benefits that can be gained increase.

- RAISE is not the Formal Method, but one method, suggesting one approach to the formal development. There are pro and against to its adoption and probably other more appropriate methods can be selected. An interesting survey on the application of different FMs to the same case study is provided in [12]. Wise management decisions and smooth transitions can allow to learn useful lessons on FMs without jeopardizing the application.

- The critical and most interesting application areas for formal methods are not only at the early stages of the lifecyle, but also in the final phases. Discovering hidden errors before delivery obviously has an enormous importance in the development of safety critical software. The selection of a FM shall consider if it provides guidelines for the developer to be easily able to define the specific test cases and prove them, either by running test or formally. This would be an enormous aid for a wider scale, less ad-hoc and more systematic adoption of formal methods.

6.1 List of Acronyms

ATC   Air Traffic Control
CDR   Critical Design Review
FM   Formal Method
PDL   Program Design Language
PDR   Preliminary design Review
RAISE Rigorous Approach to Industrial Software Engineering
RSL   RAISE Specification Language
SDD   Software Design Document
SQS   Software Quality System
SRS   Software Requirements Specification
STD   Software Test Description
STP   Software Test Plan
TCA   Traffic Conflicts Alert

References

1. Teamwork/Ada – User's Guide Cadre Technologies Inc. December 1990
2. The RAISE Language Group: The RAISE Specification Language, Prentice Hall 1992
3. The RAISE Method Group: The RAISE Development Method, Prentice Hall 1994
4. The RAISE Tool Group: RAISE Tools Reference Manual, CRI 1994
5. N.G.Levenson, M.P.E.Heimdahl: Requirements Specification for Process-Control Systems IEEE Transactions on Software Engineering, September 1994
6. R.A.Kemmerer: Integrating Formal Methods into the Development Process IEEE Software, September 1990
7. J.M.Wing, A.M.Zaremski: Unintrusive Ways to Integrate Formal Specifications in Practice Proceedings of the IV International Symposium of VDM Europe Noordwijkerhout, The Nertherlands, October 1991
8. J.Dick, J.Loubersac: Integrating Structure and Formal Methods: A Visual Approach to VDM Proceedings of the III European Software Engineering Conference Milano, Italy, October 1991
9. A.Alapide, M.Cinnella, P.La Vopa: Automatic Generation of Ada Code with the RAISE Formal Method Proceedings of the III Symposium Ada in Aerospace, Wien 1992.
10. A.Alapide, M.Cinnella, P.La Vopa: The Viability of Applying COCOMO to RAISE-Ada Projects Proceedings of the III Symposium Ada in Aerospace, Wien 1992
11. D.Craigen, S.Gerhart, T.Ralstone: Formal Methods Reality Check: Industrial Usage Proceedings of the I Internatinal Symposium of Formal Method Europe, Odense, Denmark, April 1993
12. C.Lewerentz, T.Lindner: Formal Methods for Reactive Systems Forschungszentrum Informatik Formal Methods Europe 1994 Conference Notes

Breaking Through the V and V Bottleneck

Martin Croxford † and James Sutton ‡

† Praxis Critical Systems, Bath, England
‡ Lockheed Aeronautical Systems Company, Marietta, Ga, USA

Abstract. With conventional methods of performing verification and validation - heavily reliant on testing performed late in the software production process - the late detection of errors adds substantially to project costs and delays in delivery, and introduces significant risks. This paper presents a method of software development aimed at "correctness by construction", which greatly attenuates these problems. The process described here has been applied successfully to the development of avionic software for the new C-130J ("Hercules") aircraft.

1 Introduction

In industrial software development generally, but especially for the larger and more complex systems, verification and validation (V & V) costs form an unacceptably large part of total software development cost - a figure of 50% is commonly quoted. Furthermore, this is the area where significant risks arise, or are uncovered. We would like to "design out" a large proportion of the V & V costs and risks.

Practical V & V approaches are currently all of a retrospective or "after the fact" nature. This aspect of V & V has several disadvantages:

- In an increasingly competitive aeronautical industry, the demands for greater functionality and rapid delivery of software make it imperative to "get it right first time". Retrospective verification comes too late to support this goal.

- Not only is it necessary nowadays to design and deliver advanced avionic software products to the market-place very rapidly, but the scale of aeronautical enterprises requires the elimination of risk (of delay for instance) associated with such developments. We cannot wait until system test "to see if it works".

- The achievement of test coverage, such as the Modified Condition/Modified Decision (MC/DC) test coverage required to comply with RTCA DO-178B [7] to Level A (for safety-critical systems) involves a great deal of work. The need to repeat such testing several times, after finding and rectifying errors discovered in the testing process, contributes largely to project costs. We need much earlier detection of defects.

- Retrospective V & V is very sensitive to requirements changes - which occur in every software development project. Each change demands software modifications, and if the software has already undergone V & V then, at the very least, V & V must be repeated on the changed program units. However, sound defensive practise and requirements of regulatory agencies can impose repetition of V & V on all the software in the configuration item containing the modifications. Consequently, small changes to requirements usually lead to massive repetitions of V & V.

- In an era of great safety-consciousness, not only must avionic products be safe, but they must be *demonstrably* safe. It is much easier to achieve the required level of software integrity, with convincing supporting evidence of compliance with a standard such as RTCA DO-178B to Level A through a rigorous construction process than through after-the-fact justification.

The key to breaking through the V & V bottleneck, then, is to strive for *correctness through construction,* by revision of the software development process. Lockheed Aeronautical Systems Company (LASC) and Praxis Critical Systems evolved independently to this approach based on similar philosophical foundations. LASC had focused its attention primarily on the software specification and design (and their corresponding verification) portions of the lifecycle, while Praxis had developed technology for the design and coding (and corresponding verification) portions of the lifecycle. The marriage of the two has provided comprehensive application of the correctness by construction principle throughout the software lifecycle. The first usage of this combination is on the successful development of a new avionics system for the C-130J Hercules II aircraft.

This approach, described below, has not involved replacing the conventional approach to programming by a strictly formal refinement process, but rather it builds on existing strengths, extending the constructive role of the programming language and process; its implementation is both practical and economic, using methods, techniques and tools that are available today. It will be seen, furthermore, that the measures to achieve correctness through construction naturally emphasise modularity and portability, safety and robustness, ease of extension and verifiability. These are essential characteristics of software "building-blocks", to be applicable to evolution over the life of a single product, including requirements changes during its initial development, or over a range of related products.

2 The Engineering Context

The successful use of the technology to be described here has depended not on a single choice of an appropriate method or tool, but on a number of decisions - relating to engineering context, hardware and software architecture, the form of expression of requirements, design rules, use of Ada, and formal methods - which in combination eliminate the "paradigm shifts" and changes in notation between successive development stages that usually militate against traceability and make testing so expensive. It will therefore be helpful first to set the scene, with a very brief description of the engineering context.

The C-130 Hercules, a tactical transport aircraft with both military and civilian uses, has been in production since 1955. LASC is transforming the Hercules' avionics, propulsion, flight station and certain airframe systems to create the Hercules II airlifter or the C-130J. The Operational Flight Program (OFP) software coordinates and controls the many individual systems, and operates and diagnoses the integrated aircraft as a whole. There is a primary OFP in each of two Mission Computers (MCs), and a backup OFP in each of two Bus Interface Units (BIUs). The MC and BIU OFPs also synchronise and transfer data between the various avionics hardware devices. Examples include data about electronic circuit boards, full authority digital engine control, radar and the fuel system. This data transfer is organised by the two MCs and by several hardware buses, most conforming to MIL-STD-1553.

The MC and BIU OFPs also process and transfer information needed for the flight station hardware to interface with the pilot, copilot, navigator and auxiliary crew members. This information is interdependent with the avionics, propulsion and airframe systems data that are also conveyed by the communications buses and handled by the MCs. Examples of flight station devices include head-up displays, radio control panels, and caution/warning/alert annunciators. The MC and BIU software amounts to some 200K lines of source code.

Without entering into details of system architecture, it will be clear that the MC and BIU software performs a great multiplicity of functions (to transfer information to and from a bus, originating and terminating at many different kinds of devices), but that these functions are mutually independent, and simple to describe in a precise manner. (Of course the *implementations* of these functions may use common architectural components, as is explained below.) Exploitation of the "separability" of the many functions of the OFPs contributed greatly to the simplicity of the expression of requirements, their implementation and V and V [4].

3 Correctness by Construction

The essence of a constructive approach is the "factorisation" or decomposition of a large system development into a number of small steps, each constructing a "product" according to its own rules of "well-formation" which can be enforced by a tool (in the way, for instance, that a compiler imposes the syntactic and static-semantic rules of a programming language). The well-formation rules must in themselves guarantee a certain consistency between the input and output of each step (e.g. of data flow or information flow), and facilitate complete verification of functionality. Decomposition of this kind is the key to containment of system complexity, allowing us to reason about fragments of implementation in terms of fragments of specification.

Of course, to reason about a program in terms of its constituent parts, we must be able to think of these in abstract terms, i.e. in terms of *specifications* of the functions they are intended to perform rather than their implementation details. And if these specifications are to be manipulated mechanically, they must be formulated rigorously, in a well-defined notation, as *formal specifications*. However, if formal specifications are produced for program constituents, we can perform formal verification of their code, mechanically, as this code is produced. (By formal verification we mean here mathematical and semi-automated verification of internal consistency of the software in terms of absence of data and information flow errors, as well as verification of the correct implementation of requirements.) We note the following advantages of this constructive approach:

- Formal verification of the code of a program component can be performed as soon as this is written, and in particular, before compilation and testing. We achieve early warning of many kinds of programming errors, and the expensive testing processes are usually performed once only, as *confirmation* of correctness.

- Both coding and formal verification of a program unit can be performed in isolation, using only specifications of the software components used by the unit under construction. Thus we can verify some parts of a system, while others are incomplete.

- Effects on specifications and code of program components, of changes in requirements specification, is contained to the minimum possible.

4 Requirements Engineering

The software requirements for the MC and BIU are specified using an extension of the Software Productivity Consortium's (SPC) "CoRE" (Consortium Requirements Engineering), a formal requirements modelling method based on the work of David Parnas [8, 2]. Here, the software requirements are described in a tabular form, specifying input-output relationships mathematically. This method of description is, like most, better with some kinds of system than others. CoRE is particularly well-suited for systems which have many inputs, many outputs, and relatively simple transfer functions between them. This category includes the OFPs being developed for the C-130J. An extension of CoRE by LASC represents the CoRE data by Yourdon Data-Flow Diagramming, includes the notion of "domain generics", and uses a CASE tool to maintain the CoRE data dictionary and to perform automatic well-formation checking of the CoRE model [4].

An example of a CoRE requirement is given in Figure 1. The table defines a relation. The heading of the rightmost column would normally be the name of a specific abstracted output (the relation's "dependent variable"); the names of all other columns would be the names of specific abstracted inputs (the "independent variables"). The cells below the headings in all but the rightmost column define subranges of the independent variables. The cells in the rightmost column define the function used to derive the output given the combination of subranges in the cells to its left in its row. This kind of tabulation makes it possible to positively verify coverage of the entire ranges of the inputs used to derive the output (and all the combinations of subranges). It also highlights the importance of boundary values at the "lines" between the rows.

In practice, this specification would be implemented by an Ada procedure or function subprogram. On completion of execution of this subprogram, the conditions to be satisfied, as specified by the CoRE table, can be expressed as a post-condition in first-order logic, as shown in Figure 2. (The notational conventions used here are those of SPARK, which we discuss below.)

abstracted input #1 ("i1")	abstracted input #2 ("i2")	abstracted input #3 ("i3")	abstracted output
"x"	"x"	subrange 3.1	f1(i1, i2, i3)
"x"	subrange 2.1	subrange 3.2	f2(i1, i2)
subrange 1.1	subrange 2.2	subrange 3.2	f3(i3)
subrange 1.2	subrange 2.2	subrange 3.2	f4(i1, i3)

Figure 1. Example of a CoRE Requirement

```
--# post
--#    (IsInSubrange_3_1(i3)            -> Output = f1(i1, i2, i3)) and
--#  ((IsInSubrange_2_1(i2) and IsInSubrange_3_2(i3))
--#                                     -> Output = f2(i1, i2))      and
--#  ((IsInSubrange_1_1(i1) and IsInSubrange_2_2(i2)
--#     and IsInSubrange_3_2(i3)) -> Output = f3(i3))                and
--#  ((IsInSubrange_1_2(i1) and IsInSubrange_2_2(i2)
--#     and IsInSubrange_3_2(i3)) -> Output = f4(i1, i3));
```

Figure 2. Post-condition for Example of a CoRE Requirement

5 Design

Architectural design is carried out using a Domain-Specific Design Language (DSDL), strongly influenced by the Software Productivity Consortium's ADARTS (Ada-based Design Analysis for Real-Time Systems) method [9], in particular its notions of "Class Structuring" which LASC have extended and at the same time "specialised" with rules of coherence tailored to their application domain. These rules are enforced or otherwise checked by use of Teamwork templates, ultimately represented by Ada packages. More detailed design and coding are both performed through instantiation and population of templates, with extensive use of EMACS scripts to automate the process. The "refinement" of design to the final executable code proceeds through as many as six "levels", at each of which the working material is compilable Ada text, which can be checked mechanically.

In Figure 3 is shown a greatly simplified and abstracted version of the portion of the DSDL for the devices that are attached to the data buses on the C-130J. It is recorded in something similar to Buhr notation, as the CASE tool that was used implemented a variation of Buhr; however, other notations would have been just as suitable. Underlying textual definitions were also developed for the classes (outer boxes) and their methods (inner boxes). The dashed boxes in the illustration are syntactic elements that must be "instantiated" by the detailed designers with the relevant details of each specific device in the device category covered by the DSDL. Thus, the detailed design is simply the set of instantiations of the DSDL.

This example is indicative of the highly-factored nature of the system and software architecture, which is a key element of our approach.

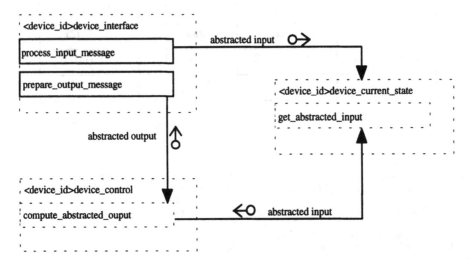

Figure 3. Simplified DSDL for Bus Devices

6 Implementation

The Ada text for all components containing significant system semantics is written using SPARK, a system of annotations (or "formal comments") and restrictions [1] that is applied to Ada to simplify demonstrating program correctness [3, 5]. SPARK was developed by Program Validation Ltd (PVL), now incorporated in Praxis Critical Systems. SPARK is formally defined (in the formal specification language "Z", plus inference rules [6]) and its use is supported by a software tool, the SPARK

Examiner, which checks conformance of Ada texts with the rules of SPARK, and performs different kinds of analyses, described below. SPARK is used in numerous military and civil safety-critical applications, e.g. avionics, railways, and nuclear power.

The method of developing the code, using templates, helps to preserve the correspondence between each "code refinement" and its predecessor, but strong additional checks are performed in the development process, as follows.

Firstly, as soon as executable code of subprogram bodies is produced, the SPARK Examiner performs their data- and information-flow analyses, and compares the results with flow relations given as SPARK annotations, these being derived from the CoRE and design documents. (At present these relations are produced manually, but in future they could be generated directly, within templates.)

Next, the formal specification descriptions (in Parnas tables) in the formal requirements specifications are embedded in SPARK program texts as post-conditions, of the kind shown in Figure 2. These annotations are expressed in a language which is essentially the language of Ada expressions, with a few extensions for instance to represent logical inference, and to describe the effects of updating operations on composite objects.

From this information, and the code, the SPARK Examiner produces the "proof obligations" which must be discharged to show that the code meets its specification. Many of these proof obligations can be proved automatically by the SPADE Automatic Simplifier, and the rest can be proved interactively using the SPADE Proof Checker. (Alternatively, they can be justified manually, by "rigorous argument"). In the C-130J project, the generation and automatic simplification of proof obligations for SPARK text has so far been straight-forward - probably because of the simplicity of the required input-output functions. Thus, by using extensions to Ada involving no more than "formal comments", and tools to check the relationship between these and the Ada code, we have been able to bind together the requirement specification, high-level and detailed design and the executable code, with strong rules of well-formation of construction, and verification procedures, all applicable prior to compilation and conventional unit test.

As an illustration of the code verification process, Figure 4 presents a SPARK subprogram which implements the CoRE table of Figure 1. Using the post-condition given in Figure 2, the SPARK Examiner generates 11 proof obligations ("verification conditions") for this code, one of which is shown in Figure 5. This is discharged automatically by the SPADE Automatic Simplifier.

```
procedure Example(i1,i2,i3 : in      integer;
                  Output    :    out integer)
is
begin
    if    IsInSubrange_3_1(i3) then Output := f1(i1, i2, i3);
    elsif IsInSubrange_2_1(i2) then Output := f2(i1, i2);
    elsif IsInSubrange_1_1(i1) then Output := f3(i3);
    else                            Output := f4(i1, i3);
    end if;
end Example;
```

Figure 4. Subprogram Implementing Example CoRE Requirement

```
procedure_example_11.
H1:     isinsubrange_1_1(i1) or isinsubrange_1_2(i1) .
H2:     not (isinsubrange_1_1(i1) and isinsubrange_1_2(i1)) .
H3:     isinsubrange_2_1(i2) or isinsubrange_2_2(i2) .
H4:     not (isinsubrange_2_1(i2) and isinsubrange_2_2(i2)) .
H5:     isinsubrange_3_1(i3) or isinsubrange_3_2(i3) .
H6:     not (isinsubrange_3_1(i3) and isinsubrange_3_2(i3)) .
H7:     not (isinsubrange_3_1(i3)) .
H8:     not (isinsubrange_2_1(i2)) .
H9:     not (isinsubrange_1_1(i1)) .
        ->
C1:     isinsubrange_3_1(i3) -> (f4(i1, i3) = f1(i1, i2, i3)) .
C2:     (isinsubrange_2_1(i2) and
            isinsubrange_3_2(i3)) -> (f4(i1, i3) = f2(i1, i2)) .
C3:     (isinsubrange_1_1(i1) and (isinsubrange_2_2(i2) and
            isinsubrange_3_2(i3))) -> (f4(i1, i3) = f3(i3)) .
C4:     (isinsubrange_1_2(i1) and (isinsubrange_2_2(i2) and
            isinsubrange_3_2(i3))) -> (f4(i1, i3) = f4(i1, i3)) .
```

Figure 5. Example Proof Obligation

In this illustrative example the correspondence between the specification and the code is almost obvious. In general the functions to be implemented are more complex, for example the abstract variables may be realised not simply by integers but by structured variables, which may themselves be subject to transformations, for instance to perform scaling, range-limiting and data-packing.

7 Compilation and Testing

Only after formal verification should the code be compiled and tested. Although the burden of proof is increased if verification is attempted for code that does not yet meet its specification, the cost savings obtained by catching errors early, and especially before system integration and costly MC/DC testing, are very great in comparison.

Compilation is performed using an Alsys C-SMART compiler. SMART is a small Ada run-time system, for safety-critical applications, and C-SMART is a certifiable version of this, with documentation designed to satisfy RTCA DO-178B Level A requirements. Since all SPARK features are supported by C-SMART, no problems of compatibility arise.

To test the end product, a set of tests has been developed rigorously from the CoRE formal specification. These tests are implemented as "scripts", to be run in a tool that simulates the environment of the computer executing the product software. The simulation tool directly employs a database created during system requirements engineering. The scripts and the database constitute a "product validation suite" that can easily be re-executed at any stage in the development and subsequent life of a product, to confirm that the product requirements are being properly met.

8 Lessons Learned

The constructive approach adopted for the C-130J MC and BIU OFP software has had the effect of keeping the development effort in pace with systems-engineering additions and modifications, and with the program schedule. This is in contrast to the "software crisis" experience of many if not most aerospace (and other application-domain) projects, where software becomes the main cause of overall project delays. The approach works well in an environment where there are difficulties in stabilising system requirements.

The constructive approach involves the entire software development team more deeply with systems engineering: it requires software developers to verify code as it is developed, possibly chasing errors and inconsistencies in the requirements, rather than relying on unit and integration testing to find problems. Of course, this is a consequence of the formal methods and the constructive approach: they simply won't allow systems-level inadequacies to propagate into the software product. While this costs some extra time in the short term, it always more than regains it later.

While most of the errors uncovered in requirements specifications and code by formal analysis would have been discovered during integration testing of the software, it has been found that tracing such bugs from traditional test results is more expensive than formal analysis of the same code. Some errors immediately uncovered by formal analysis, such as conditional initialization errors, may only emerge after very extensive testing.

The next lesson relates to software changes. When the need for domain-level requirements changes is identified, the amount of affected software can be large. Yet, because of the functional decomposition in the design, and the DSDL/template-driven implementation, C-130J experience has shown that the places where code must be changed are clear from examination of the design template(s) relevant to the affected structures. Comprehensive changes can rapidly be effected by changing the appropriate section of code in each of the implementation instances of the affected template(s). Unlike non-domain-oriented architectures, where functionality is distributed in software in an irregular way, there is objective confidence that the software changes will correctly implement the requirements changes.

Finally, we draw attention to the significance of this software project, as one of the first in which the use of formal methods has proved to be advantageous from an economic standpoint, rather than simply being desirable or even essential to achieve a particularly high level of integrity. In what way has the application, or the technology deployed, really been exceptional, to allow us to achieve this result?

The essential factors are firstly the architectural design features, which factorise this sizeable system into a large number of functionally distinct components, so that the scaling-up difficulties often associated with formal methods do not apply; secondly, the use of formal specification of the requirements of these components; thirdly, the rigidly-enforced design rules which preserved the functional separation of the components, and "kept the requirements specifications alive". Translation of the CoRE into formal specifications of program units also supported the functional separation; and finally, the technology for generating and discharging the proof obligations, based on the formal definition of the SPARK component of Ada, was crucial, in binding the code to the initial requirements.

References

1. Ada 95 Reference Manual, ISO/IEC 8652:1995(E)-RM95; version 6.0, December 1994. (See especially Annex H "Safety and Security".)

2. Alspaugh, S. Faulk, K. Heninger Britton, R. Parker, D. Parnas, J. Shore: Software Requirements for the A7-E Aircraft. Report NRL/FR/5530-92-9194. Naval Research Laboratory, Washington, D.C., 1992.

3. B.A. Carré, J.R. Garnsworthy: SPARK - An annotated Ada subset for safety-critical programming. In: Proceedings of Tri-Ada Conference, Baltimore, December 1990.

4. S. Faulk, L. Finneran, J. Kirby, Jr., S. Shah, J. Sutton: Experience applying the CoRE method to the Lockheed C-130J software requirements. In: Proceedings of Ninth Annual Conference on Computer Assurance, Gaithersburg, MD, 1994, pp.3-8.

5. J.R. Garnsworthy, I.M. O'Neill, B.A. Carré: Automatic proof of absence of run-time errors. In: Proceedings of Ada UK Conference, London Docklands, October 1993.

6. Program Validation Ltd.: The Formal Semantics of SPARK (Volume 1: Static Semantics; Volume 2: Dynamic Semantics). Praxis PVL, 20 Manvers Street, Bath BA1 1PX, U.K., 1994.

7. RTCA: Software Considerations in Airborne Systems and Equipment Certification. RTCA/DO-178B, 1994

8. Software Productivity Consortium: Consortium Requirements Engineering Guidebook, SPC-92060-CMC version 01.00.09.   Software Productivity Consortium, Herndon, VA, U.S., 1993

9. Software Productivity Consortium: ADARTS Guidebook, SPC-94107-N, version 02.01.00 Software Productivity Consortium, Herndon, VA, U.S., 1991.

Periodic Processing in Hard Real-Time Systems: Assessment of Different Design Models in Ada

Francois BOSSARD

Department of On-board Data Processing
CNES Toulouse France

Abstract. Hard real-time systems are characterized by their stringent timing constraints. The software handles several periodic and aperiodic tasks which must start at a required time and achieve before a deadline. Important issues of the schedubality theory are to provide off-line tests to ensure a system meets all its deadlines. Furthermore, optimal algorithms, such as the Rate Monotonic Scheduling (RMS) are proved to yield an efficient processor utilization.

Applying theorical outcomes to embedded software is fully attractive but many designers wonder how suitable to Ada implementations it is. Their primary concern is to foresee a right real-time design then to check the final product.

An assessment of different models affords selection among designs with a high timing behaviour predictability. On the other hand, it allows to realize actual boundaries in schedulability practice.

1. Introduction

Many hard real-time on-board systems involve periodic processes sometimes mixed with a few aperiodic processes, which are more or less time critical. Typical application cyclically samples external sensors then sends commands to actuators in order to control physical processes; in addition, some systems have to fast take into account sudden events.

Systems real-time constraints [1] consist in:
- behavioural constraints related to stimuli arrival laws;
- performance constraints bounding response times.

In hard real-time systems, the design challenge is to ensure the whole constraints will be met during operation. Such a predictability implies to be aware of system behaviour as far as possible. One development practice could be to off-line pre-calculate how the processes interleave but the method is hard and inaccurate. Unfortunately, you always cope with the same problem to determine how long tasks take to execute, since excution flows are continuously changing at run time.

The present study searches for efficient implementation models in Ada which are assessed against stringent real-time requirements.

Rate Monotonic Scheduling (RMS) is selected because it suits to mainly periodic applications without penalty. Moreover, RMS helps software to be predictable while making processor utilization better.

On purpose, two kinds of run-time supports are considered:
- standard Ada constructs;
- services provided by real-time kernels, like POSIX operating systems, or asynchronous extensions to the Ada Tasking model (CIFO, EXTRA, ...);

Both the supports are based upon a pre-emptive scheduling scheme with static tasks priorities; their main differences stand in inter-task co-operation mechanisms: Ada language provides only one synchronous co-operation while real-time kernels offer various asynchronous services (semaphores, mailboxes, events ...).

Provided Ada models stability is achieved in any configuration, predictability is presumed; then real capabilities control is enough by means of a fair validation method.

2. Rate Monotonic Scheduling Approach

This algorithm assigns a static priority to each periodic process according to its period: the task with the smallest period is given the highest priority [3]. The Rate Monotonic Scheduling is an optimal static priority assignment algorithm [2]: a task set that is schedulable by some static priority assignment algorithm will be schedulable by RMS.

The only real-time constraint which the RMS deals with is deadlines meeting assuming deadlines match the periods.

RMS provides a sufficient condition to prove a set of periodic tasks is schedulable whatever phasing is between them. The corresponding "Utilization Bound test" is a simple mathematical formula:

$$U = \sum_{i=1}^{n} U_i \leq n \left[2^{1/n} - 1\right] \quad \text{with} \quad U_i = C_i / T_i \quad \text{and} \quad \max_{n \to \infty} U = \ln(2) \approx 0,69$$

where C_i is the worst execution time and T_i the period of the task i.

Relevant information is that the processor utilization bound becomes 1 when periods are harmonic.

By applying such a formula during system development, a design can be quickly proved. However, a false test result is not clear-cut enough to invalidate the design.

In addition to the RMS, another property of periodic scheduling is the *cyclicity* which lays down that the processor makes the same thing at time t than at time t+kP; P is the Least Common Multiple of all the periods [4].

3. Design Models

3.1 Common Requirements

Functional requirements:
- start tasks periodic executions according to specified periods and phases;
- stop periodic executions on user request;
- detect scheduling faults when deadlines cannot be met;
- run concurrently with some aperiodic tasks.

Real-time requirements:
- accurately activate cyclic executions;
- achieve deterministic behaviour;
- meet deadlines;
- overcome transient overloads.

Satisfaction level depends on how stressing are the specified tasks parameters.

Development requirements:
- rely on Ada tasking or any pre-emptive scheduling kernel with static priorities;
- comply with the Rate Monotonic Scheduling model;
- accommodate tasks time parameters to changing specifications;
- make a transparent design with respect to users algorithms.

3.2 Models description

Among several models, some appear irrelevant to meet hard real-time constraints: so, centralized management only is favourite.

First model. It is built around a primary task, named "supervisor", which manages all the periodic tasks. The "supervisor" task deals with required functions in the following way:
- starts initial parts of periodic tasks;
- cyclically triggers periodic tasks by exclusively using Ada statements: on the one hand the "supervisor" task is awakened on time with "delay", on the other hand it requests tasks activations with "rendez-vous";
- controls there is no exceeded deadline with "conditional entry call" and eventually notifies the error;
- asks periodic tasks to complete by means of "rendez-vous".

Timeliness involves an accurate hardware counter to provide current time given "calendar" functions are not enough precise usually.

This model cannot stand transient overloads and loses failed cycles.

Second model. It is built similarly to the first model but relies on pre-emptive kernel services. The "supervisor" task deals with required functions in the following way:
- initializes and starts first parts of periodic tasks;
- cyclically triggers periodic tasks by using asynchronous co-operation services: on the one hand the "supervisor" task is awakened when interruption is raised by an interval counter, on the other hand it requests activation of tasks with asynchronous mechanisms such a mailbox;
- controls there is no exceeded deadline by requesting task state : eventually notifies an error;
- asks some periodic task to complete by means of asynchronous mechanisms.

An accurate hardware counter provides current time.

This model can tolerate transient overloads without losing cycles.

The programming chart of the both models is depicted in figure 1.

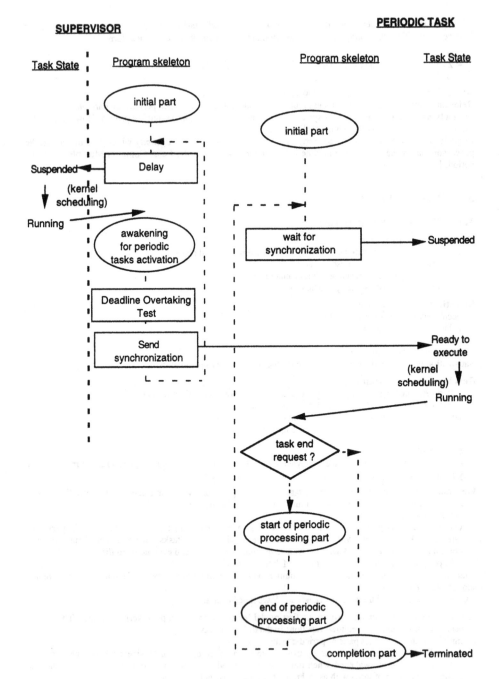

SUPERVISOR

Task State   Program skeleton

initial part

Delay

Suspended

(kernel scheduling)

Running

awakening for periodic tasks activation

Deadline Overtaking Test

Send synchronization

PERIODIC TASK

Program skeleton   Task State

initial part

wait for synchronization   Suspended

Ready to execute

(kernel scheduling)

Running

task end request ?

start of periodic processing part

end of periodic processing part

completion part   Terminated

Fig. 1: programming chart

358

Third model. It relies on a kernel service which provides cyclic synchronization events. The "supervisor" task deals only with a few functions in the following way:
- intializes and starts first parts of periodic tasks;
- starts and stops the kernel triggering service;
- asks some periodic task to complete by means of asynchronous mechanisms.

Control of deadlines is made by the triggering service.
No hardware counter is required to provide current time.
This model can tolerate transient overloads without losing cycles.

4. Application Benchmarks

The above models applied to the same original application lead to three real-time benchmarks in Ada, namely V1, V2 and V3 versions.

Static Architecture. In addition to the "supervisor" task, any benchmark includes three periodic processes and one aperiodic process; each one is assigned a static priority in the following decreasing order:
- "supervisor" task;
- aperiodic task "A"
- periodic task "P1";
- periodic task "P2";
- periodic task "P3";
- periodic task "P4".

Dynamic Architecture. An important feature is the only synchronization dependencies relate to interactions between "supervisor" task and application tasks. Other links consist in shared variables and are used to exchange functional data.
The control flows and what they aim at are expressed in the next diagram.

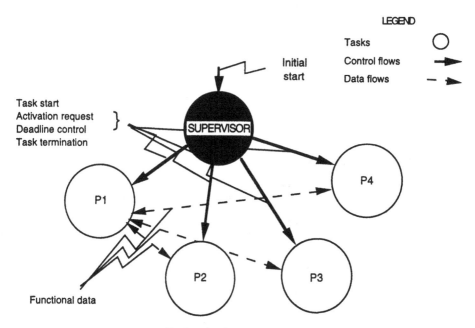

Fig. 2: tasks dependencies diagram

Real-time specifications parametrization. Benchmarks can run in a large range of real-time require-ments; furthermore deadline exceeding must be simulated to compare theorical and real scheduling limits. Therefore, relevant requirements are parameterized before running:
- execution time of the benchmark which is used to achieve periodic tasks;
- period and phase of each periodic task;
- start time and execution time of the aperiodic task.

Preplanned real-time behaviour example. Before implementing design models, some a priori checking can be made to see if the presumed tasks behaviour matches with system real-time requirements. Below, a diagram gives a behaviour sample when execution parameters are chosen to run three periodic tasks only.

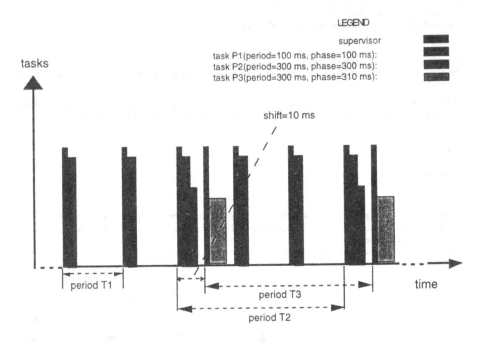

Fig. 3: behaviour time diagram

4. Real-time Assessment Method

4.1 General assessment requirements
A relevant method is required to get the best information about on-line system real-time behaviour; its outputs should reach two main goals:
- verify real behaviour complies with what the designer expects;
- check the real-time constraints are met when running on target.

Usually some compromise has to be made between issues:
- obtain a precise datation (goal: 1 microsecond);
- limit penalties in time and storage consuming;
- get a detailed observation;
- accommodate a lot of scenarios and applications;
- avoid distortion when comparing different implementations.

4.2 Assessment method operations
The selected approach is code instrumentation with immediate recording in target memory; by this way, timed mark is built while running when check points are crossed through. At the end of execution, the stored information is sent to host computer.

Finally raw data is processed later on the host computer according to user measurement profiles. Remark all these operations can be carried out automatically.

Two problems must be faced:
- choose convenient marking points with respect to general requirements;

- extract from raw data pertinent measures to highlight real-time performances.

The first difficulty is overcome by focusing on real-time statements and it is not so hard to see if the actual behaviour time diagram is suitable. After some attempts, final data flow is reliable and reusable in a lot of near contexts.

The second problem is not always addressed easily; a solution is using parameterized procedures to provide many kinds of measures. For instance, measures to assess response time or cycles accuracy are defined:
- virtual duration of some task is given by delay between its activation event and its deactivation event;
- task activation period is the interval between two successive activation events of the same task.

Figure 4 depicts a real frame of time-tagged events with some related measures.

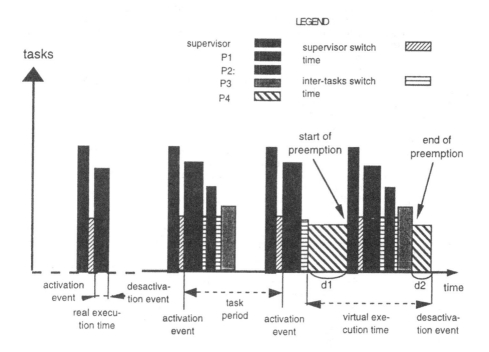

Fig. 4: tagged-time events and measures

As the above figure shows, virtual and real execution times have to be distinguished; as far as the P4 task is preempted its real execution time (d1+d2) is less than its virtual execution time.

5. Assessment results

5.1 Assessment operations

Programs generation and execution use unchanging means in the same conditions:
- an Ada cross-compiler on VAX;
- a 1750 target (MAS281) with 10 MHz clock.

The real-time executive is the space-purpose Astres1750 kernel.

Three kinds of tests are performed for most of benchmark versions:
- tests of periodic tasks only ;
- tests of periodic tasks in stressed conditions of requirements;
- tests with periodic and aperiodic tasks running together.

By changing execution parameters, each test is tailored to analyze behaviour in different real-time cases; moreover specific features are studied with respect to requirements through a set of selected measures.

5.2   Results about design models

Qualitative issues. Centralized concept around supervisor provides :
- versatility by easily changing parameters and by focusing real-time features inside supervisor; because the behaviour is controlled and understandable, adding new tasks keeps on predictability;
- efficiency is got by allowing pre-emptions while tasks switchings are limited owing to sequential activation;
- smooth termination of tasks is driven by a predetermined event;
- overtaken deadlines detection offers a reliable mean to prevent execution time errors like unwanted loops or bad code execution.

Quantitative issues. In hard real-time, it is very important to consider how are implemented the time management functions: "Delays" can strongly penalize determinism if they implemented by a periodic counting; the larger quantum counting uses, the worse cycles are; in contrast, software clock processing yields a large overhead when accuracy is required.

   "Rendez-vous" is not convenient to implement one-sided synchronizations; in this evaluation, it lasts a longer time than a mailbox communication does.

The below table 1 outlines some major results when running benchmark with the following parameters:
- task P1: period = 100 ms, phase = 100 ms;
- task P2: period = 300 ms, phase = 300 ms;
- task P3: period = 300 ms, phase = 300 ms;
- task P4: period = 600 ms, phase = 600 ms.

Measures relate to:
- tasks cycles: mean value and largest deviation during a run; discrepancy between two runs;
- tasks execution times: largest discrepancy between two runs;
- switch times: to change task after a delay suspends the current one; to change task after a synchronization mechanism suspends the current one;
- processor utilization: global rate (supervisor included); supervisor rate;
- execution times: largest discrepancy between two runs.

	Model 1	Model 2	Model 3
Mean P1 cycle (ms)	99.9	100	99.8
P1 cycle jitter (ms)	8	2.5	2.9
Cycles discrepancy (ms)	0.56	0.033	0.071
Intertasks switch time (ms)	0.2	0.23	0.23
Delay switch time (ms)	1	0.24	NS
General Processor Utilization (%)	21	10	9
Supervisor Processor Utilization (%)	11	1.5	NS
Execution times discrepancy (ms)	0.001	0.007	0.001

Table 1: major results

The above outcomes mean:
- model 3 satisfies real-time requirements finely as long as periodic rates are low;
- model 1 usually has to overcome "Rendez-vous" penalties: as supervisor makes several synchronizations in an unsteady way according to number of tasks and rates, supervisor overhead and cycles jitters cannot be avoided;
  moreover, not accurate delay implementation in the Ada kernel brings on undeterministic behaviour and long switch times;
- model 2 takes a large advantage of customized "Delay" using an interval counter in conjunction with an accurate hardware clock; predictability is good out of the avoidable cycle jitter.

5.3   Results about scheduling

Rate Monotonic Algorithm use. Provided you implemented cyclic activation mechanism, the only thing to accommodate RMS to Ada is programming tasks priorities in right order. Evaluation tests emphasize how important it is to apply this off-line algorithm; otherwise, any priorities orders lead to maximize pre-emptions and to largely increase cycles jitters.

Furthermore, the standard RMS use could be enhanced according two ways:

- selecting harmonic periods: on one hand, theorical schedulability bound is made the highest one (100%) and on the other hand predictability is better due to a fewer scheduling combinations.
- tuning phases is an efficient method to control scheduling although some overhead is added: so, provided supervisor activates the same quantity of tasks at a time, another cycles fluctuating reason is suppressed; for instance, P1 cycle jitter (refer to board 1) is decreased up to 0.11 ms with model 2.

Phases are helpful to apply precedence constraints between tasks while keeping RMS model assumptions, as well.

Finally, notice RMS theory deals with optimal deadlines meeting (see §2); it offers no guarantee about some predictability aspects:
- assuming a constant flow of execution, a cyclic task is not sure to last the same time because of possible pre-emptions;
- in the same way, even if supervisor wakes up according to accurate cyclic frame, task start time suffers fluctuations.

Schedulability test application. Each model evaluation includes the same test case to assess the practical schedulability limits; this kind of real test brings out some unexpected results such as model 2 provides a smaller processor utilization than model 3 despite the supervisor overhead (see table 1). The reason is some kernel services need internal task run without user can observe it.

Results of great concern relate to schedulability test handling:
- standard theorical test appears stripped-down: particularly, it does not take into account execution times spent to cyclically trigger tasks, to switch contexts or to run kernel tasks;
- all the parameters are assumed to be valued as worst cases; actually, such a valuation is uneasy given execution flows are uneasy to determine;
- RMS model assumptions are not always strictly complied with.

During the evaluation, several schedulability test applications are made after trying to near significant conditions as far as possible. All these applications appear too pessimistic versus the actually reached limits: explanation is worst cases are statistically far from usual cases.

The below table 2 highlights scheduling bounds when all the tasks have the same period.

Measures relate to:
- the lowest period before detecting any deadline overtaking assuming common period is decreased according to 1 ms at each run;
- the processor utilization bound: highest global rate including periodic tasks and supervisor task before detecting any deadline overtaking;

	Model 1	Model 2	Model 3
Lowest period (ms)	70	44	51
Processor Utilization bound (%)	96	95	91

Table 2: schedulability limits results

Aperiodic tasks scheduling. This study suggests a pragmatic approach rather algorithmic extension to schedule aperiodic tasks; the experimented method to run an aperiodic task among periodic tasks splits the problem in the following way:
- as far as possible, aperiodic task is assigned with lowest priority; the periodic tasks scheduling does not change and complies with RMS;
- if previous scenario does not fit into deadlines requirements, aperiodic task priority is increased whereas the behaviour of periodic tasks with smaller priorities is disturbed; the behaviour is depicted in figure 5.

In both cases, schedulability verification consists in two or three steps:
- to build a behaviour time diagram without aperiodic task by simulation or real execution;
- to analyze the time diagram off line and see if the aperiodic task fits into the worst free time without considering the smaller priorities tasks;
- to analyze the time diagram off line for each periodic task with a smaller priority than the aperiodic task; the worst case laxity of such a periodic task should be less than the largest execution time of the aperiodic task.

tasks

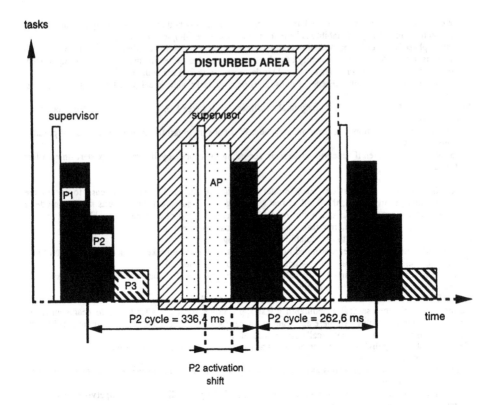

Fig. 5: aperiodic task effect on periodic tasks behaviour

Transient overload. Theorical algorithms take into account this problem but it is often a burden to implement them. This assessment only intends to analyze effects of a transient overload on tasks behaviour. Supervisor is designed to detect a task as soon as its deadline is exceeded it decides among two solutions:
- to lose the new task cycle it should start; in the best case, the next time supervisor has to start any task cycle, overload no longer exists;
- to put off the new task cycle; supervisor actually awakes the task on time but activation takes place later as soon as the faulty cycle is performed; if higher priorities task happen meanwhile, new delay is added. However, cumulative effect is prevented by rejecting several task activations while its deadline has been missed.

Finally, nothing must be done to withstand overload but waiting self recovering or handling error if it overtakes deadline more than one period.

5.4 Results about scheduling validation

Real test cases experiment show on line behaviour verification is needed with hard real time systems. A reliable method is suggested relying on the "cyclicity" property of periodic applications: a paramount issue is the behaviour observation time can be limited to the least common multiple of tasks periods.
The basic method steps are summarized hereafter:
- code instrumentation is carried out as explained at §4.2;
- a run is performed during some common application cycles; before all, it is recommended to compel worst tasks execution flows;
- preliminary verification consists in checking no deadline is missed;
- a behaviour diagram is built by picking up time tags; this diagram is helpful to analyze real time features. Notice some kinds of unbearable jitters can be suppressed by tuning tasks phases.

In addition to the basic method, it is useful to know the schedulability margin; several ways could be devised but they all assume periods and phases are parametrizable; then, it is easy to decrease either the smallest period or all the periods till some run detects overload.

Consider now application includes aperiodic tasks whose triggering events are not aware of. The foregoing off line method in conjunction with aperiodic task is applied then provided information is used to actually check schedulability. Even if heavy to operate, verification consists in several runs while trigger event sweeps the most sensitive area step by step; this approach implies forcing worst execution time and changing events times what could be simulated inside software by means of parameterized "delay".

6. CONCLUSION

Tasking models used either in Ada language standard or in real-time kernel are suited to easily implement Rate Monotonic Scheduling. RMS algorithm avoids to waste processor throughput but only deals with deadlines meetings; therefore other real-time requirements have to be achieved by further means. As far as possible, selecting harmonic periods is highly recommended to enhance RMS capacity and to make validation phase shorter ; moreover tasks phasing allows a load balance to suppress some jitters.

However some troubles are tackled to implement periodic processing in hard real time systems; major difficulties relate to manage predictability because Ada features are convenient only if used through careful designs. After experimenting several designs, centralized control seems to bring high performances; nevertheless support kernel contribution is of great concern: unskilful mechanisms design could not comply with hard requirements; then customized solution should be considered to build necessary services.

Adding aperiodic tasks entail limited disturbance and only needs some off line deadlines verification.

Schedulability test provided by RMS theory is helpful to size systems during development but results are rough and pessimistic; mean values rather worst case values should be used to check off line while unexpected overloads are taken into account on line. Finally, whatever off line methods, further on line validation is essential to rely on some real-time design.

References

1. B. Dasarathy : "Timing constraints of real-time systems: constructs for expressing them, methods of validating them" IEEE Transactions on software Engineering [1985]

2. C.L. Liu and J.W. Layland: "Scheduling Algorithms for Multiprogramming in a Hard Real-Time Environment" . Journal of the Association of computing Machinery, Vol 20 [1973]

3. Lui Sha and John B.Goodenough: "Real-Time Scheduling theory and Ada"
    IEEE Computer [1990]

4. Jia Xu & D.L. Parnas : "On satisfying Timing Constraints in Hard-Real-Time Systems"
    IEEE Transactions on software Engineering [1993]

Transaction Specification for Object-Oriented Real-Time Systems in HRT-HOOD

Pete Cornwell

Distributed Objects Research Group,
Department of Computing, Bournemouth University
Dorset, United Kingdom

Andy Wellings

Real-Time Systems Research Group
Department of Computer Science, University of York
York, United Kingdom

email: pcornwel@bournemouth.ac.uk

Object-oriented development is a structuring paradigm. It does not provide substantial support for the specification of 'end to end' control and data flow. This has implications for hard real-time system development, where applications may specify 'end to end' response times, also known as transactions. This paper introduces a graphical notation for the specification of transactions in HRT-HOOD, an object-oriented design technique for hard real-time system development. It provides an overview of the notation, and its practical application as part of a 'top-down' development process. This is illustrated through a case study, based on a naval command-control system.

1.0 Introduction

Object-based design of Ada programs has always been popular. Methods such as HRT-HOOD, HOOD and Boochs' OOD have been used to engineer a wide class of applications including hard real-time systems. One weakness of this technology is that it is primarily a *structuring paradigm*. Significant emphasis is placed on architectural structure to the detriment of 'end to end' control and data flow issues so important to real-time system design. In particular it is necessary to be able to design programs with 'end to end' response times, often called transactions. For example, reactive systems often have to respond to input within a given deadline; the computation required for that response might span across several (possibly distributed) objects. This interaction is not readily expressed in most object-based (or object-oriented) design methods.

HRT-HOOD[1] [1][2] is an object-based design method aimed at hard real-time Ada 83 and Ada 95 [3][4] systems. Although it addresses many of the timing issues associated with such systems, it does not adequately address the issue of transactions[5]. This paper considers how support for transactions can be added to HRT-HOOD. In particular, we consider how the graphical notation can be changed. A transaction in HRT-HOOD captures performance-constrained control and data flow across a set of collaborating 'black box' objects. It models the 'end to end' real-time processing of objects at the interface level, but makes no specific commitment to their implementation.

2.0 The Object

The most basic formalism is the object itself (fig 1). This construct is a module that defines a 'type' (an active, cyclic, passive, protected or sporadic abstraction), a name unique within the design, and an optional provided and required interface. A provided interface defines the operations the object *exports*, the required interface defines the operations the object must *import* from its environment.

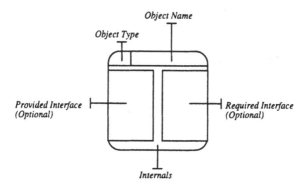

Fig. 1. Object Representation

2.1 Initiators and Terminators

An *initiator* defines a point in the design where a transaction begins. An initiator is a cyclic, sporadic or active object as these forms are capable of independently generating control flow. The transaction begins when the initiator calls a 'visible' operation defined in its required interface. For obvious reasons this is called the *initiating operation*.

---

[1]Hard Real-Time Hierarchical Object-Oriented Design is a 'top down' design technique based on HOOD™

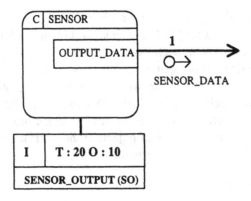

Fig. 2. An object initiator

Figure 2 demonstrates the representation of an object initiator. The initiator is associated with a transaction flag that annotates it with performance information. The flag depicted in Figure 2 has three fields. The first establishes the *role* of the object, in this case it is 'I' for initiator. The second field lists a set of *real-time characteristics* associated with the transaction these are:

- **Minimum Inter-Arrival Time (T)** - In the worse case, the transaction is initiated every N time units[2].

- **Offset (O)** - The first initiation of the transaction will not begin until an offset of M time units from system start-up has expired.

The third and final field is the *transaction identifier*. This allows the developer to reference a transaction by name. This field may also include a *shorthand identifier* enclosed by brackets. This may be used in any and all contexts where the identifier appears. Its primary role is to reduce the amount of 'clutter' on transaction diagrams.

An object initiator may initiate one or *more* separate transactions. Each transaction initiated by the object is assigned an individual transaction flag. All transactions generated by a single initiator are independent. They are assigned an individual set of real-time attributes. A set of transactions generated by a threaded object must be assigned a unique initiating operation.

An initiator may also be an operation declared in the provided interface of the parent object. In this case, the transaction is initiated by an *undefined* object initiator outside the scope of the parent object. A provided interface initiator is appended with a transaction flag in the usual manner (Fig 3).

---

[2]This may be specified as a single value, or as two values, e.g. N/M, which represents N invocations every M time units.

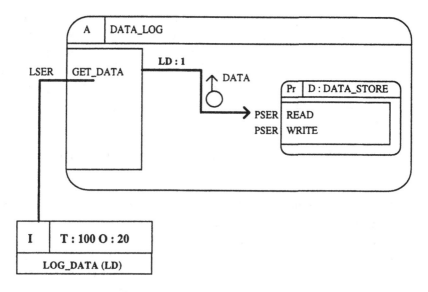

Fig. 3. A provided interface initiator

A *terminator* defines a point in the design where the transaction ends. A terminator is an 'information sink' where control and data flow is 'sunk' into an object to be used at a lower level of hierarchical abstraction, or permanently[3] leaves local scope. A terminator may be an object of any form, or an operation in the provided or required interface of the parent object.

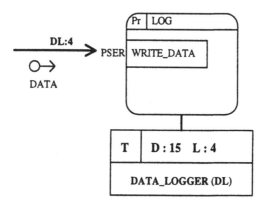

Fig. 4. An example terminator

Figure 4 depicts an example object terminator. The terminator is associated with a transaction flag that annotates it with performance information. The first field specifies that the role of the object is 'T' for terminator. The second field lists the real-time characteristics of the terminator, these are:

---

[3]Within the context of a single invocation of the transaction

- **Deadline (D)** - This specifies the 'end to end' deadline of the transaction. The transaction must complete within N time units relative to the invocation of the initiating operation. This parameter may be expanded to define Deadline$_{upper}$ (Du) and Deadline$_{lower}$ (Dl), where the transaction must complete within a given temporal 'window'. One could also imagine other requirements such as a 'percentage of deadlines met' for soft real-time systems.

- **Last Event (L)** - This defines the last event that terminates the transaction (see 2.2 *Flow Relationships*).

The third field specifies the transaction identifier. This must be identical to the identifier specified by the appropriate initiator.

A transaction may have one to many terminators. A transaction may include a set of possible execution paths. In this case each execution path may terminate at a different point in the design. For the purposes of analysis it is recommended that all terminator transaction flags are annotated with the earliest deadline that the transaction must meet.

2.2 Flow Relationships

The 'end to end' movement of control and data flow across a transaction is modelled with *flow relationships*. A single flow relationship represents control and data flow between two 'visible operations'.

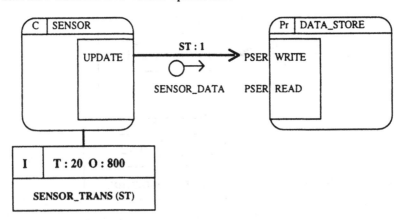

Fig. 5. An example flow relationship

Figure 5 represents a single flow relationship between two operations. A flow relationship represents a directional transfer of control between two operations. It may be further annotated with symbols representing data flow. A flow relationship may be used to represent control and data flow between client and server objects (Fig 5). It may also depict interaction between an object and the provided or required interface of the parent object (Fig 3).

A flow relationship is annotated with an *event number*. This establishes a sequence of events within a transaction. For a transaction to complete, each flow relationship must occur in the appropriate order. However, this does not imply a precedence-constrained order of execution. Figure 6 represents an example sequence of events.

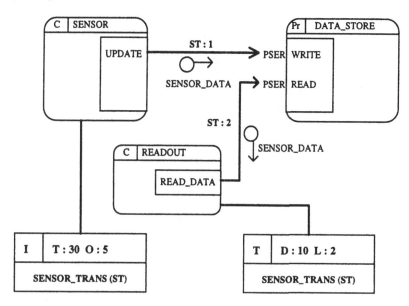

Fig. 6. An example transaction

An event number may include an optional prefix, separated from the event number by a colon. This is the transaction identifier or its shorthand equivalent. It states that the flow relationship belongs to a particular transaction. This form of identification is particularly important where two or more transactions share the same diagram.

A transaction may include a set of alternative execution paths. A set of flow relationships may share the same event number, but only one 'branch' will be executed for any given invocation of the transaction. A transaction branch may only occur *within* an object, where 'hidden' selection criteria determine the chosen execution path. A branch is represented by a set of flow relationships, *with the same event number* emerging from different operations in the required interface of an object (fig 7).

In this case, each flow relationship is uniquely identified by a *branch number*. This is a post fix annotation to the event number. The branch number is specified using a simple 'dot' notation, where the event number is specified followed by a dot and the number of the particular branch.

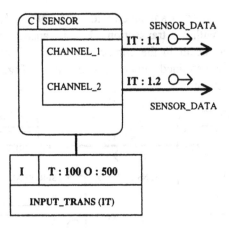

Fig. 7. An example transaction branch

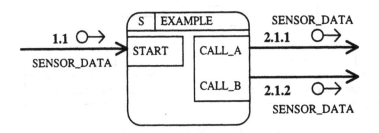

Fig. 8. An example of further branching

Figure 8 represents a complex branching example. In this case an existing branch is further sub-divided into two branching flow relationships. This is specified by adding another 'dot' after the original branch number to indicate further divergence e.g. 1.1 becomes 2.1.1 and 2.1.2 and so on.

2.3 Sub-Transactions

All active, cyclic and sporadic objects are transaction initiators. A threaded object may be part of a larger transaction. As an initiator it begins a *sub-transaction*. This is generated by an initiating operation in the required interface of the threaded object. The subsequent path of flow relationships must be *identical* to the larger transaction. However, the initiator and terminator(s) of the sub-transaction may be assigned a different set of real-time characteristics. A threaded object that participates in a transaction, and one or more sub-transactions must meet *all* 'end to end' deadlines.

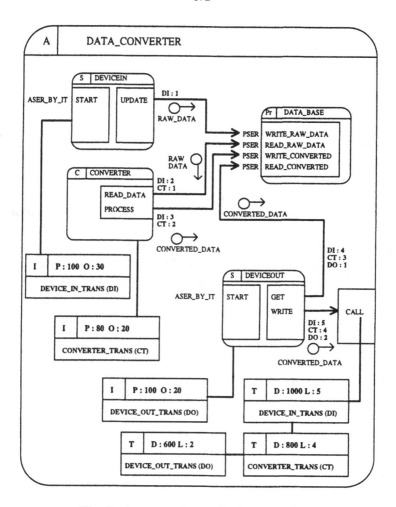

Fig. 9. An example set of sub-transactions

Figure 9 illustrates an example set of sub-transactions. The sporadic object DEVICEIN initiates the transaction DEVICE_IN_TRANS. This transaction includes two other threaded objects, the cyclic object CONVERTER and the sporadic object DEVICEOUT. Both threaded objects initiate sub-transactions. CONVERTER initiates the sub-transaction CONVERTER_TRANS. DEVICEOUT initiates the sub-transaction DEVICE_OUT_TRANS. The flow relationships generated by each sub-transaction follow an identical path to the larger transaction DEVICE_IN_TRANS. The initiator and terminator of each sub-transaction is assigned an individual set of real-time characteristics. A threaded object that participates in more than one transaction / sub-transaction must satisfy all 'end to end' deadlines. In this example the object CONVERTER must meet the deadlines of both DEVICE_IN_TRANS and

CONVERTER_TRANS. The object DEVICEOUT must meet the deadline of three transactions, DEVICE_IN_TRANS, CONVERTER_TRANS and DEVICE_OUT_TRANS.

3.0 Transaction Decomposition

The transaction notation permits the top down partitioning of real-time systems on the basis of structural and performance considerations. This formalises the HRT-HOOD world view of top-down development as an activity where architecture's are structurally decomposed and assigned performance obligations in parallel.

The flow relationships of a transaction are produced and consumed by the implementation of each participating object. A non-terminal object encapsulates a set of child objects. These participate in one or more *child transactions*. For the design to be correct the developer must ensure that both flow relationships and real-time characteristics are consistent between adjacent levels of decomposition.

The required consistency checking of flow relationships between parent and child levels of abstraction is called *flow verification*. This includes the following rules:

(1) A flow relationship that enters the provided interface of a parent object must appear as a provided interface initiator at the child level of abstraction.

(2) A flow relationship generated by an operation in the required interface of a parent object must be called by a child transaction.

(3) A single transaction can only go 'through' a parent object[4] if there is an unbroken path of child transaction flow relationships between the point of entry and point of exit.

(4) A sequence of flow relationships generated by a single parent object must be implemented by an unbroken path of child transaction flows.

(5) A child transaction responsible for generating a set of branching flow events in the required interface of the parent object, may only execute a single alternative in any given invocation period.

The consistency of real-time attributes between parent and child levels of abstraction is called *performance verification*. This includes the following rules:

---

[4]This assumes the transaction enters the provided interface of the object and leaves via the required interface.

(1) *Minimum Inter-Arrival Time*:

    (a)   The minimum inter-arrival time of an object initiator must be *equal to or less than* the invocation rate of the initiating operation by a transaction or thread at the child level of abstraction.

    (b)   The minimum inter-arrival time of a provided interface initiator must be *equal to or less than* the invocation rate of the initiating operation by external objects at the parent level of abstraction.

(2) *Offset*:

    (a)   The offset of an object initiator must be *equal to* the earliest point in time (relative to system start-up) that the initiating operation is called by a transaction or thread at the child level of abstraction.

    (b)   The offset of a provided interface initiator must be *equal to* the earliest point in time (relative to system start-up) that the initiating operation is called by an external object at the parent level of abstraction.

The verification of a transaction deadline is only possible *after* the process of design decomposition is complete. The completion of the real-time attributes section of each terminal object ODS[5], permits the calculation of response time for each cyclic and sporadic thread of control. Using the minimum inter-arrival and response time of each thread it is possible to calculate if transaction deadlines at higher levels of the design tree are met. For a detailed treatment of these issues the reader is referred to [6].

4.0 Case Study : The Close-In Weapons System (CIWS)

The CIWS is a naval point defence system for a UK type 42 destroyer. The system consists of a command-control application controlling two rotary machine cannon. These are placed fore and aft on the ship. The system is designed to engage and destroy incoming missiles within a 5000 metre radius of the ship[6].

    The CIWS receives LRR (*long range radar*) and ES (*electronic surveillance*) events from the ships sensors. These are 'fused' by the system into *target contacts*, and placed into a target list. The list is periodically scanned for targets and these are forwarded to either the fore or aft gun depending on the bearing of the contact. The target is then engaged.

---

[5]ODS - Object Description Skeleton
[6]This system was originally developed as part of a feasibility study on real-time design methods for the Defence Research Agency (UK). The design represented here is simplified for the purposes of example. A full description of the CIWS design is available in [7].

The parent object CLOSE_IN_WEAPONS_SYSTEM (fig 10) encapsulates two transactions. The first, and largest is CIWS_Trans. This is initiated by the active object TARGET_CONVERTER. The flow relationships CT:1 and CT:2 respectively, read LRR and ES events from the required interface of the parent. The flow CT:3 is used to write 'fused' target information to the protected object TARGET_LIST. This data is asynchronously read by the cyclic object SELECTOR via flow relationship CT:4. The execution path of the transaction then diverges. Depending on the bearing of the target, data is sent to the sporadic object AFT_GUN via flow CT:5.1 or FORE_GUN via flow CT:5.2, where the transaction terminates. The transaction must complete within 350ms of initiation.

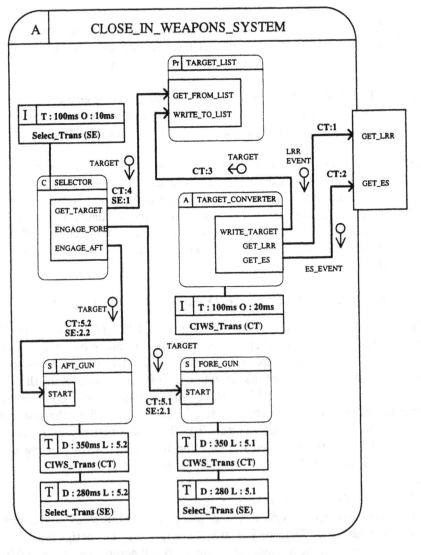

Fig. 10. The close-in weapons system

CIWS_Trans also includes a sub-transaction, Select_Trans. This is initiated by the cyclic object SELECTOR. As a sub-transaction the path of flow relationships are identical to those of CIWS_Trans. The first flow relationship, SE:1 follows an identical path to CT:4 and so on. The sub-transaction must complete within 280ms of initiation. It should be noted that the object SELECTOR must meet the deadline of *both* CIWS_Trans and Select_Trans.

For the purposes of example a decomposition of the active object TARGET_CONVERTER is presented in figure 11. The object is implemented by the child transaction Fuser_Trans. The transaction is initiated by the cyclic object CONVERTER. This flow relationships, FT:1 and FT:2 read LRR and ES events from the required interface of the parent. The flow FT:3 writes these events to the

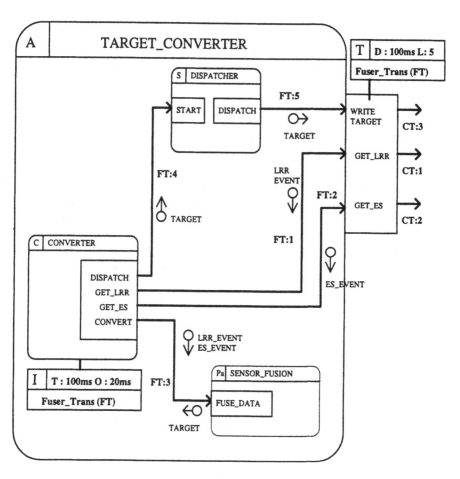

Fig. 11. The decomposition of Target_Converter

passive object SENSOR_FUSION. These events are fused and read back to CONVERTER. The target contact is written to the sporadic object DISPATCHER along flow relationship FT:4. This object then writes the target to the required interface of the parent via flow FT:5. The transaction has a deadline of 100ms.

For the decomposition to be correct the design must meet the rules of flow and performance verification. The parent flow relationships CT:1, CT:2 and CT:3 must be generated by calls to the required interface by a child transaction (*flow verification rule 2*). This rule is satisfied by the Fuser_Trans flows FT:1, FT:2 and FT:5 respectively.

A sequence of flow relationships generated by a parent object must be implemented by an unbroken path of child transaction flows (*flow verification rule 4*). This rule is satisfied as TARGET_CONVERTER is implemented by a single, and therefore unbroken, child transaction.

The parent initiator TARGET_CONVERTER has a minimum inter-arrival time of 100ms, and an offset of 20ms. This performance must be verified with respect to the next level of decomposition. The minimum inter-arrival time (MAT) of the parent must be equal to or less than the invocation rate of the initiating operation by the object implementation (*performance verification rule 1(a)*). The parent initiating operation GET_LRR is called by the flow relationship FT:1. This is generated by the child initiator CONVERTER that has a MAT of 100ms. The rule is therefore satisfied as the invocation rate is equal to the MAT of the parent at 100ms.

The offset of a parent initiator must be equal to the earliest point in time that the initiating operation is invoked, relative to system start-up (*performance verification rule 2(a)*). The earliest point in time that the initiating operation of TARGET_CONVERTER can be called is after the expiration of the offset assigned to the child transaction initiator CONVERTER. The offset of TARGET_CONVERTER is correct as the offset of CONVERTER and its parent are equal at 20ms.

5.0 Conclusions

The goal of HRT-HOOD is to provide a set of specialised abstractions for the design and performance analysis of hard real-time systems. As an object-based design technique, the current version of HRT-HOOD places a significant emphasis on top-down partitioning, and data-centred modularity. As a consequence its support for the specification of 'end to end' transactions is weak. This paper has demonstrated how the method can be extended to provide this support.

References

1. Burns, A. and Wellings, A.J. : HRT-HOOD: A Design Method for Hard Real-Time Ada, Real-Time Systems Journal, 6, 73-114, (1994)

2. Burns, A. and Wellings, A.J. : HRT-HOOD: A Structured Design Method for Hard Real-Time Ada Systems. Elsevier. (1995)

3. Ada 95 Mapping/Revision Team: Ada 95 Reference Manual, Intermetrics Inc. (1995).

4. Ada 95 Mapping/Revision Team: Ada 95 Rationale, Intermetrics Inc. (1995).

5. Vickers, A.J. : Computational Architecture - A Step Towards Predictable Software Design. Phd Thesis, University of York (1994)

6. Cornwell, P. and Wellings, A.J. : Transaction Integration for Reusable Hard-Real-Time Components. Internal Report, University of York (1995).

7. Cornwell, P., Burns, A. and Wellings, A.J. : The Design and Analysis of a Close-In Weapons Simulator using HRT-HOOD. YCS-251. Internal Report, University of York. (1995)

Evaluation of a SPARC board equipped with the Ada Tasking Coprocessor (ATAC)

F. Battini, P.L. Mantovani, M. Mattavelli

Laben S.p.A.
SS. Padana Superiore 290 - 20090 Vimodrone (MI) - Italy

Abstract. To cope with computing overheads introduced by a multithread environment, an appealing approach consists in shifting a good deal of the run time system functionalities at hardware level by means of a *tasking coprocessor* managing real-time capabilities of software applications as mathematical coprocessors manage operations for number crunching programs. Such component is available on the market, the RTech Ada Tasking Coprocessor (ATAC), and LABEN is involved in assessing the resulting performance of a SPARC/ATAC platform running an Ada software application designed for future spacecraft missions.

1   Introduction

In spite of many years of still improving compiler technology, available Ada Run-Time Supports are able to supply a rendezvous efficiency of the order of hundreds of microseconds up to some milliseconds, when executed on ordinary microprocessor systems [10].

That point is very critical for embedded real-time applications, where safety critical activities must be performed within hard time limits.   In real-time systems the most important measure of efficiency is the response time, whereas throughput, CPU utilization are critical, but of less importance [15].

Although a vertical migration from software to firmware of some operating system functionalities was already foreseen for performance improvements [15], the concept of a tasking coprocessor, acting in the real-time domain as the mathematical coprocessor for number crunching applications, had in the past outstanding practical examples, like the Transputer hardware scheduler or the Intel i960 processor.

The definitive concept is then to provide the Ada kernel software with an *Ada TAsking Coprocessor* (ATAC), in order to reduce the unsatisfactory timeliness of the Ada Run Time Support [3].

By using a special purpose hardware, able to be charged of the entire rendezvous semantics with a minimum of communication overhead, the final development goal is that the full Ada multitasking constructs can be freely used without any performance degradation, provided that Ada compiler is able to insert ATAC-like instructions for the tasking management.

The following paper explains the SPARC/ATAC evaluation approach as proposed by LABEN with reference to a space application software.

2 The SPARC/ATAC Board

To evaluate the benefits that ATAC brings to a SPARC microcomputer, a suitable evaluation board is needed. Since ESA is also funding the development of a space qualified RISC Computing Core, called ERC32 and based on SPARC architecture, such a board should be representative of what a real board for typical on-board applications could be for those aspects that can affect the ATAC evaluation, while keeping at a minimum the complexity for the non relevant aspects.
For this purpose, a suitable architecture representative of an ERC32 based microcomputer is shown in figure 1.

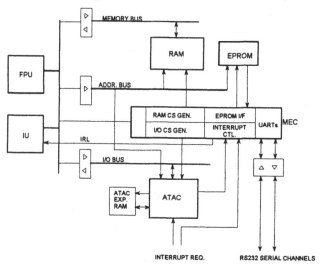

Figure 1. SPARC architecture representative of the ERC32.

2.1. CPU Core

The board is built around a MHS 90C600 SPARC CPU (IU and FPU), which are almost identical to the corresponding ERC32 devices and implement a SPARC V7 IU and FPU. The board includes an ATAC device with external memory, some amount of static RAM to store test programs, EPROM for the SPARCMon resident monitor, an interrupt controller, two RS232 serial channels handled by a pair of simple UARTS, to connect to a display and to an host computer, two timers and a VME bus interface that supports master and slave operations.
The 4 Mbyte RAM bank provides the board with the main memory to store programs and data. The use of fast static RAMs allows to access the memory with no wait states, which is an essential requirement for this system.
On the other hand to be representative of the ERC32 architecture, it is possible to introduce a programmable number of wait states in the RAM read/write operations as if an EDAC device was present in the system.

Almost all the glue and control logic is packed in a single device called MEmory Controller (MEC), which is implemented by using an Actel FPGA.
The system is clocked at 12 MHz by an on board clock generator. This clock is used to derive all the other clocks required (UART baud rate, ATAC's system and real time clocks, etc.).

2.2. The Ada Tasking Coprocessor

An ATAC 2.0 device is connected over the I/O bus as a 32 bit peripheral and appears as a memory mapped device, accessible via normal memory load/stores. Bus transactions with the ATAC are dynamically extendible to meet ATAC requirements. The clock for the ATAC is the same as the IU clock, and the real time clock is generated internally.
The ATAC coprocessor is then driven by the main processor as a memory mapped I/O device, that answers to every tasking requests with a defined response (i.e. the task identifier). The ATAC is then accessed by doing reads or write operations at a predefined address, using 64 instructions conceptually mapped on individual read/write ports with unique address [11, 12].

2.3. The Interrupt Structure

A number of interrupt inputs are made available by the board to external equipment in order to enter appropriate interrupt requests, and the whole interrupt structure of the board, which is one of the peculiar points where ATAC plays an important role is organized as follows: some interrupt lines are sent directly to the IU via the MEC interrupt controller. Some others are routed to the ATAC interrupt inputs, while the ATAC's ATTN and FAULT outputs will be sent to the MEC interrupt controller.
In this way it will be possible to measure the difference in interrupt response time with or without the ATAC.
The VME I/F routes its seven different interrupt signals to both the ATAC interrupt inputs and the MEC interrupt controller.

3   The Test Environment

To perform benchmarking and to evaluate the effects of the ATAC on the SPARC system, a suitable hardware testing environment must be set up.
Two kinds of evaluation activities are foreseen:

- the run of benchmark programs to exercise specific ATAC features, and to measure them
- the run of a program similar to a real application to evaluate the global effects of the ATAC.

In the first case, since the measurements to be made normally are time measurements (e.g. the time between an external event like an interrupt and the execution of a piece of code, or the time between the execution of two pieces of code), only laboratory instrumentation is required: no special hardware is necessary on the board. The test set-up is inclusive of:

- A logic state analyzer with support for the chosen SPARC CPU. Typically this means a special probe to be plugged in the CPU PGA socket of the board, and a software to record and display the CPU activity in mnemonic (assembler like) form. Such analyzer should also be able to measure the time between two events.
- A pattern generator or pulse generator synchronized with the logic state analyzer, to generate appropriate interrupts at given points in the flow of the program.
- A digital oscilloscope, which would also be useful to evaluate hardware aspects of the ATAC/CPU interface.
- A SUN workstation connected via RS232 to the board, for the development and downloading of the benchmark programs.

For the purpose of running an example of application program, which in this case is a simplified version of the program developed for by LABEN for the Autonomous Spacecraft Study (ASDMS) study, under ESTEC contract, the set-up will be made by the VME rack of the ASDMS breadboard provided by ESTEC, where the ad hoc developed SPARC/ATAC evaluation board will be added to a commercial SPARC board (from FORCE Computers) charged of environment simulation and not intrusive ancillary functionalities.

The evaluation board will communicate with the commercial board via the VME backplane for processor intercommunications required by the simulated environment and the system will be linked to a SUN workstation for downloading and monitoring via an RS232 channel coming from the commercial board.

The ASDMS program already provides means to collect data for performance evaluations, so no other hardware would be necessary. In any case, the same instrumentation used for benchmarking can be foreseen to perform additional measurements.

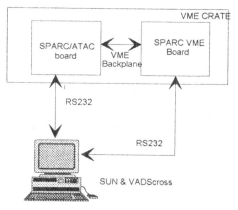

Figure 2.: the hardware set-up for ATAC benchmarks

A SUN-based Ada cross-compiler developed by VERDIX and made available by ESTEC has been used as cross compiler for SPARC board: to deal with the ATAC device integrated in the SPARC target boards produced by LABEN, a software ATAC I/F layer should be provided.

4 The Software Adaptation

An ATAC interface should provide users with real tasks, but using ATAC with the standard Ada Compilation system, explicit Ada Task declarations cannot be inserted, unless the compiler has been adapted for inserting special ATAC instructions in its own tasking system.

Therefore, the user tasks shall be declared as procedures and an ATAC interface layer is charged of managing such "threads" (to distinguish from the Ada "tasks") by means of a set of services and primitives, that give the possibility to implement a cyclic software framework, but also others scheduling policies (i.e Rate Monotonic and Deadline Monotonic Scheduling), exploiting and interfacing to the computing capabilities of the Ada Tasking Coprocessor.

4.1. The ATAC Coroutines

To avoid any reference to the Ada tasking mechanism, any task-clause should be replaced by some procedure call-clause, where context switch can be handled as a stack-saving typical of procedure calls.

Therefore threads shall be implemented by co-routines [5], whose scheduling and switch is handled by ATAC. Unfortunately, semantics of Ada procedure is different from semantics of an entry call, because a subprogram code is *reentrant* [1, 4], i.e. executable whenever required without waiting for anyone executing the same code.

Furthermore, any task has a well defined state and its execution may be blocked at rendezvous points waiting for other code execution and then may resume its running state. A procedure on the other hand can be started and executed up to the last statement and any further reference to it is just able to restart all the subprogram flow. All that to underline the fact that we have to deal with an **Abstract State Machine (ASM)** able to keep memory of its past state and to resume it at the next invocation.

As Ada packages are thought to be used as ASM, it seems sensible to identify Ada packages as a good solution for thread implementation.

4.2. The ATAC Interface layer as an Ada package

Purpose of a package-based implementation for different software threads should be to provide active objects whose status can be affected by invocation of well defined interfaces able to address the ATAC with the right instruction flow in order to manage the required context switches and the desired resources.

It is obvious that such sort of *emulation* of the Ada tasking mechanism should be supported by:

- the ATAC device mechanisms
- a suitable package that provide the application software with a set of services to access the ATAC mechanisms.

That means that the ATAC layer is a server from which the software can "buy" some services according to its tasking needs.

4.3. Process Package and Entry Calls

Let us set the following task example.
```
--      task MY_TASK is
--              entry SYNCH;
--      end MY_TASK;
--      task body MY_TASK is
--      begin
--          accept SYNCH;
--              .. body statements ..
--      end MY_TASK;
```
The ATAC interface shall be able to handle the same semantics without using any tasking clause, but only through procedure calls and suitable abstract data types as shown:

```
with ATAC;
procedure MAIN is
    << declarations>>
package MY_TASK is tasking: ATAC.TASKS:=(QUES=>1);
    procedure SYNCH(QUE: in ATAC.QID := 0);
end MY_TASK;
```

where the ATAC.TASKS object is an adequate data structure, that holds the description of some task features (here just the number of accessible queues is shown as well as the queue identifier QID) and some ATAC primitives encapsulate the save context registers related to that thread. Whatever caller would call MY_TASK, it shall execute:

```
begin
    MY_TASK.SYNCH;
        :
end MAIN;
```

that looks like an Ada standard entry call to a standard Ada task. The entry call is referring to a *procedure* SYNCH that acts as procedure interface with the *package* MY_TASK "tasking" an ATAC.TASKS.
The body of such procedure can be inserted in the *package body* or implemented in a separated compilation unit and contains the actual entry call instruction managed directly by the ATAC [11, 12].

4.4. The Message Passing Communication

Let us extending the task example written in Ada, introducing entries with parameters.

```
--      task MY_TASK is
--              entry MY_ENTRY(X: in MYTYPE; Y: out MYTYPE);
--      end MY_TASK;
```

```
--      task body MY_TASK is
--      begin
--          accept MY_ENTRY(X: in MYTYPE; Y: out MYTYPE) do
--                          << some actions >>;
--          end MY_ENTRY;
--      end MY_TASK;
```

As in the former case, the task is translated into a package, where the entries are implemented by visible procedures:

```
with ATAC;
procedure MAIN is

 << declarations >>

package MY_TASK is tasking: ATAC.TASKS:=(QUES=>1);
        procedure MY_ENTRY(X: in MYTYPE; Y: out MYTYPE;
                                          QUE: in ATAC.QID := 0);

end MY_TASK;
    :
```

To pass parameters, the message passing approach is used: whenever MY_ENTRY is called, the caller posts a message in a dedicated mailbox. A raw implementation shall declare an object composed by as many slots as the list of the formal parameters needs and the procedure body of MY_ENTRY is charged of putting its actual parameters into the mailbox.

```
separate(MY_TASK);
procedure MY_ENTRY(X: in MYTYPE; Y: out MYTYPE;
                          QUE: in ATAC.QID := 0)is
begin
   MAILBOX.X:=X; -- put the in param into mbx
   <<ATAC management section >>
   Y:=MAILBOX.Y; -- get out param from mbx
      :
end MY_ENTRY;
```

As the procedure, however, is a reentrant code and therefore many callers can request access to the same resource supplied by the mailbox object, such implementation should cope with:

- synchronization of the accesses through use of semaphores, because a new caller should be prevented to put *in* data in the mailbox till the callee has loaded down into its own registers the mailbox contents

- typical priority inversion problem related to access to shared resources [7].

The solution is provided by ATAC that provides programmers with semaphores managed as ATAC services and with *Basic Priority Inheritance* [14] scheduling. Hence a *protected object* [6] can be implemented for the mailbox using a PROTECTED type object declared within the ATAC package. Therefore, the procedure implementing MY_ENTRY shall be completed in order to deal with the mailbox as follows:

```
package body MY_TASK is
              ID: ATAC.ETID:= ATAC.set(tasking);
-----------------------------------------------------------
package MAILBOX is object: ATAC.PROTECTED;
    X, Y : MYTYPE;
    procedure P(QUE : in ATAC.QID);
    procedure V(QUE : in ATAC.QID);
end MAILBOX;


separate(MY_TASK);
procedure MY_ENTRY(X: in MYTYPE; Y: out MYTYPE;
                   QUE: in ATAC.QID := 0)is
begin
  MAILBOX.P(QUE);    -- wait for mailbox access
  MAILBOX.X:=X;      -- put the in param into mbx
   << ATAC management section >>
  Y:=MAILBOX.Y;      -- get the out param from mbx
  MAILBOX.V(QUE);    -- release resource
end MY_ENTRY;
```

4.5. The Accept Statement

Carrying on the same example of the former paragraph, the rendezvous managed by the task body:

```
--      begin
--          accept MY_ENTRY(X: in MYTYPE; Y: out MYTYPE) do
--                      Y:=X + REG;
--          end MY_ENTRY;
```

should be managed by ATAC through adequate services the package ATAC supplies the software with:

- `ATAC.accept_clause,` that signals to ATAC that the thread is waiting for accepting an entry call;
- `ATAC.end_accept` that signals to ATAC that the thread has completed accept operations and the rendezvous is accomplished;

Both services shall contain context switch operations to preempt the thread if required either before or after the do-block of the accept.

```
begin
       acceptMY_ENTRY: begin;
           ATAC.accept_clause(QID => 0);   -- wait here
           MAILBOX.Y:=MAILBOX.X + REG;
           ATAC.end_accept;
       end MY_ENTRY;
end;
```

5 The Evaluation on Space Application: ASDMS

As actual Ada coding prefers avoiding inefficient task semantics in critical functions, no ready-to-flight Ada software can be used for evaluating ATAC performance on the field.

Due to the great importance of the study assessment for the Ada Tasking systems, however, an Ada system inclusive of main OBDH functions and implemented without restrictions on the use of the Ada semantics should be provided.

Therefore, a large Ada application, developed by LABEN for the Autonomous Spacecraft Study (ASDMS) under ESTEC contract, is going to be used.

The keypoints of the proposed software are [9]:

- the extensive use of the Ada Tasking mechanism stressing a good deal of possible uses for the ATAC device
- an application with features very close to a space embedded software
- the related testing methodology for assessing performance evaluations, already identified and detailed in the ASDMS test plan [2].

As tasks included in the ASDMS task set offer a wide range of possible utilisation of the task semantics, the evaluation has been forced to implement a wider set of tasking related clause, rather than implementing a restricted set focused on execution of well defined benchmarks [8, 13].

6 Conclusions

The present paper has explained the LABEN approach to the ATAC Evaluation Study. The goal of the study is the assessment of the performance improvements on a SPARC based platform equipped with the Ada Tasking Coprocessor.

The first step of the hardware set up on a SPARC/ATAC board is under finalization, as well as the definition of an Ada coding ruleset able to manage the ATAC capabilities without any intrusive modification of an existing Ada Compile Systems.

Next steps are based on:

- the ATAC adaptation of the Ada code used for the Autonomous Spacecraft Data Management System (ASDMS)
- the application of some end-to-end tests already designed for the ASDMS Validation on such adapted Ada application
- the assessment of the improved performance introduced by ATAC with reference to the ASDMS Ada code, which uses standard Ada tasking system.

Up to now a preliminary evaluation on the usability of the ATAC device has not raised major concerns as far as the design of an Ada Platform integrated with ATAC.

Even from the software viewpoint, it seems possible to follow some Ada coding rules that allow to deal with ATAC without waiting for an adaptation of an Ada SPARC compiler for ATAC. Almost all the traditional tasking mechanisms can be provided, even by using a procedure-based approach, with some differences on the management of the task types. For sake of simplicity, handling of multiple delay options in selective wait has not been considered as well as implementation of entry families which has been avoided.

The point still open consists in a careful assessment of the overheads introduced by a ruled Ada code that may impact on potential benefits of the ATAC speed-up in the tasking mechanisms.

7 References

1.   MIL-STD-1815A Reference Manual for the Ada Programming Language.

2.   F. Battini, L.Marradi, *Verification, Validation and Testing for Autonomous Spacecraft Systems*, Proc. of Electrical Ground Support Equipment Workshop, ESTEC, Noordwijk, October 1992.

3.   Terraillon J.L., *The ATAC answer to Ada Constraint*, 2.0, Proc. of On Board Data Management symposium, Rome 1994

4.   G. Booch, Software Engineering with Ada, Benjamin Cummings, 1987.

5.   A. Burns, A. Wellings, *Real-Time Systems and Their Programming Languages*, Addison-Wesley Publishing Co.

6.   A. Burns, A. Wellings, *Bridging the Real-Time Gap between Ada83 and Ada9X*, Ada YearBook 1993, IOS Press.

7.   D.Cornhill, L.Sha, *Priority Inversion in Ada, or What Should be the Priority of an Ada Server Task ?*, November 1987.

8.   Benchmarking of Compilers and processors for Space Embedded real Time Systems, ESA STR-233-April 1991

9.   L. Marradi, F. Ciceri, D. Masotti, *The Use of Ada and Object Oriented Design in the Development of an Autonomous Spacecraft Data Management System*, Ada in Aerospace, 1992.

10.   J. Roos, *The Performance of a Prototype Coprocessor for Ada Tasking*, TRI-Ada90, December 1990.

11.   ATAC 2.0 - Final Compiler Adaptation Guide R-Tech AB October 1992.

12.   ATAC 2.0 Data Sheet, R-Tech, vers 0.99, AB March 93.

13.   Ada Mechanism Performance, R-Tech, Draft Issue 1.0, March 1993;

14.   L.Sha, R. Rajkumar, J.P.Lehoczky, *Priority Inheritance Protocols: An Approach to Real-Time Synchronization*, IEEE Trans. on Computers, 39(9), September 1990.

15.   T. Tempelmeier, *Performance Analysis of a Microprogrammed Real-Time Operating System with an Interrupt and Abort Discipline*, Microprocessor and Microprogramming, North-Holland, 19(1987), pp.233-251.

Ada and Timed Automata

Lars Björnfot

Department of Computer Systems, Uppsala University
P.O. Box 325, S–751 05 Uppsala, Sweden
E–mail: bjornfot@docs.uu.se

Abstract. The relation between the Ada tasking model and the formal model timed automaton is described. Guidelines for translating Ada tasking constructs into timed automata and vice versa are given, along with important differences and similarities in tasking semantics between Ada task and timed automata. A case study shows how a previously verified audio control protocol is translated to Ada.

1 Introduction

The tasking mechanism in Ada is based on rendezvous, a synchronous communication primitive with optional parameter passing. It is powerful, but the complexity of the mechanism is high. Even systems with a few tasks can be difficult to understand and predict, and the difficulty increases rapidly when systems scale up

Several formal methods exist for analyzing and verifying systems with concurrent processes, for example timed process algebra [1][2][3], timed automata [4] and timed petri nets [5]. Even if the formal model is simple, the complexity of the system is still a problem, e.g. finding optimal schedules or finding all potential deadlocks is often exponential, meaning that it is difficult to estimate the time it takes to find answers to such questions. State explosion is another problem, generating a set of all possible states is easy for small systems but practically impossible for large systems.

After the development of a formalism or model where state explosion can be reduced and a set of desired problems can be solved in finite time, there is still one major obstruction: there is no one-to-one mapping between the model and an implementation, i.e. the system has to be implemented using hardware, language, and operating systems that does not support the formal model.

This paper presents translation of (a subset of) Ada tasking to timed automata, that preserves the tasking semantics. Timed automata can be expressed as (is equivalent to) timed process algebra, and can be used for automatic verification of real-time systems [6]. Such a tool for automatic verification, UPPAAL [7][8] has been developed by a group at DoCS.

Important differences and similarities in tasking semantics between Ada task and timed automata are pointed out. The differences must be eliminated by modifying either or both of the language and the formal model. Since Ada is standardized it is inappropriate to add new language constructs, instead any modifications should be in the form of restrictions, i.e. resulting in a subset of Ada that can be compiled on any validated compiler. A subset of tasking with sufficiently powerful task primitives, which also offers verifiable systems, is suitable for implementing in hardware to obtain efficient task management. The distributed run-time system project [9] is one example where this is needed.

Related work include [10] where timed automata is used as a model for real-time Ada programs with tasking. The model includes processor sharing, priority preemption and process suspension. However, the translation from Ada to timed automata and vice versa is not defined. In [11] a "safe nucleus" is formally specified in Z. The nucleus provides support for a subset of Ada, extended with some Ada 9X features (before Ada 95 was standardized).

2 Timed Automata

A timed automaton (TA) is an finite automaton [12] extended with time by adding real-valued clocks to each automaton, and for each transition adding enabling conditions called guards. Time is modelled by positive real numbers. When used in a guard expression, the clocks are compared to natural values. This is a 'trick' to avoid the state explosion when representing time as discrete ticks. Real time (as opposed to CPU time) is introduced by a number of real-valued clocks. The clock rates are the same, and they may not be stopped, but they may be reset at any time.

Each transition may have a guard, which is a constraint over clock variables and naturals, i.e. a boolean expression with real-valued clocks and natural constants or variables. An action associated with a transition may only be taken when the guard is true. A guard that is always true may be omitted. Time variables should be evaluated when a state is entered. The values are used in relations such as $y=T$, which eventually may become true/false as y advances. With each arc there may be an associated set of clocks to reset when the transition is made. Integer variables (relation operators) are allowed in the guard, and the variables may be assigned values using simple algebra in the form $m:=m \cdot N+N$, where N is a natural number. Several guards are allowed (they are AND-ed), and several assignments are allowed, however at most one action is allowed per transition. It is usually obvious from the context if it is a guard, action or assignment, e.g. "<" is a relation operator in a guard and ":=" is an assignment.

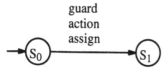

Fig 1. A guarded transition with assignment in a timed automata.

The informal semantics of the guarded transitions is that

- If a guard is false, the transition <u>may not</u> be taken.
- If the guard is true, the transition <u>may</u> be taken.
- If the guard will become permanently false, the transition <u>must</u> be taken unless there are other arcs from this state that are open or may become open.

In fig 2, the automaton has the following properties. The clock y is reset in the initial state S_0. When the guard $y==1$ is true, transition *run* must be taken. In state S_1 when the guard $y==2$ is true, the transition *reset* may be taken and the clock is reset, or at any time, the transition *next* may be taken. When the state S_2 is entered, the time variable T is evaluated. There are two mutually exclusive guards on the transitions from S_2. As long as the guard $y<T$ is true, transition *fail* may be taken, and when $y>T$ is true, transi-

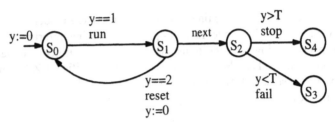

Fig 2. An example of a timed automaton.

tion *stop* may be taken. There are two possible final states, S_3 or S_4. Interaction between automata is so far not considered.

Interaction is achieved by output and input actions, where ! means an output action and ? means an input action. The purpose is to make synchronization between exactly two automata possible, so that not every automaton must participate in the synchronization. All transitions without ! or ? are internal.

3 Ada Tasking Constructs and Equivalent Timed Automata

This section contains a few reflections on the properties of Ada rendezvous, followed by a number of examples of delay, synchronization, and rendezvous. In the examples we assume there are two library level tasks, A with an entry E, and B with no entry.

3.1 Some Properties of Rendezvous

Ada requires that a task that reaches an accept statement *must* rendezvous with any task that is waiting in the corresponding entry queue. A task that reaches an entry call *must* rendezvous with a task that has been suspended on a corresponding accept statement. If several tasks execute an entry call, the calls *must* be served in FIFO order.

Several tasks may call the same entry, for example *m*. This corresponds to several automata performing the same action *m!*. However, several tasks cannot execute an accept on the same entry. Even if there is a task type, or access type, the tasks have distinct entry queues. This corresponds to exactly one automaton performing *m?*.

The parameter passing modes in Ada are not connected to whether input or output actions are used. Both start and end of rendezvous can be described with output actions at the calling side. To describe a general rendezvous, two transitions must be used.

3.2 Delay

A simple delay statement, where the amount D is constant, is modeled by resetting a clock y. At time $y=D$ the timeout transition must be taken. Time intervals in seconds are in Ada represented with the fixed point type Duration, which easily can be modelled with integers (N · Duration'Small).

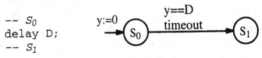

Fig 3. Delay.

3.3 Synchronization vs Rendezvous

If there are only "quick accepts" (accept without a do-part) the rendezvous is a simple synchronization. It can be modeled with a transition E, where E! means entry call and E? means accept.

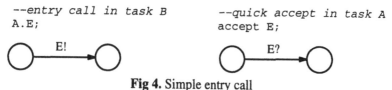

```
--entry call in task B        --quick accept in task A
A.E;                          accept E;
```

Fig 4. Simple entry call

However, it is common to have a do-part, both for parameterless and parameterized entries. If a task, for a certain entry E, has one or more accepts-do statements, the rendezvous must be modeled using two transitions, one for the start of synchronization E_s and one for end of synchronization E_e. The calling task is suspended during the rendezvous, so no other transitions are allowed than $E_s!.E_e!$. This is indicated with the dashed state in fig 5. The called task executes during rendezvous, so the "middle" state could be of any complexity. If the middle state is described by X, then $E_s?.X.E_e?$ describes the called task.

```
          A.E;                              accept E do
                                                ...
                                            end E;
```

Fig 5. Rendezvous with start E_s and end E_e of synchronization. The dashed state must not be further elaborated.

3.4 Timed Entry Calls

Timed entry calls are modeled by resetting a clock y in the initial state, and forcing a timeout transition at $y=D$. When $y>D$ the rendezvous must not be possible.

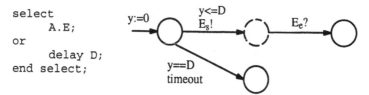

```
select
        A.E;
or
        delay D;
end select;
```

Fig 6. Timed entry call, with rendezvous or timeout.

3.5 Selective Wait Statements

The selective wait is a powerful statement that potentially adds much more complexity. An example with guards are shown in fig 7. An Ada guard is evaluated once, when the select is executed. The guard does not change when time advances, which makes it different from a TA guard. A delay alternative is handled like a timed entry call (not shown).

```
select
        accept E do
        end E;
or
        when G=5 =>
                accept F do
                end F;
end select;
```

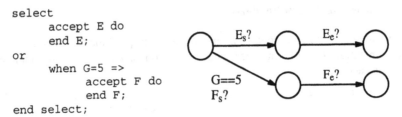

Fig 7. Selective wait statement, with a guarded accepts. The Ada guard G=5 is evaluated once, and is not dependent on any clock *y*.

3.6 Re-writing may Simplify Translation

A select with several delay alternatives does not correspond to multiple arcs with different time guards. The alternative with the lowest delay is chosen and this is translated to a transition like in 3.4. Re-writing the code to have only one delay alternative makes an automatic translation easier.

3.7 Computation Time

Separate computation time from system time used for delays etc. requires that clocks can be stopped. Stopping clocks is not implemented in the verification tool UPPAAL, so we must make the assumption that the execution time in each state of the timed automaton is sufficiently "short". This assumption is justified for a system such as the case study in section 5, where the execution during each transition consists of simple assignments, if statements, case statements etc. with a small and bounded execution time. For more complex execution time analysis it is not a justified approach. The consequences is shortly described in this section.

In [10] there are two kind of clocks associated with the timed automata: local clocks that may be stopped and thus can measure CPU time, and global clocks that cannot be stopped and thus measures system time. This requires that the run-time system is modelled, in order to decide which task to execute.

Assume that x is a local clock. The execution time for a statement or procedure call etc. could be either a lower bound, an upper bound or a range. For example in fig 8, the execution time of A is at least T_A, for B at most T_B, and for C in the range $[T_{CL} .. T_{CU}]$. The procedures A, B, and C is assumed to have a bounded execution time and no entry calls or accepts.

```
A;
B;
C;
```

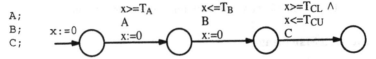

Fig 8. Guard expressions representing computation time.

Finding a bound on execution times is an important part of analyzing a real-time system. There are several methods to obtain (measure or calculate) execution times, for example [13].

4 Translating Timed Automata to Ada

The previous section presented some common Ada constructs and their translations to timed automata. Translating in the reverse direction is equally important, and this sections presents some common TA constructs with a suggested translation to Ada. Construct that are suitable for automatic translations are primarily chosen, as there are usually several equivalent translations.

4.1 State Machine

For a simple automaton with few states and few transitions it is justifiable to ignore the states and translate only the transitions, for example as in fig 9.

```
loop
    act1;
    act2;
    act3;
end loop;
```

Fig 9. Translating only the transitions to Ada

In general an automaton is not easily translatable to structured programming concepts. By enumerating all states and translating to a case within an infinite loop the general case is covered, as shown in fig 10. Note that there is no *when others* alternative.

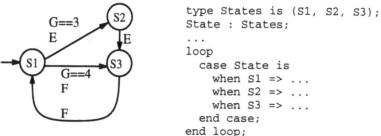

```
type States is (S1, S2, S3);
State : States;
...
loop
    case State is
        when S1 => ...
        when S2 => ...
        when S3 => ...
    end case;
end loop;
```

Fig 10. Translating into a general state machine in Ada

For each state translate the actions and state changes, for example if the variable G can have the value 3 or 4, the translation for state S1 becomes:

```
when S1 => -- actions and state changes in S1
   case G is
      when 3 => E;
              State := S2;
      when 4 => F;
              State := S3;
   end case;
```

4.2 Translating Clocks

Since in most cases the exact time when code is executed depends on in which order tasks are scheduled, the exact time must be calculated. Clocks are modelled with a variable of type Calendar.Time that holds the exact time, and used together with function Calendar.Clock that returns the current time. Declare each clock as:

```
X : Time;
```

Define a function Amount that takes natural and returns duration, properly scaled:

```
function Amount (N : Natural) return Duration is
begin
    return duration (N)/100;    --convert and scale
end Amount;
```

Guards such as x==2 is translated to the exact time when x==2 holds, X+Amount(2). This is for example used in delay statements

```
delay X + Amount(2) - Clock;   -- delay until x==2 holds
```

Resetting clocks during a transition is translated to adding the value the TA clock had when the transition was taken. For example a transition with guard x==2, reset is translated to

```
X := X + Amount(2);   -- "reset" x to the time where x==2 holds
```

4.3 Concurrent or Sequential

This section gives guidelines for the important decision: should actions be translated to concurrent or sequential code. Concurrent code is here defined as task communication which requires entries, and sequential code is any code that does not involve task communication; in both cases the code is within a task. Some transitions can be translated to either concurrent or sequential code, but in some cases one is preferable, and in some cases it is impossible to translate without changing the automaton.

Concurrent code: Declare entries for each action. Input actions, denoted ?, corresponds to accepts and output actions, denoted !, corresponds to entry calls. Single transitions are translated to entry calls or accepts while multiple transitions (from one state) are translated to select-or-accept. In a select, accepts and entry calls cannot be mixed; only multiple accepts are allowed. A particular input action cannot appear in more than one automaton, but it might be possible obtain that goal by swapping all ! and ? for this action, since it does not change the semantics.

Sequential code: For single transitions use simple statements or procedure calls, for multiple transitions use if or case statements.

The notation [C] is used to suggest a concurrent translation and [S] a sequential translation. A + or − indicates that the translation is considered good or bad, however, the guidelines for selecting concurrent or sequential translation are still rather *ad hoc*.

Unguarded transition

This means: at any time take action E. It is impossible to say when, this action is "offered" as long as the automaton remains in S1.
[C+] Simple entry call or accept.
[S−] Sequential code does not offer E at any time.

Immediate transition

Immediately take action E. If E is not possible the automaton never changes state, i.e. it stops. Ideally no time passes and $x==0$ in S2 holds but in practice x is probably slightly higher in S1 and definitely higher in S2. A guard such as $x==0$ in S2 must be relaxed

```
--concurrent
accept E;   -- or A_Task.E
State := S2;
```

Fig 11. Unguarded transition.

or ignored.

[C–] The intuitive translation is a conditional entry call or select-else, but the result during execution would depend on the state of the other task state, which is not the case in the TA. The best approach is a simple call or accept and tolerate that x==0 is not strictly true.

[S+] Do immediately rather suggests executing sequential code until a synchronization point is reached. For several consecutive transitions with guard x==0, the guard is simply ignored.

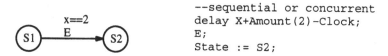

```
--sequential
E;
State := S2;
```

Fig 12. Immediate transition.

Timed transition

At exactly x=2 take E. The task must be suspended during an exact amount of time. This works equally well for concurrent and sequential code. Assuming that x is of type Time, the exact time to wake up the task is x+Amount(2).

```
--sequential or concurrent
delay X+Amount(2)-Clock;
E;
State := S2;
```

Fig 13. Timed transition.

Actions with reset

Reset x when E is taken. In some cases it is difficult to obtain the exact time.

[C+] The task is suspended in S1 until the rendezvous occurs. Reset x during rendezvous, *inside* accept-do statement, by assigning the current time. At least the clock is reset when the the call is made, but that may happen on an "inexact" time.

[S–] Assign before the sequential code (assigning afterwards would add the execution time to x). See fig 14.

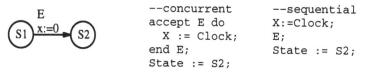

```
--concurrent          --sequential
accept E do            X:=Clock;
   X := Clock;         E;
end E;                 State := S2;
State := S2;
```

Fig 14. Reset during transition. The reset time value is not exact.

For the transition in fig 15, the value of x is known when the transition is taken, so the exact time value after reset can be calculated.

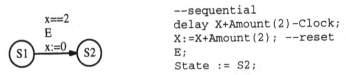

```
                          --sequential
    x==2                  delay X+Amount(2)-Clock;
     E                    X:=X+Amount(2);  --reset
  S1  x:=0   S2           E;
                          State := S2;
```

Fig 15. Reset during transition. The reset time value is exact.

For consecutive transitions with a final reset as in fig 16, exact clock value is preserved better with sequential code, by calculate the exact time and assign to x. Reading Clock during rendezvous is the best approximation for concurrent code.

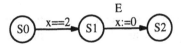

Fig 16. Reset during final transition.

Alternative transitions

[C+] Maps well to a select statement, but *only* for input actions. The task is suspended until it is called.

[S–] An if statement would work, but the case statement is more general. The function Value returns E or F. No *others* alternative must be chosen. (If neither E nor F is returned the task should be suspended, which is not possible.)

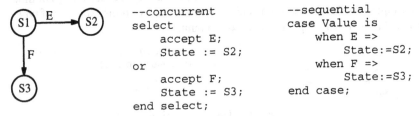

```
--concurrent              --sequential
select                    case Value is
    accept E;                 when E =>
    State := S2;                  State:=S2;
or                            when F =>
    accept F;                     State:=S3;
    State := S3;          end case;
end select;
```

Fig 17. Alternatives without time constraints.

Finally, four examples of timing constraint, <= and >=, with and without action

The examples in fig 18 and 19 for a lower bound on time, works well for concurrent and sequential code. The action in fig 19 could be a procedure or a entry call/accept.

```
      x>=2
  S1        S2            delay X+Amount(2)-Clock;
                          State := S2;
```

Fig 18. Lower time constraint with no action.

```
      x>=2
       E                 delay X+Amount(2)-Clock;
  S1        S2            E;
                          State := S2;
```

Fig 19. Lower time constraint with an action

The examples in fig 20 and 21 is for an upper bound on time. Missing this deadline would require the automaton remains in state S1 forever, but if there are other arcs from S1 with higher values on the time constraint, these are tried (in the same manner).

```
if X+Amount(2)-Clock <= 0 then
        State := S2;
else
        -- if other arcs, try them.
end if;
```

Fig 20. Upper time constraint without action (sequential or concurrent)

```
select
        accept E; -- or entry call
        State := S2;
    or
        delay X+Amount(2)-Clock;
        -- if other arcs, try them.
end if;
```

Fig 21. Upper time constraint with action (concurrent code is shown).

4.4 Eventual Context Switch

Assuming no priorities (or some default priority), we must assume that all tasks might be suspended (unless all tasks has its own CPU). For the communication this is not a problem as long as all tasks that want to communicate eventually do so, at least before the next timeout is due. For $x \in [0,1]$ all tasks must eventually be allowed to execute, and at the end of the interval ($x=1$) all tasks must be idle. The same repeats in $x \in [1,2]$ etc.

5 Case Study

The case study is communication using Manchester coding, which is part of a real audio control protocol by Philips. The protocol is formally described with four automata and has been verified [14][15]. The automata given here has been slightly changed in order to make them more realistic for implementation in Ada.

5.1 Audio Control Protocol

Manchester coding is used in the audio control protocol, to transmit bit streams of arbitrary length on a low-cost medium. Time is divided in equal sized slots and the voltage is low or high on the communication medium. The bits are encoded with rising or falling voltages in the middle of a time slot; 1 is encoded with rising voltage (Up signal), and 0 is encoded with falling voltage (Down signal). Repeated 1's or 0's requires that the signal changes at the time slot border.

Some complications of the protocol are:

1. The receiver must synchronize to the sender using the first bit in the message. Low voltage is required when no message is transmitted, and all messages must start with a 1.

2. The message length is not known to the receiver, so end of message must be deduced from a sufficiently long pause.

3. Due to the low cost medium, only Up signals (rising pulses) can be accurately detected, and all Down signals must be ignored. As a consequence, a trailing 0 is lost in messages ending with 10. The solution is to require that messages either are of odd length or end with 00.

The encoding of the message 10110 is shown in fig 22. The trailing 0 will be lost during transmission but since the length of 1011 is even and the last bit is 1, the receiver can infer that a 0 must be appended.

Fig 22. Timing diagram for Manchester encoding of the bit stream 10110

Correct messages are for example 111 (length is odd) and 1100 (ends with 00). Examples of erroneous messages are 10 (trailing 0 is lost), 11 (length is even so the receiver appends a 0) , and 01 (wrong start bit causes the receiver to be out of sync).

5.2 Description of the Four Automata

The four automata: Input, Sender, Receiver, and Output_Ack are described below. Only the Sender and Receiver automata are translated since they implement the protocol. The Input and Output_Ack automata are only needed for the verification.

Input

The input automaton (fig 23) non-deterministically generates well-formed messages of arbitrary length. It updates the integer variables k, c, and *leng* that respectively represents the parity, the binary encoding of the message, and the number of bits that has not yet been acknowledged. The action List_in tells the sender that a message is available.

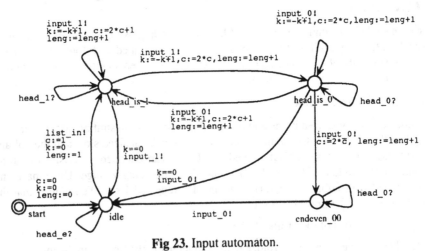

Fig 23. Input automaton.

Sender

The sender (fig 24) encodes the bits in Manchester format and communicates with the Receiver using the Up action with suitable intervals. A delay of 8 time units (two bits) between the idle and the start state ensures that messages are not transmitted too close.

Receiver

The receiver (fig 25) decodes the message from the sender by measuring the delay between subsequent Up actions. Received bits are transferred to output_ack. The inte-

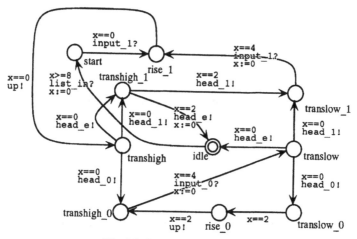

Fig 24. Sender automaton.

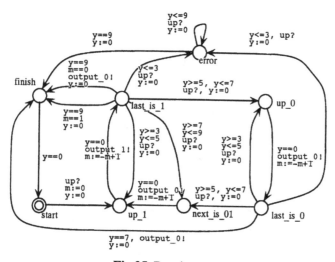

Fig 25. Receiver automaton.

ger variable *m* represents parity, i.e. whether the message length is odd or even. It toggles between 0 and 1 (using the assignment m:=1−m). If the last bit is 1 at the end of an even-length message, a 0 is appended.

The changes that hopefully make the translation more realistic compared to [15] are: The receiver is not synchronized to the sender using List_in, the receiver can *only* detect the end of a message by a long pause after Up. The output automaton does not use global knowledge of the message to force the receiver into an error state, only too close Up actions can cause such a transition. Furthermore, error recovery is implemented (as a transition to Start).

Two of the states has more complex guards. In state Last_is_1 there are five possible transitions each with a different time constraint, see fig 26. In state Last_is_0 there are four possible transitions with different time constraints, see fig 27.

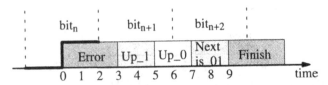

Fig 26. State Last_is_1 is entered due to an Up action. y is reset. An Up within 3 time units changes state to Error, an Up within 3 to 5 changes to Up_1 etc.

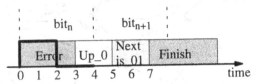

Fig 27. The state Last_is_0 is entered due to an Up action.

Output_Ack

The output acknowledge (fig 28) automaton uses the global variables *c* and *leng* together with the receiver output to determine if the bits are received correctly. Correctly received bits are removed from *c* and *leng* is updated, otherwise output_ack enters the Error state. At all times *leng* will be at most 3.

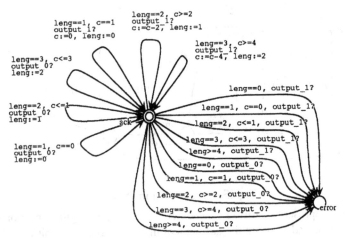

Fig 28. Output_ack automaton.

5.3 Comments on verification

The system has been verified with the UPPAAL tool. It shows not surprisingly that the protocol is correct. Correctness is based on reachability analysis and the system is correct in the sense that no violating states are reachable.

The error states in the receiver and output_ack are violating state. The error state in the receiver however is not removed when translating to Ada (although it is "dead code") since it implements failure handling which in a real program is highly desirable.

The verification does not prove the correctness of the error recovery, since the error state is never reached.

5.4 Translating the Sender and Receiver to Ada

Up and List_In are entries, all others, Input_n, Head_n, and Output_n are procedures.

First identify the waiting and non-waiting states. The waiting states has guards that for all outgoing arcs forces the automaton to remain in the state for some time, potentially causing a timeout (e.g. entry and no guard, y=2, y<=4 etc.). Non-waiting states has guards that will force the automaton to change state immediately (e.g. unguarded transitions that are not translated to an entry, y=0, etc.). The receivers waiting states are: Start, Last_is_1, Last_is_0, and Error. All others states in the receiver are non-waiting.

Reset of clocks (assignment x:=0) are translated to an addition of an exact amount to a time variable X, so X later can be used in statements such as X–Calender.Clock.

Choices in the non-waiting states are translated to if statements; at least one of the choices must be available. Choices in the waiting states are translated to one select-accept-or-delay for each transition. Luckily no guards are overlapping, this makes it easier. The clock is not reset until an entry is called or the last timeout passes.

The final program is too long to be included here, but an incomplete program is shown below, first some utility functions:

```
-- scale and convert to Duration
function Tick (Amount : Natural) return Duration is
begin
   return Duration (Amount) / 10;
end Tick;

-- substitute for delay_until, e.g. delay Ticks(X,8);
function Ticks (Clk : Calendar.Time;
               Amount : Natural) return Duration is
   Next : Calendar.Time := Clk + Tick (Amount);
begin
   return Next - Calendar.Clock;
end Ticks;

-- exact reset after a delay_until
procedure Reset (Clk : in out Calendar.Time;
                 Amount : Natural) is
begin
   Clk := Clk + Tick (Amount);
end Reset;
```

The Sender:

```
task body Sender is
   type Sender_States is (Idle, Start,
        Rise_1, Transhigh, Transhigh_1, Transhigh_0,
        Rise_0, Translow, Translow_1, Translow_0);
   State : Sender_States := Idle;
   X : Calendar.Time := Calendar.Clock;

   -- replaces Head_0, Head_1 and Head_E
   function Head (Ch : Character) return Boolean is
   begin
      return Message (Current) = Ch;
   end Head;

begin -- Sender
   loop
      case State is
         when Idle =>
            delay Ticks (X, 8); -- min interval between messages
```

```
accept List_In (M : String) do
    -- save in local string. Assume well formed messages.
    X := Calendar.Clock; -- syncronize to caller, Reset x.
end List_In;
State := Start;

when Rise_1 =>
    Receiver.Up;
    State := Transhigh;

when Transhigh_1 =>
    delay Ticks (X, 2);    -- delay_until x==2 holds
    if Head ('E') then -- Head_E
        Reset (X, 2);      -- exact reset to a known value
        State := Idle;
    else --Head_1
        State := Translow_1;
    end if;
    ...
end case;
end loop;
end Sender;
```

The state Last_Is_0 in the receiver

```
case State is
    when Last_Is_0 =>
        Again := True;

        select              -- Y <= 3  => error
            accept Up do
                Y := Clock;
            end Up;
            State := Error;
            Again := False;
        or
            delay Ticks (Y, 3);
        end select;

        if Again then
            select              -- 3 <= Y <= 5
                accept Up do
                    Y := Clock;
                end Up;
                State := Up_0;
                Again := False;
            or
                delay Ticks (Y, 5);
            end select;
        end if;

        -- similarly for 5 <= Y <= 7 (omitted)

        if Again then -- we timed out on all above
            Reset (Y, 7); -- add the exact value of last Ticks
            Output_0;     -- a procedure
            State := Finish;
        end if;
        ...
end case;
```

6 Conclusion

The main contribution of this paper is the attempt to bring theory and practice closer to each other. Formal models are commonly used to verify properties of systems but usually the level of abstraction is far away from what the programmer implements. Similarly, programming languages used for implementing real systems are usually on a level of abstraction that is too detailed and difficult to analyze.

The choice of timed automata as a formal model is based on the fact that there are quite efficient methods for verifying such systems, and equally important, the model is fairly easy to understand (at least informally). The choice of Ada as implementation language is based on the fact that it is standardized, that tasking is defined in the language, and that it emphasizes important software engineering principles, readability, maintainability, suitability for building large systems etc. By restricting the language to a subset, rather than enlarging it, standard off-the-shelf compilers can be used.

Among the Ada tasking constructs that are excluded are: Exceptions, in particular Tasking_Error and exceptions during rendezvous that must be propagated to the called and the calling task, task creation and task termination, and dynamic tasks. Task types could be allowed for static tasks. Task access types however are excluded since they are inherently dynamic.

Acknowledgements

This work is sponsored by NUTEK, project number P1221–2. I also would like to thank Paul Pettersson, Göran Wall, Wang Yi and Lars Asplund for valuable suggestions, as well as CelciusTech Systems.

References

[1]   M. Hennessy and T. Regan, "A process algebra for timed systems", Technical Report 5/91, Dept. of Computer Science, University of Sussex, UK, 1991.

[2]   X. Nicollin, J. L. Richier, J. Sifakis, and J. Voiron, "ATP: an algebra for timed processes", In Proceedings IFIP Working Group Conference on Programming Concepts and Methods, pages 402–429, 1990.

[3]   Wang Yi, "CCS + time = an interleaving model for real time systems", In Proceedings of ICALP'91, LNCS 510, Springer Verlag, 1991.

[4]   R. Alur and D. Dill, "Automata for Modeling Real–Time Systems", Proceedings of the 17th International Colloquium on Automata, Languages and Programming, volume 443, Springer Verlag, 1990.

[5]   B. Berthomieu and Michael Diaz, "Modeling and verification of time dependent systems using time petri nets", IEEE Transactions on Software Engineering, 17(3):259–273, March 1991.

[6]   W. Yi, P. Pettersson, M. Daniels, "Automatic Verification of Real–Time Communication Systems by Constraint–Solving", Proceedings of the 7th International Conference on Formal Description Techniques, Berne, Switzerland, October, 1994.

[7]   K.G. Larsen, P. Pettersson, and W. Yi, "Diagnostic Model-Checking for Real-Time Systems", Accepted for DIMACS'95.

[8]   K.G. Larsen, P. Pettersson, and W. Yi, "Compositional and Symbolic Model-Checking of Real-Time Systems", Accepted for IEEE RTSS'95.

[9] L. Björnfot, K. Lundqvist, G. Wall, and L. Asplund, "Distribution of Tasks Within a Centrally Scheduled Local Area Network", Proceedings from the First Symposium 'Ada in Europe', Copenhagen Denmark, September 1994.

[10] J.C. Corbett, "Modeling and Analysis of Real-Time Ada Tasking Programs", In proceedings RTSS'94

[11] A. Hutcheon, "Safe Nucleus Formal Specification", Project Reference CI/GNSR/27: The Design and Development of Safety Kernels, Aug 1994.

[12] J.E. Hopcroft and J.D. Ullman, "Introduction to Automata Theory, Languages and Computation", ISBN 0–201–02988–X, 1979, Addison-Wesley

[13] G. Wall, L. Asplund, L. Björnfot and K. Lundqvist, "Performance Expectations on Ada Programs",LNCS 688, pp. 227 – 239, 1993, Springer-Verlag.

[14] D. Bosscher, I. Polak, and F. Vaandrager, "Verification of an Audio-Control Protocol", In Proceedings of FTRTFT'94, LNCS 863, pp 170–192, Springer Verlag, 1994.

[15] P-H. Ho and H. Wong-Toi, "Automated Analysis of an Audio Control Protocol", In Proceedings of CAV'95, volume 939, Springer Verlag, 1995.

Testing Ada 95
Object-Oriented Programs

Stéphane Barbey

Swiss Federal Institute of Technology
Software Engineering Laboratory
1015 Lausanne Ecublens
Switzerland

email: stephane.barbey @ di.epfl.ch
phone: +41 (21) 693.52.43 - fax: +41 (21) 693.50.79

29 September 1995

Abstract. We show some of the specific problems for testing software introduced by the object-oriented features of Ada 95, and focus on specification-based testing, since this strategy is the key strategy for testing object-oriented software. We present a theory for testing software by refinement of an exhaustive test set into a finite test set using three reduction hypothesis. We also show how the Oracle problem can be partially solved using some particular features of Ada 95.

Keywords. Ada 95, Object-Oriented Programming, Testing, Test Sets Selection, Reduction Hypothesis, Oracle

1 Introduction

In this paper, we show some of the specific problems for testing software introduced by the object-oriented features of Ada 95. We consider testing programs developed with an object-oriented method, such as Fusion, OMT, or Booch, and resulting in an object-oriented architecture, i.e. a set of classes and objects which communicate by sending messages to each other. We have shown in [2] how Ada can be used to map such designs.

We focus on specification-based testing, since this strategy is the key strategy for testing object-oriented software. The architecture of object-oriented software leads often to multiple implementations of one specification: we can benefit from the test sets selected for one specification to test the various implementations, thus satisfying to the economics of testing.

In a previous paper [4], we have shown a theory to create finite test sets from a usually infinite exhaustive test set, and eventually (semi)-automatically generated assuming the availability of algebraic specifications. This strategy for selecting test sets has been applied to Ada 83 ADTs. However, the testing methods for object-based applications cannot be applied as is to object-oriented programs, because of the problems introduced by the presence of a state, inheritance and polymorphism[3]. Therefore, we need to adapt this strategy to take into account the object-oriented features of Ada 95, specifically type extension and class-wide programming.

We also take a look at operational methods (the construction of an oracle) and see how a testing harness can be build for Ada 95, by taking advantage of the child units and the generics.

2 Problems Introduced by Type Extension and Class-Wide Programming

In the case of object-oriented software, the smallest unit of testing is the class. In Ada 95, a class is considered as a modularization unit together with a type and its primitive operations. To be perfectly object-oriented, this type has of course to be refinable, i.e. tagged. An object is an instance of a class — in Ada a variable or a constant of the (tagged) type.

The primitive operations of a class could possibly be tested individually. However doing so would shift the focus of testing away from the essence of the class — the interaction between operations. Moreover, in the specification of the class to be tested, operations are rarely independent from each other and the properties of one operation are usually interleaved with the properties of other operations. Each object has a state and the behavior of the operations of the class is expressed in terms of transitions between states. Thus, every test case must be expressed in terms of a combination of operations invocations (possibly a single invocation) that lead to a certain state, and the test of an operation from this state.

Two features added to support object-oriented programming in Ada 95 open new issues in testing Ada software:

- *type extension*

  Inheritance introduces difficulties for incremental testing, assuming that we want to take advantage of the tests set selected for the parent when testing a descendant. It is not obvious to build the minimal set of primitive operations of a derived type to test (i.e. those that have a different behavior in descendant classes). It is not possible to only test the operations which are added or overridden. The obvious intuition that only new methods need testing has been proven false in [12]. Inherited operations can depend on overridden operations, and the behavior of the former can change. Moreover, the added and overridden operations can put the object in a state which could not be attained before. Therefore, the behavior of the inherited operations must also be tested in these new states.

- *class-wide objects*

  Dynamic binding hinders testing, because it prevents a static analysis of programs: dispatching calls are undecidable before run-time. Moreover, all the elements in a class hierarchy may not be known when designing a client, since it is possible to add descendants at any time, without even having to recompile the clients of the ancestor types. Moreover, type conversions inside a class hierarchy may cause errors that cannot be detected at compile-time. We have studied different uses of polymorphism in Ada 95 in [1]. Note that this issue is less important in Ada than in other object-oriented programming languages, because the level of granularity of dynamic binding is not the operation (for example, in C++, virtual or not), but the call (dispatching or not), which contributes to limit the cases of dynamic binding.

3 The Theory of Specification-Based Testing

Specification-based testing is a technique to find errors in a program by comparing the results of the execution of tests against its specification. Thus, the specification of the program is the only source for test cases, and those test cases are completely independent from the code of the program.

We postulate the availability of a complete and valid specification (either formal, or not) as a means to determine the expected behavior of the tested entity. From that specification, we determine test cases to verify the possible implementations of this specification, and an oracle to determine the test satisfaction, i.e. whether a test has discovered an error or not.

The desired properties for a test set are:

- valid: the test sets should accept only correct programs;
- unbiased: no test should detect an error in a correct program;
- finite: the test set should contain a finite number of tests;
- decidable: for every test, the decision of whether the test is satisfied or not should be decidable;
- complete: every property of the specification should be exhaustively exercised in the test set.

To select such a test set for Ada 95 object-oriented programs, we will apply an adaptation to object-oriented systems of the theory of testing developed by Bernot, Gaudel and Marre [6] for testing data types by using formal specifications. This theory is decomposed in two parts:

- *a theory of test selection*

    The theory of test selection consists in selecting from a possibly infinite set of formulae, corresponding to all the specified properties of a program, a finite set of ground formulae which is sufficient to prove the property preservations of a program with respect to its specification. Under the hypothesis that a complete specification of a class is available, convenient strategies can be applied to identify the ideal exhaustive test set.

    The reduction of the exhaustive test set to the final test set, i.e. the ground formulae, is performed by applying hypotheses to the program. Those hypotheses, called reduction hypotheses, define selection strategies and reflect common test practices.

The goal of the strategies is to select formulae showing counter-examples to the validity of the program, i.e. to exhibit the presence of errors.

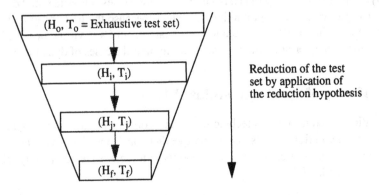

Fig. 1. Iterative refinement of the test context

Thus, as shown in figure 1, we can define test selection as the iterative refinement of a context defined as a couple (H, T) where H is the set of hypotheses, and T is the test set. The process starts from a context (H_0, T_0) which corresponds to the exhaustive test set and no reduction hypothesis. The introduction of a new hypothesis h provides a new testing context (H_j, T_j), where $H_j = H_i \cup h$, and T_j is a subset of T_i $(T_j \subseteq T_i)$. This refinement of the context (H_i, T_i) into (H_j, T_j) induces a pre-order between contexts $((H_i, T_i) \leq (H_j, T_j))$. The context refinement is performed iteratively until we reach a test set (H_f, T_f) that is finite, decidable, and preserves the properties of the exhaustive test set.

- *a theory of test satisfaction*

Once a finite set of formulae is selected, it is necessary to have a decision procedure to verify that an implementation satisfies a specification, i.e. to verify the success or the failure of every test case. This process is called an oracle [13]. A test set is decidable if, for each test, an oracle can be built to decide whether the test is satisfied or not. In our case, the oracle is based on an *equivalence relationship* that compares the outputs of the execution of a test with the expected results. The oracle decision can be an undecidable problem depending on the complexity of the proof of the equality between expressions in programming languages. For example, such oracle is very difficult to build for concurrent systems [7]. In object-oriented systems, this equivalence relationship can be difficult to build because of data hiding. The equality operation provided by the language is not a satisfying equality relationship, because it does not work well with references: instead of comparing objects, it will compare their access values.

4 The Hypothesis for Test Set Reduction

Three entities come into play when testing a class: its possible states, its defined operations, and the possible values that the parameters of its operations can take, or the possible states that the parameters can take, if these parameters are objects themselves. The exhaustive test set of a class consist of the invocation of all possible operations, starting from all possible initial states, and with all possible parameter values (see figure 2).According to the kind of specification, the tests set can be the tests of all axioms of the specification, instead of all possible calls.

Result := Object.Operation (Arguments) $\Rightarrow$

Final_State (Object) $\equiv$ Expected_Final_State (Object) $\land$
Result $\equiv$ Expected_Result

Fig. 2. Structure of a Test

The oracle must then determine it the final state is equivalent to the expected final state, and if the possible results of this operation (values or objects) are equivalent to the expected result. In the case of values (i.e. simple types like Integer, Float, String, enumeration types,...) the predefined equality can be used. For objects however, another equivalence relationship must be provided.

In Ada 95 (see figure 3), such a test for a procedure would consist in the invocation of a primitive operation in which the controlling operand (the object for which the operation is invoked) takes all the possible states, and the other operands all possible values for the other effective parameters. It can easily be generalized to operations in which several operands can be the controlling operand (for example the operation "="), because if an operation has more than one controlling operand, their value must all be of the same specific type (i.e. have the same tag). The results of the operation are obtained from the out parameters.

procedure Operation (Object: **in out** ...; Arguments: ...; Results: [**in**] **out** ...) $\Rightarrow$

$$\uparrow \qquad\qquad \uparrow \qquad\qquad \uparrow$$
Controlling operand Other operands   Results

Is_Equivalent (Final_State (Object), Expected_Final_State (Object)) **and**
Is_Equivalent (Result, Expected_Result)

Fig. 3. Structure of a test (in Ada 95)

The test of a function is a special case of the above test, in which the final and the initial state are the same (as long as no access types are involved in the arguments or in the components of the object), and the result of the function is returned instead of being passed as an out parameter.

Of course, since not all initial states can be created in one single operation invocation, getting into an initial state may imply a sequence of invocations of several operations. We present three hypothesis to reduce the exhaustive test set, by reducing the number of cases that must be tested for each of those entities, while preserving the integrity of the test set.

4.1 The Regularity Hypothesis

The first hypothesis we apply to the selection of test sets is the regularity hypothesis: if a program behaves correctly for a property instantiated to a set of terms lower in complexity than a defined bound, then it should behave correctly for all possible instantiations. This hypothesis helps limiting the size of the test set by making the assumption that one term of a certain complexity may represent all terms of the same complexity or lower complexity.

This hypothesis helps select and reduce test sets by lowering the number of states of the tested object that must be tested. Therefore, it is used to limit the number of objects of the class under test.

The possible states of an object can be grouped in equivalence classes, each member of which should be behaviorally equivalent. Test sets can be drastically reduced by finding the minimum set of those equivalence classes, since each operation is tested with all possible starting states, i.e. all possible transitions from one state to another (or to the same state) are tested.

For example, test sets for an abstract stack of generic items can be subsumed with two states: Empty and Non-Empty.

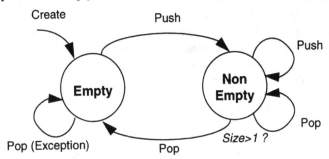

Fig. 4. The reduced set of states and transitions of an abstract stack

Assuming there are two operations defined on this abstract stack, Push and Pop, a test set can be generated by testing all the transactions of the state-based graph (i.e. <-, Create, Empty>, <Empty, Pop, Empty>, <Empty, Push, Non-Empty>, <Non-Empty, Push, Non-Empty>,...). This means that we will not test all possible non-empty stacks (a stack of 12 elements, 13 elements, 14 elements,...), but consider all those stacks to be regular.

4.2 The Uniformity Hypothesis

The uniformity hypothesis helps select and reduce test sets in the presence of class-wide objects and dispatching. The uniformity hypothesis can be stated as follows: if a program behaves correctly for a property A instantiated with a particular term T of a type S, then every instantiation of the property A with terms of the type S behaves correctly. As a consequence, if the property A is correct for one specific instantiation, it is correct for all possible instantiations.

This hypothesis is underlying in random testing, and is used to verify a property with variables of the primitive types (i.e. a type used by the tested type). However, random testing is not applicable in the case of a parameter T belonging to a class-wide type S or one of its descendants, i.e. to a derivation class. In this case, it is even difficult to generate the ideal test set, because of the need to take into account the possibility of newly defined descendants.

For example (see figure 5), in the case of the Stack, the type of the item has no interference with the behavior of the class, even if it is of a class-wide type. In the case of the Alarm System described in the Ada 95 Rationale [5], the operation Manage of a class Manager which would work for all alerts in the Alert hierarchy, would have to be tested for each kind of alert present in the hierarchy (here LowLevel, MediumLevel, EmergencyLevel, HighLevel), and not just for the root type (Alert).

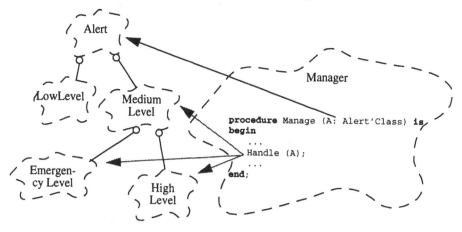

Fig. 5. A Manager for the whole Alert hierarchy

There are several ways to solve this problem. The most used one is to impose a sub-type relationship between all types in the class hierarchy. A type S is a *subtype*[1] of T if S provides at least the functionality (*conformance of behavior*) of T. Objects of type S can be used in any context in which an object of type T is appropriate. The subtype relationship ([9], [11]) ensures that the base type and the derived type have the appropriate semantics, i.e. that a program that works correctly with objects of the base type has exactly the same effect when substituting objects of the derived type to objects of the base type. Therefore, assuming that the subtype relationship has been carefully tested, it is not necessary to test the operation Manage with the states of all classes of the hierarchy, but just with the states of the root class.

If the requirements of the subtype relationship cannot be achieved, it is possible to provide test sets that test the substitutability for some properties of the hierarchy only,

---

1. this is not exactly the Ada subtype.

properties that are necessary to ensure substitutability in the context of the tested class (in the example Manager). For best results, it may be useful to take advantage of some limited knowledge of the code, such as information on the presence of dynamic binding.

4.3 The Incrementability Hypothesis

The incrementability hypothesis helps select and reduce test sets in the presence of inheritance by reducing the number of transitions that must be traversed when testing a derived type.

The incrementability hypothesis states that there is a complex, but strong relation between the testing contexts of a tagged type and its derived types, and that we can take advantage of test sets defined for a base type to reduce the new test sets to be selected to test the derived type.

Capitalizing on inheritance can be very useful in minimizing the effort of testing a derived type given the test set developed for the base type. New states and new transitions require testing, whereas pre-existing do not.

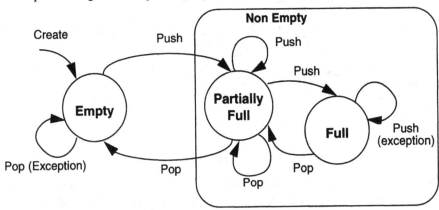

Fig. 6. The reduced set of states and transitions for an unbounded stack

For example, a bounded stack is a refinement of the abstract stack, in which the state Non-Empty is refined into two sub-states, Partially-Full and Full. Thus, some of the test sets defined for Abstract Stack just need to be re-run, because there was no difference in semantics from the parent to the derived type (e.g. <Empty, Pop, Empty>), while in other cases, new test sets need to be selected (e.g. <Full, Push, Full>).

New transitions can also be transitions which were already presenting the specification, but for which new implementations are given in a derived type.

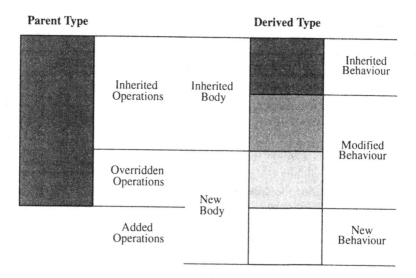

Fig. 7. Incremental testing

In Ada 95 several cases can occur when testing a derived type (see figure 7):

- Operations for which a new body is provided must of course be retested. New test cases must be selected for the added operations. For overridden operations, the test cases selected for the base type must be re-run to prove the subtype relationship, and new test cases may possibly be added to take into account the new properties of the operations. If maintaining the subtype relationship is not expected, then the existing test sets must not be re-run, but a new test set must be provided. The absence of subtyping has of course consequences on the uniformity hypothesis.

- Operations that keep their body do not automatically escape to re-testing, because their behavior may be modified by changes in the behavior of other operations. This case is obviously shown in redispatching. Redispatching occurs when the body of a primitive operation of a type contains a dispatching call to another primitive operation with the same controlling operand.

```
type Vehicle is tagged
    record
        Passengers: Natural;
        ...;
    end record;
procedure Move (V: in out
Vehicle;
                L: in Location);      procedure Move (V: in out Vehicle;
function Speed_Of (V: Vehicle)                      L: in Location) is
    return float;                      begin
                                           ... Speed_of (Vehicle'Class (V))...;
type Car is new Vehicle with ...;      -- dispatching
function Speed_Of (C: Car)             end Move;
    return float;
    -- overridden
-- procedure Move (V: in out Car;
--              L: in Location);
```

Fig. 8. Example of redispatching

For example, on figure 8, the operation Move defined for Vehicle is inherited without modification by Car. However, in its body, it makes a redispatching call to Speed_of. Its behavior for objects of the class Car is not the same as its behavior for objects of the class Vehicle. Therefore, this operation needs re-testing.

Finally, operations which do not appear in the above cases do not need re-testing: the test performed on the parent type are sufficient to show that those operations meet their specification. In most cases, this set of operations contain most of the inherited operations: for example, adding an iterator to a container class will not imply re-testing the inherited operation.

This algorithm is slightly different if the parent type is an abstract type: abstract types cannot be tested, because objects of those types cannot be declared. However, abstract types can have a specification, and therefore test sets can be generated for them. Those test sets are used for incremental testing in the same way as described above, except that all operations of an abstract types must be tested for the subtype, and not only those with a new behavior, because the operations which kept their behavior could not be tested for the parent type, and their correctness was therefore not exercised.

5 Oracle Generation

There are many ways to solve the Oracle problem. The more general approach is to define the Oracle in terms of external behavioral equivalence such as bissimulation or traces. This approach is for example used in the ASTOOT approach [8].

However, with Ada 95, we can also take advantage of the child unit constructs to get a look inside objects, in a way similar to the strategy explained in [10], except that this approach is non intrusive. This satisfies the requirement expressed sometimes that a tested unit should not be recompiled after having been tested. No recompilation is required for the parent unit when adding a test unit. For complex objects made of an aggregation of sub-objects (components), it is possible to defined several child units with observation operations that give visibility on each sub-object. Of course, extreme care must be take that those observation operations do not affect the behavior to the sub-object.

6 A Test Harness for Ada Programs

The test sets are grouped in a unit that is a child of the unit to be tested, and takes as generic parameter any type that belongs to the type of the tested class. The test set is a set of primitive operations of a new declared tagged type. A non-primitive operation Main performs the tests set.

It is necessary to make the test set package a child unit of the class that it tests so that the possible private operations of the class are visible in the test package and can thus be tested. The equivalence relationship is build inside the test type as a primitive operation of the type, and takes two wide-class parameters to hold the result and the expected result.

```
generic
    type Tested_Unit is abstract new Stacks.Stack_Type with private;
package Stacks.Test_Stacks is
    type Stack_Test_Set is tagged private;
    function Is_Equivalent (L,R:Tested_Unit'Class) return Boolean;
    procedure Test_WWWW (Test_Set: in Stack_Test_Set;
        Stack: in out Tested_Unit'Class; ...; Test_Result: out Boolean);❹
    procedure Test_XXXX (Test_Set: in Stack_Test_Set;
        Stack: in out Tested_Unit'Class; ...; Test_Result: out Boolean);
    ...
    procedure Main (Test_Set: in out Stack_Test_Set'Class);
private
    ...
end Stacks.Test_Stacks;

with Stacks.Test_Stacks;
generic
    type Tested_Unit is new Stacks.Bounded_Stacks.Bounded_Stack_Type with private;
package Stacks.Bounded_Stacks.Test_Bounded_Stacks is

    package Test_Parent_Unit is new Stacks.Test_Stacks (Tested_Unit); ❶

    type Bounded_Stack_Test_Set is
        new Test_Parent_Unit.Stack_Test_Set with private;❷
    function Is_Equivalent (L,R:Tested_Unit'Class) return Boolean;
    procedure Test_XXXX (Test_Set: in Bounded_Stack_Test_Set;
        Stack: in out Tested_Unit'Class; ...;Test_Result: out Boolean);❸
    procedure Test_YYYY (Test_Set: in Bounded_Stack_Test_Set;
        Stack: in out Tested_Unit'Class; ...;Test_Result: out Boolean);❸
    ...
    procedure Main (Test_Set: in out Bounded_Stack_Test_Set'Class);❺
private
    ...
end Stacks.Bounded_Stacks.Test_Bounded_Stacks;
```

Fig. 9. Example of harness for testing stacks

Every test procedure should use the test equivalence in a redispatching way, so that the test developed for a parent type is also valid for the derived types, and makes use of the right equivalence relationship.

```
procedure Test_WWWW (Test_Set: in Stack_Test_Set;
    Stack: in out Tested_Unit'Class; ...; Test_Result: out Boolean) is
begin
    ...
    Test_Result := Is_Equivalent (Stack_Test_Set'Class(Test_Set), ...) and ...;
end Test_XXXX;
```

Fig. 10. Example of test with dispatching equivalence

For example, on figure 10, the Test_WWWW will be valid to test both stack types and bounded stack types, because the equivalence relationship used will be the one defined in the package Stacks.Test_Stacks for stacks types and the one defined in the package Stacks.Bounded_Stacks.Test_Bounded_Stacks for bounded stacks.

The test set for a derived type consists of a child of this class, that takes as generic parameter the type to be tested, like for the ultimate ancestor. However, the test set of the derived type is created by a refinement of the test set of the parent type:

- the test set of the parent type for the derived type is created by instantiating the test set of the parent type with the derived type ❶;

- the test set of the derived type is created by inheriting from the Test_Set type of the parent type ❷;

- the test set of the derived type is then refined by overriding inherited tests (Test_XXXX) or adding new tests (Test_YYYY) ❸; some existing tests (Test_WWWW) ❶ can of course be kept from the parent's test set.

- a new procedure Main has to be defined for the derived test set (that can possibly in turn call the procedure Main defined for the parent type — Test_Parent.Main(...)) ❺. This procedure selects from the inherited test set and the additional tests which must be performed and when.

7 Summary and Conclusion

In this paper, we have shown the bases of a theory for testing object-oriented software. It is based on the refinements of a testing context from an exhaustive test set into a reduced test set, that preserves all the properties of the exhaustive test set. We have shown three hypothesis that help reducing the test set, taking into account the object-oriented features of programming languages, and in particular Ada 95. We have also shown some other features of Ada 95 can help solve the Oracle problem.

We think that this approach to testing object-oriented software has a lots of promises. It has a very strong theoretical ground, it is general, and it is sufficiently easy to be understood by the average programmer. Moreover, it is aimed at reducing the cost of testing — which can be up to sixty percents of the total development cost — by providing minimal test sets.

8 Acknowledgments

The author would like Didier Buchs for its comments on earlier versions of this paper and his thoughtful suggestions. The work reported in this paper is supported by the Swiss National Science Foundation (Nationalfonds), grant number 21-36038.92.

9 References

[1]   Stéphane Barbey. Working with Ada 9X classes. In Charles B. Engle, Jr., editor, *TRI-Ada 1994 Conference*, pages 129–140, Baltimore, Maryland, USA, November 6-11 1994. Also available as Technical Report (EPFL-DI-LGL No 94/65).

[2]   Stéphane Barbey. Ada 95 as implementation for object-oriented designs. In Charles B. Engle, Jr., editor, *Proceedings of TRI-Ada '95*, Anaheim, California, November 5-10 1995. (to appear).

[3]   Stéphane Barbey, Manuel Ammann, and Alfred Strohmeier. Open issues in testing object-oriented software. In Karol Frühauf, editor, *ECSQ '94 (European Conference on Software Quality)*, pages 257– 267, Basel, Switzerland, October 17-20 1994. vdf Hochschulverlag AG an der ETH Zürich. Also available as Technical Report (EPFL-DI-LGL No 94/45).

[4]   Stéphane Barbey and Didier Buchs. Testing of Ada abstract data types using formal specifications. In Marcel Toussaint, editor, *Eurospace Ada Europe '94 Symposium Proceedings*, number 887 in LNCS (Lecture Notes in Computer Sciences), pages 76–89, Copenhagen, Danemark, September 26-30 1994. Springer Verlag. Also available as Technical Report (EPFL-DI-LGL No 94/75).

[5]   John Barnes, Ben Brosgol, Ken Dritz, Offer Pazy, and Brian Wichmann. *Ada 95 Rationale*. Intermetrics, Inc., Cambridge, MA, USA, February 1995.

[6]   Gilles Bernot, Marie-Claude Gaudel, and Bruno Marre. Software testing based on formal specifications: a theory and a tool. *IEE Software Engineering Journal*, 6(6):387–405, November 1991.

[7]   Didier Buchs. Test selection method to validate concurrent programs against their specifications. In *SQM '95 (Software Quality Management)*, pages 403–414, Seville, Spain, April 1995. (Also Available as Technical Report EPFL-DI-LGL No 95/101).

[8]   Roong-Ko Doong and Phyllis G. Frankl. The ASTOOT approach to testing object-oriented programs. *ACM Transactions on Software Engineering and Methodology*, 3(2):101–130, April 1994.

[9]   Gary T. Leavens and William E. Weihl. Reasoning about object-oriented programs that use subtypes (extended abstract). In Norman Meyrowitz, editor, *ECOOP/OOPSLA '90 Conference Proceedings, Ottawa, Canada*, volume 25 of *SIGPLAN Notices*, pages 212–223. ACM SIGPLAN, ACM Press, October 1990.

[10]   J. Liddiard. Achieving testability when using Ada packaging and data hiding methods. *Ada User*, 14(1):27–32, March 1993.

[11]   Barbara Liskov and Jeannette M. Wing. Specifications and their use in defining subtypes. In Andreas Paepcke, editor, *OOPSLA '93 Conference Proceedings, Washington, DC*, volume 28, pages 16–28, 1515 Broadway New York, NY 10036, September 26 - October 1 1993. ACM SIGPlan, ACM Press.

[12]   Dewayne E. Perry and Gail E. Kaiser. Adequate testing and object-oriented programming. *Journal of Object-Oriented Programming*, 2(5):13–19, January 1990.

[13]   Elaine J. Weyuker. The oracle assumption of program testing. In *13th International Conference on System Sciences*, pages 44–49, Hawaii, USA, 1980.

Achieving Reusable and Reliable Client-Server Code using HOOD™ automated code generation for ADA95 and C++ targets

Maurice HEITZ

CISI 13, rue Villet, 31400 TOULOUSE, FRANCE
Phone: (33) 61.17.66.66, Fax (33).61.17.66.96.
Email heitz@cisi.cnes.fr

Abstract. This paper presents an approach for the development of reusable, reliable distributed systems using the HOOD4 code generation principles for implementing Object Oriented Designs over different target systems (ADA95, C++), possibly distributed.

HOOD4 is an extension of HOOD supporting classes and inheritance for multiple target systems. HOOD4 provides an Object Oriented framework by means of the HOOD RUN TIME SUPPORT library together with a design approach and associated code generation rules, shiedling applications from complex semantics differences between OS platforms.

We first recall the terminology between modular and Object Oriented Programming (OOP), and give a description of HOOD extensions to support OO classes and inheritance, with emphasis on the concept of virtual node. We then present the target code structure asociated to the HOOD4 entities and associated code generation rule. We conclude with the presentation of an associated development approach for developing large client-server information systems leading to efficient reusability.

Index Terms : Object Orientation, Method integration, Object Oriented Design, Object Oriented Programming, HOOD, Verification, Control expression, Real-Time, Distributed, Reliability.

---

1   Introduction

With the availability of powerful development tools for client-server applications, distributed applications are becoming more and more complex and large whereas still trying to integrate more and more the object technology. Mastering such developments is quite a challenge as projects are shrinking their time and money budgets and still have to show up within the economic competition.

In this context, the Hierarchical Object Oriented Design (HOOD) [4] addresses the development of distributed systems through a post-partitioning approach based on the concept of Virtual Node, and using extensively automated code generation.

Often presented in the past as a heavy procedure to distribution, the approach seems now to gain increasing interests since :

*   the technology is now supporting efficient inter processor communication mechanisms, rendering the post partitioning fully viable (and possibly more efficient) for loosely coupled systems
*   more and more distributed applications are re engineered towards client-server architecture.
*   distributed object technology [7,11] is going to be used for real time applications
*   powerful code generator and configuration handling tools are now used by developers.
*   the HOOD4 method has developed an object oriented framework by means of the HOOD RUN TIME SUPPORT library together with a design approach and associated code generation rules, shielding applications from complex semantics differences between OS platforms.

In this paper we present the development approach based on the code generation principles supported by the HOOD4 method allowing post distribution over ADA95[1] or C++[9] targets in a safe, reliable and test effective way.

2   HOOD4 Definition

The primary extension of HOOD4 over HOOD3 is the definition of specific formalisms for OO classes. Full support of the concept has lead also to target independent code generation support for non distributed and distributed targets, including a *virtual target machine* defined by means of HOOD RUN TIME SUPPORT (HRTS) library.

Furthermore, as the naming "HOOD object" was sometime conflicting with the term "object" meaning "class instance", a terminology brushing up has been achieved in HOOD4 [4]. In order to share the terminology of the OOP literature [6,9,7] HOOD4 avoids the terminology clash by applying the two following rules :

- the term "class instance" is always used instead of "object"
- the word "object" is always used with the meaning of "software module" (thus referring --unless otherwise specified-- either to a target code module, either to a class , either to a generic module or either to a virtual node).

2.1 Class Definition

The HOOD3[4] object can be designed as an implementation of an Abstract Data Type (ADT)[6], but ADT is missing *inheritance and polymorphism The HOOD class is more than an ADT implementation and shall refer to a concept allowing ADT+inheritance+polymorphism support*. Thus the following decisions have been taken :

- HOOD4 classes are factored entities (by *inheritance, aggregation and polymorphism*) so they should be terminal[1] "entities" at HOOD level.
- ADT on the other hand may be supported as with HOOD3 objects and may be refined, using the HOOD decomposition relationship, into sub-ADTS which eventually will become HOOD4 classes if inheritance is used. This allows "first/initial" definition of complex ADTs and to refine them into "child/sub ADTs" with a top-down approach, in parallel with their client decomposition's. When the implementation is clear and fixed enough for factorisation, definition of classes can made taking advantages of bottom-up inheritance approach.

HOOD4 Classes are graphically represented as objects but with squared instead of rounded corners (see figure 2.1). In order to avoid messy diagrams, two graphical views are defined :

- *the client-server view* shows the use relationships between objects and classes (see figure 2.1)
- *the class structure view* shows the inheritance and composition of classes. Class attributes are represented inside the class boxes. (see figure 2.1 bis).

Class instances are HOOD data that are not represented graphically. A class provides to other HOOD clients (to define data instances, or parameters) *a HOOD type of name, the one of the class*. A class provides operations whose signature has an additional parameter *me*[2] of type *target class*. Operations of a class may be constrained.

---

[1] (a class can hardly be decomposed into smaller entity, otherwise the packaging encapsulation by the object approach may be misused and lead to a too fine granularity and lead back to visibility problems)
2pointing the object on which the operation will operate, (see the this pointer in C++)

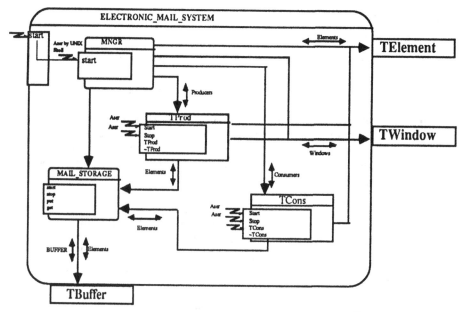

Figure 2.1 - Representation of a Client_server view[3]

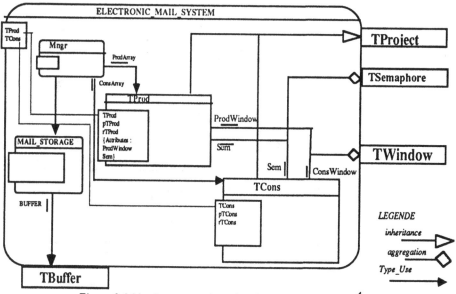

Figure 2.1 bis Representation of a Class structure view [4]

---

[3]items in the provided interface are operations
[4]items in the provided intrrface are classes or associated types.

2.2 The HOOD Virtual Node Definition

HOOD4 provides designers with the concept of Virtual Node (VN) as a mean of restructuring HOOD objects from a given HOOD Design Tree (HDT) into software units of distribution able to execute in a given physical memory partition.

A Virtual Node (VN) is thus a collection of HOOD objects defining a target software unit of execution within a same memory space (or a *heavyweight process* as defined in [2]. Virtual Nodes may be decomposed only into Virtual Nodes thus providing for hierarchical description of large and complex networks[5] of processing nodes.

In order to deal with specific communication constraints a designer may specify user-provided communication protocol between two VNs by labelling the ASER constraint of the predefined provided operation *Message_In* of the server VN. Figure 2.2 below gives an illustration of a parent VN decomposition. Note that data flows can be shown and that communication protocols are specified through the Message_In operation constraint.

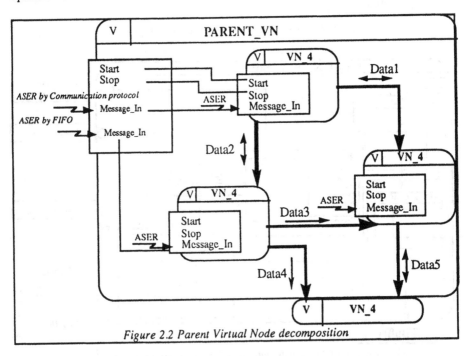

Figure 2.2 Parent Virtual Node decomposition

Section 3 below gives a detailed illustration of the target software units associated to a VN supporting reuse and multi-target code generation .

5(see section 4 below for a description of the associated development approach).

3 Code Generation Rules

3.1 Code Generation Principles

The challenge of developing flexible, testable and reusable software can be overcome by **enforcing the principle of separation of concerns all over the development**. Such an approach has several advantages over traditional ones :

- the overall complexity is broken, through logical grouping of same concerns that can be handled by specialised teams or techniques.
- Associated and specific logical properties are emphasised, thus making the test and verification activities more efficient.

HOOD4 has the key concept of operation which is **executed by a logical thread** [2] **with or without constraints**. This concept and others related to encapsulation allow software associated to operations of object or classes to be structured into three separated parts:

- **pure sequential code** is supported through the concept of OPCS[6] . It shall implement solely the functional and transformational code of an operation.
- **state integrity enforcement code** is supported through the concept of **concurrency constraints** and **state constraints**. The latter are described using an Object State Transition Diagram (OSTD) and are implemented through OSTM[7] code descriptions and associated client *precondition and post condition* code [6]referred as OPCS_HEADER and OPCS_FOOTER code. (see figure 2.3.3 below)
- **inter-process communication code** is supported through the concept of HOOD protocol constraints and is described by means **ClientObcs** and **ServerObcs code** providing a common infrastructure to all operations for communicating with [remote] threads.

The implementation principles tried mainly to enforce this logical structure for HOOD operations and have lead into the definition of several logical code parts. Moreover the target code structure was mapped in a client-server architecture as soon as the implementation required several communicating execution threads.

Associated ODS[8] fields are supported in the HOOD4 SIF (Standard Interchange

---

[6]OPCS=Operation Control Structure

[7]OSTM= Object STate Machine

[8]ODS = Object Description Skeleton

Format) allowing HOOD4 descriptions to be exchanged between different HOOD toolsets.

Code generation rules could then be derived by defining target source code fields (possibly empty) associated to the logical parts according to the type of operation constraints.

- The OPCS_ER[9] and ClientOBCS[10] parts refer to the code executed by the client thread[11].
- The ServerOBCS and OPCS_SER parts refer to code executed by a server thread
  The OPCS_HEADER and OPCS_FOOTER implement *pre* and *post conditions code* [6] that enforces state integrity of the object [8] and is executed by a server thread.
- The OPCS_BODY part refers to the functional, algorithmic, transformational code of the operation.

3.2 Target Code Architecture

Implementation of the above principles could have lead to numerous solutions according to the features of the different targets and Operating Systems. HOOD4 tried however to define common code structures whatever the target and the kind of HOOD objects. For example the non-distributed code had to be reused **unchanged** when partitioning it into a distributed one over client and server Virtual Nodes.

The design pattern associated to inter-process communication code[3] could also be reused when dealing with inter-VN communications, thus matching the remote object invocation mechanism of the CORBA Object Request Broker [7] , based on the *proxy* design pattern [10].

The definition of a HRTS layer hiding target characteristics as well as a number of recurrent services from the HOOD application helped a lot in the standardisation of logical code parts and for automating their generation. The HRTS library has been implemented in C++/UNIX[12] and Ada/UNIX, and is publicly available [5] to users (for own optimisation, porting on specific targets...).

For an object or class of name <NAME>, with protocol constraints implying a client-server architecture, three kind of target units are generated as illustrated in figure 3.2 below :

---

[9]OPCS_ER=OPCS_Execution_Request

[10]OBCS=Object Control Structure

[11]thread = basic schedulable entity=process=task

[12]the C++ version is build on-top of the ACE library and UNIX wrappers developped by D.Schmidt (Schmidt,1994)

- **a <NAME>module** *that provides the same specifications and operation signatures when non constrained. It contains OPCS_ER body code allowing clients to queue their requests and process return parameters after operations are executed within the server space.* This module isolates the client from any subsequent spreading of its provided service implementation towards additional servers. Thus client code of an object is invariant whatever the choice or refinement of the implementation of its provided services.

- **a <NAME>_RB module** *that provides an object request broker between the client and the effective <NAME>_SERVER module.* This module fully de-couples <NAME> from the server <NAME>_SERVER code. It is in this module that any optimisation with respect to network contention may take place.

- **a <NAME>_SERVER module** *that includes all the code associated to state and concurrency constraints as well as the functional code.* This allows code to be generated, which is functionally independent from any allocation schema on any execution infrastructure. The SERVER code will remain unchanged whatever the execution structure whether local, or remote or within VNs. Moreover such SERVER code can be tested and developed independently of a future or final allocation on a distributed/client server architecture.

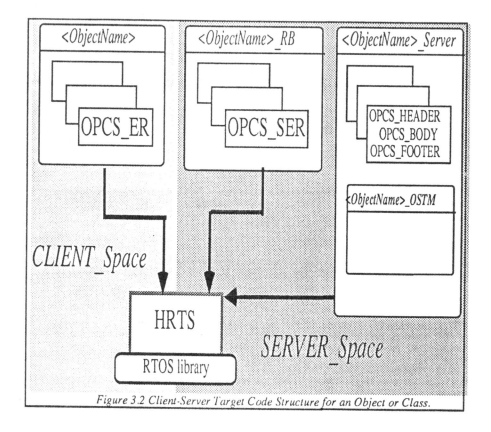

Figure 3.2 Client-Server Target Code Structure for an Object or Class.

3.3 Target Implementation and Illustrations

Let us take the well known STACK example for concise illustration of the associated
target code in Ada[13]. Some complexity is merely added by defining it as a class.
TStack[14] class has operations PUSH and POP HSER constrained, and operation
STOP state and ASER constrained, and operation START only state constrained,
semantically correct only when the behaviour expressed in OSTD of figure 3.3.1 is
enforced .

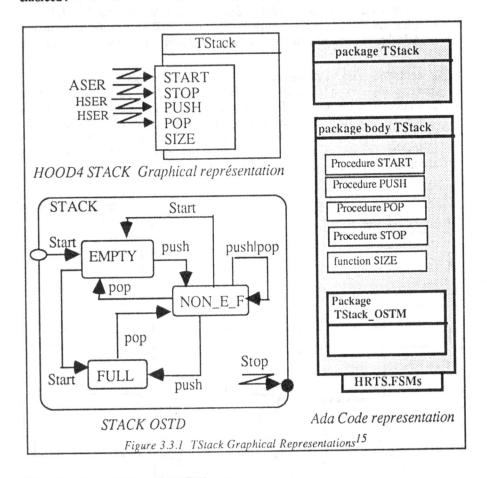

Figure 3.3.1 TStack Graphical Representations[15]

---

[13]Translation into C++ is straight since we do not use here any "tasking feature". As "thread supporting
UNIX" targets are available,translation from Ada to C+ is more direct. Full source code of this example
in C++ or Ada.may be directly obtained from the author.

[14]The following naming convention is used : a class identifier starts with T, a type identifier with "T_"

[15]Target Ada units are represented as squared boxes, with its name in the top, and required units
representented as attached small boxes.

3.3.1 State Enforcement Code

Figure 3.3.2 illustrates the target code for state constrained operations, which is standardised in an FSM[16] where transitions are only triggered by provided operation execution requests.

```
with HRTS_PE; -- for all global definitions
with TFSMs;use type HRTS_PE.T_Integer;
package Stack_OSTM is
 type T_OSTDState is (EMPTY, FULL, N_EF, STOPPED, UNDEFINED);
 type T_OSTDOperation is (START, STOP, PUSH, POP);
 NB_MAX_STATES: constant HRTS_PE.T_Integer := T_OSTDState'pos (T_OSTDState'last);
 NB_MAX_OPERATIONS: constant HRTS_PE.T_Integer:=
                                  T_OSTDOperation'pos (T_OSTDOperation'last);
 NB_MAX_TRANSITIONS:constant HRTS_PE.T_Integer:=
                                  NB_MAX_STATES*NB_MAX_OPERATIONS;
   package FSM is new TFSMs   (
                 T_Operation  =>T_OSTDOperation,
                 T_State=>      T_OSTDState,
                 NB_MAX_TRANSITIONS=>NB_MAX_TRANSITIONS );
   function Stack_FSM return FSM.TFsm;
end Stack_OSTM;

package body Stack_OSTM is
 function Stack_FSM return theFSM.TFsm is
 theFSM : FSM.TFsm;
 begin-- initial state is STOPPED
   FSM.Create(theFSM, 4, 1, STOPPED);
   FSM.Trans(theFSM, EMPTY, START, EMPTY);
     • • •
   FSM.Trans(theFSM, N_EF, PUSH, N_EF);
   FSM.Trans(theFSM, N_EF, POP, N_EF);
   FSM.Trans(theFSM, FULL, POP, N_EF);
   FSM.Trans(theFSM, FULL, STOP, STOPPED);
   FSM.Trans(theFSM, STOPPED, START, EMPTY);
   return theFSM;
 end Stack_FSM;
end Stack_OSTM;
```

Figure 3.3.2 - OSTD Implementation Illustration

3.3.2 Standard Code

Figure 3.3.3 below illustrates the code associated to a HOOD4 class module with state constraints. Note that in HOOD4 operations of a class have a special parameter with reserved name "*me*".

---

[16]FSM=Finite State Machine

```
with HRTS_PE; with Stack_OSTM;
package TStack is
 type TStack is tagged private;
 procedure Start (Me : in out TStack);
 procedure Stop (Me : in out TStack);
 procedure Push (Me : in out TStack;    MyItem  : in HRTS_PE.T_Integer);
 procedure Pop (Me : in out TStack;     AnItem  : out HRTS_PE.T_Integer);
 function Size (Me : in TStack)         return HRTS_PE.T_Integer;
private
 StackSize:constant HRTS_PE.T_Integer:=20;
 type T_StackBuffer is array (0..StackSize - 1) of HRTS_PE.T_Integer;
 type TStack is tagged record
  CurrentSize : HRTS_PE.T_Integer := 0;
  StackBuffer: T_StackBuffer;
  FSM:Stack_OSTM.FSM.TFSMs := Stack_FSM;
  end record;
end TStack;

package body TStack is
 package FSM renames Stack_OSTM.FSM;
 procedure Start (Me : in out TStack) is
 begin
-- OPCS HEADER (automatically generated)
 FSM.Fire (Me.FSM, Stack_OSTM.START);
-- OPCS BODY (extracted from ODS fields)
 Me.CurrentSize := 0;
-- OPCS FOOTER (automatically generated)
 end Start;

 procedure Push (Me : in out TStack; MyItem : in HRTS_PE.T_Integer) is
 begin
-- OPCS HEADER (automatically generated)
 FSM.Fire (Me.FSM, Stack_OSTM.PUSH);
-- OPCS BODY (extracted from ODS fields)
 Me.StackBuffer(Me.CurrentSize):= MyItem;
 Me.CurrentSize := Me.CurrentSize + 1;
 if( Me.CurrentSize = StackSize ) then
   FSM.Set (Me.FSM, Stack_OSTM.FULL); -- hanlde non deterministic states
  end if;
-- OPCS FOOTER (automatically generated)
 end Push;

function Size(me : in  TStack) return T_integer is -- non constrained operations have empty
    HEADER or FOOTER code.
begin
   return Me.CurrentSize;
end Size;-
--procedure STOP is like START
--procedure POP is like PUSH
```

Figure 3.3.3 Class TStack Standard Code Sample

3.3.3 Client_Server Code

Figure 3.3.4 illustrates the target code structure associated to a HOOD4 class when implementation requires at least one client and one server execution thread. Such target structure may be directly mapped in C++ modules and could be optimised when using Ada tasking or thread supported targets; e.g.*marshalling* [1] in OPCS_ER code and *unmarshalling* in OPCS_SER code, is not needed when threads or tasks share parameters in the same memory partition.

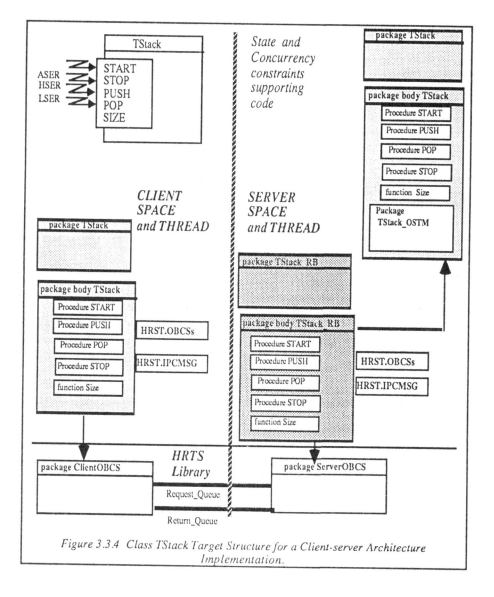

Figure 3.3.4 Class TStack Target Structure for a Client-server Architecture Implementation.

3.3.3.1   TStack Client code.

Note that TStack specification is unchanged regarding the standard code except for the private part which contains OBCS client code and IPC Message instances.

```
with Items; use Items;
package TStack is--

 spec as in figure 3.3.3

  private - but private part is different
   type TStack_D is record
    OBCS : TClientOBCS.TClientOBCS;
    Message : TMsg.TMsg;
   end record;
end TStack;
end STStack ;

package body STACK is

-- real data all in STACK_SERVER object

procedure Push (Me : in out TStack;  MyItem  : in HRTS_PE.T_Integer) is
begin
  TMsg.Initialize(Me=>Me.Message,
     Sender=>Stack_PE.STACK,Sendee=>Stack_PE.STACK_RB,Operation=>Stack_PE.PUSH,Cnstrt=
     >HRTS_PE.NO_CONSTRAINT, ParamSize  => 1 );
declare
 PtrStream:Stream_Access:= TMsg.GetParams (Me.Message);
begin
  T_Integer input (PtrStream, MyItem);
 end;
 TClientObcs.Insrem (Me.OBCS, Me.Message); -- insert and wait on return IPC message
-- no wait in case of ASER constraint
 Status := TMsg.GetX (Me.Message);
 case Status is
 when HRTS_PE.X_OK =>       null;
 when Others => raise;
   if not (Me.Message.CSTRNT=ASER) then
      me.OBCS.FREE(MSG); -- deallocate ;
   <Exception_handler>
-end Push;
-similar code for POP,STOP,START and Size
```

Figure 3.3.3.1 Class TStack Client Code Sample

3.3.3.2. TStack_RB Code

```
with Items; use Items;
with TStack_SERVER; -- exactly the same code as in figure 2.3.3
package TStack_RB is
        procedure Start ;
        procedure Stop ;
        procedure Push :
        procedure Pop :
        function Size;
end TStack_RB;
with HRTS_PE; use type HRTS_PE.T_Integer;with Stack_PE;with Stack_OSTM;
with TMsg;with TQPool;with TServerObcs;
with TStack_Server;
package body TStack_RB is
 TheStack : TStack_Server.TStack; --local
 Message  : TMsg.TMsg;
 OBCS : TServerOBCS.TServerOBCS;
 PtrStream : Stream_Access ;
procedure Stop is -- LSER constrained
 begin-- OPCS_SER code
    TStack_Server.Stop;
end Start ;
procedure Push is-- HSER constrained
 Item : HRTS_PE.T_Integer;
 begin-- OPCS_SER code
  HRTS_PE.T_Integer'read(PtrStream, Item);
   TStack_Server.Push (TheStack, Item);
end Push;
function Size return T_integer is
 aSize:HRTS_PE.T_Integer;
begin
 aSize:= TStack_Server.Size(TheStack);
 HRTS_PE.T_Integer'write(PtrStream, aSize);
 return aSize;
end Size;
Procedure RB_Dispatcher is
 PrevSender:T_HOODObject := Message.Sender begin
 TMsg.SetSender (Message, Message.Sendee)
 TMsg.SetSendee (Message, PrevSender);
 PtrStream := TMsg.GetParams (Message);
 case TMsg.GetOperation (Message) is
  when Stack_PE.START =>Start ;
   when Stack_PE.PUSH => Push; • • • • •
  when others=>EXCEPTIONS.LOG("TStack_RB"&
    T_X_VALUE'image(.X_UNKNOWN_OPERATION));
    TMsg.SetX(Message, X_UNKNOWN_OPERATION);
 end case;
    <Exception_handler>
    TMsg.SetX(Message,HRTS_PE.X_BADREQUEST);
    TServerObcs.Insert (OBCS, Message);
end  RB_Dispatcher ;
```

```
begin  -- at package elaboration
loop -- polling schema
    TServerObcs.Remove (OBCS, Message);
    case TMsg.GetSender (Message) is
    when Stack_PE.STACK=> RB_Dispatcher;
    when others =>
        EXCEPTIONS.LOG("TStack_R"&_
        X_VALUE'image (X_UNKNOWN_SENDEE));
    TMsg.SetX(Message, X_UNKNOWN_SENDEE);
    TMsg.FlushParams(Message);
    TServerObcs.Insert (OBCS, Message);
    end case;
end loop;
end TStack_RB;
```

Figure 3.3.3.2   STACK Request Broker Code Sample

By default there is only one "RB package" for a class, whatever the number of instances in clients. The "RB_Dispatcher and RB package" supports the management of protocol constraints (release the client before or after execution of server code) and leaves room for dedicated tuning according to the specific needs of a client-server application:

- The simplest strategy implements **synchronous behaviour** by means of polling and queuing client requests, and servicing one at time.
- More demanding applications may require **asynchronous behaviour** with sophisticated parallel handling of client requests. Such a pattern is illustrated by the "Reactor/Acceptor" design pattern proposed in the C++/UNIX ACE library [13]. The latter was implemented in the C++ implementation of the HRTS library.

3.3.3.4   TStack_Server Code

An <Object>_Server code is exactly the same as the standard code as described in figure 3.3.3; thus this code can be functionally validated before final implmentation on a distributed target:platform.

3.4   VN Illustration

Virtual Nodes allow a designer to encapsulate a set of co-operating classes into modules distributable over a physical network. HOOD4 generation rules fully automate the Virtual Node Control Structure (VNCS) elaboration which handle all remote communications according to the allocation of HOOD objects, as represented in figure 3.4

The code generation rules for VN enforce a client-server architecture where :

- an allocated object accesses a remote one indirectly via a local proxy object which is a surrogate object for the remote one, and whose target code is the one generated with OPCS_ER code instead of OPCS code.

- Server target code for remote server objects is generated according to OPCS_SER code.

- one ClientVncs and one ServerVncs target units are generated for each VN. This software is merely a variant of OBCS interprocess communication code dealing with "remote" communication

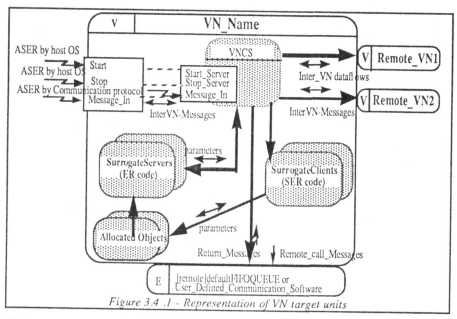

Figure 3.4 .1 - Representation of VN target units

Object and class allocation shall be carefully performed in order to limit inter-VN communication overhead. A VN may be locally or remotely called by another VN. Figure 3.4.2 and 3.4.3 illustrate the TStack client-server modules allocated onto 2 VNs :

- ClientVn is a VN that has allocated objects client of TStack, whose code is in a remote VN, the ServerVn.
- ServerVn was allocated the TStack class.

```
package ClientVN is
-- visibility on all types and class
    --defining the data exchanged with
    --server VNs and client VNs
end ClientVN;

package body ClientVN is
-- encapsulation of package TStack as ias a SURROGATE-SERVER
--   thus the code of package TStack is the one of figure 3.3.3.1 with only OPCS_ER code
-- definition of Object/operation allocation table
-- instance of a ClientObcs object with as parameters the VN allocation table, thus defining the
   CLIENTVNCS code.
```

Figure 3.4.2 Client VN Code Sample

```
package ServerVN is
-- visibility on all types and class packages defining
-- the data exchanged with server VNs and client VNs
end ClientVN;

package body ServerVN is
-- encapsulation of package TStack as ias a SURROGATE CLIENT thus the code is the same as in
   figure3.3.3.2
-- encapsulation ofpackage TStack_Server with the effective code as in figure 2.3.3
-- definition of Object/operation allocation table
-- instance of a ClientObcs object with as parameters the VN allocation table, thus defining the
   SERVERVNCS code.
....
```

Figure 3.4.3 ServerVN Code Sample

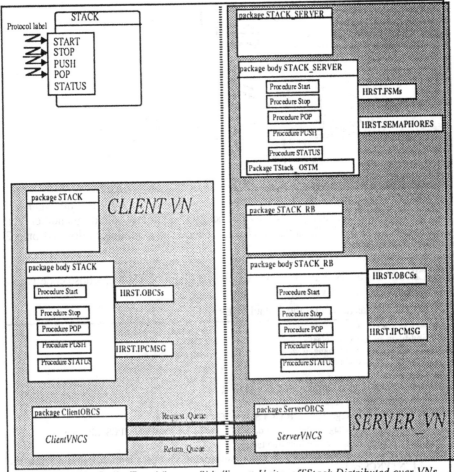

*Figure 3.4.3.2 CmlienT and Server Side Target Units ofTStack Distributed over VNs
Target Units*

4   Developing Client_Server Applications with HOOD4

The features of HOOD4 code generation for client-server architecture allow a designer to implement a post partitioning approach[1] for client-server applications :

- the design is performed and implemented first as "non distributed"
- the design is re-engineered second into distributable units by means of VNs

Developing first such a non distributed code is globally efficient in that :

- it provides at hand a **prototype of a solution that highlights the logical properties** of the system. It is then possible to reason about the target implementation constraints, instrument, and prototype them. Thus design decisions can be justified, and the testing process is more efficient.
- it provides a logical model, possibly **defining an design pattern or a** generic architecture independent of any target infrastructure, which can be reused on similar applications .
- We believe that it is always easier to develop a simplified system (and possibly redevelop it possibly later again) than to start a system integrating all constraints from scratch.

Of course, distribution constraints are placed on top of the non-distributed design especially those concerning physical memory access (parameters of operations cannot be defined as pointers). For example non constrained operations become HSER constrained ones by default when the object is allocated and remotely called by another VN.

Such constraints can either be handled at the cost of extra overhead by "deep copy" techniques, or even by configuring the VNs so as to restrict remote communications.

Inheritance and attribution at the other hand may still introduce additional complexity. We have started to establish allocation rules where a full inheritance tree must be allocated in the same server space, and where additional inheritance is forbidden on classes in client space.

The allocation of objects and the physical configuration allow furthermore to trend-off between logical level and physical/configuration with respect to the communication throughoutput. Analysis of data sharing conflicts may lead to further break-down of the objects or to re-allocation of the objects in a same VN.

5   Conclusion

The work presented is only a first step towards more automation in the development of distributed applications. We want to thank B.DELATTE and JM WALLUT from CNES, who funded this HOOD4 validation work. We also are grateful to D.Schmidt for his work on ACE support [12], without which we would not have been able to have a first implementation of the HRTS. A parallel implementation in Ada could not yet fully succeed in using the RPC and distribution facilities of Ada due to the lack of a full ADA95 implementation, at the time this paper was written. This work should however be completed by end of 1995.

We believe that our approach is a viable one within the economical constraints of nowadays projects. The benefits expected are many fold :

- at primary level, **systematic reuse** of the HRTS library and ACE frameworks :
    - HRTS EXCEPTIONS module for exception logging, tracing and management.
    - HRTS FSMs module for FSM implementations
    - HRTS OBCS modules for inter-process communication implementations
- **effective separation of functional code from dynamic and pre/post condition code.** This should lead to dual parallel developments with prototyping, verification of dynamic code in parallel of functional code development.

As a result, the suggested HOOD4 development approach for complex systems should lead to solutions matching the following constraints:

- *independence with respect to target hardware configuration*, a requirement which is more an more expressed on large projects.
- *portability for several targets*, growing demand on large projects where identical software pieces are running on different platforms.
- *reusability on frozen parts of a given application domain* (reuse of high level architecture and or parts of the designs),
- *maintainability*, which is directly improved if above constraint are already fulfilled.

6   References

1   Ada9X Mapping/Revision Team (1994), *Annotated Draft Version 5.0 of the Programming Language Ada, and Rationale for the Programming Language Ada, Version 5.0,,* Intermetrics, ISO/IECJTC1/SC22 WG9 N 207

2   Burns A; A.Wellings (1989), *Real-Time Systems and their Programming Languages,* 1989 Addison-Wesley Press

3   Gamma E, R.Helm, R.Johnson and J.Vlissides (1994), *Design Patterns : Elements of Reusable Object Oriented Software,* MA : Addison-Wesley

4   HOOD Technical Group(1993,1995), B.DELATTE, M.Heitz, JF MULLER editors, *"HOOD Reference Manual",* Prentice Hall and Masson,1993*and "HOOD Reference Manual release 4",* to be published 1995.

5   HUG ,*"HOOD User Manual",* (1995) C.Pinaud, M.Heitz editors HOOD USERs GROUP A.I.S.B.L." C/O SpaceBel Informatique, 111, rue Colonel BOURG, B-1140 BRUSSELS, Belgium   tel (32).2.27.30.46.11   fax (32) 2.27.36.80.13

6   Meyer B,(1990)*"Object Oriented Software Construction"* in *ISBN 0-8053-0091,* Benjamin Cummings

7   OMG,(1991)*The Common Object request Broker : Architecture and Specification* , OMG doc.

8   Sourouille JL, H Lecoeuche(1995), Integrating State in an OO Concurrent Model, *Proceedings of TOOLS EUROPE95 Conference,* Prentice HAll

9   Strousoup B(1991) *The Annoted C++ Reference Manual,* Addison-Wesley Press

10   Vinoski S(1993) *Distributed Object Computing with CORBA,* C++ Report, vol 5,

11   Vinoski S, Schmidt D(1995) *Comparing Alternative Client Side Distributed Programming Techniques,* C++ Report, 1995 May/June 1995 issues

12   Schmidt D, ASX ('1994): *An Object-Oriented Framework for Developping Distributed Applications,* Proceedings of the 6th USENIX C++ Conference, Cambridge, MA, April 1994

13   Schmidt D,Stephenson P(1995) *Using Design Patterns to Evolve System Software from Unix to WIndows NT* C++ Report, 1995 March 1995

7   Appendixes

The full target code of the samples described in ADA throughout this paper may be obtained on request to the author both in C++5since we had no space here) and ADA. They can also be obtained by ftp as well as the full HOOD Reference Manual from the HOOD repository at the following URL:
estwns.wm.estec.esa.nl:8001/hood-page.html.

Round Table Discussion : "Tools and Design Methods"

held on October 4, 1995

Participants:

Chairman: Mr. Finn Hass, C.R.I. A.S

Messrs.

R Gerlich, Dornier Satellitensysteme GmbH
M. Heitz, CISI
J. Barrington-Cook, Logica UK Ltd.
H. Schneeweiss, CADRE Technologies

Mr. Hass introduced the participants and explained the subject of the discussion. Originally he had anticipated the debate to centre on the comparison on the various design methods available. After having contacted the Panel members, he came to the conclusion that the problem that was most present in the minds of every one at the present stage was the possibility of a conflict of interest between the vendors of the tools that are developed to implement the various methods, and the software developers, who are supposed to use them.

He therefore proposed to focus on this particular aspect of the problem.

Mr. Gerlich opened the discussion.
He started by bluntly asking the basic question: are tools developed and marketed to support the users or are they to support the vendors?

In the real life, Mr. Gerlich said, software engineers are working on the requirements of projects. Developers are not, in general, free to use methods and tools as proposed by the vendors. They have to comply with the requirements of the customers regarding standards, lifecycle, software management approaches, etc. On the other hand, one can see that vendors propose a large variety of methods and tools - often very expensive. In addition, one may even wonder whether there is really a process control for the method tools, since there is often no real progress from one method to another, no tool being ever complete and most of them being constantly subject to modifications. In this context, must one not consider that what is offered by the vendors is much too complex and that a drastic simplification is needed to adjust to what industry really needs?

Mr. Lee (Logica) intervened from the floor to express an even more radical position. Mr. Lee considered that, for to a large extent, when tool vendors evoke the need of bringing some order in the present situation, they react more in function of their own interest than in that of the users. In projects, people have to make do with an ad hoc collection of tools and most often than not would be unable to afford the best tools proposed by the vendors.

In the real projects, what is needed is a variety of tools and methods. The nature of projects change thoroughly from the one to the other. Therefore is it not a nonsense to try and fine a method that would support such a variety of approaches. In Mr. Lee's view, it is probably futile to think that one can try and unify the methods used in Software when this has proven impossible in all other fields of industrial activity. "Maybe we should stop trying to find the Nirvana hoping for a panacea: a new tool covering all need, and be content with our lot"!

Vendors, and in particular Messrs. Kruchten and Schneeweiss reacted to that by observing that, if it is true that an excessively large variety of tools, each based on a particular method, are nowadays proposed on the market, some consolidation has already taken place in the recent past. Tool developers have borrowed ideas one from the others and great steps have been made towards more unification.

Vendors are criticised because they have an interest in maintaining high prices, in proposing products the maintenance of which is expensive or proprietary data exchange standards, but this is beginning to change. There is an attempt at standardisation between tool vendors, although it is still in its first steps.

Several users (Messrs. Simoens, Barrington-Cook and Lee, in particular) observed at that point that the main investment is not the purchase of the tool, but the education of the people who have to use it. The introduction of a tool in an organisation is a cost intensive process that has to be monitored carefully. After that, the cost of ownership is much less than the cost of entry. The consequence is that the users have difficulties to cope with tool modifications or with the introduction of new methods and tools. A company must be very careful before taking the decision of changing a tool.

This led to a discussion, the conclusion of which was that it would be wise for users never to purchase a tool without at the same time buying consultancy services from the tool vendor.

Mr. Schneeweiss was then given the opportunity to explain the difficulties with which tool vendors are faced.

In the beginning, he explained, were the traditional methods - which, it should not be forgotten, are still largely used, including in very large projects. The problem of tool vendors was, at that time, relatively straightforward, although it must be noted that tools are not always used, certain organisations, some of which very large (Mr. Schneeweiss gave the example of an aeronautical project) using the classical methods without any tool.

Then came the Object-Oriented approach. The choice of methods to tackle with this approach is large, and for a CASE vendor, it is a tremendous job to keep track of the various existing methods and to select the most appropriate one. The tool

vendors face another difficulty: it is that the language preferred by the users may be different (Ada 83/Ada 95/C++, Smalltalk...). It must be admitted that it is not without reason that users are complaining that
- too many methods are floating around,
- in many, there is a lack of formal aspects, a poor integration of models, a poorly defined development process,
- they are in constant evolution,
- Ada specific support may be lacking.
However the problems of tool vendors are not easy.

Messrs. Schwarm and Kruchten expressed their sympathy for the difficulties of tool vendors, but said again that the cost of tools was excessively high. Why has no tool vendor thought of selling large quantities of inexpensive tools to be used on PCs, in the manner in which Microsoft is doing it? It is true that the present number of licences sold is small, but it would increase if the prices would go down, and, in addition, a secondary market: students, could develop. Naturally, the up-front investment for developing such cheap products would be high. But the hardware industry has for long recognised the necessity of high up-front investments to address the mass market. Can the tool vendors not do the same?

The tool vendors representatives were dubious but admitted that this was perhaps the way into the future. In any case, it was observed, the present market is becoming difficult: several tool vendors have already disappeared. This will perhaps make a new approach, like that mentioned, necessary..

The floor was then given to Mr. Heitz, who addressed a still more basic question: why methods?

Methods, he answered, have been invented for large teams of Software developers. If one has only a small team, maintaining homogeneity is easy, and methods can be dispensed with.
There are cases where people write code directly from requirements, and this works well.
With large teams however, chaos is always threatening, and methods are needed to have an homogeneous and efficient process and to maintain quality.
The methods are used
- to planify and predefine processes,
- to provide formalisation:
  - in the extraction of relevant properties,
  - in performing tests,
  - in ensuring reliability and security,
  - in providing reusabilty.
And tools are there to automatise activities such as the capture of properties, and the retrieval of such properties for verification, documentation, code generation, etc.

In Mr. Heitz view, the problems with present tools are that they provide only poor process models, and that they try to do too much, addressing at the same time all problems, from analysis to design, coding, quality assurance, documentation, etc.

What is needed, in Mr. Heitz view, is a series of small methods, treating one property only, and, as a consequence simple to handle. One small method and one tool could be used for each step of the SW development from requirement to the final coding, in an incremental manner.

These simple tools should be designed in such a manner that they can be associated (which implies a coordination in the approaches to communication, storage, etc.)

The audience tended to agree with the first part of Mr. Heitz presentation.

Messrs. Lee and Barrington-Cook insisted on the importance of the people in software development and expressed the view that the purpose of a method is not to improve the best people in the companies, but to raise the level of the medium people.

The best ones will always find a way, and when using a method will always improve on it. The problem is to achieve a good level also with medium specialists.

Mr. Gerlich compared the development of a SW with the building of a house. He noted that when building a house, there are fixed rules, that one has just to apply. In SW development, there are no rules as clear as in the building industry: every one thinks that he can go his own way. Hence the necessity of methods.

Messrs. Kruchten and Schwarm remarked that in the early days of the Software industry, people were very motivated and worked for very long hours. Nowadays, SW developers consider their job as any other job and expect to work no more than 8 hours a day like every other profession. Therefore one cannot go on working like in the past. Rules and methods are needed. Management has to be more realistic and take this evolution into account. They also wondered if it would not be useful to have, for software developers, recognised qualified specialists in the same manner as what exists in the building industry.

Mr. Barrington-Cook proposed another analogy than the house-building industry: it is the chemical industry.

Every child, he said, can make a chemical experiment using one of the kits that are on sale in many shops, but every manager knows that installing a chemical plant is a very different story, and that years of systematic preparation are necessary. In the same manner, every possessor of a PC can produce lines of code. But developing a professional software is something different. This is what the managers should realise. Methods are there to make possible the preparation of professional products, which is not possible without having a lot of intermediate step that have to be carefully controlled.

Regarding the second part of Mr. Heitz presentation, the interest of developing small tools, the opinion was not unanimous, some tool vendors, in particular, having doubts that this would really help.

The last presentation was made by Mr. Barrington-Cook. Mr. Barrington-Cook showed how there is a difference between the theoretical view on how a software is developed and how it is done in practice. In theory, one expects the work to proceed continuously from one step to the other, from the user requirement to system integration and testing through the various well-known intermediate steps. However, developers tend to apply a more complicated process, in which they sometimes come back from one stage to the previous one and, finally, distribute their work in a manner that is different from what is expected by theoreticians.

For this reason, one can thing that, finally, a unique tool would perhaps be less adapted to the real situation than a mix of tools - possibly the small tools envisaged by Mr. Heitz.

Mr. Hass terminated the discussion by observing that no conclusion was really possible. Practice is usually more complex than what is assumed by the methods, the software development is much more difficult to rationalise than hardware activities and a permanent dialogue between users and tool vendors is clearly needed to help the profession to organise itself in an efficient and modern manner. He thanked the participants for their contributions and suggested to resume the debate next year in the light of the progresses that will have been made in the meantime.

LAMPBADA

"Logiciel d'Aide à la Mise au Point de Bibliothèques ADA".
(ADA Libraries Validation Tool)

D. De GABAÏ
AEROSPATIALE Cannes

A library of software components written in the Ada language schematically consists of packages, each such package containing declarations of data types, data, and subprograms.

Rereading generally suffices to validate declarations of types and of data. On the other hand, validating a sub-program requires that it be executed a certain number of times, with inputs supplied and outputs verified.

Let us distinguish two types of tests, the so-called "first tests" and "non-regression" tests. The latter merely consist in executing some pre-established test sequences, with inputs pre-defined and results awaiting comparison with a validated reference.

The main difficulty encountered in validating a library lies in building test sequences and checking results that will serve as references. This phase is generally a trial-and-error one, calling for use of already validated sub-programs in building the inputs and validating the results obtained.

The principal use of the tool presented here is to ease out the "first test", i.e. the all-too-often time-consuming and difficult task of building up test sequences and reference results.

But another, most worthwhile application of LAMPBADA is what may be called the "supercalculator" one. Since he can thereby interactively access all of an Ada library's components, the user can tap all of the computer's power and use all of the software components by mere pocket-calculator actions, with no need for writing and compiling a complete program.

1. The test tool

As said in the introduction, LAMPBADA is a tool for interactively building test sequences and verifying the results obtained. It naturally enables such test sequences be played back to ascertain non-regression of software components affected by changes.

This is exemplified in the three sub-sections 1.1, 1.2 and 1.3 hereunder as the validation of a simplified complex number package. This imaginary package is specified as follows:

```
PACKAGE p_complexes IS

  TYPE t_real IS DIGITS 15;

  TYPE t_complex IS RECORD
    re: t_real;
    im: t_real;
  END RECORD;

  i: CONSTANT t_complex:= ( re => 0.0, im => 1.0 );

  FUNCTION complex ( re: t_real;
                     im: t_real:= 0.0 ) RETURN t_complex;

  FUNCTION complex ( module, arg: t_real ) RETURN t_complex;

  FUNCTION re    ( c: t_complex ) RETURN t_real;
  FUNCTION im    ( c: t_complex ) RETURN t_real;
  FUNCTION "ABS" ( c: t_complex ) RETURN t_real;
  FUNCTION arg   ( c: t_complex ) RETURN t_real;

  FUNCTION "+" ( left : t_real;
                 right: t_complex ) RETURN t_complex;
  FUNCTION "-" ( left : t_real;
                 right: t_complex ) RETURN t_complex;
  FUNCTION "*" ( left : t_real;
                 right: t_complex ) RETURN t_complex;

  FUNCTION "+" ( left, right: t_complex ) RETURN t_complex;
  FUNCTION "-" ( left, right: t_complex ) RETURN t_complex;
  FUNCTION "*" ( left, right: t_complex ) RETURN t_complex;
  FUNCTION "/" ( left, right: t_complex ) RETURN t_complex;

END p_complexes;
```

With such simple software components, careful rereading of the code is arguably the best validation approach. But suppose we wish to validate the last four operators, assuming all other functions to be validated.

1.1. First test

The idea is to build a test sequence, i.e. a number of calls on the sub-programs to be validated, supplying input parameters and storing the output parameters each time, and to check accuracy of the results obtained, writing them down in a reference file. Then, one needs only to delete in the history file all instructions no longer needed in the non-regression tests, and to store the command file thus created.

Consider the example of the validation of all 4 complex-related operators.
We first initiate the program by keying in **lampbada**, then give a session name that will be used to name the history file, for instance **complexes_test1**. Throughout the rest of the example, the bold print is used for the user's inputs and the normal print for the LAMPBADA outputs, while the italics are comments for our reader's benefit.

```
Session Name: complexes_test1
LAMPBADA> @use p_complexes  -- avoids the prefixed notation
LAMPBADA> 2.0 + i           -- definition of a number
RETURN:= 2.0 +i. 1.0        -- result of the sum
=> c1                       -- storage of the result
LAMPBADA> 3.0 - 2.0*i
RETURN:= 3.0 +i. -2.0
=> c2
LAMPBADA> c1 + c2           -- test on 1st operator
RETURN:= 5.0 +i. -1.0
=> c3
LAMPBADA> re(c1) + re(c2) - re(c3)
RETURN:= 0.0                -- verification of result
=>                          -- non-storage of 0.0
LAMPBADA> im(c1) + im(c2) - im(c3)
RETURN:= 0.0
=>
LAMPBADA> c3 - c2           -- test on 2nd operator
RETURN:= 2.0 +i. 1.0
=> c4
LAMPBADA> c4 = c1           -- verification of result
RETURN:= TRUE
=>
LAMPBADA> c1 * c2           -- test on 3rd operator
RETURN:= 8.0 +i. -1.0
=> c5
LAMPBADA> ABS(c1) * ABS(c2) - ABS(c5)
RETURN:= 0.0
=>
LAMPBADA> arg(c1) + arg(c2) - arg(c5)
RETURN:= -9.853E-16
=>
LAMPBADA> c5 / c2           -- test on 4th operator
RETURN:= 2.0 +i. 1.0
=> c6
LAMPBADA> @save complexes_test1.ref -- writing of file
LAMPBADA> @quit
```

Steps have run in the following sequence:
- define two complex numbers c_1 and c_2
- calculate their sum c_3 and check the result
- calculate the difference $c_3 - c_2$ and check the result
- calculate product c_5 and check the result
- calculate quotient c_5 / c_2: the result is indeed c_1
- save all validated results in the complexes_test1.ref file

This file contains all values of variables c_1 through c_6 and will stand as reference for the non-regression tests.

The session's history file has been saved under the name complexes_test1.lamp, and it has the following content:

```
@use p_complexes
2.0 + i
>>> c1
3.0 - 2.0*i
>>> c2
c1 + c2
>>> c3
re(c1) + re(c2) - re(c3)
>>>
im(c1) + im(c2) - im(c3)
>>>
c3 - c2
>>> c4
c4 = c1
>>>
c1 * c2
>>> c5
ABS(c1) * ABS(c2) - ABS(c5)
>>>
arg(c1) + arg(c2) - arg(c5)
>>>
c5 / c2
>>> c6
@save complexes_test1.ref
@quit
```

One needs only to delete the result verification instructions and rename the file of saved results (which becomes, for instance, complexes_test1.res) to obtain the command file for use in the non-regression tests. This command file, renamed, for instance, complexes_test1.com, is as follows:

```
@use p_complexes
2.0 + i
>>> c1
3.0 - 2.0*i
>>> c2
c1 + c2
>>> c3
c3 - c2
>>> c4
c1 * c2
>>> c5
c5 / c2
>>> c6
@save complexes_test1.res
@quit
```

1.2. Non-regression tests

A non-regression test merely consists in playing back a defined sequence of tests and comparing the results obtained with a validated reference. With LAMPBADA, one needs only to execute a command file that constitutes the test sequence, then to compare the results file with the reference file which was created and validated during the first test.

To go back to the complexes example, one needs only, once under LAMPBADA, to key in the command Əexec complexes_test1.com and compare the two files, complexes_test1.res and complexes_test1.ref.

Compared to a conventional test program, this economises a tremendous amount of time and memory space:

- whereas link-compiling plus link-editing time is on the order of 40s for a conventional program, with LAMPBADA it amounts to zero;

- the program-developing time, too, is shorter with LAMPBADA as the code is reduced to the bare minimum - witness the deletion of the entire input-output part - and, in addition, errors are more rapidly corrected, as one needs only to delete the related lines in the command file;

- the memory space occupied by a command file is smaller than with an Ada source file, but, more importantly, if one wishes to economise the compilation time on every non-regression test, one has to save the executable files, whose volume nears 1.5 Mbytes per program, to be compared with the 4.5 Mbytes of the LAMPBADA executable, which gives access to several hundreds of sub-programs.

1.3. Evolution of tests

As one adds capabilities to an already-existing package, or as one detects some abnormal behaviour in an untested case, one is led to add tests to the test sequences associated with such package.

With LAMPBADA, this can be done in either of two ways:

- edit a command file to host the additional tests, execute that file and then validate the results from the new tests;

- alternatively, execute an old command file, interactively build the new tests, validating their results each time, then complete the old command file from the history file that has just been stored.

With a conventional program, one would have to feed the code the instructions related to the new tests, compile and execute the program, and then create yet another program to validate the new results by another computation method.

2. Supercalculator

For the user, a somewhat tedious experience classically consists in writing and compiling a program that uses some functions of a library, especially if this user does not know the Ada language. This is where LAMPBADA comes in, with interactive access to the library and some language flexibility.

2.1. Management of data

The data that LAMPBADA can handle come in all the types defined in the utilised library: they may be scalars, arrays, records, access types.

In addition, the expression of every physical quantity's real value is complete with the appropriate unit. Where such value is used in a computation, the dimensional equation is verified, and all necessary conversions automatically performed. The handling of data may be exemplified as follows:

```
LAMPBADA> 42.0 km + 195.0 m
RETURN:= 42.195 km      -- the unit is that of the 1st term
=> distance             -- storage of the result
LAMPBADA> distance / 3.0 hr
RETURN:= 3.907 m.s-1  -- the unit belongs to the SI system
=> speed
LAMPBADA> 0.0 km.hr-1 + speed -- change of unit
RETURN:= 14.065 km.hr-1
=> speed
LAMPBADA> distance + speed     -- operation illegal
Exception dimension_error raised
LAMPBADA> 0.0 W + 80.0 kg * 9.8 m.s-2 * 1.0 km / 1.5 hr
RETURN:= 145.185 W
=> power_of_a_man_climbing_1000m_in_90min
```

Subsection 1.1 showed how all of the variables defined by the user during a session can be written in a file with help of the @save command.

In fact, this command writes in a file all of the variables the user has created in the current package, i.e. that which is implicitly opened as a LAMPBADA session is initiated. However, further user packages can be created to make several sets of data available. Thus all of a package's data can be saved in a file.

Likewise, a data file can be read in either of two ways:
- by merely adding the read data to those in the current package
- alternatively, by creating a package to host the file's data, which enables virtual manipulation of a file's data with no interference from the other data.

The data packages defined by the user can be viewed as data packages that are virtually in the library. Their components are accessed either by the documentation prefixed with the package's name or by using the @use clause, as we did in subsection 1.1 for the complex package.

The user selects the current package, in which all unprefixed variables will be written. The user can, of course, switch to another current package during session. One must note that the @use clauses are associated with a given package; and hence switching to another current package modifies visibility on the other packages.

2.2. Call on sub-programs

At first sight, one may consider that the commands understood by LAMPBADA are either specific commands that begin with @, or Ada instructions.

Thus, a sub-program is called merely by its name, and giving the required parameters. Such parameters can be entered either by position or by name, as in the Ada language. If the example of complexes is used again, we may write:

```
LAMPBADA> complex( 1.0 )
```

to define the complex of real part 1 and imaginary part 0, or

```
LAMPBADA> complex( re => 0.0, im => 1.0 )
```

to define number i,or

```
LAMPBADA> complex( 1.0, arg => 90.0 deg )
```

which, again, yields number i.

In the third case, a slight difference w.r.t. the Ada language is that the argument is given with an angular unit. In fact, for each sub-program, the parameters' units are defined in the interface package associated with the sub-program's package. Subsection 3.3 will give a more detailed idea of what interface packages are, but we may say that they add, over the library's components, the treatment of physical units.

We may of course write more complicated expressions, such as:
```
LAMPBADA> re( complex(1.0) + complex( 0.0, im => 2.0 ) )
```

One flexibility-enhancing feature of LAMPBADA is the possibility to omit some parameters when calling on a sub-program: the missing parameters are replaced with the string "..". For instance, we may write:
```
LAMPBADA> complex( arg => 90.0 deg, .. )
```
The missing parameters are then called:
```
module => 1.0
```
and the result displayed:
```
RETURN:= 0.0 +i. 1.0
```

We may alternatively write:
```
LAMPBADA> complex( .. )
```
but in this case two possibilities arise from the existence of two functions with just one name, which requires that we choose one of the overloads, as shown in the next subsection 2.3.

2.3. Resolution of overload

Overload is resolved by the principle described in the language's norm, i.e. the types of the effective parameters are matched with those of the formal parameters.

However, overload resolution by LAMPBADA presents two particularities, which stem from the tool's interactivity:

- the deliberate omission of some parameters when calling on a sub-program conveys the notion, when it comes to overload resolution, of a default value for every formal parameter; the differentiation occurs when the missing prameters are required of the user, as the default values of those parameters which have one is proposed at that time;
- where several possibilities remain after resolution, the user has the final choice, with all remaining possibilities proposed to him as profiles.

Let us get back to the example in 2.2. to illustrate the resolution process:

```
LAMPBADA> complex( .. )
1: FUNCTION complex ( re: IN t_real; im: IN t_real:= 0.0 ) RETURN t_complex
2: FUNCTION complex ( module: IN t_real; arg: IN t_real ) RETURN t_complex
Enter 0 to abort evaluation
Choice (0..2) ?
```

If the user's choice is 1, this will be followed by:
```
re => 1.0
im => ( 0.0 )
```

The default value, displayed between brackets, is used failing any replacement value given by the user.

If the user's choice is 2, this will be followed by:
```
module => 1.0
arg => 0.0 deg
```
In both cases the result is displayed and can be stored in a variable:
```
RETURN:= 1.0 +i. 0.0
=>
```

Of course, an expression may lead to several overload resolutions, which will then receive similar treatment, cascade-wise.

2.4. Example of use

Since most pocket calculators do feature complex operators, LAMPBADA's contribution to that kind of computation is not obvious. Therefore, we are proposing here a somewhat more complicated example of computation using a library that offers, among others, components for:
- the vectorial and 3-D geometrical calculations
- the handling of dates and of the Julian calendar
- some astronomical calculations.

We intend to calculate the Sun's and the Moon's positions for an Earth-based observer at a given date, as well as the angle formed by the two luminaries.
Let the observer's position be 7 deg. longitude and 43.5 deg. latitude North. The goal is to indicate Sun and Moon positions by two angles easily measurable by the observer, namely azimuth and elevation, the former being the angle between the local North and the celestial body's direction projected on the horizon, the latter the angle above the horizon.

Figure 1 shows the definition of the observer's local reference frame.

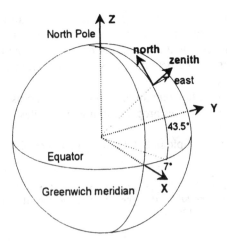

FIG 1: Earth frame and observer's local fram

Figure 2 shows the definition of the azimuth and elevation angles

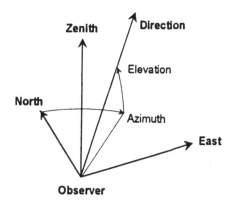

FIG 2: Azimuth and Elevation

All calculations are performed in the Gamma 50 reference frame:
- the origin is at the Earth's centre,
- the Z axis is the Earth's rotation axis, pointing North,
- the X axis lies at the intersection of the equateur and ecliptic planes.
Thus, we have a reference frame whose axes do not rotate with the Earth.
The algorithm is as follows:
- calculation of the Earth-restrained frame (whose vector X is on the Greenwich meridian)
- calculation of the observer's local frame
- calculation of the azimuth and elevation angles
- calculation of the Sun/Moon angle as seen by the observer.

Here is what comes on display during the session, with the same conventions as in subsection 1.1.here-above. The @use clauses on the utilised packages are assumedly implemented.

```
LAMPBADA> clock                    -- current date
RETURN:= 1994-10- 7 at 10h 46mn 42.9s
=> date
LAMPBADA> julian_date( date ) -- date conversion
RETURN:= 16350 at 38802.9s
=> jul
LAMPBADA> sid: t_real:= sideral_angle(jul)
LAMPBADA> earth_frame: t_frame:= gamma50 * rotation(sid,z)
LAMPBADA> earth_frame * rotation(   7.0 deg, z )
                      * rotation( -43.5 deg, y )
                      * translation( 6378.0 km * vector_x )
```

```
RETURN
  origin:= km,
           -4615.4
            -319.3
           4390.3
    trihedron:=  -0.724    0.069    0.687
                 -0.050   -0.998    0.048
                  0.688    0.000    0.725
=> local_frame
LAMPBADA> zenith: t_vector:= local_frame.trihedron(x)
LAMPBADA> north : t_vector:= local_frame.trihedron(z)
LAMPBADA> east  : t_vector:= local_frame.trihedron(y)
LAMPBADA> s: t_vector:= vector(local_frame.origin,sun(jul))
LAMPBADA> m: t_vector:= vector(local_frame.origin,moon(jul))
LAMPBADA> angle( north, s, -zenith )
RETURN:= 169.08 deg
=> sun_azimuth
LAMPBADA> 90.0 deg - angle( zenith, s )
RETURN:= 40.67 deg
=> sun_elevation
LAMPBADA> angle( north, m, -zenith )
RETURN:= 140.10 deg
=> moon_azimuth
LAMPBADA> 90.0 deg - angle( zenith, m )
RETURN:= 19.49 deg
=> moon_elevation
LAMPBADA> angle( s, m )
RETURN:= 32.55 deg
=> moon_sun_angle
LAMPBADA> @quit
```

On 7 October 1994 at 10hr 46min 42.9s, for the Earth-based observer,
the Sun stood 40.67 deg above the horizon, with a 169.08 deg azimuth angle,
the Moon stood 19.49 deg above the horizon, at azimuth 140.10 deg,
and the angle between the two was 32.55 deg.

3. Architecture

LAMPBADA is a software tool which provides interactive access to the software
components in a given library. Therefore, the executable is built by linking
LAMPBADA to the units in the considered library.
Figure 3 shows the architecture of the LAMPBADA software.

The kernel of LAMPBADA is invariant.
The library's components are accessible via some interface (IF) packages.
Data management is effected with help of the input-output (IO) packages.

3.1. Kernel

The kernel of LAMPBADA contains all of the general mechanisms:
- syntactical analysis of commands
- interpretation of the "pseudo Ada" commands
- resolution of the overload
- management of data
- tools utilised in the interface packages.

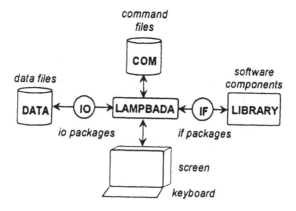

FIG 3: LAMPBADA's architecture

3.2. Input-output packages

LAMPBADA does not directly handle the data defined by the user, but only a representation of those data as strings of characters.

Thus, each individual type of data defined in the library relates to one input-output package, which package principally offers the following capabilities:
- procedures for writing on the screen and in strings of characters
- features for reading on the keyboard and in strings of characters
- management of units for the type considered.

These input-output packages are written with a code generator which is fed a complete description of the types considered as well as the handling principle for the associated units. The Ada code generated is directly compilable. Only a few minutes are needed to describe a given type of data and generate the code of the associated input-output package.

3.3. Interface packages

Each package in the library made accessible by LAMPBADA relates to one interface package. Such interface package supplies LAMPBADA with all elements needed to build the objects base related to it.

The interface package is the one that effectively calls on the sub-programs of that package to which it is associated. Such call requires a sequence of steps to be taken:
- convert into real data the data supplied by LAMPBADA as strings
- check the units of the data according to the protocol defined in the interface
- call on the sub-program with the effective parameters thus obtained
- convert the output parameters into strings of characters
- calculate the units obtained by the method defined in the interface.

Just like the input-output packages, the interface packages are written with a code generator which, for each package in the library,is fed with the descriptions of:
- all types of data declared in the package
- all data declared, complete, as applicable, with the associated physical units
- the profiles of all sub-programs, along with the constraints on the units expected as inputs and the methods to calculate the units of the results.
Depending on the package's complexity, this complete description may take from a few to a few tens of minutes.
Here, too, the Ada code generated is directly compilable.

One main interface provides the list of all interfaces accessible by a given executable of LAMPBADA.

4. Conclusion

LAMPBADA is a tool devised to serve the dual purpose of testing/validation and interactive utilisation of an Ada library.

Its use as a test tool economises both time and memory space, as a test sequence is no longer a compiled, complete program, but a command file. Not only is this command file simpler than an Ada program, particularly due to the fact that the whole "input-output" part is directly handled by LAMPBADA, but it moreover requires no compilation. Hence the huge savings on storing the test sequences.
The tool's interactiveness offers the user the possibility of a trial-and-error approach to building tests, and, more importantly, of validating the results obtained by calling on already validated sub-programs. Such calls, now no longer required in the non-regression tests, need only be deleted in the LAMPBADA session's history file, which thus becomes a command file to be stored to this aim.

The tool's second application is the interactive utilisation of an Ada library. LAMPBADA becomes a "supercalculator" the functions of which are all of the library's sub-programs, and in which he data are of any of the types declared in the library.
The physical data, to rule out any misinterpretation, are always given with explicit units in the text. All conversions of quantities and verifications of dimensional equations are performed automatically.
The user can read and write data files, call on sub-programs, execute command files, crea te or destroy variables.

In sum, LAMPBADA is a kind of command interpreter associated with a set of packages. The LAMPBADA-dedicated commands are used for managing the data, the packages and the tool, as against the other commands, which are pseudo-Ada instructions Certain Ada instructions, like, for instance, the exception-raising ones, are not allowed, whilst some other instructions are made more flexible, name only the possibility of omitting parameters when calling on a sub-program.
Thus, LAMPBADA makes it easier to use an Ada library whenever "small" calculations make use of "powerful" functions.

Springer-Verlag
and the Environment

We at Springer-Verlag firmly believe that an international science publisher has a special obligation to the environment, and our corporate policies consistently reflect this conviction.

We also expect our business partners – paper mills, printers, packaging manufacturers, etc. – to commit themselves to using environmentally friendly materials and production processes.

The paper in this book is made from low- or no-chlorine pulp and is acid free, in conformance with international standards for paper permanency.

Lecture Notes in Computer Science

For information about Vols. 1–957

please contact your bookseller or Springer-Verlag